INTERNET TECHNOLOGIES AND CYBERSECURITY LAW IN NIGERIA

INTERNET TECHNOLOGIES AND CYBERSECURITY LAW IN NIGERIA

Oluwatomi A. Ajayi

malthouse MP

Malthouse Press Limited

Lagos, Benin, Ibadan, Jos, Port-Harcourt, Zaria

First Published 2024
ISBN: 978-978-60617-1-9

Published by

Malthouse Press Limited

Lagos Port Harcourt Zaria

5, Adele Street, Off Warehouse Road,
Apapa, Lagos Mainland, Lagos, Nigeria
E-mail: malthouselagos@gmail.com
Facebook:@malthouselagos
Twitter:@malthouselagos
Instagram:@malthouselagos
Tel: 0802 600 3203

International Distributors:
African Books Collective Ltd, Oxford, UK
Email: orders@africanbookscollective.com
Website: http://www.africanbookscollective.com

PREFACE

Internet and Cybersecurity technologies have become the bedrock of modern societies comprising of different professionals who manage *Internet* security risks, computer systems, network applications and data infrastructure. Clearly, *Internet* and cybersecurity management is vital in this digital savvy world as Industry statistics keeps revealing that the world is getting more connected ever than before. Now we can boldly say the *Internet* has brought us to the information age that is enabled by computers, mobile devices and other technology tools which assist us to perform daily tasks such as researching online for information, transacting business, networking with others and monitoring world or local events. Unfortunately just like every human activity, cybercriminals are getting daring. They openly run dozens of scams across social media platforms. They work individually or in clusters and use every platform available to them to defraud people. The Internet has revolutionized many aspects of life, including how law enforcement agencies will solve crimes. Thus the rise in cybercrime have no doubt complicated matters for law enforcement officers who are trying harder to stay ahead of existing and emerging cyber threats, which has therefore called for a more robust cybersecurity measures.

Essentially, understanding the principles of cybersecurity require that we know the foundation of the meaning of the prefix 'cyber'. This is a word depicting any Internet-enabled activity involving the use of computer networks or electronic mobile devices. In this context therefore, we can say cybersecurity is all about protecting our security and privacy from online bad actors who have become security threats because they seemingly hold the view a that any crime committed online would be hidden perfectly from the prying eyes of the law even after instigating a wide range of cybercrime on individuals, organisations and governments. It got extremely bad when we read how Russia-sponsored hackers unleashed cyber-attacks against Ukraine which forced Ukraine to establish its own information technology army to protect its cyberspace.

Nonetheless, the *Internet* world is both a simple and complex platform depending on how we utilise the space, since this is an age of AI-authored books, AI-generated human speech and facilities. We can however navigate through, if we nurture ourselves with the in-depth knowledge on cybersecurity. This is what this book has set out to do. It will not only seek to identify the many risks associated with cybercrime and the nature it takes, but will also reveal how hackers exploit vulnerabilities and how to stem the tide of cybercrime through institutional guidelines, legal response and cybersecurity education. Sadly, some of us indulge in cyber pranks without even knowing our actions also constitute cybercrime!

As cybercrime continues to come in different dimensions and in the face of increasing criminal use of the *Internet*, the only option open to us, is to continue to invest in cybersecurity research, improve cybersecurity practices and follow international best practices as much as we can, so we do not become a prime target to cyber criminals.

I dare say that if cybersecurity is a vast industry with diverse specialities, then this book will be suitable for technology policymakers, cybersecurity students and practitioners, security, law and technology experts including cyber education enthusiasts who are interested in staying ahead of cyber risks. On the lighter side, the book is also meant to serve as a warning to potential cybercriminals because once we raise awareness about any subject matter, there is tendency for people to keep to the law.

Oluwatomi A. Ajayi
April 2024

FOREWORD

I want to express my heartfelt gratitude to Tomi Ajayi, Esq., LLM, the author of this great book, *Internet Technologies and Cybersecurity Law in Nigeria*, for extending the honour of writing the Foreword to me. I consider it a privilege to be entrusted with such a significant role.

Over the past few decades, in the blink of an eye of history, our world has undergone a complete metamorphosis. One invention of man that has smoothened the transformational phenomenon is the computer. Today, computers dominate the world. The impact of computers on humanity has been tremendous. Indeed, the current age is appropriately christened the Computer Age, the Age of Information and Communication Technology (ICT), or the Electronic Age.

Another significant feature of the modern world is the Internet. The Internet is a system that allows various computer networks around the world to interconnect. Internet connects the person sitting in the remote corner of the home or office to the entire world through the information highway called the web, cyber, etc. Also, dangerously but inadvertently, the Internet connects people to cybercriminals waiting to hit gullible and unwary users. The Internet, which is a direct product of the current technological revolution, is open to all. The openness of the Internet has expanded the scope of criminal opportunities and has spawned new categories of crimes and criminals, popularly known as cybercrimes and cybercriminals, respectively. Unlike conventional communities though, no police officers are patrolling the information superhighway. As such, it is left open to everything from Trojan horses, viruses, and all forms of attack. The Internet, in essence, has become a lawless arena where bullies, deviants, criminals, and terrorists are accommodated and can roam freely with recklessness.

In an increasingly interconnected world, where the digital realm intertwines with every facet of our lives, the significance of cybersecurity cannot be overstated. This book, which focuses on cybercrimes, cybersecurity threats, and response, cyber education and, general workings in the cyber world, depicts how technology has not only ushered in unprecedented opportunities but also exposed the world to new and evolving threats that transcend borders and boundaries. As we embark on the journey through the pages of this book, we are confronted with the realization that the battle for our digital safety requires constant vigilance, adaptability, and a deep understanding of the ever-changing landscape of technology. Cybersecurity is not merely a technical discipline, it is a critical enabler of trust, innovation, and the preservation of our way of life. In the words of the author, it is "a collective responsibility between the governed and the government" to ensure a safer cyberspace.

Within the chapters of this book, you will find a wealth of knowledge, insights, and practical guidance from the author who is an expert in the field. From the fundamentals of encryption and network security to the intricacies of threat detection and incident response, this book serves as a comprehensive resource for both the novice and the seasoned professional. The book is not just about the tools and techniques of cybersecurity; it is a call to action. It is a reminder that in this digital age, our collective security is a shared responsibility. It is a plea for organizations, governments, and individuals to prioritize cybersecurity as an essential component of our modern society, even as it serves as a note of warning to cybercriminals.

As we delve into the depths of this book, I encourage you to reflect on the role that each of us can play in safeguarding our digital future. The stories of cyberattacks and breaches serve as cautionary tales, but they also illustrate the resilience and ingenuity of those who defend against them. Let these stories inspire you to become a guardian of the digital realm.

In closing, I commend the author for her dedication to shedding light on the complex world of cybersecurity. May this book empower you, the reader, to navigate this challenging landscape with confidence and competence. Together, we can build a more secure and resilient digital world for generations to come.

Hon. (Justice) Alaba Omolaye-Ajileye, Rtd
Visiting Professor, Faculty of Law
National Open University of Nigeria HQ,
Jabi-Abuja FCT
April 2024

ABBREVIATIONS AND ACRONYMS

AD	Anno Domino
AfCFTA	African Continental Free Trade Area
AGF	Attorney-General of the Federation
AI	Artificial Intelligence
AIG	Assistant Inspector General of Police
APT	Advanced Persistent Threats
ARPANET	Advanced Research Projects Agency Network
AT	Assistive Technology
ATM	Automated Teller Machine
BITB	Browser in the Browser
BEC	Business Email Compromise
BSR	Business for Social Responsibility
BVN	Bank Verification Number
CAPTCHA	Completely Automated Public Turing test to tell Computers and Humans Apart
CBI	Central Bureau of Investigation
CCPCJ	Commission of Crime Prevention and Criminal Justice
CCTV	Closed Circuit Television
CDR	Call Detail Records
CEH	Certified Ethical Hacker
CISO	Chief Information Security Officers
ChatGPT	Chat Generative Pre-trained Transformer
CTFs	Capture The Flags
CODES	Coalition for Digital Environmental Sustainability
COE	Council of Europe
COVID 19	Coronavirus
CSAM	Child Sexual Abuse Materials

CSS	Cascading Style Sheets
DDoS	Distributed Denial of Service
DIA	Defence Intelligence Agency
DNA	Deoxyribonucleic Acid
DROWN	Decrypting RSA with Obsolete and Weakened eNcryption
DSL	Digital Subscriber Line
ECOSOC	Economic and Social Council
ECOWAS	Economic Community of West African States
ECtHR	European Court of Human Rights
EDR	Endpoint Detection and Response
EFCC	Economic and Financial Crimes Commission
ESI	Electronically Store Information
FBI	Federal Bureau of Investigation
FCA	Federal Court of Australia
FIR	First Information Report
FRN	Federal Republic of Nigeria
FUD	Fear, Uncertainty and Doubt
GDPR	General Data Protection Regulation
GOOGLE	Global Organization of Oriented Group Language of Earth
GPS	Global Positioning System
GSM	Global System for Mobile Communications
HCI	Human-Computer Interaction
HTTP	Hyper Text Transfer Protocol
HTTPS	Hypertext Transfer Protocol Secure
I2P	Invincible *Internet* Project
IC3	*Internet* Crime Complaint Center
ICCS	International Classification of Crime for Statistical Purposes
ICS	Industrial Control System
ICT	Information and Communications Technology
ID	Identification or Identifier
ID4D	Digital Identification for Development Project
IDN	Internationalised Domain Name
IETF	*Internet* Engineering Task Force

INTERPOL	International Police Organization
IoC	Indicators of Compromise
IOCE	International Organization on Computer Evidence
IRS	Internal Revenue Service
ISP	*Internet* Service Provider
IT	Information Technology
ITU	International Telecommunication Union
JPEG	Joint Photographic Experts Group
KEV	Known Exploited Vulnerabilities
KYC	Know Your Customer
LAN	Local Area Network
LLMs	Large Language Models
Mbps	Megabits per second
MITM	Man-in-the-Middle
NAPTIP	National Agency for the Prohibition of Trafficking in Persons
NAS	Network-Attached Storage
NBS	National Bureau of Statistics
NCC	Nigerian Communications Commission
NCPS	National Cybersecurity Policy and Strategy
NDEPS	National Digital Economy Policy and Strategy
NDR	Network Detection and Response
NeFF	Nigerian Electronic Fraud Forum
NIA	National Intelligence Agency
NIMC	National Identity Management Commission
NIST	National Institute of Standards and Technology
NNBP	Nigerian National Broadband Plan
NOTAP	National Office for Technology Acquisition and Promotion
NPL	Nigerian Passport Learning
OAuth	Open Authorization
OSEA	Online Sexual Exploitation and Abuse
OSINT	Open Source Intelligence
OT	Operational Technology
OTP	One Time Password
PaaS	Platform-as-a Service

PC	Personal Computer
PDA	Personal Digital Assistant
PDF	Portable Document Format
PII	Personal Identifiable Information
PIN	Personal Information Number
PHA	Potentially Harmful Application
PRIDA	Policy and Regulatory Initiative for Digital Africa
QR	Quick Response
TCP	Transmission Control Protocol
Raas	Ransomware-as-a-Service
RADPA	Round Table of African Data Protection Authorities
RAM	Random Access Memory
RDP	Remote Desktop Protocol
RSA	Rivest-Shamir Adleman
SaaS	Software-as-a Service
SIM	Subscriber Identity Module
SOP	Standard Operating Procedures
SPD	Sensitive Personal Data
SSID	Service Set Identifier
SSS	State Security Service
STEM	Science Technology Engineering and Mathematics
TLS	Transport Layer Security
ToR	The Onion Router
UFED	Universal Forensic Extraction Device
UGC	User-Generated Content
USB	Universal Serial Bus
USSD	Unstructured Supplementary Service Data
UN	United Nations
UNESCO	United Nations Educational, Scientific and Cultural Organization
UNICEF	United Nations International Children's Emergency Fund
UNPFA	United Nations Population Fund
VRP	Vulnerability Rewards Program
WAN	Wide Area Network

WI-FI	Wireless Fidelity
XSS	Cross Site Scripting
YAHOO	Yet Another Hierarchical Officious Oracle
ZKP	Zero-Knowledge Proof

TABLE OF CASES

TABLE OF LAWS

Administration of Criminal Justice Act 2015
Administration of Criminal Justice Law of Lagos State 2015
Advance Fee Fraud and Other Fraud Related Offences Act 2006
Advertising Practitioners Act 2004
African Union Convention on Cybersecurity and Personal Data Protection 2000
Child's Right Act 2003
Code of Practice for Interactive Computer Service Platforms/*Internet* Intermediaries 2022
Criminal Law of Lagos State 2015
Criminal Code Act 2004
Cybercrimes (Prohibition, Prevention, etc) Act 2015
Cybercrimes (Prohibition, Prevention, ETC) Amendment Act, 2024
Economic and Financial Crimes Commission (Establishment) Act 2004
Evidence (Amendment) Act 2023
Evidence Act 2011
Federal Competition and Consumer Protection Act (FCCPA) 2008
Independent Corrupt Practices and other Related Offences Act 2000
Lagos State Domestic and Sexual Violence Agency Law 2021
Money Laundering (Prohibition) Act 2011
National Broadcasting Commission Act 2004
National Cybersecurity Policy and Strategy 2021
National Digital Economy Policy and Strategy 2019
National Information Technology Development Agency Act 2007
NCC Consumer Code of Practice Regulations 2017
Nigeria Broadcasting Code 2020
Nigerian Communications Act 2003
Nigeria Data Protection Act 2023
Nigeria Data Protection Regulation 2019

Nigeria Police Act 2020
Nigerian Data Protection Regulation Implementation Framework 2020
Sales Promotions of Nigeria Code of Advertising Practice Sales Promotion and other Right/Restrictions 2004
Talinn Manual on the International Law Applicable to Cyberwarfare 2013
Terrorism (Prevention and Prohibition) Act 2022
The 1999 Constitution of Nigeria
The Penal Code Act, Laws of the Federation 2004
UN Protocol to Prevent, Suppress and Punish Trafficking in Persons 2000
United States Communications Decency Act 1996
United States Convention on the Rights of Persons with Disabilities 2008

CONTENTS

CHAPTER 3 - CYBERSECURITY THREATS

CHAPTER 4- TYPES OF CYBERCRIME

CHAPTER 5 - OTHER ACTS OF CYBER THREAT

CHAPTER 6 – CYBERSECURITY TOOLS & DATA PROTECTION

CHAPTER 7 – CYBERCRIME INVESTIGATION AND EVIDENCE

CHAPTER 8 - FRAMEWORK & POLICIES

CHAPTER 9 - CYBER VIOLENCE AGAINST WOMEN

CHAPTER 10 - DIVERSITY, EQUITY & INCLUSION IN TECHNOLOGY

CHAPTER 11 - PROACTIVE CYBERSECURITY STRATEGIES

Chapter 1

INTRODUCTION TO INTERNET

Human societies have long been built around information, since the creation of man. Thereafter, the world has never been known to be blank or empty. So, how was information communicated between people before the advent of the Internet, computers and smartphones? No online activity was ever envisaged or envisioned until technology evolved surpassing physical boundaries and connecting humans in the cyberspace. However digital age did not magically appear. Communication started right down from the Stone Age where early humans expressed themselves either by speech, signs or gestures.[1] The movement later shifted up to the agrarian age, thereafter to the industrial revolution age and subsequently to the information age and currently, to the artificial intelligence age. In other words, the evolution of traditional means of communication or sharing of information or content between humans from ancient civilization to the digital age showed there was no information gap, rather there has always been different tools of communication regardless of the methods available. Historically, the first known analogue computer was called the '*Antikythera Mechanism*' which developed from the knowledge of astronomy and mathematics courtesy of the Greek astronomers in the early first century BC,[2] while the mathematician and inventor Archimedes (circa 287-212 B.C.E) crafted and built the analogue computer, although this claim still remains inconclusive and unconvincing till today.[3] Thereafter in the 7th or 8th century AD, early Islamic scientists and astrologists produced the first astrolabe, an ancient astronomical instrument and circular metal calculators which were used to

---

1 „The oldest forms of human communication" <https//www.sahistory.org.za/article/> accessed 20 December 2022

2 Prof. Tony Freeth. „Scientists unlock mysteries of world's oldest „computer"<https:// www.bbc.com/news/science-environment-56377567 > accessed 21 December 2022

3 Owen Jarus. „World's first computer, the Antikythera Mechanism, „started up" in 178 B.C., scientists claim" <https://www.livescience.com> accessed 14 April 2022

track or predict the actual position of the sun, moon and planets as they repeatedly moved in cycles.[4]

The dynamics changed with the progression of the advent of digital technology brought about by the proliferation of Internet-enabled phones which facilitated access to information, networking, education, entertainment and other key variables of digital life. The Internet is known as the interconnection of computer networks. As inter-reliance on the Internet keeps getting increasingly essential to our common future, the transition from physical to virtual interaction continues to grow but the more we connect, sadly the more likely we encounter cyber criminals and become victims ourselves.

Clearly, majority of us have significant presence online. For example, this research was confirmed by the National Bureau of Statistics (NBS) which has stated that there were 222.6 million telephone subscribers and a total of 154.9 million active Internet subscribers as at the end of 2022 in Nigeria.[5] The COVID-19 pandemic equally has revealed to the world the importance of Internet presence because people were able to conduct their daily engagements online while professionals embraced remote work. With our smartphones or computer, electronic mails, we are connected to each other. According to *Earthweb*, the average person receives over 100 emails every single day while 80% of users check their mail daily.[6] Some have also imbibed the digital nomad lifestyle taking a foray into the cyberspace where they turn to source for news and seek for informed opinion. We also search the web daily for information enabled by browsers such as Google, Chrome, Microsoft, Opera, Mozilla, Firefox, Apple, Safari, Edge and other networks. In. ***Google LLC v. Defteros,***[7] the Court mentioned that the role of Google is to assist persons searching the web to find certain information and to access it.

Social media is a platform to reach a broader audience. That is why we disseminate information on social media platforms or networks such as Facebook, Twitter (X), Instagram, Linkedin, YouTube including messaging

[4] „Computer Science" < https://www.encyclopedia.com> accessed 22 September 2022

[5] „222.5 Nigerians use telephones – NBS" <https://www.vanguardngr.com/2023/04/222/> accessed 25 April 2023

[6] Jason Wise. „How many Emails Does the Average Person Receive Per Day" <https://earthweb.com/> accessed 01 November 2022

[7] (2022) HCA 27

platforms like WhatsApp and Telegram. There are also doomscrollers who devote their time to source for negative or bad news despite their disheartening and depressive effects, an act referred to as 'doomscrolling or doomsurfing.'[8] Experts have equally raised alarm over the adverse health impact of the growing addictive use of smartphones and the Internet among Nigerian youths. They have associated what they call obsessive use of technology with depression disorders and several other mental health issues.[9] This is not strange because many people go through challenging life transitions making them rely heavily on social media for solution. Companies and organisations have similarly continued to digitize their platforms while almost everyone has become Information and Communication Technology (ICT) compliant or digitally literate. Statistics say there are approximately 108.75 million digital users in Nigeria and the project has continued to increase.[10]

It is thus interesting to emphasise that the cyberspace is a virtual world where most people seek for news and informed opinion since the presumption is that citizens become better when they have access to information. United Nations (UN) in effect recognises that having universal access to information means that everyone has the right to seek, receive and impart information and beyond this, the right of access to information is considered an integral part of the right to freedom of expression. This right aligns with Goal 16: Target 10 of the Sustainable Development Goals (SDGs) which expect citizens to get public access to information with government protecting their fundamental freedoms in accordance with national legislation and international agreements. This is based on the premise that the Internet plays a crucial role in this fundamental freedom. Since the Internet employs millions of people all over the world, it is expected that majority will continue to pursue their online activities and as they do that, they are also likely to become potential victims of online-related crimes. Unfortunately, the cyberspace is vulnerable to many malicious cyber activities where perpetrators target people for purposes of making financial gain, inflicting

---

[8] Kenneth B. Rosen. „How to Stop Doomscrolling With Psychology" <https://www.wired.com/story > accessed 30 March 2022

[9] Ebuka Onyeji. „Addictive use of smartphones, Internet worries Nigerian health officials" <https://www.premiumtimesng.com> accessed 04 February 2022

[10] Mubarak Umar. „Data privacy day: Celebrating citizen"s right to privacy and protection in Nigeria" <https://www.thecable.ng/> accessed 04 February 2022

sabotage or disrupt business operations for personal satisfaction while devastating government infrastructures that affects essential services and private individuals.[11]

In 2022, the United States Federal Bureau of Investigation (FBI) report ranked Nigeria as the 16th country worst affected by cybercrime.[12] Recent statistics have also shown that in Nigeria, the number of password-stealing malware attacks[13] has doubled in 2022 when compared to year 2021.[14] In fact, the level of cyber-criminality has gone up higher both in the real and virtual world so much so that criminals with their sophisticated tools and intellect are working daily to outwit technology itself. Indeed, since information stealers have equally infiltrated into our computer systems, Internet-facilitated crime has assumed a high dimension in this modern world where e-commerce websites are compromised by hackers who steal sensitive data every day. In the words of the Head of the International Police Organisation (INTERPOL) National Central Bureau Nigeria and Vice-President INTERPOL (Africa), "the top five threats identified by the African Cyber-Threat Assessment Report 2021 are online scams, digital extortion, business email compromise, ransomware attacks and botnets."[15] These five threats do not exist in isolation; some countries are also having serious issues with Internet connectivity that is seriously crippling their digital connection with the outside world. For instance, countries like Spain have experienced more than 150,000 cyber-attacks since the beginning of COVID-19 pandemic. That explains why the US Federal Trade Commission disclosed that year 2021 was a goldmine for scammers due to its loss of several millions of dollars to fraudsters cashing in on shopping scams, cryptocurrency scams, loan scams, romance scams and other social media scams before the pandemic eased off.[16] In addition, website defacements, hacktivists data leaks and cyber-attacks have become visible and being used

---

[11] Shanfiq Ashrah, Veera Sundram and Jafaar Pyeman. „ Strong password can prevent you from becoming cybercrime victim" <https://www.nst.com.my/opinion/letters/2022/04 > accessed 18 April 2022

[12] Wale Odunsi. „Internet Crimes: Nigeria is 16th Worst Country- FBI" <https://dailypost.ng/ 2021/03/17> accessed 07 April 2022

[13] Malware is an umbrella term for viruses, worms, ransomware and spyware.

[14] Sami Tunji. „Password-Stealing Malware Attacks Rise by 145.65% in Nigeria - Report" <https://punchng.com> accessed 01 June 2022

[15] Interview with Nigerian Vice-Presidential candidate for INTERPOL, Garba Baba Umar conducted on 23 November 2021. <https://globalinitiative.net/analysis/interpol/ > accessed 24 December 2021

[16] Charlie Osbourne. „iPhone, Android users lose life savings to romance fraud, cryptocurrency operation" <https://www. zdnet.com/article/> accessed 17 March 2022

as digital weapons. The cyber warfare between Russia and Ukraine is another example signalling how far ransomware gangs can go on to attack each country's critical infrastructures to the extent that a dangerous software created by one country could enable its security services to listen-in, read messages and access sensitive data of another country.[17] The United States and China have also once threatened themselves with spying and intellectual property theft. In Nigeria, many young people are involved in cyber fraud and other unlawful online activities. Statistics revealed by the Economic and Financial Crimes Commission (EFCC), shows that cyber-attacks are among the fastest growing crimes across Nigeria with 80% of its 978 convictions being cybercrime-related offences.[18]

According to the 2022 FBI annual Internet Crime Report, a total of 848, 376 Internet crime complaints were filed in 2021 which is a 7% increase from year 2020 statistics with the top three cybercrimes in 2021 being phishing scams, non-payment/non-delivery and personal data breaches.[19] In 2024, the World Cybercrime Index identified Nigeria as the 5th cybercrime capital in the world.[20] These worrying trends demonstrates that it is important for the government and its regulatory agencies to do all in their powers to curb cybercrime because just from one's home or office, a criminal can disrupt the Internet of an entire country! Indeed we are all potential victims, notwithstanding the fact that our Internet activity is monitored daily by an Internet service provider (ISP) with our browser plugins and cookies also tracking our activities across multiple websites, including the information saved on our emails, online purchase receipts and electronic medical records which are all threatened by cyber-criminals who take advantage of our online activities, especially so long as we continue to share our personal details on social networks without caution, and worse if our electronic gadgets or software are not secured.[21]

---

[17] Matthew Sparkes. „UK prime minister"s office smartphones targeted by Pegasus spyware" <https://www.newscientist.com/ article/2316485 > accessed 20 April 2022

[18] Juliet Umeh. Cybersecurity: Why Organisations must Intensify Awareness. <https://www. vanguardngr.com/2021/10/ > accessed 22 February 2022

[19] David Anders. „Internet Crime Cost People More Than $6.9B in 2021, FBI Says" <https://www.cnet. com/tech/computing/Internet> accessed 28 March 2022

[20] „World-first Cybercrime Index ranks countries by cybercrime threat level" <https://www.ox.ac.uk/news/2024/> accessed 20 April 2024

[21] Melanie Lockert. „How do hackers use your information for identity theft" <https://www. creditkarma.com/ > accessed 23 November 2021

Daily the number of photos and videos containing child sexual abuse materials are found on the Internet. Sometimes the personal information innocently put on the Internet is used to attack celebrities, political-exposed persons or vulnerable persons. Private individuals are also affected when they fall victim to scammers who fraudulently lure them to reveal their social media and banking details through their compromised or stolen mobile phones. In as much as the Internet gives everyone the opportunity to express themselves, it equally creates opportunity for cybercrime, because cybercriminals remain concealed in their space and find it easy to facilitate criminal activities without being detected or arrested in time. Regardless, cybercrime is a different crime of a different world. It is different from other traditional crime where we can physically hold somebody culpable for his crime unlike in the digital landscape where cyber criminals are in a hidden environment.

During the COVID-19 pandemic lockdown, the physical world almost came to a standstill and people had to go virtual with many workers shifting to remote work while companies transferred their workload online. In light of this, the question arises; what position should we adopt and should we examine the behavioural pattern of those who perpetrate online crimes? Practically, there are preventive measures to adopt since cybersecurity awareness is all about taking a pro-active security protection. With that, it will then become difficult for a cyber-attacker to exploit any form of users' online vulnerabilities. In Nigeria, the foremost legal framework on cybersecurity is the Cybercrimes (Prohibition, Prevention, etc.) Act 2015. However the recent Cybercrimes (Prohibition, Prevention, Etc) Amendment Act, 2024 has amended the 2015 Act to insert some consequential words that were inadvertently omitted in the 2015 Act.

Thus, this book is structured into 11 chapters. Chapter one introduces the topic on the Internet while Chapter two defines cybersecurity and its components. Chapters three, four and five identifies the indicators of cybersecurity threats, types of cybercrimes and other acts of cyber threats. Chapter six discusses data privacy and access. Chapter seven interrogates cybercrime investigation and evidence while chapter eight examines the domestic and international legal framework governing cybersecurity. Chapter nine outlines the factors constituting cyber-violence against women. Chapter ten focuses on the concept of diversity, equity and inclusion while chapter eleven concludes the book and offers recommendations for proactive cybersecurity strategies. The purpose of this book is to drive advancements that make a lasting impact on the field of cybersecurity and Internet technology, shaping policy and playing pivotal role.

I. MAN AND INTERNET

The ubiquitous influence and the massive volume of global Internet traffic are fundamental to the interface between people and the Internet which has significantly improved. Despite man's effort to catch up with this rapidly development technology, the Internet has taken its toll on us. Over the years, information processing has always been central to living systems. Before the electronic mail became popular, we relied on physical paper to record, share or store information. We also dispatched letters by hand or through the post office. In other words, what predated the Internet age facilitated a harmonious relationship between man and his physical environment where man was and still is traditionally contented to network physically with his friends and business associates, although access to specific information about certain subjects were clearly hidden from many people. In Western countries, this was traceable to factors bordering on gender and racial discrimination until the court decided against pronouncing on inexplicitly stated or ambiguous rights. Even after personal computers began emerging in homes and offices in the 1980s, physical networking did not change much because many people did not readily embrace the electronic mail system until it became a reality in 1993.[22]

With the advent of the Internet, the status quo changed as all classes of people and races started connecting and enjoying access to information in the subject matter they all desired to learn regardless of their physical various locations.[23] This could not have been possible without the use of computer technology which humans resorted to generate and disseminate broadcast information. Applying this to the digital age, how then has man intervened with his electronic devices that came with the revolution of

---

[22] Jason Wise. „How many Emails Does the Average Person Receive Per Day" <https://earthweb.com/> accessed 01 November 2022

[23] *Griswold* v. *Connecticut* (1965) U.S. LEXIS 2282 cited in the article written by Alexandria M. Lord. „ The Revolutionary 1965 Supreme Court Decision that Declared Sex a Private Affair. < https://www.smithsonianmag.org > accessed 20 May 2022

technology? Undoubtedly, the Internet is in our face all the time and digital technology is intertwined with our lives as a result of the computer which interfaces with us through screens, printers, speakers, pads, keyboards and other computer accessories that we often use in our everyday world.[24] The logical explanation is that a person will readily interact with any tool he explores daily and when he does that, he dissects the tool and they blend together. In a way, the close relationship between Internet and its users can productively impact his space, as long as the user chooses the tool of the Internet to be so. That is the power of a computer.

Section 418 of the Criminal Law of Lagos State 2015 describes a computer as a device that computes, especially a programmable electronic machine that performs high-speed mathematical or logical operation or electronic machines that assemble, stores, correlates or otherwise processes information. Similarly, the Evidence Act 2011 in Section 258 defines a computer as any device for storing and processing information. Both interpretation of a computer depicts a nexus between man and his computer such that man will avail the computer tool to express itself according to the way he controls it. This aligns with the theory of Human-Computer Interaction (HCI) in psychology which states that there is an interface between human users and computers but that due to the multidisciplinary nature of HCI, it is individuals from different professional backgrounds that will contribute to the success of the computer. These professionals will include scientists, social scientists, lawyers, computer engineers and other digital experts. On the professional level, HCI seeks to focus on the function of technology as it affect people's use of a specific technology as well as to teach people how to design usable technologies and how the field of technology affects the workforce.[25] Regarding the intersection, an American psychologist, Dr Joseph Carl Robnett Licklider (1915-1990) formulated the 'man-computer symbiosis' which postulates that when we put a computer in the hands of a human being, the interaction between them brings a major opportunity to further accelerate and transform the world of information.[26] From the literal perspective however, HCI could even mean we are just

[24] „Computer Science" < https://www.encyclopedia.com> accessed 22 September 2022
[25] „What is Human Computer Interaction? <https://hci.cc.metu.edu.tr/en/ > accessed 02 February 2022
[26] Keenan Mayo & Peter Newcomb. „The Birth of the World Wide Web: An Oral History of the Internet" <https://www.vanityfair.com/news/2008/07/> accessed 12/12/2021

interacting with our computer or our digital devices playfully. Clearly, the relationship between the Internet and man does not have a limited boundary and this is part of the reason this relationship has given rise to a set of people who are called digital nomads. These are remote workers who travel to different locations on a regular basis, using technology to work from their various locations as long as they have a Wi-Fi connected laptop or smartphone.[27] Unfortunately where Internet users go virtually, scammers are likewise bound to follow virtually. Further concerns have also been raised about the virtual wars that occur when two different countries seize the virtual domain belonging to one another. This has impacted negatively on the freedom of expression of users in the affected countries. In Nigeria, Section 39 of the 1999 Constitution provides that every person shall be entitled to freedom of expression, including the freedom to receive and impart ideas and information without interference.

Interestingly, Human Computer is also a profession. This discipline relates to the sociology of the Internet which seeks to find out how the Internet play persuasive roles in managing or facilitating communication and interaction with how the Internet affects the social life of users since the Internet has become indispensable in human daily lives as a tool to stay connected even at a distance. No wonder there are Internet influencers who have established credibility in their online trade while enjoying access to massive followership, thus enabling them to persuade their followers to support certain specified activities.

In the words of N.R. Narayana Murthy, an Indian billionaire businessman and founder of an Information Technology firm, "Technology is all about using the power of science to make life better for people, to reduce cost, to improve comfort, to improve productivity, etc."

2. HISTORY OF INTERNET

In the 1960s, the modern Internet pioneered by the Advanced Research Projects Agency Network (ARPANET) was established by the United States Department of Defence Advanced Projects Agency (DARPA) which is a military agency set up for the development of emerging technologies solely for academic and research purposes in order for scientific users in

[27] Matthew Karsten. „How To Become A Digital Nomad" <https://expertvagabond.com?digital-normad-tips/> accessed 25 February 2022

universities or research institutes can communicate with each other. Historically, ARPANET thus became the first design of what is known as the Internet today because it deployed packet switch technology with built-in error connection and package assembly to send and receive data. No wonder, ARPANET is called the grandfather to the WWW. The Internet was later adopted in 1983 after a team of military engineers in the Defence Agency created an access for computers located on different networks to communicate with each other via a 'Transmission Control Protocol/Internet Protocol' (TCP/IP).[28]

With our electronic devices, we have all become Internet sleuths, searching the Internet daily for negative and positive information. The Internet is made up of a massive network of specialized computers called routers. This enables us to access the web irrespective of distance which is no longer a barrier in family and business communication. For digitized education and the need to promote personalized learning, schools have embraced the Internet to connect their students to tools and resources. Libraries are able to share books all over the world creating larger virtual platforms to engage readers. Healthcare systems are adopting telemedicine approach for improved patient efficiency in order to reach millions of people who require faster and convenient health services.[29] Many people are also shopping online.[30] There are online tax payment reminders, job offers and recruitments and information alerts. During the outbreak of the COVID-19 pandemic, the lockdown provided an opportunity for health workers to interface with many people across the world as almost every sector moved online while non-essential workers were equally conducting their businesses from home, with others becoming hybrid workers thus providing valuable support to offline workers. The economic sector was not left behind as many companies and organisations moved their transactions online including the judicial sector which switched to virtual hearings. This is a court hearing conducted by audio-visual means, where cases are conducted without the need for participants to attend the court in person.[31] It is an indisputable fact that, every sector benefits from technology. For some people, it is using their

---

[28] Gavin Wright. „ARPANET" <https://www.techtargets.com/searchnetworking/> accessed 29 March 2022

[29] „National Online Recovery Day" <https://nationaldaycalendar.com> observed every 22nd September.

[30] „Safer Internet Day U.S" <.https://nationaldaycalendar.com> observed every February 8.

[31] Many States issued Practice Directions for Remote Hearings and Guidelines for Sitting During Covid-19 Pandemic in 2020 which are still operational till date

technical skills to advance their careers in IT. Anyone cleaning, operating or repairing our smartphones or computer systems like computer engineers and maintenance technicians would also be online most of the time. Those who are active browsers on the Internet are generally referred to as cybercitizens, cybersurfers, infonauts, netizens, cyberians or cybernauts.

Like many adults, children also have a close relationship with their computers and e-devices. That is according to a national survey which indicated that half of children in the U.S.A., for example, are said to own smartphones by age 11 and nearly 9 out of 10 teenagers have their own electronic devices.[32] In recent times, some states have enacted laws banning children under 14 from having social media accounts,[33] but according to the 2022 study carried out by the European Institute for Gender Equality (EIGE), the age of 13 is the minimum legal age for children to open a personal profile on most social media platforms.[34] These children are not left out and that is why most of them have developed a dependency on their electronic devices and as a result have been exposed to pornography and other vices, whether or not by choice. As teenagers continue to 'live' on social media, so have rates of depression, anxiety, and suicide have risen, leading scientists to investigate the potential connection between children and social media. That is why Experts believe that exposure to social media at a young age could lead to deleterious mental health concerns.[35] In fact, children who are so proficient in technology are called digital natives.[36] It is interesting to note that the cloud is also the Internet. When something is in the cloud, it means it is stored on Internet servers instead of our computer hard drives. An Internet of things (IoTs) cloud itself is a massive network that supports IoT devices and applications which includes the underlying infrastructure, servers and storage needed for real-time operations and processing. For example, Google Drive is a free cloud-based[37] storage service that enables users to store and access files online.

---

[32] Anya Kamennetz. „Report: More Than Half Of U.S. Children Now Own A Smartphone By Age 11" <https://www.npr.org/2019/10/29/> accessed 10 August 2023

[33] Check the States of Florida, Texas, Alaska, Arkansas, Louisiana and others

[34] EIGE"s Research on „Combating Cyberviolence Against Women and Girls, 2022

[35] Corryn Wetzel. „Negative Effects of Social Media may Impact Adolescent Girls and Boys at Different Ages" <https://www.smithsonianmag.com > accessed 29 March 2022

[36] Awake Magazine. „Technology; Your Master or Your Servant?" (No. 2. 2021 Edition)

[37] Erica Mixon, Ivy Wigmore. „What is Google Drive?" <https://www.techtarget.com> accessed 03 June 2022

The summary of it all is that if the Internet continues to connect us together in a world that is brought about by communication technologies, of which individuals and groups are organized around digital information network, then we can rightly say we are living in a network society. This principle of network society is credited to two sociologists who are Jan Van Dijk in his Dutch book titled *The Network Society* in 1991 and Manuel Castells in his research on *Globalization, Network Society and Internet Studies* in 1996, propounded the theory of network society which basically indicates the impact of informationalism on the society as it relates to the spread of the networks of digital technologies which depends upon whether people can harness technological improvements for their own collective good and leverage technology for the beneficial future of humanity.[38]

3. WHAT LIVES INSIDE THE INTERNET?

We are living in the digital age and the Internet is the gateway for users. This is the time when large amount of information are widely available to many people through the tools of computer technology.[39] We all want to stay informed and connect with family, friends, business associates, professional colleagues and even strangers. There is no discrimination on the Internet as the good and the bad makes use of this technology and live on the Internet just like how the good and the bad live in the physical world. In November 2022, the world's population was estimated to have reached a record of 8 billion people[40] out of which are 5 billion Internet users.[41] These Internet users visit different social platforms almost every day – a place where we may either experience Internet burnout or Internet satisfaction.

There are different types of websites which comprises of the surface website, dark website, deep website and the emerging dark artificial intelligence (AI) website.

i) **Surface Web**

The Surface Web represents just a small fraction of the whole Internet that is readily available to the general public and searchable with standard web

[38]Prachi Juneja. „Network Society- Rise of Digital Networks" <https://www.managementstudyguide.com.network-society.htm/> accessed 10 November 2022

[39] David Thomas. „What is the digital age"< https://www.ventitech.com/blog/> accessed 03 June 2022

[40] „Day of 8 Billion" United Nations" <https://www.un.org> accessed 10 December 2022

[41] „Internet and social media users in the world 2022" <https://www.statista.com> accessed 10 December 2022

search engines. The surface web is also called the visible web or indexed web because it not a concealed web. Users get information easily on the surface websites where users access the public search engines in their regular day-to-day activity and therefore do not need any special configuration on their electronic devices to browse the surface web.[42] That is why cybercriminals find it easier to operate on the surface web like stealing other people's personal information and data for financial gain. In other words, they use the Internet as a marketplace for cybercrime to lure unsuspecting public members into phantom contract deals or fake employment offers. However, these cybercriminals are more vulnerable to being caught easily too. Examples of surface web are Facebook, YouTube, Wikipedia and other regular blogging websites.[43]

ii) Dark Web

This is a website which is not indexed by search engines but require special software or authorization to gain access into the dark web which is a network of websites that are full of illegal activities that needs specialized browsers like the 'The Onion Router' (ToR) or the Invincible Internet Project (I2P) for users to get in. The content of dark web is accessible only to browsers that require specific network configurations since they are intentionally hidden or concealed inhabited mostly by malicious hackers who make use of the web to scam their victims. Other features of the dark web is that it provides anonymity of users by keeping their communications private; Users must gain access to the web through a special password or encryption; It is often depicted as a sinister forum that accommodate fraudulent dealings in credit cards, narcotics and drugs, stolen cultural artefacts/artworks, stolen passwords and other account information, contract killer services, guns, child pornography and sexual abuse materials, counterfeit money, FraudGPT, stolen software, black market use of cryptocurrency and other crimes. Sadly, there have been instances where hackers steal data or private information of other people and then reveal such sensitive information on the dark web forum. As a result of this, victims whose data are stolen go through mental

---

[42] „EI-ISAC Cybersecurity Spotlight" <https://www.cisesecurity.org/insights/spotlight/> accessed 06 September 2022

[43] Kelsey Taylor. „Detailed Introduction About the Surface, Deep & Dark web Levels Explored" <https://www.hitechnectar.com/blogs/> accessed 28 November 2022

health issues and financial hardship.[44] Basically the underlying factor is that those using the dark web forums usually want to evade detection and be secure in their cocoon. That is why dark web criminals bear fake names which are not their original names in real life. Apart from using dark websites to publish stolen data, a suspect once used the dark web to request for a "hitman that can deliver murder-for-hire services" and had to pay bitcoin to the dark website so that his illegal transaction could not be traced to him.[45] Similarly, a transnational child sex offender in UK who sexually abused children was convicted for using the dark web to advise and encourage other paedophiles on how they might best commit equally horrific crimes.[46]

It should be noted that the dark web is not all about crime or an entire online underworld where criminals live.[47] For instance, an established network like Facebook has a dark website where Internet users can get in through 'the onion router' (ToR) browser. Normal people use ToR to protect their privacy from unscrupulous marketers, identity thieves and irresponsible corporations while others use ToR to protect their children online, to research sensitive topics and to circumvent censorship. Law enforcement officers also use ToR for online surveillance and sting operations.[48] In addition, Human Rights Activists, Whistle-blowers, Bloggers, Journalists, Opposition Politicians and people living in authoritarian countries equally use the dark web if they want to remain anonymous or if they do not want others to monitor their digital footprints.[49] It is of interest to note that cybercriminals are not immune from cybercrime because they also scam themselves on the dark web but they cannot report to the Police for obvious reasons.[50] More importantly, ToR was developed by the US Naval Research Laboratory and funded by the US government.

---

[44] Emily Ritchie. „Medibank Cybercrime Updates" https://wwwmedibank.com. au/livebettere/ newsroom/ post/ > accessed 12 November 2022

[45] Richard Webster. „Tampa woman sentenced for murder-for-hire order planned through the dark web" <https://www.acenewstoday.com/ > accessed 22 April 2022

[46] Hamish Mureddu-Reid. „Dark web paedophile who coached abusers jailed"< https://www.bbc. com/news/> accessed 23 June 2023

[47] Avant Academy. „What Is the Dark web and How to Access It?"< https://www.avast.com/dark-web > accessed 07 March 2022

[48] Tor Inception <https://2019.www.torproject.org/about/tor...> accessed 22 April 2022

[49] Eva Galperin. „Internet Experts Debunks Cybersecurity Myths" <https://www.wired.com/video/watch/> accessed 07 March 2022

[50] Danny Palmer „Cyberscammers are scamming each other and revealing dark web secrets along the way" <https://www.wired.com/story/> accessed 08 December 2022

iii) **Deep Web**

The Deep Web, also known as the invisible web or hidden web is oftentimes regarded as the portion of the Internet that is hidden and not visible to the conventional search engines such as the Google or Yahoo networks that we use every day. Deep web content therefore is any content that we cannot easily find from a public search engine except we use a password or a username before we can access the content. Examples are email messages, chat messages, bank account balance, Amazon order history, electronic health records and other content used by financial institutions, web mail, cloud storage and some restricted media that is not easily accessible on the Internet.[51] In the context of a cyber-attack, a cybercriminal was jailed for two years for committing thousands of cybercrimes including creating his business on the deep web (an area of the Internet that search engines cannot find) to set up an online hackers shop; to launch attacks on Google; to sell people's malware products enabling users to spread viruses; to conduct and steal data and to offer a web attack service for anyone who had a grudge against an individual or company.[52]

iv) Dark AI – The enthusiasm for AI is growing bigger. AI is a field of computer science that focuses on creating intelligent machines that is capable of performing tasks that require human intelligence. Despite the advantages of AI, cybercriminals are also using AI to perpetrate bad activities. That is why it is associated with darkness as anything dark is considered a mystery or evil in nature. In this sense, dark AI could be implied to mean a dangerous and unethical application of artificial intelligence without any ethical limitations, just as the which dark Web accommodates anonymous and illegal activities to thrive online, dark AI poses severe threats to society, enabling malicious actors to engage in heinous acts such as identity theft, cyber blackmail and extortion as well as enabling paedophiles and predators to share content. The deep web also encourages spread of misinformation and malicious propaganda, loss of privacy and cyber warfare.[53] To regulate AI-generated content or to ensure its content are verified for accuracy, leading

---

[51] Andy Patrizio. „What is the deep web?" <https://whatis.techtarget.com/definition/deep-Web > accessed 07 March 2022

[52] BBC News. „Hacker Alex Bessel; jailed for cybercrime offences" <https://www.bbc.com/news/ukj/> accessed 07 March 2022

[53] Yael Hsu. „ The Rise of Dark AI" <https://blogs.timesofisrael.com/> accessed 20 July 2023

companies in AI have resorted to manage the risks posed by AI technology through the following ways - engage in security testing of their AI systems by internal and external experts before information is released to the public; update automated errors by reviewing them with human eyes before content is published; ensure that people are able to spot AI by implementing watermarks; publicly report AI capabilities and limitations on regular basis; research the risks such as bias, discrimination and the invasion of privacy as well as invest in AI detectors that can help distinguish a fake content from the authentic content.[54]

It should be noted that information or content posted on websites are not totally secured irrespective of whether some websites are not visible to locate. We are not to assume that we are anonymous even when using secured websites because our computer can be compromised while browsing.[55] We should also be mindful that some Internet users do not usually have direct control over their websites. For example, some schools have been able to block access to many websites for security purposes or they could take such a position just to protect their students' privacy from online predators and cyber bullies. Our network administrators or Internet service providers can equally block our websites for legitimate reasons. When a website is blocked or banned, users are restricted or denied access to information or resources available on the website, although this could be a temporary ban. Globally, September 28 is annually observed as the "Banned Websites Awareness Day." It is a day to raise awareness of how censorship negatively impacts intellectual freedom.[56]

4. INTERNET ACCESS AND HUMAN RIGHTS

The Internet remains a level playing field for everyone and in today's world; Internet access is considered an essential service just like water and electricity. Everyone needs access to a seamless, affordable and high-speed Internet where people will have to connect with each other from their various locations. This process is largely driven by the concept of human

[54] Shiona McCallum. „Seven AI companies agree to safeguards in the US" <https://www.bbc.com/news/tecnology-66271/> accessed 21 July 2023

[55] „EI-ISAC Cybersecurity Spotlight" <https://www.cisesecurity.org/insights/spotlight/> accessed 06 September 2022

[56] „Celebrate Banned Websites Awareness Day on the Wednesday of Banned Books Week" <https://www.nonstopcelebrations.com> accessed 06 September 2022

rights which are inherent and universally applicable to everyone in the physical and online world. Human right takes a justice-centred approach which is a rights-based approach. Applying a rights-based approach in Internet-related matters is expected to deal with issues concerning misuse of the Internet, data privacy of citizens, cybersecurity and safe Internet, digital divide, lack of access to technology and gender inequality among several factors. Globally nearly 6 out of 10 people are said to be excluded from the Internet while some countries in the developing world do not enjoy unhindered access to the Internet since Internet access require infrastructure to be in place. This could be attributed to the category of people living in rural areas as they are likely to experience restricted access to the Internet because rural areas may lack existing cable or fibre-optic Internet.[57]

Access to the Internet comprises of two distinct dimensions. Firstly, it promotes the ability to view and disseminate content online without fear or favour and secondly, it is the ability to use physical infrastructure, such as our mobile phones or computer, to gain access or create pathways to such online content.[58] The dimensions of access to the Internet falls under the term 'Internet Freedom' which is defined as an exercise of internationally recognized human rights online, such as freedom of expression, freedom to seek or impart information or ideas and freedom of peaceful assembly online.[59] Access to the Internet is therefore closely linked to the right of freedom of expression or speech and the right to privacy. In ***Copland* v. *United Kingdom,***[60] the Court defined private life as the privacy of communication which covers the security and privacy of mail, telephone, email, information (data) privacy, online information and other forms of communication where the purpose is not meant to suppress free speech and expression. Internet access has been held to be a right that requires protection of the law because it relates to freedom of expression. In ***Kalda* v. *Estonia,***[61] the European Court of Human Rights (ECtHR) held that the

[57] Human Rights Watch. „Digital Disruption of Human Rights" <https://www.hrw.org/news > accessed 07 March 2022

[58] „Is there a Right to the Internet under International Law?" <https://www.mediadefence.org/> accessed 09 March 2022

[59] Freedom of the Net 2022 <https://freedomhouse.org/country/united-kingdom > accessed 10 March 2022

[60] (2007) ECHR 253

[61] Application No. 17429 (January 2016) <https://hudoc.echr.coeint/eng?i=001-160270 > accessed 09 March 2022

applicant's right to freedom of expression had been violated by a prison's refusal to grant the applicant access to Internet websites containing legal information and this had consequently breached his right to receive information. However, access to the Internet is a derivative right even though it has not been expressly stated as a full-fledged fundamental right. Despite this, the United Nations Educational, Scientific and Cultural Organisation (UNESCO) adopted some recommendations in 2003 on 'Communication and Information' while recognising that basic education and literacy are prerequisites for universal access to cyberspace, further recommended that all member states should support universal access to the Internet as an instrument for promoting the realization of human rights as defined under the Universal Declaration of Human Rights (UDHR).[62] According to UNESCO, a universal access to cyberspace refers to an equitable and affordable access by all citizens to information infrastructure (notably to the Internet) and to information and knowledge essential to collective and individual human development.[63]

To this end, in 2011, the Freedom Online Coalition consisting of a group of countries that were deeply committed to human rights and fundamental freedoms as proclaimed in the UDHR was established in The Netherlands. The purpose of the Online Coalition group was meant to balance the freedom of expression, access to the Internet, the protection and promotion of the rights of its users as well as to ensure that Internet freedom issues are placed on the international agenda as a strategy to drive concrete policy changes and outcomes.[64] Thereafter, in 2012, the UN Human Rights Council (UNHRC) passed a resolution calling on all countries to facilitate access to the Internet for their citizens. The Sustainable Development Goals (SDGs) adopted by the UN in 2015 also expanded the right of access to the Internet by recognizing the spread of ICT and global interconnectedness.[65] Consequently, a non-binding UN Resolution on the Internet was passed in July 2016 and adopted by more than 70 countries where the UNHRC articulated the need for access to Internet an essential

---

[62] „Recommendation concerning the Promotion and Use of Multilingualism and Universal Access to Cyberspace" <https://www.unesco.org/en/lagal-affairs/> accessed !2 April 2022

[63] Ibid.

[64] See <https://freedomonlinecoalition.com> accessed 25 February 2022

[65] See Goal 5(b) and Goal 9(c)

human right.[66] While describing the Internet as being a great potential tool to accelerate human progress, it also condemned any measures that encourages policing of the Internet or acts that intentionally prevent or disrupt access to information online, which may likely threaten free speech and lead to speech censorship or regulation of content posted by Internet users as these actions will negatively impact on the technology companies which may be forced to remove extremism and hate speech on their platforms, thereby infringing on the rights of websites and other digital platforms.[67]

Although there is no explicit provision under human rights law or treaties which says everyone has a right to the Internet, the right to express oneself on the Internet can be deduced from the framework of the UDHR and the International Covenant on Civil and Political Rights (ICCPR), which states that everyone has the right to seek, receive and impart information and ideas of all kinds, regardless of where the country is situate and the type of the media involved.[68]

As an integral part of the human rights to freedom of expression, the Internet remains a platform for human freedom, expression and creativity. No member state must therefore interfere with the freedom to express oneself nor should citizens face constitutional challenges over this freedom, because where free speech is suppressed, it will inevitably weaken democratic institutions. In ***Shreya Singhal v. Union of India,***[69] the Supreme Court struck down Section 66A of the Information Technology Act 2020 relating to restrictions of online speech as unconstitutional on the ground that the provision violated the freedom of speech under the Constitution. According to the Court, the Internet gives any individual a platform which requires very little or no payment through which to air his views. In ***Faheema Shirin RK v. State of Kerala & Ors,***[70] the Court stated that the right to access the Internet is a part of right to education and right to privacy under the Indian Constitution because Internet access not only enhances the opportunities of students to acquire knowledge but also enhances the quality

---

[66] Utkarshshara. „Right to Internet and Fundamental Rights" <https://www.legalserviceindia.com> accessed 08 April 2022

[67] ***Gonzalez* v. *Google LLC*** No. 18-16700 (9th Cir. 2022)

[68] Azad Essa. „What can the UN do if your country cuts the Internet? <,https://www.aljazeera.com/features/2017/5/8/> accessed 08 April 2022

[69] AIR 2015 SC 1523

[70] AIR 2020 Ker 35

of education. Similarly in ***Amnesty International Togo v. The Togolese Republic,***[71] the ECOWAS Court of Criminal Justice held that access to the Internet should be seen as a right that requires protection of the law and that any interference with the right has to be provided for, by the law specifying the grounds for such interference. In effect, this judgment is a depiction of the exception in every human right law which provides that human rights are not absolute on grounds of national security, public order, public health, public morals and the rights or reputations of others. All these exceptions are legitimate reasons for suspending fundamental human rights where it is deemed necessary. This explains why Section 45 (1) of the 1999 Constitution provides that in the interest of defence, public safety, public health, public morality and public order, fundamental human rights may be restricted.

The freedom of expression itself has further demonstrated the very porous nature of the Internet being a public resource platform that has millions of entry points. It is open and accessible to everyone, no doubt. That is why it is possible for different people to be accessing the Internet at the same time from different locations such that a single Internet connection can carry hundreds of connections for internal and external users.[72] This obviously calls for regulation. For instance, in a bid to regulate social media and online publications as it relates with national security in Nigeria, the National Information Technology Development Agency (NITDA) released a Code of Practice for Interactive Computer Service Platforms/Internet Intermediaries in 2022 with the aim of protecting the fundamental rights of Nigerians and non-Nigerians living in Nigeria which provided guidelines for interacting on the digital ecosystem.[73]

5. THE ADVENT OF WWW

Information is crucial in the 21st century. The World Wide Web (WWW) is the leading information retrieval service of the Internet as well as the largest repository of information and knowledge made accessible to an indefinite number of people. According to history, American computer programmer, Ray Tomlinson (1941-2016) invented the email in the 1960s which existed

---

[71] ECW/CCJ/APP/61/18 (2020)

[72] Andreas M. Antonopolous. „How to deal with the ‚porous perimeter" <https://www.networkworld.com/article/2333497?> accessed 25 February 2022

[73] <https://nitda.gov.ng/> 2022/06 PDF

long before the WWW, often known as the Internet.[74] Regarding the creation of the web, British Scientist, Tim Benners-Lee invented WWW in 1989 as a platform to help scientists share their data and transform governments, businesses and societies, while computer scientists Vinton Cerf and Bob Kahn have also been credited with inventing the Internet communication protocols. The intention of these web inventors is that all people should be able to create and access information.

WWW rests on the foundation of worldwide or global interconnectedness which gives people the ability to understand and function in an increasingly multicultural, international yet interconnected environment for easy exchange of ideas and knowledge between people or to make flow of goods, capital and services easier. The Internet and the WWW remain the biggest decentralized communication system humanity has ever seen. Decentralization means that the Internet is controlled by several networks and global technology giants. There is no monopoly and this is why decentralization ensures that the Internet remains a public resource that is healthy and available to all of us.[75] In other words, no one network can own or control the Internet, neither can it be switched off for everyone. Clearly, the web gives users the access to a vast array of documents, images, sounds, animations and movies that are connected to each other by means of hypertext or hyperlink. In HTTPS which stands for Hypertext Transfer Protocol Secure, if you see a link with a blue underlined word and you click on it and it takes you somewhere else, that is hypertext. Whereas with hyperlink, all a user needs do is to select a word from a text, then you will receive additional information or related references within the text.[76] World Wide Web acts as a domain that can operate with or without hypertext. However HTTPS is much more secured than HTTP, its extension.

The WWW working process is accessed through the Hyper Text Transfer Protocol (HTTP) which allows two computers to exchange information. This HTTP relies on the Transmission Control Protocol (TCP) to set up the connection between two machines which in turn uses the Internet Protocol (IP) to send and receive data. Your IP address follows a set

---

[74] Sudeshna Dutta. „National Technology Day 2023: Date, Theme, History, facts, Ouotes, Theme" <https://www.edudwar.com/> accessed 05 January 2023

[75] Who controls the Internet? <https://www.Internethealthreport.org/ > accessed 25 February 2022

[76] Britannica, The Editors Encyclopaedia. "World Wide Web" (2019) <https://www.britannica.com> accessed 12 February 2022

of rules regulating the information that are sent to our devices is when they need to connect. The IP does the hard work of actually moving the data across the Internet since everything on the Internet has an IP address such as <www.malthouse.com>.[77] TCP is responsible for ensuring that data can be sent reliably over the Internet. It works through a number of software ports or receptacle that acts to keep data separate on the same computer in order to make it possible to browse a web page, receive email and listen to streaming music at the same time. TCP also ensures that all data sent from a computer is received by its destination. Thus for the Internet, the two most important protocols are the TCP and the IP. They are so inextricably linked that they are often written together. However, IP is only concerned with moving data while TCP ensures the data arrives.[78]

In view of the strategic importance of the Internet enabled by the rising use of technology, the world celebrates the World Wide Web day every first day of August of every year because without the web, the belief is that the earth would be a lonely or secluded place while not forgetting that before the WWW was created, people have had to spend a lot of money to contact others that were far away. Fewer people also used the Internet until the WWW which was designed from the very start to be an open environment, hit the ground. The WWW awareness day which came into being in 1990 is a day to appreciate their inventors, Sir Tim Berners-Lee and Robert Calliau who developed the HTTP.

In summary, we can conveniently contact ourselves through voice calls, chats and calls at the click of a button. The Internet has proved to be the fastest-growing medium of communication for information, movies, videos, songs, games and academic topics that are easier to download on devices. In this vein, statistics have estimated that there are over 1.6 billion live websites around the world with the top five being the large technology companies such as Google, YouTube, Facebook, Baidu and Wikipedia while 40,000 search queries are processed by Google every second.[79] These large technology companies provide hugely valuable services to billions of people across the world. In addition to giant technology companies dominating the

---

[77] Michael Gariff. „What is an IP address and how can you change it with VPN?" „<https://www.zdet.com/article/> accessed 10 July 1999

[78] FutureLearn Open University on Cybersecurity. December 2022

[79] <https://nationaltoday.com/world-wide-web-day/> accessed 13 February 2022

global sector Internet, there are also many other websites that are blog websites, small business websites, personal websites and government-owned websites.

6. BROADBAND COMMISSION FOR SUSTAINABLE DEVELOPMENT

The Internet works through a series of networks that connect devices around the world through telephones lines where users are provided access to the Internet by the Internet Service Providers (ISPs) which is based on the fact that easier connectivity in all ramifications do have the capacity to accelerate economic development and improve the overall quality of life and wellbeing of citizens. This is driven by the widespread use of mobile broadband and Wi-Fi in that has paved the way for this connection to be wireless.[80] What makes this possible is the 'Broadband' which is a type of active Internet connection that is provided by ISPs. In other words, your ISPs connect your home to the Internet through a modem which in turn re-connects our homes to the broader Internet and determines the maximum Internet speed by providing broadband services to us at a fee. With a symmetrical connection and speed, Internet subscribers' can upload or download larger files faster, eliminate Internet bottlenecks and enjoy seamless cloud services.[81] That is why the Broadband connectivity is relevant for interactive immense learning, research, hybrid study and more which is critical for closing the digital divide and ensuring that government addresses the technological needs of its citizens and businesses.[82] The term 'Broadband' simply means a high speed Internet that is faster than the average dial-up connection which requires using more than one band to transfer data. This is quite different from a Wi-Fi connection which is one of the means by which one can connect to the broadband to access the Internet without needing a physical connection between two devices. Wi-Fi provides wireless high-speed Internet access. Broadband due to its high-speed quality or far superior speed enable communities in rural and urban areas, regions and

---

[80] Michael Aaron Dennis. „Internet Computer Network" <https://www.britannica.com/technology/Internet> accessed 21 June 2022

[81] It should ensure symmetrical connection – a connection with equal download and upload speeds unlike an asymmetrical connection which does not have equal download and speed.

[82] „Dublin progresses smart city vision with free public wifi" <https://www.smartcitiesworld.net/> accessed 21 June 2022

nations to connect faster regardless of the large amount of data transmission.[83] With this, the speed element will make citizens enjoy their browsing experience seamlessly. Interestingly, fibre broadband has emerged to serve communities effectively as possible because it has the potential to be much faster and has a bigger bandwidth than other broadband options.[84]

Tracing the evolution of Broadband, in 2010, the Broadband Commission was established by the International Telecommunication Union (ITU) and United Nations Educational Scientific and Cultural Organisation (UNESCO) with the aim of boosting the impact of Broadband on the international policy agenda, thus expanding broadband access in every country, with the purpose that the Broadband Commission is to bridge digital divide among people of all classes and enhance universal and seamless connectivity to the world population, borne out from the glaring digital divide between those living in the rural and urban areas or those that classified under gender and socio-economic categories. This is based on the principle of 'net neutrality' which seeks to ensure equal treatment for all Internet traffic, without discrimination and devoid of any preferential treatment or restrictions by the ISPs.

The Broadband Commission is also to ensure that networks of the Internet must connect with one another effortlessly, as a tool for socio-economic development. To achieve this purpose, the Commission launched a new framework of Seven Targets 2025 to facilitate 'Connecting the Other Half' of the world's population. These seven targets seek to expand Broadband infrastructure and Internet access for the use of populations around the worlds o they can align with the 2015 UN Sustainable Development Goals (SDGs). The seven ambitious targets are built on the technology of the Fourth Industrial Revolution (4IR) which seeks to connect the world by mobile devices with unprecedented power, speed, storage, capacity and access to knowledge.[85] Essentially, the purpose of the targets is to connect billions of people and achieve the goals of Broadband access in the following ways:

1. make Broadband policy universal;

---

[83] „Broadband Definition" <https://www.investopedia.com> accessed 13 February 2022

[84] „Broadband or Fibre? Whats the Difference & Which Do You Need?" <https://www.airband.co.uk/> accessed 20 August 2022

[85] Aklaus Scwarb. „The Fourth Industrial Revolution: What it means. How to respond" <https://www.weforum.org/agenda/> accessed 05 December 2022

2. make Broadband affordable;
3. get people online;
4. acquire digital skills;
5. use digital financial services;
6. get businesses online, and;
7. achieve gender equality.

To work in tandem with these seven targets in the country, the Nigerian National Broadband Plan (NNBP) 2020-2025 was launched by former President Mohammadu Buhari in 2020, to increase the Internet and Broadband penetration across the country. There are four critical pillars in the Broadband Plan, namely Infrastructure, Policy, Incentives, Demand Drivers and Funding which all work together to address various socio-economic challenges faced by the country.[86] Among other things, the new Broadband Plan is designed to deliver data download speeds across Nigeria with a minimum 25Mbps in urban areas and 10Mbps in rural areas, with effective coverage available to at least 90% of the population by year 2025 at a price not more than ₦390 per 1GB of data (i.e. 2% of median income of 15 of minimum wage).[87] As of November 2022, Broadband penetration was said to have hit a new high speed of 46%[88] while in June 2023, it was revealed that Nigeria has achieved 50% Broadband penetration target.[89]

It should be noted that the yearly observance of the World Telecommunication and Information Society Day every May 17 since 1969 marked the establishment of the ITU[90] and the signing of the first International Telegraphic Convention in 1865. The purpose of the yearly observance is to help raise awareness of the possibilities the Internet and other opportunities ICT can bring to societies and economies through focusing on the importance of many issues in the area of ICT. According to the ITU Secretary-General, equitable access to digital technologies is not just a moral responsibility, but it is also essential for global prosperity and sustainability. In 2022 observance of the World Telecommunication Day was

---

[86] „Nigerian National Broadband Plan 2020-2025" <https://www.ncc.gov.ng> accessed 05 December 2022

[87] Olufemi Adeluyi. National Digital Economy Policy And Strategy (NDEPS): 2020-2030 published by the Federal Ministry of Communications and Digital Economy

[88] Temitayo Jaiyeola. „Broadband penetration hits 46.24%" <https://thepunchng.com> accessed 03 January 2023

[89] Juliet Umeh. „Nigeria has achieved 50 out of 70% broadband penetration target, says Danbatta" <https://www.vanguardngr.com/2023/06/> accessed 30 July 2023

[90] The ITU is the UNO specialized body for the Internet, telecommunication and broadcasting.

focussed on commitment to expand digital access across all regions as well as to all ages.[91] In 2023, the theme was 'Empowering the least developed countries through ICTs'. In ***Foundation of Media Professionals v. Union Territory of Jammu & Kashmir***[92] otherwise called the 4G Landmark Case, the petitioner contended in the first place that it can easily be inferred that a lot of people will suffer if there is a ban of high-speed Internet and in the second place that as an Internet operator company interested in providing a high-speed Internet access for its customers, it must not engage in predatory pricing by charging below cost to outrun the other competitors. In fact, the European Commission considered the action as an abusive behaviour against France Telecom SA (formerly Wanadoo Interactive SA) during the critical take-off period of Broadband service in France where France Telecom was sanctioned for engaging in abuse of a dominant position when it deliberately restricted market entry causing harm to consumers. The European Court of Justice in its ruling held that dominant operators cannot use their market power to stifle competition.[93]

7. PEOPLE WHO LACK INTERNET ACCESS

Internet technology has no doubt revolutionised the world. Yet some people are still resistant to the cyber age and averse to the use of technology. These set of people do not rely on digital technologies as they hold a rigid opinion that nothing can be compared to physical interaction. These set of people could be called digital immigrants because they were probably brought up before the advent of digital technology and so do not see any reason why they should embrace virtual interaction. (In the local Nigerian parlance, this category are said to fall into the 'old school' category). Equally, there are those who do not have access to the Internet and other ICT technologies. Statistics say nearly 3 billion people or 37% of the world's population have never used the Internet despite the COVID-19 pandemic lockdown that drove people online.[94] Similarly, 60% of school-age children in

---

[91]Member Communique on Celebrating World Telecommunication and Information Society Day. ,<https://www.itu.int/en/mediacentre/Pages/MC> accessed 06 May 2022

[92] (2020 SCC Online SC 453)

[93] ***France Telecom SA* v. *Commission of the European Communities (T-340/03) EU:T20007:22(30 January* 2007**). Antitrust: Commission welcomes judgment of the Court of Justice in French broadband case" (Memo/09/147) <https://ec.europa.eu/commission/presscorn.../ > accessed 14 April 2022

[94] More than a third of world"s population have never used the Internet." <https://www.theguardian.com> accessed 30 April 2022

urban areas do not have Internet access at home and around three-quarters of school-age children in rural households do not have Internet access at all. Mostly affected are school-age children in the sub-Saharan Africa and South Asia.[95] There also lies a gap between those who are benefiting from the Internet and those who are not. A widening gap can exist if Mr. X can access the Internet faster than Mr. Y. Of particular note is the research that says it is expected that about 360 million smartphones will be on the African continent by year 2025.[96] In any case, currently about 60% of Nigeria's population are connected to the Internet.[97] Having said that our phones or computers rely on Internet access to perform, we should be mindful that many are still excluded from the Internet and the factors could be attributed to the following reasons:

- Rural people who are living without Internet connection;
- Poor people who cannot afford to own Internet-enabled devices such as desktop computers, laptops, smartphones, video games and other electronic devices;[98]
- Some people are simply not familiar with technology and therefore not interested in using the Internet even though they can afford it. They believe it is not necessary for them to be in the public spotlight;
- Temporary Internet outage due to cyber-attacks. For example, thousands of Internet users across Europe were thrown offline due to a likely cyber-attack at the beginning of Russia's offensive in Ukraine causing partial network outage;[99]
- Some criminals are barred from using a computer or smartphone. For example, a sex offender could use the Internet but will not be allowed to have a social media account and all of his time online will be monitored by a probation officer;[100]

---

[95] „Two thirds of the world's school-age children have no Internet access" <https://www.unicef.org > accessed 30 April 2022

[96] Reuters Journalism Institute Report. <https://reutersinstitute.politics.ox.ac.uk/news/> accessed 30 April 2022

[97] SERAP 2022 Report titled "We are all Vulnerable: Crackdown on Data and Digital Rights in Nigeria."

[98] The presumption is that the poor do not use online access for civic engagement

[99] Agence, France–Presse. „Thousands Without Internet After Massive "Cyberattack" In Europe: Report" <https://www.ndtv.com/world-news/> accessed 05 March 2022

[100] Sarah Lageson. „Sex-Offender Laws Sent a Man to Prison Over a Prayer Livestream" <https:/ /www.wired.com/story/> accessed 23 February 2022

- Those who fail to register their SIM cards in accordance with their home government's regulation. This could be a deliberate act on the part of some citizens who simply distrust their government and feel hesitant to hand over their details required for capture in their Voters' cards, international passports, BVN and NIN. In Nigeria, repeated registration exercises is also a discouraging factor;[101]
- Citizens may be restricted from the Internet when government decides to suspend access to the Internet for security reasons emanating from civil unrest,[102] transmission of hate messages, or series of cyber-attacks, such a government may be justified to do so up to an extent.[103] Section 45 of the 1999 Constitution provides that in the interest of defence, public safety, public morality and public order, fundamental human rights may be restricted;[104]
- If the directive given by the Federal Government to telecommunications companies is to block outgoing calls on all unlinked mobile telephone lines after the deadline for verification expires, this action can deprive citizens of Internet use;[105]
- Digital divide attributed to lack of digital infrastructure. People have to be connected before they derive benefit from ICTs. They also need to know how to make use of their devices otherwise they cannot enjoy all the benefits that digital literacy offer. For example, they cannot obtain digital information. They cannot shop online. They cannot learn online. They cannot trade their skills online. They cannot participate democratically in citizen or professional elections and they cannot communicate faster with their friends and family;
- Strict Internet censorship rules and crackdown on Internet users just to suppress dissent could cause complete or partial Internet blackout. Some countries like China, Iran North Korea and Russia consider the Internet

[101] Ope Adebayo. „Why are African governments blocking phone lines of citizens? <https://www. aljazeera.com > accessed 08 April 2022

[102] NDTV. „Internet Ban Extended Till July 10 In Violence-Hit Manipur" <https://www.ndtv.com/india-news/> accessed 08 July 2023

[103] ALJAZEERA. „Internet Shutdowns raise free speech concerns in India" <httpss://www. aljazeera. com/news/2017/9/18/> accessed 08 April 2022

[104] The Information Technology Act 2000 of India empowers the government to block information from public access in the interest of sovereignty and integrity, public order and prevention of incitement and friendly relations with foreign states.

[105] ***SERAP* v. *FRN*** (FHC/L/CS/711/2022)

as a threat to their regime security apparatus. In extreme circumstances such as threats to critical infrastructures, Russia has once considered 'YouTube' a tool of Western Information Warfare used against their country;

- When network companies conduct maintenance shutdown for brief period to carry out maintenance checks and repairs, Internet users will lack access in that short duration;
- A phobia is a strong and irrational fear of something that does not generally pose any significant danger. There are those who suffer from cyber-phobia or technophobia and this category represent digital phobic persons who dread technology or are always reluctant or afraid to try out any new technology, smartphones, computers or the Internet. There are also those who have suffered from the use or misuse of their data;
- There are people who take a dislike to new technologies. They are often referred to as 'Luddites'. A Luddite is an opponent, antagonist, opposer and resister of technology.
- Bail conditions may include granting severe restrictions on a defendant's use of his electronic devices and Internet. In a United States case involving fraud charges levelled against the defendant, the Court ruled that the defendant should get a new phone; that the new phone should not be Internet capable; that the new phone's communication functions should be restricted to text messages and voice calls, with all other messaging applications prohibited; that he should get a basic laptop that has limited functions; and that the laptop should have only a monitoring software to track user-activity. The defendant was also forbidden from using other electronic communication devices.[106]

In essence, efforts must be made to close the digital divide among citizens by providing an enabling tech environment that will guarantee meaningful access to Internet infrastructures, applications and services. This will surely boost the development of digital economy, digital professionalism, digital inclusive citizen engagement, digital participation, digital skills and digital accessibility, after all the duty to provide meaningful digital access to the populace rest on the government to make citizens digitally inclusive

---

[106] Lu Cohen & Akriti Sharma. (ed. Sam Holmes) „Sam Bankman-Fried, prosecutors reach new bail agreement" <https://www.reuters.com/legal/> accessed 30 March 2023

through their regulatory policy framework. This duty is derived from the theory of 'social contract' propounded by the German Philosopher, Jean Jacques Rousseau (1712-1778) who advocated that governments should intervene to ensure that any society's economic benefits should be fairly and meaningfully distributed to all citizens regardless of their status. This also aligns with Section 21(b) of the 1999 Constitution which provides that the State shall encourage development of technological and scientific studies which enhance cultural values. This implies that 'No one should be left behind.'

8. ETHICS ON THE NET

Netiquette is made up from the two words; '*net* and *etiquette.' The* Net is a shortened form of Internet while etiquette is derived from the meaning of ethics - good manners or good behaviour. In the online world, netiquette refers to the socially acceptable rules of online conduct which represents the importance of cultivating proper manners and behaviour required or expected from Internet users. Netiquette rules are therefore a set of rules practiced and advocated in electronic communication over any computer network.[107] Netiquette rules as ethical principles are based on a foundation of rules whether on law or morals. Rule followers are said to be responsible while those who disobey rules are called irresponsible. Ethics as a moral philosophy is a skill to cultivate because ethics and responsibility skills equip us with the knowledge to comprehend and become conscious of our ethical role and responsible behaviour online. These skills involve understanding the laws that govern online behaviour, as well as regulate issues surrounding plagiarism, copyright infringement, online safety and taking responsibility for our actions.[108]

The ethics of Internet users are being called into question when it clashes with the right of free speech. Ethics are moral principles that govern a person's behaviour which helps conduct his activity in a fair manner. Ethics generally cautions us not to break any code of conduct rules. That is, ethics embody the values of what we must do and what we must not do. Ethics encourages us to comply with rules. Human beings acquire ethics and they

[107] „What is Netiquette? 20 Netiquette Rules" <https://www.kapersky.com/> accessed 15 January 2023

[108] Matthew Lynch. „What are the 7 Skills of Media Literacy?"< https://www.theedadvocate.org/> accessed 22 May 2023

carry them wherever they go either to their physical or online community. Just as we have physical identity, we also have digital identity. A lot of unethical practices are common in the online world which pushes people to behave irresponsibly although demographic factors such as age, gender, education, race, income, ethnicity, religion, political affiliation affect how we behave on the Internet.

It is important that an Internet user should know first that he is a digital citizen who depends on his digital tools to exercise his right to speak without government interference while enjoying his right to online privacy. This means you have an unrestricted access to the Internet but you must be law abiding and so you should be able to use your discretion to "know obscene information when you see it."[109] This is the essence of having a regulatory framework which is meant to ensure digital citizens behave responsibly on the Internet despite the freedom of expression and the fundamental right to access information. A digital citizen is someone who has an identity on the Internet. For example, when you apply for a new job, many employers will try to find and evaluate your social media presence in order to check if you are a suitable candidate. Advertisers also use our publicly available information gathered from our social profile and search history to determine what products to market to us.[110] Due to the fact that Internet platforms potentially make human rights violation easier and by extension puts us in a situation of particular vulnerability, digital citizenship is accompanied by many rights and responsibilities which are intended to protect us as we interact online. These human rights are basically captured under the law governing freedom of expression, privacy and freedom of association. So, whether you are on Facebook, Twitter (now called X), WhatsApp, Instagram or on any social media networking service with your smartphones, you must conduct yourself in a responsible manner as listed hereunder.

Remember it is up to you to avoid engaging in risky activities online. Social media users may need to use terms that are not offending in order to avoid platform censorship because your network moderation filter

[109] Culled from. Justice Potter Stewart's famous words "I know it when I see it" in ***Jacobellis v. Ohio*** 378 U.S. 184 (1964) regarding a case involving an exhibition of an obscene content in a film.

[110] Charlie Osborne. „How to delete yourself from Internet search results and hide your identity online" <https://www.zdnet.com/article/ > accessed 11 May 2022

algorithms can suppress or remove any offending term you post. Be guided by the law that penalizes the display of criminal acts in whatever form it takes. For example, in some countries forwarding animal cruelty image or peddling videos depicting violence on the Internet are prohibited.[111] Under the United States Communications Decency Act 1996, Section 230 absolves Internet intermediaries (ISPs, Bloggers) that republish content posted by Internet users or comments left by readers. In other words, the law is saying the person who creates and post online content is the one directly responsible for it. Thus, a defendant cannot be liable for defamatory material unless he is found to have published that material.[112] Therefore, a user must weigh the risks and opt to take or not to take them because whether we like it or not, the Internet shapes public opinion. As outlined below, a good Internet behaviour focuses on safe, ethical and respectful relationship with other online users which broadly consist of the following;

- Online behaviour operates in tandem with prescribed ethics and code of conduct;
- All online content should be treated the same in accordance with the principle of "net neutrality or open Internet" – This means that you control what you see and do online without the interference of Broadband providers;
- Users are free to choose their online experience;
- There are laws to protect the rights of Internet users;
- You can decide to freely move your personal data from one online platform to the other;
- Right to create and share digital content or media;
- Right to privacy in digital communities;
- Right to express your ideas and opinions freely and right to report anyone or anything that seems inappropriate;
- Right to use decent language and behaviour when interacting with others.

What Are Our Online Responsibilities?

Mobile phones and computers have become our digital companions. Despite the fact that social media does seem uniquely harmful to some people, we

[111] „Reporting Internet Abuse" < https://www.americanhumane.org> accessed 07 June 2022
[112] ***Google LLC* v. *Defteros*** (2022) HCA 27

still consider them as repository of knowledge and a platform in which we can express ourselves and find friends unhindered. It keeps us in constant communication with the world, yet we are not to misuse the technology in our hands otherwise this could make people publish false or spread misleading claims online. Be aware of your responsibilities and be cautious so your keyboard does not become an instrument of crime, because what you spew online can spill over into real world violence. Being careful will help you to know the danger signs and guide your choice to act responsibly. In India for example, the government has, in their new rules, prohibit objectionable religious content alongside transmitting child/adult pornography, trademark infringements, fake information and anything that could be a threat to the sovereignty of the nation that users can flag to social media platforms.[113] The primary responsibilities of an Internet user are listed below:

- Respect the opinions and ideas of others;
- Adhere to your employer's Internet restrictions;[114]
- Do not use or share other people's work without their consent;
- Do not impersonate others online;
- Misinformation and dis-information are toxic. Do not share denigrating graphics or violent content,[115] threats or online hate speech[116] that will trigger religious violence just because you want to trend on social media;
- Do not indulge in harmful video pranks just to increase your followership on your social media account or increase your income;[117]
- Do not engage in investment or romance scam under the pretext of being bored otherwise you may get yourself into trouble;
- The online community can easily be deceived. Do not believe everything you see on the Internet;

---

[113] Express News Service. „Grievance appellate committees will be set up to redress social media users" complaints: Centre to Delhi HC „<https://indianexpress.com/article/cities/> accessed 03 January 2023

[114] *United States* v. *Norsal* 676 F.3d 854 (9th Cir. 2012)

[115] The accused person shared posts encouraging violence against Jews and Muslims, posted quotes from Hitler in a private chat group and disseminated terrorist publications". See „Far-right fitness guru jailed over terror manifestoes"<https://www.bbc.com/news/> accessed 24 June 2023

[116] See the UN Strategy and Plan of Action on Hate Speech 2019 where hate speech is defined as any kind of communication that attacks or uses pejorative or discriminatory language with reference to a person or a group on the basis of who they are, in other words based on their religion, ethnicity, nationality, race, colour, descent, gender or other identity factor.

117 Atty Gilberto Lauengco„Online Pranks that Cross the Line" <https://www.pna.gov.ph/opinion/pieces/> accessed 16 August 2023

- Do not share the picture of children who are involved in cases involving sexual offences, crimes and rituals or witchcraft either as victims, witnesses or defendants;[118]
- Do not share old videos to create panic and fear among the populace especially if the purpose is to create confusion, hate and anger;
- Responsibility to report cyberbullying, defamation, threats and inappropriate use of digital resources.[119] For instance, Facebook has a defamatory reporting form for defamatory content that violate their community standards. All it takes is just for an individual to report and Facebook will investigate;
- Cease posting defamatory/derogatory information or publishing offensive articles against another person and apologise immediately you are called to order, otherwise the victim can instruct his lawyer to write you a 'cease and desist letter' or threaten you with a lawsuit;[120]
- Do not raise false alarm or create fictitious story out of a non-existent crime;
- Be civil. No swearing of profanities. No toxic posts or comments as direct insults. Refrain from cyber harassment or threatening others online.[121]
- Do not share obscene information except if it is for the public good or in the interests of science, literature, art and general learning.[122] In ***U.S. v. Matthews***,[123] the defendant was convicted for sending and receiving child pornography over the Internet. The defendant asserted that he did so for journalistic and research purposes, but could not produce any notes indicating he was writing an article on child pornography or doing a research on the role of law enforcement in policing child pornography on the Internet;
- Facebook for instance can restrict a user's accounts if it feels the offending user has posted something inappropriate, abusive or violent, or has been sending spam friend requests or messages to people he does not

---

[118] See The Ilorin Declaration of 1998 (Code of Ethics for Nigerian Journalists)

[119] „Digital Rights and Responsibilities" <http://laurabiancoedtech.weebly.com/ > accessed 28 February 2022

[120] *Nicholas Okoye* v. *Ladun Liadi, Google Inc & Ors* LD/170/2012

[121] *Eloms v. United States 575 U.S. 723 (2015)*

[122] See Section 153 of the Criminal Law of Lagos State 2015

[123] *209 F.3d 338 (4th Cir. 2000)*

know or has been engaged in any online activity that goes against Facebook community standards. The restrictions are normally temporary but repeat offenders may sometimes get a long-term ban.[124] Similarly, a user can also be restricted on Linkedin or his content may be removed or his account suspended if he has violated Linkedin User Agreement or Professional Community Policies. Twitter (X) had once suspended the social media account of anti-Police website for violating its rules against inciting violence;[125]

- An online user must remember the expression 'digital permanence' which means that what goes on the Internet stays on the Internet forever. Your uploaded or posted videos, blogs, photos, clicks or links, tweets, website visits, Google search, views of YouTube items, and Facebook posts are your digital footprints which are designed to live forever.[126] So watch it! Do not allow your data to fall into wrong hands;[127]
- Some institutions provide guidelines for their officers on how to use their personal social media accounts. In law enforcement agencies, officers are to abide with the specific standards of conduct which govern Police behaviour in online platforms mandating them to maintain a low profile on social media because making or sharing a hasty, unwise comment or response to a post can compromise their agency reputation while such erring Police officer could be sanctioned for officer misconduct. For instance, the combination of the Nigeria Police Social Media Policy 2020, the Nigeria Police Act 2020 and the Nigeria Police Guidelines for Recruitment, Promotion and Discipline of Supernumerary Police 2013 are set out to caution Police Officers from committing social media misconduct, and further restricting all Police personnel from making, sharing or commenting on any post that ridicules, maligns or disrespects any race, gender, ethnicity, tribe, religion, nationality and politics. Officers

---

[124] Alex Finnis. „Why is my Facebook Account Restricted?" <https://inews.co.uk/news/technology/ > accessed 30 May 2022

[125] Emma Colton. „Twitter suspends „KillerCops" account that put bounties on police officers after massive LAPD data release" <https://www.foxnews.com/us/> accessed 31 March 2023

[126] Dave Moore. „Once on the Internet, always on the Internet" <https://www.normantranscript.com> accessed 28 April 2022

[127] Google has announced on 21 April 2022 that the public can submit removal requests of personal information such as email address, home address and phone number which pops up in search results in a bid to protect privacy. Google will also consider removal requests for images of minors, deepfake pornography and other explicit content. <https://www.wired.com/story/remove-personal-info-from-google-search-results/> accessed 07 May 2022

are also prohibited from identifying themselves as Police officers on their social media accounts. The policy is meant to uphold ethical standards and regulate the activities of all Officers on social media platforms so they won't undermine the agency's mission otherwise citizens will likely interpret an Officer's personal opinion as his agency's opinion.[128] Thus, the interest of one's employer is important when commenting upon matters of public concern.[129] However, usage of social media platforms such as Linkedin and WhatsApp groups for promoting professional and educational goals is permitted for Officers to build capacity and network for the benefit of Police Force personnel.[130] Basically, the general rule to Officers is "Apply caution in your speech when you are on social media.[131] This is especially so because the Police institution is a regimental organisation, and discipline is the pivot on which it revolves;[132]

- Judges should use social media with restraint because their social media post could compromise their impartiality and consequently undermine the dignity of the judiciary.[133] Judges while not forbidden from having personal social media accounts are expected to respect their country's judicial code of ethics. A social media tip sheet published by the American Bar Association's Judicial Division includes issuing reminders to Judges not to post the dates or locations of judicial meetings, or give a hint about the likely outcome of a case and to be generally careful about what they endorse with clicking on '*Likes*';[134] Their freedom of expression is therefore, subject to additional specific restrictions, which also apply to activities outside courtrooms.
- Social media influencers in Nigeria are also to ensure they comply with the Nigerian Code of Advertising Practice. The adverts they pass across must be verified claims and ethical. Misinformation is a crime;

---

[128] Michael Rubinkam. <Phily Officers fired over social posts can pursue First Amendment claim" > accessed 12 June 2023

[129] ***Pickering* v. *Board of Education of Township High School.*** 391 U.S. 563 (1968)

[130] Perez Brisibe. „Inspector General of Police regulates social media use for officers" <https://www.vanguardngr.com/2020/06/> accessed 20 February 2020

[131] ***Moser* v. *Las Vegas Metropolitan Police Department*** (2021) WL 98249 (9th Cir. 2021)

[132] Okpako Omudhowo. *Policing – The Science of Discretion* (2021, Nereva Publishing & Educational Services) Benin City

[133] „The Case of the Judge Who Sent Controversial Twitter Posts" <https://globalfreedomofexpression.columbia/> accessed 04 March 2023

[134] Carly Lewis. „Survivors Suffer When Judges Misunderstand Social Media" <https://www.wired.com/story/judges/> accessed 04 March 2023

- Some Western countries can request the removal of certain information from Google search results. This delisting request is done on a case-by-case basis. But you must provide the Uniform Resource Locator (URL)[135] you want to remove and explain why Google should remove it. This request will be reviewed by weighing and comparing the information with your rights in accordance with the data protection law in your jurisdiction. Note that Google does not consider every delisting request;[136]
- Obey all intellectual property laws. Do not infringe other people's work online. In the case of ***UTV Software Communication Ltd v. 1337x,***[137] the Delhi High Court held that there is no difference between an infringer in the physical world and the infringer in the online world;
- Most important of all, be a rule follower. A rule follower seeks to know the law and follows that law to the letter. Be mindful of the laws of your country, especially the different aspects of cybercrime because if you break the law, the Police can summon you to appear for questioning.[138] The essence is to deliver justice for online victims, improve public safety, and create an orderly Internet world, but if a law violates your right of free speech, you can approach the Law Courts for redress.

---

[135] The URL is location and address of a webpage. Example of a URL address is: https://www.jw.org

[136] Chalie Osbourne. „How to delete yourself from Internet search results and hide your identity online" <https://www.zdnet.com/article> accessed 11 May 2022

[137] (2019) SCC Online Del. 8002

[138] A TikToker was sentenced to 3 years in jail for defaming a popular actress, Eniola Badmus. See the published report in<https://www.intelregion.com/entertainment/> dated 05 April 2024

Chapter 2

INTRODUCTION TO CYBERSECURITY

1. WHAT IS CYBERSECURITY?

In the technology sector, there are concerns over cybercrime or cybersecurity incidents. A cybercrime is a crime that involves a computer since the computer may have been either used as a tool to commit a crime, against another person or the computer itself may be the target. Computer therefore provides an opportunity for criminal minded or even legitimate Internet users to explore the 'benefits' of crime. In ***R* v. *Gold*,**[1] a hacker accessed the contents of an electronic information service after visiting a computer exhibition where the system was being demonstrated by an engineer. Thus our computers, its components and the purposes for using them must be protected by all means in this cyber-age. Protecting our computer devices against cyber-attacks or misuse extends to protecting other components of the computer systems which includes the hardware, software, data, Internet-connected applications, network and programmes. A cyber-age is an age of computer or Internet digital. Where cyber-activity or operation takes place in the cyber domain, we should envisage and predict cybersecurity risks or cyber-attacks from threat actors. The prefix 'cyber' refers to all Internet-enabled activities relating to computers and information technologies while the term, 'security' is the state of being free from threat or danger. A combination of the two words 'cyber' and 'security' put together as cybersecurity imply that all activities enabled by the use of computers or information technologies should be free from dangers by taking effective measures to protect our security and privacy from bad actors who are also referred to as, cyber-criminals, cyber-thieves, digital bandits, hackers and invasive advertisers.

---

[1] (1988) 1 AC 1063

In this circumstance, cybersecurity could be defined as a body of technologies, processes and practices designed to protect programs, networks, software, USB drives and data from all forms of cyber-attacks or unauthorised access. Cybersecurity could also be defined as a computer or information security where you have to add security features to strengthen your computer programs or the protection of your computer systems and networks from information disclosure, theft, vandalism, invasion of privacy or damage to hardware, software and electronic data.[2] For instance, if your computer shares the same memory hardware with other computers, your information could be stolen by those who are sharing the system with you. So you need to fortify your computer system or device from any potential security breach or vulnerability. Cybersecurity in essence has become a critical intervention tool to mitigate cyber-threats generated by malware, viruses, trojans and other cyber threats from damaging computer systems and networks.[3] For example, in order to ensure that users are secured online, it was reported that Google has been busy removing apps infected with malware[4] that were downloaded from its playstore by millions of users.[5]

The definition continues. Cybersecurity further refers to the safety measures undertaken either to investigate cybercrime incidents or evaluate the extent of the nature and scope of the crime in order to protect a computer system or personal device against network intrusion or unauthorised access from criminals such that when there is cybersecurity legal framework or cyber-policing in place, it prevents our sensitive information or data getting into wrong hands and if it does, there are legal mechanisms to intervene for redressing the wrongs or punish the perpetrators.[6] This requires that international and local safety standards institutions must be available and capable to address and enforce the regulatory policy and rules. For instance, in an effort to help healthcare organizations protect their patients' personal health information, the National Institute of Standards and Technology (NIST) updated its cybersecurity guidance for the healthcare industry. The purpose is designed

---

[2] Computer Security. <https://www.britannica.com> accessed 20 June 2022

[3] Sharon Shea. 'What is cybersecurity?' <https://www.techtarget.com/searchsecurity/definition/ > accessed 20 June 2022

[4] Malware is an umbrella term for viruses, worms, ransomware and spyware.

[5] 'Google removes malware-infected apps from Play Store' <ncsc.gov.uk> accessed 04 August 2022

[6] Cybersecurity vs. Data Privacy <https://amtrustfinancial.com/blog/ > accessed 02 February 2022

to help the industry maintain the confidentiality, integrity and availability of electronic protected health information - a term which covers a wide range of patient data, prescriptions, laboratory results, records of hospital visits and vaccinations.[7] According to the NIST, cybersecurity is the ability to protect and defend the use of cyberspace from cyber-attack measures. Despite the complexities and challenges that are impeding cyber activities, the primary goal of cybersecurity is to safeguard and implement defensive measures or strategies that can effectively thwart or mitigate all forms of cybercrime.

Cybersecurity can be divided into the following categories:

Network Security – This is when we secure a computer network from intruders or we ensure the security of IoT devices and critical infrastructures from bad actors.

Application Security – This is when we keep our software and devices free of threats or cyber theft.

Information Security – The four core pillars are privacy, confidentiality, integrity and availability. These pillars protect essential trade secrets of organizations and their intellectual property.

Operational Security – This is when we deploy solutions to determine how and where data can be stored.

Disaster Recovery and Business Continuity -This seeks to interrogate how organizations will respond to cybersecurity incidents or any other cyber-attack in a timely manner.

End-Use Education – This is a call on everyone to embrace cybersecurity education by following good security practices through training, awareness and precaution to prevent tech theft.[8] In other words, we all have a role to play in making sure our cyberspace stays safe.

A combination of all the above-named six categories is focused on boosting information security, protecting devices, defending threat intelligence or external attack and generally helps to respond to any potential real-time, unplanned and unanticipated cyber incidents. The four underlying factors governing cybersecurity are to:

Govern: Identify and manage security risks;

---

[7] Alexandra Kelley. 'NIST Revises Cybersecurity Guidelines Specifically for HIPAA' <htpps://www.nextgov.com/cybersecurity/2022> accessed 22 July 2022

[8] 'What is Cybersecurity? ' <https://www.kaspersky.com/resource-centre/> accessed 22 July 2022

Protect: Implement controls to reduce security risks;

Detect: Investigate and understand cybersecurity events to identify cybersecurity incidents;

Respond: Mechanism response through investigation, countering and recovery from cybersecurity incidents.[9]

According to the UN Security Council, the global annual expenditure on cybersecurity reached a total of $1 trillion in year 2020 – 50% higher than in 2018-with most expenses focused on damage repair and recovery.[10] *FutureLearn* has claimed that the estimated global cost of cyber-attacks is predicted to rise as high as $10.5 trillion by 2025.[11] With this alarming figure, robust cybersecurity frameworks have adopted the combination of Technology (application of scientific knowledge); Processes (series of progressive steps) and People (Human beings are the most intelligent species on the planet) to curtail cybercrime where all these inclusive factors are taken into consideration.

Note that every November 30, the world observes the Computer Security Day which serves as a reminder for all Internet users to protect their computers and keep them secure. It is a fact that our computer devices hold a lifetime of data, irreplaceable photos, journals, novels, passworded and other valuable information which exposes us to cybercrime. The question is, how do we then secure our data? The response is let us enable Windows Update. Install and keep running antivirus software. Turn on windows firewall. Use strong passwords and do not write them down. Back up critical data. Log off the computer when not in use and amplify awareness on computer security issues.[12]

2. HISTORY OF CYBERSECURITY

'Cyber' is a prefix associated with all web or Internet-enabled operation and virtual activities in this computer and information age. The word 'cyber' was first coined by American mathematician and philosopher, Professor Norbert

---

[9] ACSC. 'The cyber security principles' <https://www.cyber.gov.au/acsc/view-all-contents/> accessed 20 June 2022

[10] Press Release of the Security Council on 'Explosive Growth of Digital Technologies of Creating New Potential for Conflict, Disarmament Chief Tells Security Council in First-Ever Debate on Cyber threats' <https://www.un.org/press/en/2021/sc14563.doc> accessed 23 February 2022

[11] 'Cyber Security Foundations: Start Building Your Career in Cyber Defence' <https://www. futurelearn. com/experttracks/> accessed 23 July 2022

[12] 'Computer Security Day' <https://nationalcalendar.com> accessed 30 November 2022

Wiener (1894-1964) who formulated the science of cybernetics. Cybernetics is derived from *kybernetes,* a Greek word which stands for 'those who steer or govern'. According to Professor Norbert Wiener, cybernetics is the 'science of control and communication in the animal and machine' – a definition which relates the science of cybernetics to the study of automatic control of any system by using technology. In subsequent years, cybernetics has come to be interpreted as the science of the control of complex systems in technology or the science of all forms of control and information processing.[13] However, in modern times, cybernetic technology has been defined as a process that examines the intended and unintended consequences of technology for people and the planet. It aims to ensure that humans and the environment should be at the forefront of technological innovation and that new systems are safe in a changing world.[14]

Another historical inventor in the cyber-technology world was Auguste Kerckhoffs (1835-1903), a German Professor of Languages who is still regarded as the father of computer security after he published an article in the Journal of Military Science which laid the foundation for modern cryptography-the art of writing or solving codes.[15] Cryptography is a method of protecting information and communication through the use of codes such that only those for whom the information is intended can read and process the information. For example, cryptanalysists can decrypt cryptographic algorithms or codes and their workings. Fundamentally, cryptography is a specialised area of mathematics that is concerned with protecting information so that it can be transmitted and received securely. That explains why the term is derived from the Greek word *kryptos*, which means hidden. Cryptography is closely associated with email encryption and decryption or other plain-text messages which helps prevent data loss even if a mobile device, hard drive or storage medium fall into wrong hands.[16] Note that in real life, we use cryptography every day even if we don't realize this. Our social media messages, online banking, email and shopping all rely on

---

[13] Erik Gregersen. 'Cybernetics. '<https://www.britannica.com/science/cybernetics> accessed 26 August 2023

[14] Lauren Play. 'What is Cybernetics' <https//www.anu.edu.au/news/all-news/> accessed 02 December 2022

[15] HEC Paris <https://china.exed.hec.edu > accessed 23 February 2022

[16] Cryptography definition. <https://www.kaspersky.com/resource-center/ > accessed 23 February 2022

cryptographic algorithms that are designed, tested, approved and adopted by artificial intelligence (AI) regulatory authorities in jurisdictions globally.[17]

Under the African Union Convention on Cybersecurity and Personal Data Protection 2000, cryptology is defined as the science of protecting and securing information particularly for the purposes of ensuring confidentiality, authentication, integrity and non-repudiation. Its tools consist of a wide range of scientific and technical tools (equipment or software) which permits enciphering or deciphering.

As with most inventions, computer evolved through the works of many notable figures among who are named as follows:

- The British Mathematician, computer pioneer and inventor, Charles Babbage (1791-1871) is credited with having conceived the first automatic digital computer, a general-purpose computing machine called the 'Analytical Engine'[18] which was designed to perform more complex computations;
- Augusta Ada Byron also called Ada Lovelace' (1815-1852) interest in mathematics propelled her research on computer programming where she made a distinction between numbers and symbolic operations in computing. In fact, her research notes till date are regarded as the earliest and most comprehensive account of computers. Ada Lovelace contended that computers as the phenomenon of technology can perform any abstract operation which can automate many of the laborious task humans do. She also believed that by and large, computing machines can go beyond just calculating numbers;[19]
- John Vincent Atanasoff (1903-1995), a Mathematics and Physics professor is known as the father of computer after inventing the ABC computer which was recognised as the first digital computer in the world, although the computer had exact specification and function;[20]
- The British Mathematician Alan Turing, (1912-1954) who is credited to be the father of computer science after creating the 'Universal Turing

[17] Matthew Sparkes.'US chooses encryption tools to protect us from quantum computers' <https:// www. newscientist.com/article/2327054> accessed 05 July 2022

[18] Michael R.Swaine. 'Analytical Engine' <https://www.britannica.com/technology/> accessed 29 June 2022

[19] Justyna Zwolak.'Ada Lovelace: The World's First Computer Programmer Who Predicted Artificial Intelligence' <https://www.nist.gov/blogs/> assessed 25 March 2023

[20] William Harris & Chris Pollette. 'Who Invented the First Computer?' <https://science. howstuffworks.com/> accessed 25 March 2023

Machine' which discovered the full power of modern computation and helped in cracking the Nazi Germany's 'Enigma Code' thus laying the groundwork for modern computing and test of computer behaviour. Alan Turing not only invented the concepts underlying modern computer software and hardware, he also laid the foundation for modern forensic science;[21]

- An American mathematical Engineer, Claude Elwood Shannon (1906-2001) is regarded as the founding father of the electronic communication age after he published a landmark paper bordering on the concept of information theory, digital computer and digital circuit theory in 1937;[22]
- A programmer Bob Thomas developed '*Creeper*', the first computer virus in history while Ray Tomlinson, the famous creator of e-mail developed the antivirus software called *Reaper*. This influenced the history of cybersecurity which started in the 1970s;[23]
- The evolution of modern cybersecurity awareness started in the United States in October 2004 when the world began to notice cybersecurity threat as a huge concern, having discovered that the more people used the Internet, the more the risk factors soared with hackers becoming a nuisance on the web while people had their data stolen and networks compromised. This prompted the Cybersecurity and Infrastructure Security Agency (CISA) and the National Cyber Security Association (NSCA) to take steps to raise cybersecurity awareness on this issue.[24]
- An American Engineer and pioneer of computing technology, Late Gordon E. Moore (1929-2023) postulated the 'Moore's Law' which set in motion, the principle of digital revolution when he predicted that computing processing would double every two years which would lead to an exponential growth in computing power. Till today, Moore's Law has made a profound impact on AI.[25]
- Radia Perlman, an American computer programmer was most famous for inventing the algorithm behind the Spanning-Tree-Protocol (STP) which is

[21] Mark Perlin. ' DNA Matters: What Forensics Owes to Alan Turing' <https://www/forensicmag.com /587733> accessed 29 June 2022

[22]< https://cosmoslearning.org/documentaries> accessed 10 March 2022

[23] James Bores. 'When Did Cybersecurity Start?' <https://hackernoon.com > accessed 11 December 2022

[24] <https://www.daysoftgheyear.com/days/cyber-security/> accessed 20 October 2022

[25] Wylie Wong. 'Moore's Law Lives On – and AI Chips Prove It' <https://aibusiness.com/verticals/> accessed 30 June 2023

fundamental to the operation, growth development of the Internet and because this, she has been nicknamed the mother of the Internet for her innovations that have made a huge impact on how networks self-organise and move data.[26]

7. INTERNATIONAL REPORT ON CYBERSECURITY

In the wake of an increasingly sophisticated cyber threats facing our public safety, a cyber-attack could potentially disrupt essential public services, expose personal or financial data of citizens, cripple cyber infrastructures of organizations and disable the economy of a country relating to its public safety, national security and international stability necessary for the sustainability and restoration of the cyberspace. In the field of cybersecurity, this is known as Critical Cyber/ICT Infrastructure.[27] According to the 9th edition of the European Union Agency for Cybersecurity (ENISA) Threat Landscape 2021 (ETL) report, "cyber-threats" continue to rise due to "an ever-growing online presence, the transitioning of traditional infrastructures to online solutions, advanced interconnectivity and the exploitation of new features of emerging technologies." While industries are busy adopting modern and sophisticated defensive systems, cybercriminals are also busy circumventing authorised procedure and exploiting the most basic tricks to achieve their criminal goals. In addition, several independent surveys have claimed that up to 90% of security breaches are the result of inadvertent errors caused by human beings. The published ENISA Insight Report focuses on:

a. the rise of cybercrime across the world and why cities must understand the threat;
b. identifying vulnerabilities when it comes to people as well as systems and mitigating them;
c. the importance of shared responsibility and becoming 100% cybersecurity aware;
d. real-world examples of cities around the world which have taken a security-by-design approach to cybersecurity;

[26] 'Radia Perlman- Spanning Tree Protocol-Computing and Telecommunications' <https://lemelson.mit.edu/resources/> accessed 01 August 2023

[27] See the African Union Convention on Cybersecurity and Personal Data Protection 2000

e. cybersecurity recommendations and why it has become an on-going challenge.[28]

In another research conducted by the UK Cybersecurity Services in 2022 which surveyed about 521 cybersecurity decision makers in the communications, utilities, finance, government and transport and aviation sectors, it was revealed that "all critical infrastructure organisations must be prepared to suffer a ransomware attack and have strategic response plans in place to deal with bad actors targeting both Information Technology (IT) and Operational Technology (OT) systems. Failure to prepare cyber-response plans can result in the loss of IP, interruption to operations, and significant financial and reputational damage which often leave victim organisations with no choice but to pay demanded ransom, an illegal act further exacerbating cyber-crisis.[29] That is why modern organisations are building capacity to anticipate, respond and recover from cyber-attacks. This capacity is called cyber resilience which is the ability to measure how well an organization can manage a cyber-attack, cyber-threat or data breach while continuing to operate its business effectively at the same time.[30]

8. FOCUS OF CYBERSECURITY

The nature of cybersecurity is not only about professionals sitting in front of computers every day. Embarking on cybersecurity policy initiatives also encompasses the features of what should be done to protect the security of the cyberspace from bad actors whose cyber-attacks daily surge affect thousands of organisations and millions of people all over the world.[31] Cybersecurity tends to focus on Information about security and privacy in the digital world as well as best practices for staying safe and secure online. The field of security informatics recognises that cybersecurity loopholes exist with criminals consequently exploiting the shortcomings to breach computer systems because there is no geographical limit to cybercrime. It transcends

[28] Insight Report: Securing Smarter Cities' <https://www.smartcitiesworld.net /whitepapers/whitepapers /insight-report-securing-smarter-cities> accessed 13 April 2022

[29] 'UK critical national infrastructure at risk of ransom attacks' <https://www.smartcitiesworld.net/data-privacy-and-security/> accessed 22 June 2022

[30] Juliana De Groot. 'What is Cyber Resilience?' <https://digitalguardian.com/blog/> accessed 24 February 2022

[31] Sagar Samtani. 'How AI is shaping the cybersecurity arms race' <https://www.theconversation.com > accessed 24 February 2022

borders since all an offender needs to do is to use his computer as an instrument to perpetrate illegality or crime.

According to the UN Security Council, the explosive growth of digital technologies around the world is opening up new potential domains for conflict between State and non-State actors to carry out attacks across international borders. In view of the several challenges posed by cyber-intruders, malware and other threats, members of the UN Security Council have raised an alarm regarding the increase in malicious incidents in recent years ranging from disinformation campaigns to the disruption of computer networks thereby contributing to diminishing trust and confidence among States.[32] It should be noted that as long as cybercriminals hijack our devices, our personal identities may be stolen; there will be victims of data breaches and credit fraud among other vices. Therefore we should be prepared to protect or defend our networks against these cyber-attacks. This means we have to be cyber-proactive by cultivating safety measures like pass-wording our laptops and mobile devices, preventing/combating cybercrime in whatever way that is backed by law or policies to assist us in implementing the necessary security measures by tackling issues relating to:

1. Digital safety;
2. Information security and awareness;
3. Digital forensics and digital evidence;
4. Cyber law;
5. Mitigation of cyber-attack;
6. Cyber vigilance;
7. Data protection;
8. Maintaining cyber resilience.

The purpose of highlighting these issues is to protect and prevent criminal elements from attacking or intruding into our cyberspace or our computer system to cause damage. All these safety measures will go a long way to protect our computer networks and infrastructure against intrusions.[33] Essentially, the focus of cybersecurity is to ensure that with cybersecurity tools, cybersecurity laws and resources are implemented correctly and effectively with policy makers keeping abreast of the issues

---

[32] *ibid*

[33] Chuck Brooks. 'Canadian government and industry need to enact a Zero Trust cybersecurity strategy' <htpps://www.thestar-com cdn ampproject org/c/s/> accessed 09 April 2022

while the industry professionals are to ensure that organizations comply with cybersecurity regulations and practices as laid down by law, including keeping to self-regulations on how to assess risks, evaluate and monitor security control and mitigate the risks and threats in business organisations that will help them prevent potential future attacks.[34]

Cybersecurity tools are defined as the different applications or software programs used by companies or organizations to protect their systems and networks from unauthorised access.[35] This tools of cybersecurity can help spot anomalies, take steps to mitigate potential cyber threat activity, assess situational awareness, address vulnerabilities and respond to disruptive and destructive attacks that could be launched by cyber criminals as well as enable us to deal with cyber threats of any form. It is common knowledge that cyber-attacks can be costly for individual organisations and governments. For example, Ukraine has encountered several DDoS attacks affecting their banks, websites and other government infrastructures.[36]

3 WHO IS RESPONSIBLE FOR OUR SECURITY?

Security simply depicts the presence of peace, safety, gladness and the protection of human and physical resources or the absence of crisis and threats to human dignity.[37] Security could also be regarded as the protection of assets from threats or the mitigation and protection of system entities and assets against threats while safety is about being protected from harm or actions that may cause harm.[38] Under the law, cybersecurity is related to human rights because the unauthorised collection and use of personal data online threaten the right to privacy coupled with the fact that cybersecurity threats is also a leading threat to international security.[39] The truth is cybercriminals are everywhere on the Internet and we all stand to be potential victims and vulnerable to these threat actors if we do not protect

---

[34] Auger G., Scott J., Helmus J., Nguyen K., '*Cybersecurity Career Master Plan'* (2021 Packt Publishing)

[35] 'Cybersecurity Tools: Definition, Importance and Examples' <https//au.indeed.com/career-advice/> accessed 31 July 2023

[36] Danny Palmer. 'Ukraine Crisis: Russian cyberattacks could affect organisations around the world so take action now' <https://www.zdnet.com/article/ > accessed 22 February 2022

[37] Muyiwa Afolabi. 'Concept of Security'< https://www.researchgate.net/publication/3038992/> accessed 04 February 2022

[38] Geir M. Koien. 'A philosophy of Security Architecture Design' <https://link.springer., com/article/ 10.10007/s11277 > accessed 04 February 2022

[39] Deborah Brown & Anriette Esterhuysen. 'Why cybersecurity is a human rights issue, and it is time to start treating it like one' <https://www.apc.org/en/news/> accessed23 May 2023

our online security. First note that there is nothing we can do to prevent online or cybercrime just can physical crime but we can do our best to manage, mitigate and regulate it. The online culture has come to stay and so, the management of cybersecurity has now become a shared responsibility. Indeed, Cybersecurity is a vast industry with diverse specialities but the individual in the first place can protect himself by being informed and alert since nobody teaches us how to lock our doors. Nobody tells us to be careful when we cross the street or generally train us how to be security conscious. In the same vein, it should also be part of us to be cyber vigilant and know how to keep our password secure or know when to hang up when we realize we are talking to a scammer on the phone or when we are straying into dangerous websites that can steal our personal information. Nobody teaches us to be cautious when shopping online either. When we are told to enable two-factor authentication in order to add an extra layer of security, we do not hesitate to comply. By doing so, we can reduce our risks online but we do not have to be professionally trained in the basics of security management before we know how to protect ourselves. Those who can also protect us are the law enforcement agencies, the government, data regulators, community and even everybody. But if we discover that our computers or phones have been hacked, we can seek the help of qualified forensics expert to check the device in order to do a forensic analysis which can be relevant for evidential purposes.

As the saying goes, security is everybody's business. A cautious behaviour can help thwart potential hackers and the power of collective cyber vigilance against cybercrime is vital. That is why security agencies expect the public and private sector to report any suspicious activity online or cyber intrusion in order to "understand what is happening, prevent it from happening to others and hold those responsible accountable."[40] In Nigeria, the obligation to provide security is constitutional. Section 14(2) of the 1999 Constitution provides that the security of the people shall be the primary purpose of government. In other words, the Constitution has made it the duty of the State to provide security of its citizens.

In the virtual world where there are little restrictions, who then can us secure because we all are vulnerable to cybercrime? For a start, cyber-

[40] Andy Greenberg, 'North Korea Hacked Him. So He Took Down its Internet' <https://www. wired. com/story/> accessed 13 February 2022

security ignorance can be disastrous if we fail to be cyber capable or vigilant. What you see is what you believe online, but it is up to you to be cyber-smart. Statistics have claimed that as of July 2022, there were 2.934 billion monthly active users of Facebook worldwide[41] with a large percentage of these users overly trusting in what they see online such that when a friend request is sent to them, they quickly accept. For example, we check only the profile and the scanty information that comes with a friend request, but we do not know the maker of the request in the physical world. Yet we click on the acceptance button, in a way permitting unknown individuals to gain access into our space. In ***Commonwealth v. Carrasquillo,***[42] the defendant had accepted a friend request on Snapchat from an undercover agent who was able to access and recorded the defendant's post. The undercover agent then alerted other police officers about the post, who located and apprehended the defendant. The Supreme Court ruled that the defendant's privacy rights were not violated and there is no expectation of privacy after accepting a friend request. This shows that we are all potential victims. Let us therefore make security a habit and not leave it to chance. Do not leave any room for vulnerabilities when embracing cybersecurity awareness.

Taking concrete action against cybercrime involves going the extra to lodge a report to the appropriate authorities. What are the extant laws? Section 21(1) of the Cybercrimes Act 2015 as amended in 2024 provides that a person or institution can immediately inform the National Computer Emergency Response Team (CERT) Coordination Centre through their respective sectoral CERTs or Security Operations Centres (SOCs) of any attack, intrusion and other disruption liable to hinder the functioning of another computer or network while Section 21(3) of the same law provides that any person who fails to report any such incident to the National CERT within 72 hours of its detection, commits an offence.

A multi-sector approach governing cybersecurity response comprises of the individual, the government, private and public organizations. The characteristics of a multi-stakeholder approach are; (1) it is open and accessible; (2) it is inclusive of stakeholder's views; (3) it is consensus-driven;

[41] Facebook Statistics and Trends <https://datareportal.com.essential/ > accessed 31 December 2022
[42] SJC-13122 (Mass. Feb, 2022)

and (4) it involves transparency and accountability.[43] These four features are driven by constant education, monitoring, and close collaboration, especially as hackers themselves are becoming more daring, using advanced tools for exploiting vulnerabilities. So, what does this entail? It means we all have to be aware of our cybersecurity responsibilities and be cyber vigilant. Anyone can be a victim of cybercrime. The more cybersecurity is advancing our different sectors, the more cybercrime is on the increase. Be cautious about putting your personal information online as it stays on the Internet forever since our digital footprints expose us to cyber-crooks who may want to attempt to link our password, email or usernames to our IP address and geo-location. Be cautious of procuring or downloading just any software. Do not open any Uniform Resource Locators (URLs) from unknown sources while using your mobile devices. Use strong and different passwords. Turn on the two-step verification (2SV). Stay clear of websites that appear to be using outdated software. Every Internet user should possess the ability to spot potentially suspicious activity. Stay safe and heed the warning that tells you "*your connection is not private! Attackers might be trying to steal your information from passwords, messages or credit cards. GO BACK TO SAFETY or Advance*" Remember if we are careless on the Internet, we leave ourselves vulnerable to cybercrime.

4 KEY DEFINITIONS

a. Cyberspace

The cyberspace was first conceived by William Gibson, a science fiction author who defined the cyberspace in 1982 as the formation of a computer network in the world that has artificial intelligence.[44] Thereafter, it has passed through many definitions, although restricted to the Internet. Like some have defined the cyberspace as a global domain consisting of the interdependent network of information systems infrastructures including the Internet, telecommunications networks, computer systems and embedded processors and controllers. The cyberspace is also called 'all the spaces online that uses the Internet' such as the WWW and social media platforms. UNESCO has equally defined the cyberspace as the virtual world for digital

---

[43] See M. Shears, Daniela Schnidrig & Lea Kaspar. 'The Multistakeholder Approaches to National Cybersecurity Strategy Development' (2018) <https://www.gp-digital.org> accessed 20 January 2022

[44] 'William Gibson On Coining the Word 'Cyberspace' <https://www.kuow.org/stories/> accessed 12 January 2022

or electronic communication associated with global information infrastructure.[45] Other people have defined the cyberspace as an electronic or digital world; an interconnected technology environment; any facility that is linked to an Internet; a place where technical communication takes place; a virtual computer world; an electronic medium that is used to facilitate online communication; a place where people play online games and share opinions; or an environment of the Internet such as the home of Yahoo, Facebook, Google and other virtual platforms. Essentially, a user must first learn to access and navigate the cyberspace for information and other communication activities. The advantage we derive from the cyberspace includes, provision of social networking, entertainment, opportunities, instant communication and educational or informational resources.[46] Unfortunately, the cyberworld is also overshadowed by a real-world threat of information stealing malware distributed by hackers, cyber-bandits, virtual creepers and digital thieves who can facilitate data breach and hijack cryptocurrency transactions, capture discord authentication tokens, and even pilfer login data saved on browsers. What used to be vibrant spaces for sharing and creating innovating mods have now turned into trapdoors for these cyber marauders.[47] All these have devastating consequences on individuals and business organizations operating in the cyberspace.

b. Cybercrime

This is defined as any criminal activity which takes place on, or over the medium of computers, Internet or other technology recognized by the Information Technology Act.[48] Simply put, cybercrime is a technology-facilitated crime committed through the use of a computer as an instrument to further illegal ends. Historically, the first cyber-attack occurred in France in 1834 before the invention of the Internet when attackers stole financial market information by accessing the French telegraph system. However, the modern history of cybercrime began in 1962 when Allan Scherr, a PhD student of Massachusetts Institute of Technology (MIT) committed the first

---

[45] 'Recommendation concerning the Promotion and Use of Multilingualism and Universal Access to Cyberspace' <https://www.unesco.org/en/lagal-affairs/> accessed !2 April 2022

[46] Cyberspace Advantages and Disadvantages. <https://www.vapulus.com/en/cyberspace > accessed 12 January 2022

[47] Kurt Knutsson. 'Massive distribution of malware exposes gamers to theft and data breaches' <https://cyberguy.com/security/> accessed 15 June 2023

[48] < https://www.bbau.ac.in > accessed 12 January 2022

cybersecurity attack after he launched a cyber-attack against MIT computer networks, stealing passwords from their database.[49] From then on, cybercrime gradually became a global epidemic transcending national borders. Despite the advantages we derive from the Internet, our presence on cyberspace comes with negative consequences and poses threat to users creating opportunities for criminals to access our information, sending virus attacks to our devices or distributing malware. Cybercrime can come in the forms of identity theft, cyber stalking, phishing scams, distribution of pornography or other illegal content, hacking websites, online harassment, social engineering and many other online crimes that people have fallen victims to. Not only is cybercrime disruptive and hugely damages our personal or professional lives, it can also ruin organizations, institutions, companies and governments. Reports have traced cybercrime to stolen credentials obtained through phishing, social engineering or brute-force attacks; and ransomware threats that leverages on the anonymity of the dark web which could also be driven human error and improper handling of data.[50] So, why do cybercrime happen? Of course, it is caused by bad actors who daily search for weaknesses of users and hack into their systems. These bad actors are also called digital criminals, hackers, thieves, and invasive advertisers who gain easy access into our systems and privacy to infect your systems or perpetrate other crimes for many reasons especially when the user is negligent or careless. According to a research conducted by an international team of researchers, cybercrime cost the world $6 trillion in 2021, reflecting a 300% hike in online criminal activity in the last two years. This is due to the widespread adoption of web applications emanating from *eCommerce*, *iBanking* and e*Governments* that have become a prime target of cybercriminals who want to steal individual or company information and disrupt business activities.[51]

c. Cybercrime Law

Generally, the law defines our rights, obligations and limitations. A law develops to tackle a societal problem and to prevent it. Relating the law to

---

[49] Arctic Wolf. 'A Brief History of Cybercrime' <https://arcticwolf.com/resources/blog/> accessed 20 April 2024

[50] Sarmad Hassan.' 7 Key Takeaways From Verizon's Data Breach Investigation Report 2023' <https://antidos.com/blog/verizons-data-breach/> accessed 30 July 2023

[51] 'A Simple Tool to Protect Websites from Cyber Hacking' <https://www.forensicmag.com/587616/> accessed 24 June 2022

the online world, cybercrime law refers to the legal framework for dealing with crimes committed on the Internet through the use of a computer or circumventing any rules of conduct/law/policy/code that deals with Internet technologies which regulates the cyber industry and practices for sustainable applications. The regulatory laws help to reduce the harm and impact caused by cybersecurity attacks, sanctions cyber perpetrators and helps deter future attacks. Cybercrime law deals with just about any activity done through electronic means. According to the United Nations Office on Drugs and Crime (UNODC), cybercrime law identifies standards of acceptable behaviour for ICT users; mitigates or prevents harm to people, data, systems, services and infrastructures, enables the investigation and prosecution of crimes committed online and facilitates cooperation between countries in cybercrime matters.[52] A person could be prosecuted under the cybercrime law if he is alleged to be misusing technology in various ways such as gathering unlawful information through acts of voicemail interception. Abuse involving cyber-surveillance, abuse involving texts, photos, non-consensual image sharing, phone hacking, cyberstalking, online harassment and many other online crimes. Cybercrime Law therefore raises issues of cybersecurity concerns, providing the measures to reduce cybersecurity risks, prevent the known threats including the readiness to detect and respond to unknown threats. The legal framework in Nigeria is the Cybercrimes (Prohibition, Prevention, ETC.) Act of 2015 as amended in 2024 which provides in Section 1, that the objective of the law are: (a) to provide an effective and unified legal, regulatory and institutional framework for the prohibition, prevention, detection, prosecution and punishment of cybercrimes in Nigeria; (b) ensure the protection of critical national information infrastructure; and (c) promote cybersecurity and the protection of computer systems and networks, electronic communications, data and computer programs, intellectual property and privacy rights. There are other extant laws regulating cybercrimes in Nigeria such as the EFCC Act 2003, Evidence Act 2011, ICPC Act 2000 and the recent Nigeria Data Protection Act 2023, among several others, In some foreign jurisdictions, AI laws/guidance/regulations have been enacted in China, Canada, European

---

[52] UNODC. 'Cybercrime Module Series: Cybercrime' <https://www.unodc.org/e4J/en/cybercrime/> accessed 25 February 2023

Union, United Kingdom and USA, among others to tackle AI-enabled cybercrime.

d. Cybercrime Security

If almost any computer system is hackable, then we need a process to keep the IT systems secure. Thus, with emerging data security threats, cybersecurity is a continuous process as long as we all have something to do online, cyber risks and threats will also come.[53] Therefore, the activity of cybercrime security can best be defined as the defending of computers, servers, mobile devices, electronic systems, networks and data from malicious attacks that may found their way into business organisations and personal devices.[54] It is generally known that many individuals and organisations have experienced terrible cyber-attacks since the advent of Internet connectivity having opened a way for vulnerability, attack or compromise. In view of this, cybercrime security does not only ensure cybersecurity tools or techniques are used to ward off all attacks, it also includes making deliberate effort to apply various technologies to protect systems or networks, and other information from cyber-attacks or unattended access and destruction. In ***Australian Securities & Investments Commission v. RI Advice Group Pty Ltd***,[55] the Federal Court held that a financial institution has obligations under the law to manage cyber resilience and cybersecurity risks adequately. The findings were revealed after nine cybersecurity incidents involving hacking, ransomware and phishing emails were discovered after an unknown malicious agent gained access to an authorised representative's server.

Beyond this, are there any cybersecurity measures in place that can counter-attack cyber-threats? Note that keeping one's online profile private and creating a strong password are part of the proactive steps that can help us avoid cyber traps. Futhermore, cybersecurity technologies such as detection systems, antivirus software and industrial firewalls are preventable tools and techniques that can counter cyber-attacks. The tools help secure our information and protect our systems from virus attack and other

---

[53] Joseph Chukwube. 'Privacy vs. Innovation: Balancing Data Protection and Technological Advancements in 2023' <https://hackernoon.com/> accessed 21 July 2023

[54] Rohit Chatterjee. 'Difference Between Cybersecurity & Information Security'<https://analyticsindiamag.com> accessed 20 May 2022

[55] (2022) FCA 496

security vulnerabilities. Awareness is vital. The knowledge of cybersecurity aided by cybersecurity professionals will help us master the basics of cybercrime investigation in order to bypass cyber scams. In cybercrime security, a digital forensic scientist and other systems analyst are called upon to investigate and prevent cyber-attacks. They usually understand the task of collecting data while exploring the fundamentals of malware analysis to help them understand how malicious software can cause harm.

e. Cybersecurity Professionals

The field of cybersecurity requires that we should engage those who have a comprehensive understanding of privacy management, data security regulations and cyber-legal framework which are all ICT-driven. These security experts or system administrators are digital forensics and incident response professionals who deal with the dangers posed by ransomware, malware, advanced persistent threats (APT) and other vulnerabilities. The range of contemporary cvybersecurity field is broad embracing many fields such as software programmers, security researchers, security engineers, cloud security analysts, governance, risk and compliance analysts, technology geeks, ethical hackers, bug hunters, licensed private investigators or threat intelligence analysts, and data privacy lawyers.[56] All these professionals are generally experts whose backgrounds are in cybersecurity education, academia, tech industry and law enforcement. As cybercrime increases, so the need for cybersecurity specialists rises. A variety of different professional backgrounds in the tech industry ranges from computer engineering, coding and other fields of Internet technologies including law are needed to build the cybersecurity industry. That is why the discipline leverages a multidisciplinary approach that is needed in all technology-related fields including those who have professional credentials in privacy and data risk management, local/global cybersecurity and data. Collectively, these professionals are called Chief Information Security Officers (CISO) as they provide expertise and oversight to security operation centres since 'they know the sites to do their research, what information is available and how to find people.' They are knowledgeable in cybersecurity laws, internal cyber rules, frameworks and standards to ensure compliance with emerging or

[56] 'Magnet Forensics Survey: Digital Forensics to Increase to Combat Cyber Threat' <http://www.forensicmag.com/584624/> accessed 28 March 2022

changing security and privacy laws. They send immediate alerts in case of any suspicious activity that a network exhibits by detecting quickly and highlighting possible vulnerabilities. In this vein, a cybersecurity professional is a specialist in information technology and security who has a strong foundation in computer knowledge management which helps to prevent or contain attempted security breach and damage control.

Evidently, IT is a specialised field in computer science and cybersecurity, therefore the expert must have the ability to handle cyber incidents and lead remediation tasks. He also collaborates with law enforcement agencies to stem cyber-attacks because his expertise focuses on security protocols and best practices. As an information security analyst, he is there to defend cyber threats, cyber intrusions, data breaches, cyber hacking, computer glitches and other crimes committed against computers or cybersecurity. He attends security-related conferences in order to update his knowledge.[57] Cybersecurity is technical. His expert on the subject matter gives him the skill and experience to mitigate mishandling of evidence. He gives advice on how best to secure cloud infrastructure through vulnerability assessment and penetration testing. Both tests work together to encourage optimal network and application security. He is trained to recognize the Endpoint Detection and Response (EDR) method relevant for protecting devices such as desktops, laptops and mobile devices from attacks.

In spite of the fact that a research study has outlined six pitfalls that threaten security professionals,[58] it is still believed that IT professionals are the unsung heroes of modern businesses because of their great insight they possess into the technical universe which brings numerous opportunities to individuals and businesses alike. This explains why IT professionals who have technical knowledge of the job are celebrated annually on the 3rd Tuesday in the month of September of every year.[59]

f. Information Security

In the literal sense, all information are not only the ones stored on computers alone. However, any information that is stored in an information

[57] Aratrika Dutta. 'How to get a government job as a cybersecurity professional' <https://www.analyticsinsight.net> accessed 17 March 2022

[58] Julie Haney. 'Users are not Stupid: Six Cyber Security Pitfalls Overturned.' <https://www.nist.gov/news-events/news/> accessed 21 March 2023

[59] 'National IT Professionals Day' <https://nationaldaycalendar.com> accessed 20 September 2022

domain or Internet-connected device is strictly information security-driven. The Nigerian Data Protection Regulation (NDPR) of 2019 recognises that many public and private bodies have migrated their respective businesses and other information systems online and that information solution in both the private and public sectors currently drive service delivery through digital systems. These information systems have thus become critical information infrastructure which must be safeguarded, regulated and protected against atrocious data breaches from unauthorised access, use, disclosure, disruption, modification or destruction of information in order to meet the integrity, confidentiality and availability needs of online networks.[60] These three components are popularly referred to as the *CIA Triad*[61] because they form the core pillars of information security. *Confidentiality* means that our information should only be read by only the right people. *Integrity* means that our information should only be changed by authorised persons while *Availability* means that our information should be read and used whenever we want. The goal is to protect assets, devices and services from being disrupted and exploited by unauthorised users otherwise known as threat actors. In order to ensure efficient operation of information security, organisations put in several policies such as accredited PASS ID card or PASS code issued to authorised persons to gain access to buildings, user IDs, passwords for network login and finger print or retinal scanners as control policy and measures to serve as intrusion detection systems and regulatory compliance.[62] What is the difference between cybersecurity and information security? While cybersecurity consist of measures to protect attacks in the cyberspace such as data and storage devices, information security is intended to lay the foundation of data security to protect data from any form of threat regardless of whether it is analogue or digital.[63] An information security analyst monitors his company's networks for security breaches and investigates when a breach occurs while a cybersecurity analyst is a trained cyber-professional who specialises in network and IT infrastructure security. He understands the nature of cyberattacks, emerging cyber technology issues, criminal threats, malware, and actively seeks to anticipate and prevent these attacks.[64]

---

[60] NIST SP 800-16 Under Information Systems Security

[61] Confidentiality, Integrity and Availability

[62] <https://csrc.nist.goc> glossary/>

[63] Rohit Chatterjee. 'Difference Between Cybersecurity & Information Security'< https:// analyticsindiamag, com> accessed 20 May 2022

[64] 'Cybersecurity Analyst Career Guide' <https://www.wgu.edu/career-guide/information/> accessed 18 May 2022

9. CAUSES OF CYBERCRIME

Security researchers have contended that anyone with a phone, computer and other electronic communication devices can commit cybercrime against co-users of the Internet because cyber platforms offer unbridled freedom to criminal-minded persons who use the opportunity to play both non-serious and harmful pranks, especially when an Internet user knowingly or unknowingly click on a link that contains malicious scripts. Unknown to many of us, there are certain vulnerabilities that are related to a URL of a domain such that when attackers launch malicious code into a user's browser session, the user's session is hijacked giving the attacker an opportunity to do whatever he likes with the user's system. From there, the hacker can redirect the user to visit malicious websites. He then records the user's online activity or downloads malicious files into the user's system and subsequently hacks his device.

The triggers of cybercrime could be attributed to lack of training and retraining of computer personnel, persistent misinformation available to online users, lack of cybersecurity awareness, ignorance of online users, greed of perpetrators, insider attacks from employees who may want to leak confidential data to competitors, lack of security assistance, storing data in small places, complex coding, availability of confidential information in online platforms and getting an enabling easy access system. To perpetrators of crime, cybercrime is lucrative and highly organised. For example, a Venezuelan cardiologist was alleged to have set up a cybercriminal enterprise in which he held out his software to be used as an economic and reputational interest for cyber-attacks.[65] Cybercriminals thrive in their sophisticated knowledge of network vulnerabilities which they exploit due to the ignorance of companies and individuals and lack of cybersecurity education coupled with the inexperience of IT employees who sometimes make mistakes as a result of cybersecurity burnout or cyber optimism bias, the absence of modern anti-analysis and detection avoidance mechanism, and the use of out-dated software or programs as well as the failure of victims to report to the police who may not even respond promptly. Note that hackers can hack into computer systems even without knowing your information or

---

[65]Julian Bingley. 'US prosecutors allege Venezuelan doctor is ransomware mastermind' <https://www.zdnet.com/article/> accessed 18 May 2022

password and that is why cybercriminals have found the Internet a convenient hiding place to hide their identity.

It is also instructive to note that some victims of cybercrime also lay the foundation for cybercrime to take place. This can happen when parents for instance, indulge in the act of 'share renting' – an act where parents share too much information about their children on social media which gives the children unnecessary exposure to online predators who may use their images and information to stalk and exploit the children or sell the information to the dark web. Cyber criminals may also make the children a target of cyberbullying, harassment and other risks.[66] If this ends up as violation of privacy, a Court can order the parent or grandparent to take down the photos of the children concerned. According to the European Union's General Data Protection Regulation (GDPR) directive, photos of children up to the age of 16 can only be posted online with the consent of their parents.[67]

Negligent cybersecurity practices occurring from failure to plan for proactive strategies to prevent systems vulnerability, human errors, theft of data, creating fake authentication tokens and impersonation of users are several of the many forms of Internet misuse which can affect us all. For example, Remote Desktop Protocol (RDP) is often exploited via unsecured networks, such that if an individual uses a vulnerable network to access an RDP server, a cybercriminal could infiltrate the process and gain unlawful access to the server.[68]

Criminal behaviour on the Internet could further arise by opportunity which may expose a person to commit a particular crime. In other words, we all can be careless and leave loopholes for others to commit crimes without them actually planning to do so. This is based on the concept of 'routine activity theory'[69] which assumes that crime can be committed by anyone who has the opportunity to do so. An opportunistic cybercriminal capitalises on unpreparedness, often exploiting common human traits such as

---

[66] Yetty Williams. 'Just Before You Post Your Children Online' <https://www.bellanaija.com/2023/03/> accessed 22 March 2023

[67] Akinwale Akinyoade. 'Grandma Ordered to Delete Grandchildren's Photos from Facebook or Pay Fine' <https://guardian.ng/life/> accessed 22 March 2023

[68] Katie Rees. 'Can Remote Desktop Protocol Be Hacked?' <https://www.makeuseof.com> accessed 23 March 2023

[69] Bradford W. Reyns. 'Routine Activity Theory and Cybercrime' <https://www.taylorfrancis.com/chapters/edit/> accessed 18 May 2022

trust and familiarity.[70] For instance, ladies who share their nude pictures with their partners or close friends may end up becoming victims of revenge porn. Challenges in tracking, apprehending and prosecuting cybercrimes also encourage cybercriminals to continue.

Cybercrime could also be as a result of what is called a user-generated content (UGC) when it is misused. UGC is a published information which comes in form of photos, video, blog, discussion forum post, poll response or comment that an unpaid contributor provides to a website, with little or no scrutiny. UGC is associated with perils. A scammer for instance can misuse this UGC opportunity to post false or misleading information about a product or someone else online.[71]

According to a professional content writer and founder of *Digitage*, cybersecurity threats have become more sophisticated, caused by malicious actors who have jumped on the AI revolution to launch deadlier, subtler and more precise attacks than they ever have, with insider threats increasing daily while employees have increased the complexity of maintaining high-level security coupled with the budgetary constraints faced by many organisations which have deprioritised data security.[72]

Cybersecurity risks and data breach could also be triggered by e-waste hacking. This is when we improperly dispose our electronic devices, thereby enabling hackers to use the discarded devices and thus gain access into our files that are still intact. In other words, once our devices leave our hands and lands in the trash, cybercriminals can infiltrate our network, recover the data from them and retrieve sensitive information.[73]

Nevertheless, whatever angle one looks at the causes of cybersecurity, the power of a cybercriminal expands, if he goes unchecked. Really we know scammers desire us to be uninformed of their deceptive tactics. But on 'Slam the Scam Day' which is observed every March 9 of every year, we are informed about the need to protect ourselves from social media scams and

[70] 'Hacker Personas' A Deeper Look into Cybercrime' <https://i.cm.com> accessed 20 June 2023

[71] Jon Christian. 'Scammers are Creating Fake Students on Harvard.edu and Using Them to Shill Brands' <https://futurism.com/fake-harvard-students/> accessed 30 June 2023

[72] Joseph Chukwube. 'Privacy vs. Innovation: Balancing Data Protection and Technological Advancements in 2023' <https://hackernoon.com/> accessed 21 July 2023

[73] Zac Amos. 'What is E-Waste Hacking?' <https://hackernoon.com> accessed 28 April 2024

scammer tactics so we don't fall prey to their schemes.[74] This awareness day is encouraging us to be proactive on early cybersecurity interventions.

10. EFFECTS OF CYBERCRIME

In 2023, parliamentarians and stakeholders from the African Internet Governance Forum congregate at Abuja and expressed their concerns over the issue of cybercrime in Africa when they disclosed that cybercrime has become a potential threat to implementing the African Union Agenda 2063 and its digital transformation strategy.[75] About 97% of surveyed leaders of financial institutions in Africa rank cybercrime as the leading threat to the financial services industry alongside worsening economic conditions.[76] It should be recalled that the Nigerian Communications Commission (NCC) in 2022 revealed that Nigeria loses about 500 million US dollars annually to cybercrime, a figure which amounts to about 0.08% of the country's GDP.[77] In 2024, EFCC also claimed that Nigeria has lost $706 million to cybercrimes in 2022. Generally the commission of a crime has a lot of impact on not only the victims of crime but also on organisations, the country and even the perpetrators of crime. Thus, crime has its negative impact on the society as a whole. Where cybercrime is involved, firstly, a direct victim will suffer economic harm which can affect his health condition and emotional psychology while the secondary victims who are his family dependants may also feel the impact of the same economic loss. Secondly, the country is a potential victim of crime as the threat posed by crime can manifest in the economic, political and social life of the people. For example, crime will drive investors away. Nigerians will get tagged as lawless criminals. The country will incur cost right from the stage of apprehension of criminals, investigation of the crime and prosecution of the case. The government will also incur costs whenever it resorts to the establishment of more security outfits, extradition of suspects' enlargement of personnel and equipment to fight crime and criminals. Thirdly, crime could impact negatively on all

[74] 'National Slam the Scam Day'<https://nationaldaycalendar.com> accessed 09 March 2023

[75] Zakariyya Adaramola. 'Cybercrime Poses A Big Threat to Africa's Digital Transformation Strategy-AIGF' <https://dailytrust.com/> accessed 22 September 2023

[76] Abraham Augustine. 'Financial Institutions in Africa say Cybercrime is a Bigger Risk than Political Instability' <htpps://techcabal.com/2023/05/10/> accessed 20 August 2023

[77] Innocent Odoh. 'Federal Government, Stakeholders Herculean Task Against Cybercrime' <https://leadership.ng/> accessed 23 April 2023

organisations such that investors are not happy diverting their resources towards the crime of fraud perpetrated by hackers or yahoo boys. Finally, the perpetrator of crime when caught will be arrested, tried in a Court of law, convicted and will be jailed. Apart from feeling the guilt of shame, his family members will also bear the cost of his defence.[78]

Every person or every organization connected to the Internet is a constant target of cyber intrusion having recognised that criminals use the computer to commit crime and to avoid being caught. These are criminals who intrude the cyberspace with criminal intent. In this vein, the Cambridge English Dictionary defines a cyber-intruder as someone who uses the Internet to illegally enter a computer system without permission.[79] This comes with many consequences: Viruses can impair the operation of computers. With no territorial limits, these viruses spread to organisations across the world wiping networks and costing companies a lot of money in damages. There are dangers of malware erasing our entire computer systems. By altering or deleting data, attackers will quickly clean compromised websites and if this happens, the incident becomes very hard to investigate. Cyber-attacks tarnish victims' names, scaring off their customers and ruin their businesses. A criminal can mount a very sophisticated attack against a large number of organisations or individuals. The effects are devastating for the victims and communities in the following ways;

a. It causes total country-wide service outage and damage;
b. By breaking into one's system and stealing our confidential data information, an attacker can also alter our sensitive financial data;
c. Intercepting your system exposes the personal information of employees of organizations. That is, employee information like their names, addresses, contacts, credit card, text messages, telephone numbers, email addresses, photos, audio recordings, call logs, files and social security numbers may be compromised or leaked out to blackmail victims;
d. The attack on programmable logic controllers (PLCs) exploits engineering workstations. The Evil PLC attack is a good example to cite here. By 'weaponising' one PLC, an attacker may in turn compromise an engineer's workstation. The attack targets engineers working every day on industrial

[78] Okpako Omudhowo. '*The Plight of the Victims of Crimes in Nigeria*' (Booksmith Publishers 2023)
[79]< https://dictionary.cambridge.org > accessed 20 September 2022

networks, configuring and troubleshooting PLCs to ensure the safety and reliability of processes across critical industries such as utilities, electricity, manufacturing and automotive, among others;[80]

e. Using network of hijacked computers to send spam and to launch Distributed Denial of Service (DDoS) attacks;
f. Hacking into the Internet infrastructure of foreign governments to collect the information off their networks;
g. Using your computer to access your data to attack others or redirect it to attacker servers;
h. Theft of intellectual property. Stealing confidential information, trade secrets or fund transfer details;
i. Watering hole attacks are conducted by a set of cybercriminal gangs. cyber-espionage groups and notorious Ransomware-as-a-Service (Raas) gangs in order to compromise very specific targets and disrupt the operation of large firms;
j. Stealing your credit card information in order to make unauthorised purchases;
k. Stealing your sensitive data saved on your device to monitor your activity like camera use, audio conversation, location and banking data;
l. Increase of child predators who know children are also accessing the Internet;
m. Under business impact due to misinformation and disinformation can lead to financial loss, operational disruption, customer antipathy, loss of important business partners and loss of intellectual property;[81]
n. Global peace and security is threatened when the spread of online violent extremism is involved;
o. Network providers or companies will/may have to temporarily shut down or take their services down so they can address their security issues or fix the vulnerabilities. For example, the European Court of Human Rights (ECtHR) once fell victim to a cyber-attack after publishing a ruling on the fate of an incarcerated Turkish political leader. It was reported that

---

[80] Sharon Brizinov, Mashar Sapir, et al. 'Evil PLC Attack: Using a Controller as Predator Rather than Prey' <https://claroty.com/team82/research/> accessed 20 August 2022

[81] The Investopedia Team. '6 Ways Cybercrime Impacts Business' <https://www.investopedia.com/financial-edge/011> accessed 08 January 2022

hackers struck at the Court's website and knocked the information off for 16 hours before the website was restored;[82]

p. Police officers and cybersecurity professionals may sometimes have a harder time investigating digital crimes while uncaught suspects are less likely to cooperate in investigations;
q. Companies and organisations that cooperate with online blackmailers stand the risk of getting targeted repeatedly;
r. The attack can extend to the family members of victims.

In conclusion, we can say that even with the best of precautions, cybercrime still happens and will still happens on the Internet, but we can minimize it. In other words, we cannot completely eliminate the risk of our devices being infected by cyber-attack but we can protect our systems by keeping up with software updates and restart/refresh our devices regularly. The advantage is that this can flush out certain types of malware. Our system becomes clean.[83]

---

[82]Sarah Coble. 'Cyber-Attack on European Court of Human Rights' <https://www.infosecurity-magazine.com/news/> accessed 25 February 2022

[83]Lily May Newman. 'Hacker Lexicon: What is a Watering Hole Attack?' <https://www.wired.com/story/> accessed 08 January 2022

Chapter 3

CYBERSECURITY THREATS

The negative impact of cybersecurity threats, breaches and vulnerabilities consist of a broad spectrum of social engineering attacks which could be active or passive. Social engineering attacks can take place online, on the phone through human interaction or when criminals launch their attack in person by using a false identity. Social engineering is defines as the tactic of manipulating, influencing, or deceiving a victim in order to gain control over a computer system, or to steal personal and financial information. Examples of active social engineering attacks are when hackers download virus into computer systems, when scammers direct Internet users to malicious websites; when hackers hack into devices, claiming to be someone the victim trust so as to get the victim to send money to them or when these hackers gain unauthorized access to confidential information, using it for their financial benefit.[1] Social engineering can also be passive. This is when these "social engineers" wait and watch you enter your Pin at ATM stands and they quickly make a mental note of your credit card or memorise your usernames and passwords in order to gain access to your records thereafter. This illegal act is called 'shoulder surfing'[2] Cyber scam may also occur when hackers bait Internet users by posting enticing adverts that can lure them to download harmful websites or malware-infected programs on their systems. Sometimes, Internet users are harassed by fake threats or warnings that their computer will get infected with malware thus tempting users to download what hackers call the latest software. (These are called attacks by baiting and scareware). Social engineering attacks come in a variety of types and classifications as follows:

[1] 'What is Social Engineering'? <https://www.f--secure.com/en/articles/> accessed 02 April 2022

[2] Mark Guntrip. ' Three Types of Social Engineering Attacks to Know' <https://www.proofpoint.cxom/us> accessed 02 April 2022

I. 'YAHOO YAHOO'

Yahoo is one of the most popular Internet portals and web service provider that incorporate a search engine. Yahoo is a notable e-mail service provider. For instance, users subscribe to Yahoo mail to communicate with others. Sadly in Nigeria, the name 'Yahoo' has been given a negative connotation, with it being associated with Internet scammers. 'Yahoo Boy' has therefore found its way into the Nigerian lexicon and is defined as a man who carries out fraudulent online with the use of his computer. The name has gone viral on national headlines as no day passes without us reading about these online fraudsters who are better known as 'Yahoo Boys'.[3] Citizens are infuriated with these so-called scammers who use different illegal techniques to commit Internet fraud. For example, these boys are known to use their devices to access people's sensitive information without permission; they fraudulently debit other people's money and diverting the proceeds to other countries where they have a syndicate; they are identity thieves who pass themselves off as legitimate recipients or set up fake social media accounts; and these boys are hackers whose materials such as laptops, automated master cards, phone numbers and Biometric Verification Number (BVN) of bank customers are found in their possession. Although these boys try to conceal the details of their activities online, some even go as far as boasting online that they can access a bank's database, extract the data of the bank customers' and send e-mails to such banks to demand for money. Eventually, when these criminals are apprehended, they are charged to court for gaining unauthorized access with intent to facilitate the commission of a crime. In Lagos State, the offences are contrary to Sections 21(5), 278(1) and (2), 285, 385, 386, 387, 388 and 389 of the Criminal Law of Lagos State[4] including Sections 6 and 16 of the Cybercrimes (Prohibition Prevention, etc. Act) 2015, further amended in 2024. Yahoo boys also fraudulently impersonate other people using different e-mails with the intention to obtain money or deceive victims based in foreign lands to part with their money either for romance or business scam which is contrary to Section 22(3)(b) of Cybercrimes (Prohibition, Prevention Act) 2015 and punishable under

[3] Matthew Ogume. 'Court convicts six Yahoo Boys' in Abuja. <'https://guardian.ng/news/> accessed 01 September 2023

[4] Guardian Nigeria. 'How we apprehended Access Bank's account hacker'- EFCC' < https://editor.guardian.ng/news/> reported on 07 February 2022

Section 22(3) (d) of the same Act. In Abuja, the Federal Capital Territory, Yahoo boys are mostly charged under Sections 321and 324 of the Penal Code. As at January 2023, the Economic and Financial Crimes Commission (EFCC) disclosed that it secured thousands of convictions against a huge number of Internet fraudsters known as Yahoo Boys.[5]

2. HACKING

Every computer system, electronic device or network can be hacked by Internet criminals who exploit vulnerabilities so as to gain unauthorised access into computer systems, mobile phones, and networks. Vulnerability is simply a weakness or flaw that hackers take advantage of, in order to cause damage to victims or their devices. When cybercriminals manipulate devices, such action demonstrates they have circumvented the affected security authentication process. Security vulnerability types can be categorised into network, operating system, human and process.[6] Essentially, hacking of an electronic device indicates that a criminal has tampered with someone else's computer system after identifying the weakness and it is from there that he then proceeds to exploit the security to further gain access to the victim's personal or business data. So, when someone gains unauthorized access into another person's existing account, then we can say such account has been hacked. However, not all hacking is malicious[7] and not all hackers are criminals as generally labelled. Although hacking and hackers are computer technology terms, the terms hacking and hacker has become associated with bad activities.

Historically, the word *hack* used to refer to someone who roughly and indiscriminately chopped off an object with an axe, until at some point in the 21st century when the meaning of *hack* evolved into another terminology that meant innovation and productivity. In 1975, the word '*hack*' progressed from a verb to a noun in a bid to recognise a computer enthusiast who didn't just hack, but was a hacker. This implied that a hacker was somebody who only relished and excelled at hands-on computer programming but not concerned

---

[5] 'EFCC makes big statement 3,785 Yahoo Boys, others jailed in 2022' <https://pmnewsnigeria.com/2023/01/04/> accessed 04 February 2023

[6] Eric Dosal. 'Top 5 Computer Security Vulnerabilities' <https://www.compuquip.com/blog/> accessed 13 June 2022

[7] Lawrence Wiliams. 'What is Hacking? Types of Hackers/Introduction to Cybercrime.' <https://www.guru99.com> accessed 15 February 2022

about the theory of computer science. Thereafter in the 1980s, hackers were described as people who understood computer systems and could criminally breach the security of a company's computer system. Consequently, a distinction was made between hackers who wore white hats and hackers who wore black hats. In the 2000s, when cyberattacks became a frequent occurrence, the word *hack* began to be used synonymously with 'attack'.[8] Another version of the word *hack* was traced in 1955 to the students of Massachusetts Institute of Technology (MIT) who used the word as a slang for a shortcut – '*something for which computer science students at MIT were always searching,* because the first computer hackers were these same MIT students who were daily interacting with a machine.[9]

Hacking could be used in a positive or negative context. If it used in a positive context, then we would be referring to a civic or ethical hacker while the negative context would depict a criminal hacker. In a positive context, civic hacking portray that not all hacking is illegal or malicious and not all hackers are bad. In real life, we have read about a former convicted hacker who later practiced ethical cybersecurity.[10] Ethical hacking is important since it is capable of tackling cyber-attacks which occur frequently. The role of ethical hackers as security professionals are to identify weaknesses in computer systems or networks; come up with countermeasures that protect the weaknesses; use the methods deployed by unethical hackers to penetrate into systems and identify vulnerabilities before malicious hackers exploit them.[11] In the US for example, the Joe Biden Administration unveiled a new policy that empowered US agencies to retaliate against hackers with counter-attacks while the Department of Justice launched 'a hack back squad' to stop tech theft.[12] Ethical hackers are also called 'Penetration Testers' because they perform penetration tests or attacks on systems to detect vulnerabilities in order to help companies

---

[8]Jesslyn Shields. 'How the Word 'Hack' Became so Hacked' <https://people.howstuffworks.com> accessed 05 May 2023

[99] Adam Volle. 'Hacker Computing' <https://www.britannica.com/topic/hacker/> accessed 28 August 2023

[10] 'Who is Kevin Mitnick? World's most wanted hacker dies at 59'< https://www.the statesman.com/> accessed 23 July 2023

[11]Veda. 'Top 10 Ethical Hacking Certifications to become a Security Expert' <https://www. analyticsinsight.net/ > accessed 02 April 2022

[12] Ryan Naraine. 'US National Cyber Strategy Pushes Regulation Aggressive Hack-Back Operations' <https://www.securityweek.com/> accessed 04 March 2023

protect themselves from cybercriminals. Ethical hackers are legally authorised to control or limits surveillance from threat actors. This presupposes that ethical hackers must get written permission from the owner of computer systems before they commence their hacking activity in a bid to protect the privacy of organisations and transparently report all the identified weaknesses in the computer system to such organisations and inform hardware or software vendors of the identified weaknesses. Ethical hacking is legal if they fall into the category of government-backed hackers or if the hacker abides by the rules stipulated by The International Council of E-Commerce Consultants.[13] It is interesting to know that certified ethical hackers (CEH) are now recognised as professionals.

On a negative dimension, criminal hackers are Internet fraudsters, social engineers or scammers who are skilled in computer programming. As bad computer hackers, they use the computer to commit fraudulent acts of infractions such as privacy invasion, forgery of electronic signature, stealing corporate/personal data and password cracking algorithm just to gain access into a computer system. Hackers break systems and look for vulnerabilities to exploit others. For example, these scammers can hack into a user's Facebook account and change his phone numbers or email. When hackers hack your device, they get access into your Internet Port or Protocol (IP) address, steal your sensitive information on your device, track your activity and may perform a DDos on your device. When they do this, we may refer to them as 'crackers'. Crackers are people who hack a system by breaking into the system and violate it with the bad intentions to damage and destroy files, plant viruses or steal credit card numbers.[14] Beyond this, criminal hackers can steal our identities by obtaining our personal financial information online, even through our phones. Some hackers can plant or fabricate fake evidence on computers to implicate victims until forensic evidence proves otherwise.

Furthermore, bad hackers subvert systems to harvest credentials after getting hold of a victim's usermail and passwords. However note that hackers do not have to know our passwords before they hack into our systems. This is because they are armed with intrusive tools of technology.

---

[13]Lawrence Williams. 'What is Hacking? Types of Hackers/Introduction to Cybercrime.'< https://www.guru99.com> accessed 15 February 2022

[14] <https://www.pcmag.com/encyclopedia/term/cracker/> accessed 10 May 2022

For example, the "Access Bank Hacker" made a viral video in which he boasted about him gaining access into the Access Bank's database to extract the data of over 2,000 bank customers, including their BVN, phone numbers and bank account numbers. He allegedly sent an electronic mail to the management of the bank demanding money from them. After he was apprehended by the Police, several documents, HP laptop, chips and discs were recovered from him. In another related incident, a lady visited a cyber café to fill her National Youth Service Corps (NYSC) registration. When she logged in her details into the NYSC portal, she discovered that her details have been used by another hacker, thus preventing her from performing the mandatory NYSC programme.[15] In India, the Hack-For-Hire Groups have been targeting lawyers and their clients across the globe by using phishing attacks to gain access to confidential legal documents.[16] Like all software, there are many cyber adversaries out there. Hackers can even steal our data from a mobile device through a power bank. Artificial Intelligence (AI) or Machine Learning (ML) can also be hacked where the attacker will be able to access the source code which allows malicious application to sneak in.

As earlier stated, the term 'hacking' has a negative connotation which makes Internet users feel uncomfortable. That is why the image of a solitary hacker that is illustrated is always that of a shadowy man sitting in front of a computer in a darkened room. Hackers don't have faces and they are always covered up. A civic hacker has said this image gives a wrong impression to the populace because the ability to spend long periods on his computer to do his research forces him to do many hours at his computer, much of it solitary.[17] Yet there are others who have the ethical hacking knowledge to assist others who do not have such skills. That is why the world observes the National Day of Civic Hacking on September 10 of every year. It is a day created for people to use their hacking skills for the common good of the society.[18] Notwithstanding, hackers are categorised as follows:

---

[15] NYSC Controversy: Kwara Poly Blames Hacker, Corps Declares Imposter Wanted' <https://newswirelawandevents.com> accessed 10 May 2022

[16] Matt Burgess. 'Security News: Gun Database Breach Leaks Details on Thousands of Owners' <https://www.wired.com/story/> accessed 03 July 2022

[17] Kevin Townsend. 'Hacker Conversations: Youssef Sammounda, Big Bounty Hunter' <https:// www.securityweek.com/> accessed 02 August 2023

[18] <https://www.daysoftheyear.com/days/national-day/> accessed 30 October 2022

a. Black Hat Hacker

This is a cybercriminal who breaks into computer systems or networks with a malicious or criminal intent to manipulate vulnerabilities in computer systems and software. He steals sensitive or personal data and compromises computer systems or networks after exploiting a flaw with a view to profiting financially from such data breaches. He can also decide to sell discovered vulnerabilities to criminals on the dark web. No wonder he is called a 'pain in the neck' since he does not have any ethical code. In cybersecurity terminology, a black hat hacker is also referred to as a bad or threat actor who hacks for financial gain. That is why he could decide to send malware to electronic devices, demand for ransomware or intercepts communications. Black hackers prefer to hide under any secure software such as a proxy server and channel their communications through lots of different countries in order to evade detection.[19] A black hat hacker is therefore, someone who compromises the security of a computer system without obtaining permission from an authorised party, which is usually done with the intent of illegally accessing computers or networks.[20] An illegal hacker also includes any person who knowingly accessed a computer without authorisation or exceeding authorised access.[21]

b. White Hat Hacker

This is a cybersecurity expert or ethical security hacker who uses his skills to find and solve vulnerabilities in organizational networks or computer systems by legal means. He is known as a friendly or civic hacker who is legally authorised to hack systems in order to help prevent an external attack or fix loopholes occurring in an organizational security settings. He is called the good kind of hacker or a certified ethical hacker (CEH) because his motive is to help businesses to prevent cybersecurity and thwarting attacks by coming to their rescue.[22] Organisations are therefore encouraged to employ active defence techniques to protect their systems. For example, the government of Ukraine sent out a call for defence volunteers with hacking skills to help protect the country's critical infrastructure from Russian invasive cyber-

---

[19] James MacKay. 'How Do Hackers Normally Get Caught' <https://www.metacompliance.com> accessed 29 April 2023

[20] Ejaz Khan. 'Top 10 Notorious Balck Hat Hackers' <https://www.wonderslist.com> accessed 29 April 2023

[21] See the Computer Fraud and Abuse Act 1986

[22] CNBCTV. 'Nomad and Solana attacks demonstrate how white hat hackers are helping counter crypto exploits' <https://www.cnbctv18.com/cryptocurrency/ > accessed 13 August 2022

attack. These defence volunteers are classified as ethical hackers because they would focus on protecting critical assets of national and state infrastructures from bugs.[23] A bug is a flaw or vulnerability in the software or hardware design that can be potentially exploited by cyber-attackers. Thus, a bug hunter is a white hacker who takes the responsibility route to uncover and report software flaws to companies in exchange for a reward called a bug bounty program or vulnerability rewards program (VRP).[24] White Hat hackers also share knowledge on how one can avoid intrusions, disruptive and destructive attacks, as well as how damage done by attacks can be minimised and controlled. In so doing, white hackers are usually co-opted into red teams or blue teams in cybersecurity industry because the purposes of the two teams are to find vulnerabilities, strengthen network security, develop response plan, build capacity in detecting and containing attacks, among addressing other security challenges.[25]

c. Grey Hat Hacker

This is a cybersecurity expert who looks for ways to hack into computer networks without having the malicious intent of a black hat hacker. The motive of the grey hat hacker is borne out of personal enjoyment or curiousity since he is just interested in finding vulnerabilities that are inside computer systems. This is often done without the owner's permission. If however, issues are found, he reports the findings to the owner. Grey hat hackers are a hybrid, somehow falling in-between the dark side of black hat hackers and well-intentioned white hat hackers because their motives are usually good, although they still engage in technically illegal hacks when opportunities arises for such, and when they do, they may sometimes violate laws or ethical standards by demanding payment in exchange for providing full details of what they have uncovered. The grey hat hacker could also be compensated depending upon the organisation concerned.[26]

[23] Charlie Osbourne. Report: Ukraine calls for volunteer hackers to protect critical infrastructure. <https://www.zdnet.com/article/> accessed 25 February 2022

[24] Damir Mujezinovic. 'What are Bug Bounty Programs? Here's Everything You Need to Know' <https://www.makeuseof.com/> accessed November 2022

[25] Coursera. 'Red Team vs. Blue Team in Cybersecurity' <https://www.coursera.org/articles> accessed 18 September 2023

[26] J.R. Tietsort. 'The 15 Types of Hackers (And How To Protect Yourself)' <https://www.aura.com/learn/> accessed 22 February 2023

d. Green Hat Hacker

He is new to the hacking world but more focused on gaining knowledge on how to perform cyber-attacks. He is usually a young person, a newbie or a neophyte who is eager to gain acceptance into the ranks of the hacker world. He is sometimes called a Trainee Hacker.[27]

e. Red Hat Hacker

This is a hacker who acts as a digital activist or a vigilante and uses his hacking knowledge to convey a message. He does not work for any established organisation. His reasons for hacking might be political, social, religious or ideological. A red hat hacker's main goal is not to violate laws, but he will do so if it will enable him to build justice.[28]

f. Blue Hat Hacker

He is a cybersecurity expert hired by companies to bug-test new software or system network. His role is to use his skill to identify vulnerabilities in new organizational software before it is released for use. The blue hat hacker does this by using a variety of techniques and tools, such as penetration testing port scanning and vulnerability.[29] He is similar to a white hat hacker.

g. Purple Hat Hacker

He practices his hacking skills on his private computer from his comfort zone just to improve himself. He does not pose a minimal risk to anyone but he believes hacking into his own device is the best way to test his skills and to upgrade himself. IT hacking **is his domain knowledge. Domain skills are hard skills that are acquired by practical experience or personal research.** By doing this he can even begin to teach others how to pursue a career in IT.

h. State Sponsored Hacker

State sponsored hacking is a government-backed hacking. This hacking is a form of digital incursion that works to promote a country's interest at home or abroad. This hacker is appointed by the government of a country to gain

---

[27] Marshall Gunnel/ 'Green Hat Hacker' <https://www.techopedia.com/definition/< accessed 28 August 2023

[28] Ray Fernandez. 'Red hat hacking: Understanding the vigilante hacker' <https://moonlock.com/red-hat-lacking/> accessed 30 July 2023

[29] 'What is a Blue Hat Hacker?' <https://www.privacysense.net> accessed 30 July 2023

access to another nation's computer systems. His aim is to monitor and prevent international threat, so that bad actors won't cripple the financial systems of a country.[30]

i. Script Kiddies

They are part-time amateurs who do not have the skill or expertise like experienced hackers. To make up for this, they turn to the existing malware created by other hackers to carry out their attacks or to cause disruption. Organisations with unsecured networks and systems are at risk with script kiddies.

i. Hacktivist

He is someone who hacks into government-owned networks and systems just to draw attention to a political or social cause. He uses hacking as a form of protests retrieving sensitive government information which is used for political or social purposes. Some hackers in this category have been known to hack into banks with the purpose of donating a large amount of the money to charities or to bring the media's attention to their region.[31]

j. Botnet Hackers

They are large-scale hackers or malware coders who create bots to perform high volume attacks across many devices as possible such as targeting routers, cameras and other Internet of Things (IoT) devices. The bots operate by looking for devices to plant themselves in. When we have unsecured devices on our network, it creates a perfect entry points for bots, especially if we have never change the factory-set passwords.[32]

k. CryptoJackers

Cryptocurrency is a virtual currency, only existing online with no physical notes and coins. Mining cryptocurrency is a lucrative yet time-consuming and process-heavy endeavour. This cost and process is what cryptojackers bypass so that they can exploit system vulnerabilities and steal computer resources as a way to mine for crypto currencies. They spread malware by

---

[30] <https://www.cyberpolicy.com/cybersecurity/> accessed 22 February 2023

[31] Uzair Amir. ' Hacker Steals and Donates #10k in Bitcoin to Kurdish Group' <https://www.hackread.com/ > accessed 01 June 2021

[32] J.R. Tietsort. 'The 15 Types of Hackers (And How To Protect Yourself)' <https://www.aura.com/learn/> accessed 22 February 2023

planting infectious viruses across the web which works quietly in the background without the victim's knowledge. Cryptojackers are tough to spot. Their motive is not to steal victims' data but rather to use their system as a vehicle for cyptocurrency mining or cryptomining.[33]

m. Elite Hacker

Elite hacker is the most advanced hacker because he is often the first one to discover cutting-edge attack methods that hinders a cyber-attacker from destroying the computer security systems of an organisation by leveraging AI to solve problems relating to cybercrime. Due to his techie background and skill sets in the hacking world, he is regarded to be an expert or innovator who can break into information systems and pull in data and information with ease. Elite hackers are regarded as the champions of modern-day hacking who can significantly use their expert skills in both white hat hacking and black hat hacking.[34] Elite freelance hackers involved in white hat hacking make a lot of money after helping their clients to solve the flaws in their software code.

n. Phreaker

Phreaking is an illegal act of hacking into telecommunications particularly the exploitation or manipulation of weaknesses in telephone networks just to gain access to make free long distance calls or unauthorised calls. A phreaker is therefore a hacker who identifies and exploits weaknesses in telephones instead of computers.[35] Some of the techniques of telephone phreaking exploitation are blue boxing, red boxing, call forwarding and caller ID spoofing.[36]

o. Insider Hacker

He exposes or exploits an organisation's confidential information because he is a person who has the insider knowledge of an organisation's proprietary information but can intentionally misuse the information to negatively impact

---

[33] J.R. Tietsort. 'The 15 Types of Hackers (And How To Protect Yourself)' <https://www.aura.com/learn/> accessed 22 February 2023

[34] Chandana. 'Types of Hackers' <https:// <www.simplilearn.com/types/> accessed 25 February 2023

[35] 'What is Phreaking in Cybersecurity?' <https://www.alibabacloud.com/topic-centre/> accessed 25 February 2023

[36] Charlee Iddon. 'Phreaking Purpose & Examples' <https://study.com/acadermy/lesson/> accessed 27 May 2023

the integrity of the business. He is also called a whistleblower hacker because he may be acting on a personal grudge to the detriment of his current employers.[37] An Inside hacker is different from an intruder hacker who is usually a stranger or an outsider.

p. Attention Hackers

These are Internet users who knowingly produce and share misinformation content out of personal exuberance so they can attract the attention of Internet users to their online content. Attention hacks therefore indulge in the act of trolling or groyping to achieve their purpose. These attention-seeking users devise outlandish or divisive words on the Internet and take steps to direct maximum attention to themselves. The motive could be to make money or gather more followership. Examples include sending messages to mainstream talk shows in the hope they will read out the content on air, leaving an insulting message on the Internet in order to annoy someone, fooling high profile figures into re-sharing their content on other social media accounts and sharing conspiracy theories in unsuspecting television and radio phone-ins (known as groyping).

q. Prompt Hacking

This is a type of attack that exploits the vulnerabilities of Large Language Models (LLMs) by manipulating their inputs or prompts. A LLM is a specialised type of artificial intelligence that has been trained on vast amounts of text to understand existing content and generate original content.[38] LLMs have the potential to revolutionise how we interact with computers while a prompt is the initial user-provided input that an algorithm will complete. Unlike traditional hacking which typically exploits software vulnerabilities, prompt hacking relies on carefully crafting prompts to deceive the LLMs into performing unintended actions. It should be noted that there are three types of prompt hacking which are prompt injection, prompt leaking and jail breaking which can all sabotage our systems if we are not careful.[39]

---

[37] Panda Security. '14 Types of Hackers to Watch Out For'<https://www.pandasecurity.com/en/medicentre/> accessed 12 February 2022

[38] See the Gartner Glossary

[39] 'Prompt Hacking'<https://learnprompting.org/docs/> accessed 24 June 2023

3. INFORMATION DISORDER

In today's world, we all desire a healthy-dose of information sharing and that explains why people keep searching online for the true news. When information is thrust out into the limelight, many people give it different interpretations, sometimes leading to what is called the strategy of *'Fear, Uncertainty and Doubt'*, often shortened to *FUD*. This FUD strategy is founded on lack of evidence, contested evidence and ambiguity which tends to influence one's perception when others disseminate negative, dubious or false information. This is further compounded by the era of widespread misinformation that we find get to read on the Internet. To help dispel prevalent myths and misconceptions on the social media landscape, citizens have the right to know the truth about what is happening or about what happened. According to UNESCO, the spread of disinformation and misinformation is made possible largely through social networks and social messaging. Nigeria in 2021 hosted the West Africa Information Disorder Conference with the aim of engaging media professionals, academics, researchers and the public on the subject of information disorder and the efforts at combating the scourge because misinformation is a danger to every society.[40] The popular adage says 'bad news travels fast.' This means people tend to circulate bad news very quickly which expectedly will go viral on the Internet. Misinformation borne out of conspiracy theories and unfounded rumours easily spread through myriad sources on the Internet, based on the number of clicked likes, comments and shares. However it turns out, and depending on the trending topic, the solution is to always fact-check any trending news with organisations that have authoritative information released from their official quarters. International Fact-Checking Day is observed globally every April 2 annually which is considered as a tool that filters fact from fiction, particularly relevant for the huge segment of the population that either lacks the capacity to discern true and false information or for those that cannot be bothered to interrogate claims they encounter online and offline.[41] For example, if we need to confirm trending health news online, it is best to check the websites of either the WHO, your local

[40] Premium Times. 'Aregbesola to deliver keynote address at Information Disorder West Africa Conference' <httpps://www.premiumtimesng.com> accessed 20 May 2022

[41] Caroline Anipah. 'Fact-Checking is at the Heart of Good Governance and Democracy-Building' <https://factcheckingday.com/articles/49/fact-ch..> accessed 20 May 2022

medical association or your government's Ministry of Health which are verified and authentic sources, not Wikipedia which could have been edited by unknown contributors or quack health practitioners who deliberately distort information.

Internet users are therefore enjoined to be media literate and vigilant. Media is a communication tool for disseminating information whether on the traditional media or the social media. To be considered literate on the media, Internet users should possess the ability to identify different types of media, and understand the messages other media users are sharing. Media literacy also means the ability to critically analyse the news presented in the mass media and to determine their accuracy or credibility. However, a user must develop certain skills which include inquiry, search and research, critical thinking, analysis, evaluation, ethics and responsibility, plus reflection and self-assessment.[42] Information disorder could be classified as follows:

a.Mal-information

Mal-information is information that is based on reality but used to inflict harm on a person, social group, organisation or country.[43] Mal-information can also be defined as genuine information published with intent to harm, the clearest example of which is revenge porn or leaks. In a way, bad actors are manipulating the context of the information rather than the real information itself which the victim finds difficult to debunk.[44] Examples of mal-information is when you share real images and claim that they represent something that they do not or when you share images of different events from different date to create a false /misleading narrative or to discredit certain individuals. Combining pictures together is called photomontage when you create making a composite photograph by cutting, gluing, rearranging and overlapping two or more photographs into a new image in order to pass a wrong message or mislead people. In casual terms, an act of photomontage could also be referred to as 'photoshop.' That is, when an imagery is manipulated to deceive or convince Internet users to think of something or

[42] Matthew Lynch. 'What are the 7 Skills of Media Literacy'< https://www.theedadvocate.org/> accessed 20 May 2023

[43] Karen Santos-D'Amorim, Majory K. F.-de Oliveira. 'Misinformation, Disinformation and Malinformation: Clarifying the Definitions and Examples in Disinfodemic Times' <https://www.redalyc.org/journal/147/147681/> accessed 10 June 2022

[44] Hossein Derakhshan. 'The Era of Faked CCTV has Truly Arrived' <https://www.wired.com/story/> accessed 08 March 2023

somebody in a certain way whether favourable or unfavourable[45] or when you change the date and location of a genuine photograph and link it to another event in a different part of the world in order to harm the reputation of a rival or adversarial group or you mistranslate someone else's words or the use of selective quotes which changes completely what was meant.[46] Sharing unsubstantiated claims of certain herbal drugs and falsely claiming it can cure coronavirus just to peddle bogus treatment is an example of mal-information. Despite the global scope of Wikipedia, mischievous people still spread mal-information on Wikipedia or in their personal blogs and alter historical narratives which tend to promote ideas that are not credible or amplify information that contradicts well-established scientific consensus on sensitive topics. These online platforms deliberately or inadvertently promoting false information should not be allowed to thrive. Information quality is important. That is why it has been contended that law enforcement agencies will need to enhance the skills and technologies at their officers' disposal if they are to keep pace with the criminal use of mal-information and misinformation. To dispel mal-information or disinformation, efforts must be made to deploy artificial intelligence, technical and organizational safeguards to track all forms of fake news to remove inaccurate content and provide research-backed information.[47]

b. Misinformation

The digital world is rife with misinformation. Some stories look or sound believable yet they are fake. Some stories start out as rumours and later developed into conspiracy theories. Subsequently, people who think the stories are true continue to spread them without fact-checking or verifying the source. The Code of Practice for Interactive Computer Service Platforms/Internet Intermediaries of 2022 defines misinformation as the unintentional dissemination of false information. It is information that is false but not created with the intention of causing harm. We know how accidental spread of inaccurate information can cause fear panic and hate, confusion in

---

[45] Lauren Olson. 'Composite Images: What Are They, and How Can You Make Your Own? <https://www.pagecloud.com/blog> accessed 20 September 2022

[46] Hossein Derakhshan. 'The Era of Faked CCTV has Truly Arrived' <https://www.wired.com/story/> accessed 08 March 2023

[47] 'Europol report finds deepfake technology could become a staple too for organized crime' <https://www.europol.europa.eu/media-press/> accessed 10 June 2022

the society, however misinformation can be curbed by increasing digital literacy especially for people who are most vulnerable to misinformation. During the COVID-19 lockdown, there was lot of misinformation flying around and that was why the WHO coined the term 'infodemic' due to the increasing rate of misinformation in the online and physical environments.[48] According to the WHO, an infodemic is when there is too much information including false or misleading information in digital and physical environments during a disease outbreak which causes confusion and risk-taking behaviours that can harm our health.[49] Misinformation could also become harassment when some mischievous people on the social media for example, decided to create a stigma about monkeypox after sharing fabricated images of the infection on social networks. Misinformation can emanate from Google and other information search giants and that is why they have pledged millions of dollars to fight online misinformation and fake content. Google's ranking systems also aims to reward original, high-quality content that demonstrates qualities of what they call *EEAT* - an acronym for Expertise, Experience, Authoritativeness and Trustworthiness which will serve as a useful guide to deliver reliable, high-quality results to users.[50] Or is it not a fact that we trust Google as a reliable information reservoir and organiser that can provide answers to all the questions we ask. No matter where the stories are coming from, it is always still advisable to do due diligence because many of the online content could equally be wrong or subjective,[51] so we can help our personal research by ensuring that we back any online information up with papers written by experts or other peer reviewed research articles. This will assist us to create a distinction between fact and fiction especially where medical misinformation is concerned. In October 2022, the 193-Member States of UNESCO unanimously adopted the Abuja Declaration as a remedy to tackle false news, disinformation and misinformation. In the current scheme of things, it is necessary that we build a workforce that knows how to identify and track those who are maliciously manipulating

---

48 'Fighting Misinformation: Where it happens: striking first and often' <https://shareverified. com/ 2022/06/08/> accessed 10 June 2022

49 'Infodemic' < https://www.who.int/health-topics/infodemic> accessed 10 June 2022

50 Maggie Harrison. 'Google Made an AI-Generated Fake the First Result for Tank Man'<https:// futurism.com/the-byte/> accessed 22 September 2023

51 'Is Google always right? A sad truth about our perception of Google' <https://www.softscripts. net/blog/2018/07/> accessed 10 June 2022

people through the social media.[52] To stop circulating fake content, peddlers of fake news can also be sanctioned. That is saying, network companies should explore other options either by sacking their journalists and replace them with AI tools. Any fake story can be pulled down or deleted while the networks can also employ human fact-checkers to correct errors and ensure the quality of the content posted online.[53]

c. Disinformation

Disinformation can come through fabricated claims, cherry-picked information, doctored imagery or video, account-hacking including bots and trolls. Disinformation has three main characteristics which are: (1) It is created on purpose with the intent to deceive; (2) It is inaccurate; and (3) it is shared in order to cause harm. In this vein, the Code of Practice For Interactive Computer Service Platforms/Internet Intermediaries 2022 defines disinformation as a verifiably false or misleading information that, cumulatively, is created, presented, and disseminated for economic gain or to deceive the public intentionally and which may cause public harm. Disinformation is information that is false and deliberately created to harm a person, social group, organisation or country.[54] Such information creates confusion and propaganda or question scientific studies in an absurd way. Disinformation can be generated by creating content videos to look exactly like original; using screenshots that appear from legitimate news outlets to create false news; spreading a misleading campaign against vaccines, and appropriating the identities of mainstream media brands to distort news. Disinformation can have many different motives ranging from economic, political or religious perspectives. This is common whenever countries are preparing to hold elections where some individuals misuse social media platforms to perpetuate ethnic hate speech or direct personal attacks on politicians and incite others to commit violence and create communal conflict. During the COVID-19 pandemic lockdown, a Nigerian man was sentenced to two months imprisonment for posting false information on his

---

[52] 'Lab will train NJ High Schoolers in cyber Forensics'<https://www.forensicmag.com> accessed 16 December 2022 '

[53] Maggie Harrison. 'MSN Deletes Fake News About Mermaids & Bigfoot…' <https://futurism.com/msn/> accessed 07 December 2022

[54] See: 'Journalism, Fake News and Disinformation: A Handbook for Journalism Education and Training' published by UNESCO in 2018

Facebook page where he wrote that fever was killing many people in Kogi State. Consequently, the prosecution was able to prove that the false information was capable of causing panic or inflicting injuries on the society.[55] It should be noted that every November 27 of every year has been declared as the worldwide Disinformation Awareness Day because disinformation is perceived as a global threat to both democracy and public health. Disinformation also represents a growing threat to law enforcement. To curb disinformation, we need to verify our sources from scientific research articles and expert opinions on the subject matter and also be mindful of the academic qualifications and experience of the writer.

In view of the fact that there are too many false claims and misconstrued assertions, exaggerated facts, political truths and countless myths and fake news on the Internet, we have been advised to debunk whatever misinformation and inaccuracies that may come our way. All of us should strive to be debunkers in this information-based world. A debunker is a person who discredits false or suspicious claims and helps expose or put a stop to the spread of false information.[56] To this end, a healthy information ecosystem requires everyone to do their part in elevating facts.[57]

d. Digital Information Manipulation

In an AI-enabled world, digital information manipulation has been on the increase with AI-generated content and AI-generated human speeches becoming a daily occurrence. There is no doubt that AI has made it more convenient to shape information in a deceitful way. Manipulation of information is a widespread online editing of media to make it appear different. Manipulation covers dis-information, mis-information and mal-information. With AI, it can come in the form of videos and pictures. Digital manipulation of pictures and photographs emerged with the invention of computerized photography and the aim is to attract more viewers and readers. It is popularly referred to as 'photoshopping' because it is associated with image editing, cropped video footage that is intended to deceive although not intended to harm people. Manipulation is also common in this

[55] Gbenga Oladogun. 'Kogi man fined, jailed over Facebook post on COVID-19' <https://punchng.com> accessed 16 June 2022

[56] 'Debunking Day- March 11, 2023'< https://www.nationaltoday.com/debunking-day/> accessed 11 March 2023

[57] 'About International Fact-Checking Day' <https://factcheckingdaycom/ > accessed 11 March 2023

digital age of advanced Internet-enabled devices where phone camera apps have beautification settings to change a person's body features. What a woman looks like in the physical world may be altered to "slim the face and hide blemishes."[58] The advantage of a manipulated image is that it is considered influential and will have a great impact on viewers because the image is made to look more potent than it originally is. It could also save models the cost of doing makeup or surgeries so that they look beautiful during photo shoots.[59] On the other hand, it is unethical for individuals and institutions to alter images to fool their audience. For instance, manipulating physical attributes of individuals has an effect of causing emotional harm to that person when other people discover he is not physically what he is in the image.[60] Alteration or manipulation is also regarded as a scientific misconduct in scientific research.

e. Swatting

This is an unreasonable or unscrupulous act/conduct of Internet callers who make deceitful calls to first responders who are Police officers, fire fighters, paramedics or community volunteers who intervene in emergency situations or arrive first at a crime scene. Swatting occur when a person falsely reports a crime or emergency to law enforcement officers or medical personnel usually through an Internet-based telecommunication relay services in order to elicit emergency response. Swatting is the practice of making false reports to the public safety agencies of situations that would necessitate a significant and immediate response from armed law enforcement agencies.[61] In ***United States v. Mir Islam***,[62] the defendant pleaded guilty to crimes involving theft and online information, conveying false information about the use of explosives and cyberstalking. The rationale is that this bad conduct on the long run will not only divert first responders from actual life-threatening emergencies and waste their valuable time and resources, but it will also

---

[58] 'National Online Safety Course'<https://nationalonlinesafety.com> accessed 02 January 2023

[59] 'Benefits of Photo Manipulation Services' <https://www.truppglobal.com> accessed 02 January 2023

[60] 'Ethics of Digital Manipulation Research Paper' <https://ivypanda.com/essay/ethics/> accessed 02 January 2023

[61] Alexander Martin. 'Alleged 21 year old founder of cybercriminal market place arrested in U.K' <https://news.sky.com/story/ > accessed 14 April 2022

[62] 932 F. 3d 957 (D.C. Cir, 2019)

cause severe emotional distress to a large number of citizens.[63] Nowadays, technology presently has the ability to detect false callers through a track caller identification tool and hopefully, this will deter anonymous informants against making false calls.[64]

f. Deepfake

The process of deepfake technology begins with collecting visual and audio data about the target individual through publicly available information such as social media appearances.[65] Created by specialized programmes, deepfakes are video, audio, text and image content generated by AI that appear real and meant to mislead the public. Sadly, this is growing at an alarming rate. The technology is a tool of disinformation deliberately produced by bad actors to photoshop images, videos or sounds of a person, place or event that appear authentic.[66] They are deceptive videos, images and voices that are created by or with the help of AI algorithms to mislead an audience, to manipulate images, portray individuals in doing or saying things which they never did or said. The digital age has contributed to the disturbing trend of deepfakes where one person's likeness is altered for it appears to be someone else.[67] Deepfake technology are being used to frame someone and it has gotten more sophisticated as criminals are now using AI models to instantly create or edit near photo-realistic scenes or they go far as creating AI voice cloning to steal money. For example, a United Arab Emirates bank manager was fooled by criminals who used the deepfake voice of a company executive to transfer millions of dollars to his possession.[68] Voice replication AI and AI-powered face swapping technology have enabled deepfake technology for creating fake videos of individuals[69] and voice cloning scams.

---

[63] 'New York man Sentenced to 24 Months in Prison for Internet Offenses, Including 'Doxing', 'Swatting'. Making a False Bomb Threat, and Cyber-Stalking' <https://www.justice.gov.usao-dc/pr/> accessed 20 June 2022

[64] *United States v. Rose* 2022 WL 4115945 (5th Cir. 2022)

[65] Alka Jain. 'AI Scam Alert! How to spot fake video calls deepfake technology to stay safe' <https://www.livemint.com/technology/tech-news/> accessed 33 July 2023

[66] Nadia Smaili, Audrey de Rancourt-Raymond. 'How to combat the unethical and costly use of deepfakes' <https://theconversation.com/> accessed 22 June 2022

[67] Jeremy Hsu. 'Deepfake videos create false memories-but so do fake articles' <https://www.newscientist.com/article/2383218/> accessed 22 July 2023

[68] Tony Tran. 'Bank Robbers Steal $35 Million By Deepfaking Boss's Voice' <https://futurism.com/the-byte/bank-robbers/> accessed 24 December 2021

[69] Stephanie Condon. 'Amazon's Alexa reads a story in the voice of a child's deceased grandma' <https://www.zdnet.com/article/> accessed 27 June 2022

Today, those AI voice scams and fake video calls are on the rise, leading to an increase in cybercrime. "With scammers, sometimes all it takes is you picking up the call and saying a few worlds can help scammers grab your voiceprint and use that to authenticate payments with a finance institution or to authorise a transaction.[70]

Although some deepfakes can sometimes be harmless, it may have harmful consequences if used in pornography and election videos. After Russia invaded Ukraine, a deepfake video of Ukrainian president calling on his country's troops to surrender to Russian forces reportedly went viral. Obviously, the video was intentionally meant to deceive the Ukrainian troops.[71] Video manipulation software influenced by deepfake technology is also posing problems for remote courts which find it challenging to verify evidence from litigants and witnesses.[72] Deepfake therefore raises cybersecurity concerns for individuals and organisations when cybercriminals use generative machine learning to create believable fake nudes and child sexual abuse or create photorealistic artificial bodies, faces and voices and substitute the face or bodies of anyone in videos. To check the accuracy and authenticity of videos and audios, some deepfake detection tools in image forensics can provide useful insights into detecting inconsistencies and manipulation in imageries or the tools can help make a distinction between a synthetic audio/video from the real ones.[73] Similarly, machine learning recognition technology allows a user to edit any text/font or enable him to make a face swap algorithm to replace a face on a meme. For example, Android phones have audio lab apps where users can edit, convert and compress audio recording including other inbuilt features such as split audio, reverse audio, voice change, karaoke effect, video trim, channel manipulation to create false noise and wave generator. In this digital age, criminals are using deepfake to apply for remote technology jobs which grant them access

---

[70] Richard Webster, 'Artificial Intelligence: Voice cloning scams are on the rise, here's how we protect ourselves' <https://www.acenewstoday.com> accessed 13 June 2023

[71] Victor Tangerman 'Hackers deepfaked a Video of the Ukranian President Telling His Soldiers to Surrender' <https://futurism.com/ > accessed 17 March 2022

[72] Neil Rose. 'Deepfake warning over online courts' <https://www.legalfutures.co.uk/latest-news/>accessed 12 May 2022

[73] Roberto Caldelli et al. 'Optical Flow based CNN for detection of unlearnt deepfake manipulations' <https://zenodo.org/record/4707894# > accessed 12 May 2022

to corporate IT networks.[74] On the whole, the deepfake technology or the deepfake content which is facilitating the proliferation of crimes must be curbed through the same advances in artificial intelligence.[75]

g.Shallowfakes

These are controversial citizen videos which have been falsely presented in an out- of-context manner or crudely edited from the original video. The false effects are achieved by using video-editing software or smartphone applications to change the speed of the video segments or crop some clips together in order to remove relevant parts.[76] The shallow fake manipulation is not as strong as the deepfake technology, because it only requires a traditional manual alteration and selective editing and it is done solely to capture only part of story before grouping many different videos together. Shallow fakes are also called cheap fakes and the purpose is just for the videos to go viral on the Internet possibly to highlight a specific statement or to change a statement.[77]

4. DIGITAL PRYING

In the olden days, you would have to follow and physically monitor someone, read his diary or inquire from family and friends to know what another person is up to, but not anymore in this digital age where a person's movement can be tracked without him knowing. Digital prying is called an Internet of Things (IoT)-facilitated violence, when a cyber-attacker uses IoT as an instrument to harass, stalk, control or abuse through spyware, smart doorbells, security cameras and other electronic devices to covertly obtain data about an individual's activities.[78] The Spyware technology is a form of digital prying and an example of intrusive surveillance of a communication system. The Spyware app is malicious software designed to grab a person's personal details such as his financial accounts without his consent. In many

[74] Liam Tung. 'FBI warning: Crooks are using deepfakes to apply for remote tech jobs' <https://www.zdnet/article/fbi> accessed 29 June 2022

[75] 'The Europol Report finds deepfake technology could become staple tool for organized crime' <https://www.europol.europa.eu/media-press/> accessed 10 June 2022

[76] 'The Online Information Environment' <https://royalsociety.org/topics-policy/> accessed 22 February 2022

[77] Kalev Leetaru. 'The Real Danger Today is Shallow Fakes and Selective Editing Not Deepfakes' <https//www.forbes.com/sites/kalevleetaru/2019/> accessed 12 May 2022

[78] European Institute for Gender Equality Report on Combating Cyber Violence against Women and Girls 2022 <doi:10.2839/827864>

western countries, the federal Police agencies uses powerful spyware technology to access text messages, email, photos, videos, audio files, calendar entries and financial records for criminal investigation purposes.[79] The Stalkerware app is a form of spyware technology deployed to actively monitor a person through his mobile device. The apps can be used to track spouses, ex-partners, children and employees on their work devices. With Stalkerware app, you can track a location by GPS, eavesdrop on calls and social media conversations, steal logs, monitor browser activity and compromise a device's camera and microphone to listen/take photos of a real-world environment, although the apps may be difficult to detect on smartphones.[80]

5. DISTRIBUTED DENIAL-OF-SERVICE (DDOS) ATTACK

It is important that we should be able to access our data anytime or if our authorized personnel wish to do so but sometimes there are bad actors who flood our servers with traffic of emails just to prevent other users from accessing their online services and sites. This means a criminal is denying us access to use our system or network. Here, a denial of service attack is likely to jeopardise a computer's action especially where it is carried out by a disgruntled ex-employee possibly seeking to carry out revenge on his employer by leaking personal information through denial-of-service attacks.[81] The criminals involved in this DDoS generate a volume of spurious messages so that the victim's site will be clogged and consequently be unable to accept messages from genuine users wishing to place orders for goods or services. They can also bombard the victim's site with spurious data which may cause the victim's computer to crash. In ***DPP v. Lennon,***[82] the respondent admitted he downloaded a mail-bombing program called *Avalanche* from the Internet to flood his former employer's emails.

DDoS attack can come in other ways. Where a person who uses an old system can no longer be updated, hackers will find it easier to launch a

[79]TCR Staff. 'Expert Labels Spyware a Global Threat to Democracy, Human Rights' <https://thecrimereport.org/2022/08/09/ > accessed 09 August 2022

[80]Charlie Osborne. 'How tech is a weapon in modern domestic abuse—and how to protect yourself' https://www.zdnet.com/article/ accessed 11 February 20222

[81]Rohit Chatterjee. 'Difference Between Cybersecurity & Information Security'<https://analyticsindiamag,com> accessed 20 May 2022

[82] (2006) EWHC 1201

'teardrop attack'. So, running an old software can expose your system to cyber risks.[83] A 'ping of death attack' otherwise called a teardrop DDoS attack can also occur when an attacker crashes, destabilizes or freezes computers or its services by targeting them with oversized data packets (UDP flood DDoS attack or exploits the recipient device by overwhelming the system with Internet Control Message Protocol (ICMP) echo requests, also known as pings.[84]

DDoS attack can also come by Telephony Denial of Service (TDoS) attack. This is when a person makes continuous repeated calls to someone's telephone number with the intent of occupying the telephone line so that other callers will not get through to the owner of the telephone line.[85] In 2003, a Michigan entrepreneur called Alan Ralsky became known as the 'spam king' after sending millions of bulk e-mails for a variety of businesses. Some people who received his bulk e-mails decided to retaliate against Alan Ralsky by signing his address up for junk e-mail across the web. At the peak of the revenge scheme, Ralsky's home received hundreds of pounds of junk mails each day.[86] A recent example of DDoS attack happened during the Russia/Ukraine crisis, when the Russia's cyber army carried out repeated DDoS attacks against Ukraine government websites, overwhelming them with spurious traffic in order to take them offline. Consequently, the DDoS attacks rendered Ukraine's websites unreachable after Russia increased the fake traffic while Ukraine's own cyber warriors also retaliated in kind.[87]

Finally, when hackers deliberately slow down a website or cause a significant disruption to a targeted website, then we can say a '*Slowloris*' DDoS attack has taken place. Other types of DDoS attack include HTTP flood DDoS attack, Syn flood attack and MAC flooding.

6. BUSINESS E-MAIL COMPROMISE (BEC)

BEC is known as cyber-enabled financial fraud that targets employees with access to company finances and trick them-using a variety of methods like

[83] 'What is a Teardrop Attack> Definition, Damage & Defense' <https://www.okta.com/identity-101/> accessed 15 May 2023

[84] 'What is a Ping (ICMP) Flood DDOS Attack?' <https://www.radware.com> accessed 15 May 2023

[85] Ian J. Lloyd. Information Technology Law. (Oxford University Press 2011)

[86] Josh Clark & Patrick Kiger. '12 Big Cases of Revenge'< https://history.howstuffworks.com/> accessed 15 July 2022

[87] Gian M. Volpicelli. 'How Ukraine's Internet Can Fend Off Russian Attacks' <https://www. wired. com/story/ > accessed 03 March 2022

social engineering and computer intrusions – into making wire transfers to bank accounts thought to belong to trusted partners but instead controlled by criminals themselves.[88] BEC is a sub-set of phishing threats or phishing attacks perpetrated by a cybercriminal to gain access to email accounts, which he then uses to send fraudulent emails instructing victims to wire money to bank accounts he controls. BEC involves a cybercriminal who compromises a legitimate email account, and then tricks a business or individual to send their data or transfer funds in order to steal their money before selling the victims' identities and credentials on the dark web.[89] BEC scams are considered a sophisticated ruse which targets business and individuals who are duped into transferring funds to the scammer's account under the belief that they are performing a legitimate transaction.[90] Hackers who do BEC rely on fake, spoofed or compromised email domains to relay messages to targets with the aim of fooling them into making a wire transfer. As a top category of cybercrime measured by funds lost, the scams are technically simple but are often laced with deceptive story that fools even well-trained employees. The FBI has warned that scammers have ramped up video meetings as a tool to trick unsuspecting victims into handing over their money.[91] Scammers were also able to invade many virtual meeting platforms during the COVID-19 pandemic lockdown when people were home and working remote. The FBI has revealed that BEC fraud cost organisations and individuals at least $43.3 billion between 2016 and 2021 with victims in 177 countries.[92] A person involved in BEC scheme and held culpable by a Court of law could be imprisoned, extradited, fined to pay restitution to victims or forfeit the properties that he obtained with the proceeds of the cybercrime scheme.[93]

---

[88] FBI. 'International Business E-Mail Compromise Takedown' <https://www.fbi.gov/news/stories/> accessed 27 May 2022

[89] Jessica Lyons Hardcastle. 'FBI: Cyber-scams cost victims $6.9b-plus worldwide in 2021' <https://www.theregister.com/2022/05/fbi/ > accessed 27 May 2022

[90] Liam Tung. 'FBI: Email fraud keeps getting worse. Here's how to protect yourself' <https://www.zdnet.com/article/ > accessed 11 May 2022

[91] Liam Tung. 'FBI: Now scammers are using fake video meetings to steal your money' <https://www.zdnet.com/article/ > accessed 21 February 2022

[92] Jessica Lyons Hardcastle. 'FBI: Cyber-scams cost victims $6.9b-plus worldwide in 2021'<https://www.theregister.com/2022/05/fbi/> accessed 27 May 2022

[93] Edward Kovacs. 'Nigerian Man Sentenced to 8 Years in US Prison for $8 Million BEC Scheme' <https://www.securityweek.com/> accessed 20 July 2023

7. CLOUD ACCOUNT COMPROMISE

A cloud account compromise involves the act of attacking or maliciously gaining control over a legitimate user's cloud-based e-mail or collaboration service account. Whether the act is from social engineering, phishing or other cyber-attacks, an account becomes compromised when a threat actor gains access to credentials or other means to perform actions on behalf of the targeted user. A cloud attack is a cyber-attack that targets cloud-based service platforms such as computing services, storage services, or hosted applications in a platform-as-a-service (PaaS)[94] or software-as-a-service (SaaS)[95] model. Cloud attacks can have serious consequences, such as data breaches, data loss, unauthorized access to sensitive information and disruption of services.[96]

8. SALAMI ATTACKS

It is a type of cybercrime in which an attacker steals money in small amounts. Also called penny shaving attack, salami attack is a financial gain attack or a financial crime. This is when the attacker installs computer chips that cheat consumers overstating the amount without anyone knowing. Salami attacks are common in digital payments where the attacker uses an online database to obtain a customer's information such as bank/credit card details. Overtime, the attacker deducts insignificant amount from each account while these insignificant sums gradually add up to a large sums of money. It is computer crime where a criminal steals money or resources a bit at a time. When a fraudulent programmer arranges to collect fractions of pennies in a separate account, such thefts are very difficult to detect because the belief is that thefts are not easily discovered if they are done in bits. Sadly, majority of victims do not report the losses, often due to the small amount involved.[97]

9. MAN-IN-THE-MIDDLE (MITM) ATTACK

A Man-in-the-Middle (MITM) or Person-in-the-Middle (PItM) attack is a type of cyber-attack where an attacker intercepts communications between two

---

[94] A cloud computing model that provides customers a complete cloud platform- hardware, software and infrastructure for developing, running and managing applications.

[95] Allows users to connect to and use cloud-based apps over the Internet.

[96] 'What Are Cloud Attacks?' <https://www.aquasec.com/> accessed 21 May 2023

[97] Anshuman Singh. 'What is Salami Attack and How to protect against it. <https://www.naukri.com/learning/article/> accessed 20 September 2022

parties, impersonates both of them and manipulates the information exchanged between them. It is a type of eavesdropping attack where an attacker essentially positions himself between the sender and receiver, allowing him to intercept and modify the communication flow. That is, the attacker masquerades secretly and intercepts two parties who are communicating with each other. One example of a MItM attack is through active eavesdropping carried out by a cyber-attacker who makes independent connections with the victims and relays messages between them to make them believe they are talking directly to each other over a private connection when in fact the entire conversation is controlled by the attacker. MItM attackers can also intercept a message to save for another date and replay the old message in order to obtain access to a system. MItM attacks can occur through the use of public Wi-Fi networks and use of phishing scams by e-mail. In recent times, the NCC has alerted Nigerians about how hackers can unlock and steal vehicles due to the vulnerability caused by the MItM attack.[98] These attackers can use the MItM attacks to inject malicious code into the communication flow, allowing criminals to infect the victim's device with malware, ransomware or other malicious software.[99]

10. REMOTE KEYLOGGERS

A keylogger can infiltrate your safe computer either through phishing, social engineering, file sharing, software download or vulnerable browser.[100] A keylogger is a form of spyware. A spyware is a type of malicious software that is installed on a computing device without the end user's knowledge. A keylogger is a program that records every keystroke made by a computer user in order for the hacker to gain fraudulent access to passwords and other confidential information. Keylogging software tracks each key that is struck on a keyboard of your laptop and smartphones revealing every conversion, every click and every tap that is capable of giving hackers access to your personal data. This simply means that it is the action of recording the keys struck on a keyboard without the knowledge of the user and this

[98] Na'ankwat Dariem. 'NCC Alerts Nigerians, Reveals How Hackers Can Unlock , Steal Vehicles' <https://von.gov.ng/2022/05/15/ > accessed 15 May 2022

[99] Jabir Ahmed. 'MItM Attack' (Linkedin) 29 April 2023

[100] 'Demystifying a Keylogger- How They Monitor What You Type and What You Can Do About it?' <https://home.sophos.com/en-us/security-news/> accessed 02 February 2022

mainly affects our mobile device or laptop because the cybercriminal needs to first access your device, before installing a piece of software to record everything that you type on your keyboard such that if you log into any of your personal e-mail or bank accounts, every key will be recorded while the hacker will have this information and be able to hack your account.[101] It should be noted that not all keyloggers are illegal as some are often used by IT departments to troubleshoot problems and systems. Sometimes keyloggers help us keep an eye on employee activities including what our children are doing on the computer. There are two types of keyloggers. Some keyloggers are hardware devices embedded within your internal PC hardware while the second type is software that can be easily installed on victims' devices which does not harm the phone or laptop. In 2021, keyloggers gained access into a JAMB intranet site to alter the profile of its *ad hoc* staff. According to JAMB, a keylogger is software which grants access to the profile of anyone who has logged in using a public cybercafé even after the person has logged out and gone.[102]

11. ROGUE SOFTWARE

In cybersecurity and antivirus, the word, 'rogue' refers to software or systems that operate without clear oversight or strict security protocol. Fake or rogue antivirus software is a form of malicious software that infiltrates your system, with the hacker pretending to have discovered an infection on the victim's computer or misleads users into believing that there is a virus on their computer. Thereafter, the hacker starts demanding for money in exchange for providing a fake malware removal tool, which actually introduces malware into the computer.[103] Rogue security software is deployed via conventional file downloads. This means if you download files from an untrusted website, your computer or device may become infected with rogue security software.[104] Note that rogue security software does not protect our devices against cybersecurity threats; it is in fact a malware or

[101] Jessica Truong. 'How to Hack TikTok Accounts: 5 Common Vulnerabilities' <https://hackernoon.com > accessed 25 February 2022

[102] Emmy. 'How Hackers Accessed JAMB Website, Diverted Over N1om' <https:// diamond fountainmedia.com/>accessed 10 February 2022

[103] Rogue Antivirus Software. <https://www.kaspersky.com/resource-centre/ > accessed 10 February 2022

[104] Logix Consulting. 'What is Rogue Security Software?' <https://logixconsulting.com/2020.08/24/ > accessed 10 February 2022

scareware which displays fake warnings to trick Internet users into paying for non-existent antivirus solutions.

12. SNIFFING ATTACK

This is an illegal extraction of unencrypted data which captures network traffic through packet sniffers. They are used by cybercriminals to steal customer data and compromise network security. Sniffing attacks can be active or passive. When the attack is active, it becomes a security risk which enables network threat types such as man-in-the middle attacks, spoofing attacks and insider threats among others.[105] For passive sniffing attack, it can be difficult to detect sniffers because they often remain passive by simply listening in, collecting and capturing data, but not interacting with it. However, if you use anti-sniff detection software, it can protect your data.

13. INTERNET TIME THEFT

Although not considered a very serious threat, this is when employees use the Internet for non-work purposes or when an unauthorized person uses Internet hours paid by another person. These employees could be using the Internet time for general browsing, doing online shopping, playing games or music, enjoying themselves on social media and reaching out to their customers while at work. An Internet time thief could also be an hacker who gets access to another person's computer without the person's knowledge. It is easy to commit Internet theft if the victim uses an open Wi-Fi connection which requires no password for Internet access. What the owner of the Internet time only suffers is financial loss because he is paying for the Internet time.[106]

14. LOGIC BOMBS

This is a form of cybersecurity sabotage also sometimes referred to as slag code, code bomb and cyber bomb. It is a malicious code inserted intentionally into a program or software to harm a network. Other forms of malware such as viruses, worms, or Trojan horses also contain logic bombs. The logic bomb virus is a subtle code which is harmful but capable of causing

[105] Peter Arntz. 'What is IP sniffing?' < https://blog.malwarebytes.com/explained/2021/12 > accessed 02 February 2022

[106] '5 Types of Time Theft' <https//www.future-systems.net/blog/> accessed 28 August 2022

explosive damage that is difficult to trace or mitigate. The malicious code remains undetected until it after executing its specified function.[107]

15. SIGNAL JAMMING

A jammer is a signal blocking or blurring device. It is possible to jam any wireless transmission, especially if a person suspects that someone is trying to spy on his online activities with a hidden camera in a neighbourhood. A signal jammer can block or disrupt the said hidden camera. Being in possession of Phone jammer or GPS blocker device is illegal in most countries because it is a form of cyber-attack which can cripple online services and cause an outage that affects call centres, hinder receiving emails or posting online chats in the particular area where businesses are carried out. What are the consequences for Internet users? Those living in the area will experience poor network reception. This could interfere with aviation, maritime, industrial, automotive and personal systems which rely on GPS data to navigate their operations. Users can also lose their GPS location and related information. However, users can alert their network operators when these anomalies occur so that they can create an incident response plan before services are restored depending on whether the affected company paid ransom in exchange to recover their operations. Users will then be reassured that their personal data is safe.[108]

Case Study

A father in France is facing a hefty fine and possible jail time following his well-intentioned attempt to keep his children off the Internet late at night. His use of a signal jammer was so effective that it not only kept his children off the Internet, but also extended to those in a nearby town as well. Consequently, a report on this was made to the French Frequency Agency that something was affecting the Internet and cellular services every midnight. The search for the cause of the jammer led investigators to a house near the coast where the Father was caught and admitted he was in fact using the signal jammer to prevent his teenage children from accessing

---

[107] Rahul Awati & Laura Fitzgibbons. 'What is a Logic Bomb?' <https://www.techtarget.com/searchsecurity/defition/> accessed 30 August 2022

[108] Mission Secure. 'The Cyber-attack on Garmin: Exposing GPS vulnerabilities. <https://www.missionsecure.com > accessed 19 February 2022

the Internet instead of sleeping in the night. The case has since been handed over to the appropriate authorities.[109]

[109] Tim Sweezy. 'A Father Who Used A Signal Jammer To Keep His Kids Offline At Night Now faces Jail Time' <https://hothardware.com/news/ > accessed 20 February 2022

Chapter 4

TYPES OF CYBERCRIME

The International Classification of Crime for Statistical Purposes (ICCS), 2015 define crime as a punishable contravention or violation of the limits on human behaviour as imposed by national criminal legislation. The ICCS framework further states that any cybercrime-related action serves to identify various forms of crime committed with use of a computer or through electronic dissemination.[1] In this context, we can say that any activity endangering or attacking cybersecurity is a cybercrime. Simply put, cybercrime is any crime committed by electronic device or arising from a computer misuse. Cybercrime consist of a range of computer-related activities that is directed as an attack against any electronic device, or against individuals or against property, organisation, community and countries. With the advent of the Internet, criminals are also using technology to commit crime with sophisticated cyber tools and digital knowledge while the primary motivation is usually economic and political. Cybercrime can be carried out in so many ways such as hacking which is unauthorised access by intruding into a computer information system to exercise illegal control over it with the purpose of endangering network security or infringing another person's personal information. It is also possible for a person to use his computer to commit other crimes that does not have any relationship with the Internet, such as theft, embezzlement and misappropriation of public funds, among others. Anyone who renders assistance technical support or any assistance either by distribution, sale or offering for sale of hardware, software or other tools used for committing the act is also liable for cybercrime.

Cybercrime is perpetrated by one individual or more whether known, unidentified or anonymous to the victim. From the social psychology perspective, cybercrime thrives on the concept of 'De-individuation' which

[1] The Framework of the UNODC

refers to certain persons who do not want to be identified, for example on the massive Internet where their anonymity is guaranteed, so they want to hide in a group and behave differently. These persons are more likely to engage in online crimes.[2]

In Nigeria, all acts of cybercrimes or cyber-attacks fall under the exclusive legislative list. The governing framework is the Cybercrimes Act of 2015, but few provisions of this law have been further amended in 2024.

I. CYBER & PHISHING ATTACKS

The Tallinn Manual on the International Law Applicable to Cyber Warfare in 2013 defines a cyber-attack under international humanitarian law as a cyber-operation whether offensive or defensive, that is reasonably expected to cause injury or death to persons or damage or destruction to objects.[3]

Cybercrime is spurred on by an ever-growing online presence and the exploitation of new features of emerging technologies which has become a growing threat to many online users of which devastating consequences have equally affected the physical environment in many ways. For example, cyber-attacks potentially disrupt essential public services, expose personal and financial data, and disable the economy of a city. This is bad for cities which essentially rely on interconnected networks to operate and deliver facilities that people and businesses need.[4] When these criminals get inside our systems, they access our data, copy and export it. Cyber-attacks can range from hacking into systems and social media, phishing attacks, malicious software including ransomware, identity theft, social engineering and denial-of-service attacks. This is a painful experience for victims both personally and financially.[5] Cyber-attacks could cost organisations the trust that people repose in them. It can hamper economic growth and damage critical infrastructure. For example, the Joint Admissions and Matriculation Board (JAMB) in Nigeria suffered a cyber-attack resulting into a shift in the 2022 Unified Tertiary Matriculation Examination (UTME) while about 48 lecturers

[2] Elizabeth Happer. 'What is Deindividuation in Psychology?' <https://www.thoughco.com/> accessed 25 October 2022

[3] <https://www.ccdcoe.org/research/tallinn-manual/ > accessed 20 April 2022

[4] Gianni Minetti. 'Cybersecurity: a lifelong journey for smart cities' <https://www.smartcitiesworld.net> accessed 14 February 2022

[5] Ann Brady. 'Counter-Attacks on Cybersecurity' < https://www.iso.org/contents/news/> accessed 12 May 2022

and security officers were arrested for compromising the Joint Universities Preliminary Examinations Board (JUPEB) examinations website. Similarly, the Police arrested some suspects with incriminating exhibits for attempting cyber-attacks on 10 banks in Lagos State with the intent to pull out huge sums of money. It was alleged that a bank worker who colluded with the suspects was asked by the suspects to leave critical gateways open on the bank's server so that the syndicate can gain unauthorized access into the bank's network and move money out using Python application and Zoom.[6] Competing crime groups could also infect e-commerce sites with skimming attacks. Skimming occurs when devices illegally installed on automated teller machine (ATM), point-of-sale (POS) terminals, or fuel pumps capture data or record cardholders' personal information number (PINs). Criminals use the data to create fake debit or credit cards and then steal from victims' accounts.[7] Over the years thousands of network sites and computer systems have been hit by hacking exploits causing them to run malicious code and load malicious scripts. Hackers take over your website modify and even update so they can be in control of your files. You need to get an expert with special training to trace or detect the vulnerable entry points. Another option is to use antivirus software.[8]

Examples of Global Cyber-Attack

1. Attack on the servers of International Committee of the Red Cross Hack 2022
2. The Chrysler Jeep Hack 2015
3. Stuxnet Cyberworm Attack 2010
4. IPhone Hack on Uyghur Muslims 2019
5. Target Data Breach (Gregg Steinhafel) 2013
6. The Bangladesh Bank Cyber Heist 2016
7. The WannaCry Ransomware 2017
8. Tesla Vehicles Hack 2020
9. The *Center Hospitalier Sud Francilien* (CHSF) attack 2022
10. Manchester United Football Club cyber-attack 2020

---

[6] Akewushola Afeez. 'France-Based Nigerian Leads Cyber-attacks on 10 Banks in Lagos'< https://theinformant247.com > accessed 23 June 2022

[7] 'FBI Scams and Safety' <https://www.fbi.gov/> accessed 12 February 2022

[8] Dan Goodin. 'Hackers Rigged Hundreds of Ecommerce Sites to Steal Payment Info '<https:// arstechnica.com/information-technology/> accessed 12 February 2022

11. The Medibank Data Breach 2022

With so many logins and passwords to remember, it is tempting to reuse credentials. You can prevent any cyber-attack by using a strong password or update your password, and facilitate training and education on potential threats arising from social engineering attacks. You must know how to validate backup and use anti-malware/software protection. If the cyber-attack is more than you can handle, engage cybersecurity experts who are specialists in cyber intelligence, purple team,[9] security 'capture the flag (CTF),[10] cyber resilience technology, stacks and design, threat modelling and threat intelligence.

Cyber-Attacks exposes users to different type of threats such as malware, man in-the-middle attack, drive-by download, malvertising, rogue software, DDoS, password attack, phishing and breach of personal data. With these forms of cyber-attacks, a company can lose its credibility, reputation and productivity; It can negatively impact those who do not have cyber liability insurance; your files are corrupted; you encounter privacy violation, data breach and litigation. In the Medibank cyber-attack, customers' data released into the dark website included the good list, the naughty list, abortions and alcohol dependants.

a. Phishing Attacks

Phishing attacks are cybersecurity attacks. In ***National Association of Software & Services Companies* v. *Ajay Sood,***[11] the Delhi High Court defined phishing as a form of Internet fraud involving a deliberate misrepresentation or theft of identity in order to perpetrate theft of data. This means we all stand the risk of being victims of phishing scams when we compromise our emails to cyber thieves whether intentionally or not. In other words, phishing is a type of social engineering attack often used to steal user data, including login credentials and credit card numbers. Ordinarily, it comes in the form of a seemingly legitimate e-mail sent by a hacker with an attachment for the user to open with the purpose gaining access to his data, maybe to do illegal money transfer or conduct online

---

[9] A cybersecurity testing exercise or a group of cybersecurity experts who enhance information sharing with other teams.

[10] CTFs means Capture The Flags. It is s a computer security competition which focuses the expertise in attacking or defending computer resources

[11] 2005 (30) PTC 437

shopping until the user finds out about it.[12] Some phishers also disguise themselves as mailer daemon where the e-mail recipient is informed that his e-mail could not be delivered except he clicks a phishing site.[13] When you are receiving phishing e-mails, the motive is to mislead you to give or grant unhindered access to a bogus app that permits cyber-attackers to read and write your e-mails or files, create inbox rules, read your contacts and tamper with your calendar items. Phishing emails appear to come from someone you trust, such as an online service provider, bank, Credit Card Company or a popular website. These e-mails typically try to track and convince you into giving away your sensitive information such as your usermail, passwords or credit card details in order to extract your passwords or money from you. The phishing mails may also try to install malware[14] onto your computer by getting you to click a malicious link or open an infected attachment. For example, the NCC warned the public of *TangleBot,* a new virus infecting Android mobile devices through short messaging service (SMS). In recent times, scammers could also use Chat GPT to write phishing emails.[15]

Phishing techniques are used to capture credentials. Section 58 of the Cybercrimes Act 2015 defines Phishing as the criminal and fraudulent process of attempting to acquire sensitive information such as usernames, passwords and credit card details, by masquerading as a trustworthy entity in an electronic communications through e-mails or instant messaging in form of an e-mail from what appears from your bank asking a user to change his password so that such information can be used to defraud the user. Phishing schemes mimic the appearance of legitimate websites to gather victims' online credentials, including usernames, passwords, financial account information, social security numbers and other types of personal identifiable information.[16] Phishing, spamming and spreading of virus are prohibited under Section 32 of the Cybercrimes Act, 2015.

---

[12] Isha Upadhyay. 'Top 10 Challenges of Cyber Security Faced in 2021'<https://www.jigsawacademy.com> accessed 18 June 2022

[13] Soren Schulte. 'Treacherous Cyberscams: Phishers disguise themselves as mailer daemon' <https://www.retarus.com/blog/th/> accessed 20 June 2022

[14] Types of Malware –include spyware, trojan horse, keylogger. worm, virus, adware, remote access, etc.

[15] Chris Stokel-Walker. 'ChatGPT can be made to write scam emails and it slashes their cost' <https://www.newscientist.com/article/2361490/ > accessed 03 March 2023

[16] Press Release. 'Nigerian Man Sentenced for Online Fraud Schemes' <https://www.justice.gov/usao-ma/pr/> accessed 10 May 2023

b. *Types of Phishing*

Phone Phishing – This is when your phone is hacked and you see new apps that you did not download or you see calls in your phone that you didn't make or there has been a data usage that you cannot account for.

Spear Phishing – This is an email spoofing, fraud sent by a trusted sender such as your bank, or a hospital specifically targeting a company and attempting to solicit sensitive information.

Vishing/Voice Phishing – These are fraudulent phone calls impersonating banks, investment companies, governments or medicare officers urging the recipient to reveal certain sensitive information. It is the use of voice-altering software or the use of other social engineering tactics where callers impersonate legitimate companies to steal money, personal and financial information. For example in a CEO fraud attack, attackers can impersonate the CEO of a company just to convince customers that they need access to sensitive information.

Smishing – This is a phishing attack sent out by text messages or short message service (SMS) urging the recipient to click a link that downloads malware into his device. For example those messages come with a link to a malware telling phone users to click on a link that is falsely designed to genuinely contain information on COVID vaccination, power outages or to update certain information.

Whaling – This is a form of phishing where the sender claims to be a high authority. This is someone who you ordinarily would not communicate with, such as a King or the CEO of a Bank, who is asking you to reveal your information.[17]

Impersonator Attack - is an attempt to gain unauthorized access to information systems by masquerading as authorized users. An impersonation attack is a form of social engineering where an attacker pretends to be someone else or impersonates a legitimate user or group of users to gain access to information that they are not authorised to have.[18]

---

[17]Julie Emory. 'Cybersecurity 101: Phishing and what you should know to stay safe online https://www.dailyuw.com/news/discoveriesa/ > accessed 08 March 2022

[18]Ahona Rudra. 'What is an Impersonator Arrack?' <https://powerdmarc.com> accessed 11 November 2022

Browser-in-the-Browser (BITB) Attack - This is an advanced and more sophisticated phishing attack that can trick users into believing that a fake website is real. It mimics a legitimate website window within the browser where hackers will want to conduct successful phishing attacks.

Scareware – This is a malicious computer programme which pops up on your device to warn you that your device has been compromised by a virus and causes you anxiety to trick you into buying and downloading unnecessary and potentially dangerous fake antivirus software.

Pharming – This is a form of online scam that re-directs people to fraudulent websites mimicking authentic websites. Pharming scams try to convince people to interact with fake, lookalike websites in order to harvest their personal data like emails and passwords, or infect their computers with malware. Pharming which derives its name from the two combined words '*phishing and farming*' is similar to phishing but pharming scams cast mush wider nets. The difference is phishing attacks are often carried out through fake emails, while pharming occurs via fake websites. The two primary examples of pharming are malware pharming and DNS server poisoning. How do you spot pharming? – For example, when a person with ulterior motive says you have won a lottery and then send you a link for payment or a redirect notice requiring to pay, take a conscious look at the website's URL. Does the URL begin with http or https? When a URL begins with https, it means you are on a secured connection. But if the URL has only http, the connection is not guaranteed as secure and the website might be unsafe. Check the spelling of the URL just in case the spelling in the domain is altered by one letter or character. Examine the webpage carefully and use strong antivirus software, strong password, and password manager, as well as anti-malware software backed with cyber capture technology which automatically identifies and evaluates suspicious files.[19]

2. ONLINE IDENTITY THEFT (OIT)

Many people share the intimate details of their lives and activities online including that of their family members. Beyond this, our online personal information is in places that we do not have control over as long as they are

[19] Danielle Bodhar. ' What is Pharming and how to protect against it' <https://www.avast.com/c-pharming> accessed 01 February 2022

generated from our personal computer, driver's licence, paperwork, government tax database, personal digit assistance (PDA) device, cell phone, educational institutions, bank and Internet records, mail, trash, and flash drives. Even, a 'Google' search exposes our personal data of social media users to vulnerabilities. This has made our personal data to be vulnerable to hackers who may want to use them for unlawful or illegal purposes

But what happens when cybercriminals are bent on stealing our online information? Personal data refers to any information relating to a person's identity, such as their name, family, religion, physical location and other unique description identifying the person. This information identifies who we are and it is unique. Note that the process of OIT begins when scammers collect the publicly available visual and audio data of online users. Criminals might decide to steal our identity and use the information. Identity theft is a type of impersonation otherwise called spoofing. Identity spoofing is the action of assuming the identity of another human or non-human identity and then using that identity to accomplish a goal. That is, when a scammer assumes the identity of others to commit a fraud.[20] Section 58 of the Cybercrimes Act 2015 defines identity theft as the stealing of somebody else's personal information to obtain goods and services through electronic-based information. On identity theft and impersonation, Section 22(1) of the Cybercrimes Act 2015 provides that any person engaged in the services of any financial institution who commits identity theft of its employer/service providers with the intent to defraud, commits an offence.

It should be noted that our online identity includes who we are on our social media handles such as Linkedin profile, X, Facebook account, Instagram, and other search engines. Thus, anyone who decides to steal your online identity whether in the form of your digitalised account or personal identifiable information (PII) will be guilty of online identity theft. In the context of data privacy, PII is information that can be used on its own or with other information to identify, contact, or locate a single person, or to identify an individual in a context.[21] Therefore any criminal who steals our online identity can also steal our sensitive personal data (SPD) which is defined as any data relating to religious or other beliefs, sexual orientation,

---

[20] 'Identity Spoofing' <https://fraud.net/d/identity-spoofing> accessed 28 February 2022

[21] See Section 1.3 (xx) of Nigeria Data Protection Regulation 2019

health, race, ethnicity, political views, trades union membership, criminal records or any other sensitive personal information.[22]

As technological advancement advances, online identity theft will also be on the rise. Other types of identity theft are mail identity theft, social security number identity theft, Biometric theft, online banking theft, social media, photo/video theft and malware identity theft. These cyber thieves steal and collect our information without our consent. A typical example is when scammers use the names and positions of company employees for online impersonation and fraudulently use those stolen identities during hiring process. Hackers can also use stolen personal information to take over a victim's financial accounts, open new accounts, or to obtain fake documents.[23] Furthermore, identity theft occurs when someone uses another person's PII like their names without their permission to commit online crimes such as Catfishers who often use stolen images. Online identity theft or Catfishing is therefore a deceptive activity where a person creates a fake identity often taken from other people's social media account in order to create a new identity.[24] OIT could also happen when a perpetrator uses someone else's picture to commit crime on social media or when people post pictures they don't have permission to share on social media. Basically, a person enjoys copyright protection of his photograph which means we need to obtain the person's consent before we display his picture otherwise we may be infringing or violating the owner's rights. However a lot of users rely on the exception of "fair use" (to teach, for research as commentary or criticism or news). Unfortunately some people go as far as posting a person's picture or headshot to perpetrate the crime of fraud, since cyber criminals can easily download these pictures and use them for Internet scams, fake social media profiles, revenge porn or fraud.[25]

For the legal punishment of identity theft and impersonation, Section 22 (2) of the Cybercrimes Act 2015 provides that a person who fraudulently or dishonestly makes use of the electronic signature, password or any other unique identification feature of any other person or fraudulently

[22] Section 1.3 (xxv) Nigeria Data Protection Regulation 2019

[23] Liam Tung. 'FBI warning: Scammers are posting fake jobs ads on networking sites to steal your money and identity' <https://www.zdnet.com/article/fbi > accessed 28 February 2022

[24] What is Catfishing? <https://www.cybersmile.org > accessed 28 February 2022

[25] Christa Leste-Lasserre. 'Fake faces created by AI looks more trustworthy than real people' <https://www.newscientist.com/article/2308312/ > accessed 16 February 2022

impersonates another entity or person, living or dead with intent to gain advantage for himself or another person is liable on conviction to imprisonment for a term of *five* years or a fine of not more than ₦7 million or both.

Essentially, the questions usually posed by social media users are: What is this crime of online identity theft and what are the components? How can digital forensics help to stop the theft? Can social media users really control their pictures that are posted in the cyber domain? How is the investigation going to be carried out since identity theft does not have a typical crime scene nor a blood or fingerprint? Nonetheless, there are forensic traces like the evidence of indicators of compromise (IoC) which align with Edmond Locard's principle of exchange that can unravel the perpetrator that was behind the online identity theft. Are there any remedies for online identity theft? A victim of identity theft is best advised to contact digital experts or cybersecurity experts who will perform online identity checks and track down the IP addresses and geographic locations of Internet users. These experts working in conjunction with the Police can help the victim to retrieve his money and get the last location of the scammers. Social media users are also advised to perform an audit of their online presence to determine whether their pictures or names are linked to something they do not know anything about. Simply Google your name once in a while to check the online results. In any case, investigating identity theft crime is not always easy and it takes time. So, to avoid being catfished, we are advised to:

1. Verify or confirm identities;
2. Keep a track of the bills you own and their due dates;
3. Monitor your bank statement;
4. Do reverse image searches to check whether a person's photographs appear somewhere;
5. Install the most recent windows fixes or use antivirus software and firewall to keep your computer safe;
6. Avoid websites with a bad reputation;
7. Be careful of your contact information on dating apps and other enclosed networks where your identity can be stolen;
8. Educate yourself and stay informed;
9. Apply security update;

10. Report suspicious any behaviour. Doing all these also helps protect potential victims as well.

Impact of Online Identity theft

The list of online identity thefts in recent years is growing daily. As the amount of time we spend uploading private information on our gadgets keeps increasing daily, it has also raised potential opportunities for cyber threats. Thus, we need to identify the potential threats. The loss of your mobile devices or phones or who you hand over your phones to, has far-reaching implications because your phones stores your most private information ranging from your photos, banking, passwords and your family or employee/employer information. If someone uses your identity to commit a crime and gives your information to the Police, note that when they get arrested you could be implicated too, you could lose time and money or there could be tax debt. Be aware that we are all vulnerable to OIT.

In this digital age of artificial intelligence (AI) or machine learning (ML), the tools can conveniently create computer-generated human faces that people can't distinguish from real human faces. These fictional, computer-generated human faces are so convincing that they can fool social media users, except a trained eye. Worse off is the fact that AI-synthesized faces have become so sophisticated that many people think they are more trustworthy than actual humans. This has adverse effects for it could encourage the production of many deepfaked images and videos that are indistinguishable from reality and further cast doubt on real photos and videos.[26]

Photographs

Of course, there is a reason why people take photographs and that is to keep records. Our images are out there on the Internet, so are criminals seeking to explore the vulnerabilities in technology. You do not have to be a celebrity before your photos are stolen. Most times, cybercriminals do it randomly like when thieves physically steal our smartphones; they have access to our information and can steal our data. The risk is higher for those who post their selfies on social media platforms and dating apps. When

[26] Tony Tran. 'Scientists warn that new AI-generated faces are seen as more trustworthy than real ones' <https://futurism.com/the-byte/ > accessed 18 February 2022

hackers crack our passwords and gain access into our Facebook page, they can steal our photos, copy fingerprints from photos and use them to steal our identity and may even go as far as selling it on the dark web. They are known to break into online dating websites to steal photos. There are even scammers who buy photos and videos from specialised websites that cater to such theft operations, without the knowledge of the owners of the photographs.[27] If hackers gain access into your phone, they can use simple file restoration programmes to get your deleted photos. So, why do criminals steal our photos? The motives vary from blackmail, to setting up fake profiles, to impersonate, to cover their footprints, to use for fraudulent purposes and to go after other people's credit card information. Scammers steal pictures to deceive and defraud vulnerable lonely women. Stealing online photos serve as an economic value to cyber criminals. In 2004, more than 100 private photos of celebrities were leaked online after the images were reportedly stolen from iCloud accounts.[28] However, posting other people's photographs online could be regarded as invasion of privacy, depending on what the motive is all about. The typical example here is known as the *Streisand Effect*, a phenomenon that is derived from the case of ***Streisand v. Adelman, et al.***[29] where the plaintiff filed a lawsuit against a photographer who took 12,000 pictures of the California Coast in which the plaintiff's oceanfront mansion appeared. The defendant photographer thereafter posted the photos on the Internet, contending that the images were free for non-profit and had been used by government entities for scientific research. The plaintiff claimed that the photo violated her privacy because it showed how to access her residence. At the time the lawsuit was filed, the photograph had been downloaded only six times but after the lawsuit, the photo was viewed more than 400,000 times and shared by many. The Court dismissed the suit and held that the plaintiff's complaint constitutes an effort to silence the defendant's speech about a matter of public concern on the protection of California's coastline.

---

[27] 'ProPublica Team. Human Trafficking Victims Also Forced to Cyberscam'< https://hackernoon.com> accessed 24 December 2022

[28] Victoria Woollaston. How DID hackers steal celebrities' private iCloud photos? Tech experts suggest wide range of security flaws for data theft. <https://www.dailymail.co.uk/sciencetech/article/> accessed 05 May 2022

[29] Case No. SC077257, May 2003) Californai Supreme Court

How Does the Court Regard Photos?

The Court has stated that a person's image constitutes one of the chief attributes of his or her personality, and that it reveals the person's unique characteristics and distinguishes the person from his or her peers. The right to the protection of one's image is thus one of the essential components of personal development, presupposing that an individual has the right to control the use of his image, including the right to refuse publication thereof.[30]

To prevent photo theft, a retired detective has advised that online dating users should not be sending photos to people through their iPhone as those images can reveal information about their location, home address and one's daily routine because the information could be misused by people with bad intentions. Instead you take a screenshot of the photo because the screenshot will not record your location.[31] Be aware that deleting a photo from a device does not mean it has been totally deleted from your online storage account especially if you are using *iCloud's my Photo Stream* feature, although deleting your old images can free up hard disk space. In the course of criminal investigation, Police can recover permanently deleted photos from iPhones/Android phones with their data recovery tools.[32] No technology is ever truly secure so how can you protect your data? Most times, a strong password can make all the difference. Never share your password with anyone, especially by email. When you are using public computers, do not click on 'remember me' option. Update your software and app. Use the two-factor authentication as an extra layer. It is an extra layer of protection. Lock your phone or laptop when not in use so that others will not have access to it. Do not use public Wi-Fi. Create unique e-mail accounts. Do not overshare your details on social media networks. Keep personal information personal. People do not need to know your birthday, BVN numbers, NIN numbers, or your mother's maiden name, etc. Be careful of spy apps. Some network flaws can leave your sensitive, personal photos open to theft and could potentially put you at risk. Do not download

---

[30] See the case of *Von Hannover* v. *Germany* (No. 2) [2012] ECHR 228, reported in the Casebook on Data Protection by Olumide Babalola

[31] Amber. 'Retired Detective Explains Why Online Dating Users Should Never Text Their Photos To Matches' <https://www.independent.co.uk/life-style/online > accessed 10 June 2022

[32] Jignasa Sinha. 'How a Deleted Photo helped Delhi Police crackDTC employee's murder last year' <https://indianexpress.com/ article/cities/delhi/> accessed 22 January 2023

attachments because the emails can be laden with virus. Generally do not be eager to try any new offer on the Internet otherwise you will fall prey to criminals who pretend they are genuine.[33] It is important to note also that photographs are treated as intellectual property. After the death of a social media user, all his online content, account and pictures will pass on to his legal heirs.[34]

Thumbprints

Finally, another form of online identity theft is the theft of thumbprints. Research has revealed that millions of fingerprint records are stolen online when hackers get hold of personal files stored in our devices and hijack the device-stored fingerprints. This is made possible by the increased use of biometric scanners on phones and computers. Stolen fingerprints can be used to spy, expose secret conversations, disrupt investigations or poison international negotiations.[35] In India, fraudsters are stealing thumb prints from land registry websites to create duplicate prints on silicon, and using it to commit fraud by withdrawing money from victims' bank accounts. Con-men do this by creating forged biometric thumb impressions.[36] Nonetheless, cybersecurity experts are trying their best to make fingerprints harder to duplicate because once biometric information is stolen, it can be used for repeated fraud.

3. CYBER-FRAUD

Fraud in the physical context is when deception or trickery is used to gain a dishonest advantage over another person. In the cyberspace, a cyber-fraud is a crime committed via a computer with the intent to corrupt another person's personal and information stored online. It is also an Internet fraud enabling a criminal to use Internet services to defraud victims or create a fake domain or generally to take advantage of others, usually to gain monetary advantage. The crime of cyber fraud manifests in several ways.

---

[33] Claire Bahn. 'Personal Photos: Can Hackers Access Your Selfies?' <https://onlineprofilepros..com > accessed 04 March 2022

[34] Nandagopal Rajan. 'What happens to your online data after death?' <https://www. businesstoday.in/magazine/> accessed 12 May 2022

[35] Jose Pagilery. 'OPM hack's unprecedented haul: 1.1 million fingerprints. <http://money.cnn.com/> accessed 12 May 2022

[36] Pavneet S. Chadha. 'In new-age data theft, fraudsters steal thumb prints from land registries' <https://indianexpress.com/article/cities/delhi/ > 13 May 2022

Cyber-fraud could come in form of a cyber-scam if you pose as another person on the Internet to defraud unsuspecting victims or if someone sends you an e-mail with an attached link asking you to disclose or confirm your bank account information. It is cyber-fraud when fraudsters post job offers on social media claiming a 'work from home' opportunities at higher salaries and flexible timings exist. Job seekers would then contact them for details of the hiring process while the fraudsters would charge an amount of money from these potential job seekers. Unfortunately these fraudsters will later become unreachable after payments are made.[37] Cyber-fraud can also happen when someone receives a phishing e-mail from a hacker containing a web link leading to a phishing website fraudulently crafted to mimic the legitimate office. After a user logs in his credentials, the hacker captures it and controls the spoofed web page granting the intruder full access to the account. The hacker thereafter sends fraudulent wire transfer to request for money, while intercepting the legitimate e-mails and marks them as read. For example, criminal actors are taking advantage of the crisis in Ukraine to target members of the public with fraudulent donation scheme. Similarly, a Nigerian businessman was arrested in the United States for cyber fraud and charged with computer fraud/wire fraud of which criminal elements include -; obtaining funds through fraudulent means by engaging in fraudulent business emails, phishing and other computer-based schemes; sending phishing emails to one or more businesses in an effort to login credentials of employees; obtaining legitimate credentials of other individuals to commit fraudulent acts; targeting other businesses of individuals to obtain money and properties; accessing protected computers without authorization; sending fraudulent wire transfer requests; using fake invoices and viewing and downloading files belonging to other individual and business victims; obtaining and compiling credentials of hundreds of victims and; engaging in email compromise schemes.[38]

In Nigeria, activities of cybercriminals have taken a new turn, as they become more daring and innovative, unleashing more terror on their prey. Cybercriminals do this by using AI or ML to break through the defences set

---

[37]Express News Service. 'Promised work from home, 1,700 people from across the country duped by bogus call centre' <https://indianexpress.com/article/cities/delhi/> accessed 30 December 2022

[38]Press Release. 'Nigerian Businessman Pleads Guilty to $11 Million Fraud Scheme' <https://www.justice.gov/usao-edva/> accessed30 November 2022

up by companies while cybercrimes and financial fraud have put at risk electronic payment transactions, estimated to be worth an average of ₦30.2 trillion monthly which is further aggravated by a dearth of IT staff to promptly respond to cyber-threats.[39] On the whole, cyber-fraud generally causes other big losses to numerous victims,[40] but with the awareness and knowledge of cybersecurity, it will protect us from becoming a victim of financial Internet scams. We also have to make a conscious effort to be vigilant by observing the cyber-hygiene tools

4. CYBER DEFAMATION

Defamation law seeks to protect and restore the reputation of victims. The legal right to protect one's reputation has been recognized since at least 16th century England through the common law torts of libel (which is called written defamation) and slander (which is called a spoken defamation).[41] The tort of defamation protects a victim from defamatory statement and enables him to seek compensation against the defamer.

Cyber defamation and by extension defamation prosecutions have increased with the advent of the Internet in this age of promoting free speech. Cyber Defamation is false speech and documents made in electronic form to smear the reputation of others on the Internet. Apparently it is a form of mudslinging. That is, when someone says bad and often untrue things about someone in order to make Internet users have a low opinion of them. It is presumed that if Internet users know that they are sharing information online, they should know they are posting to an international audience. Expressing one's views on social media comes with limitations. That is why we should refrain from making disparaging remarks about others that could amount to an infraction in law. If we are disseminating publicly through a global communication channel, we should realize that a broadcast containing libellous statements published on the Internet against an individual/group/business which are vile, untrue, malicious, derogatory, unfounded and wicked either deliberately or by mistake and in effect

---

[39] Adeyemi Adepetun. 'Cybercrimes raise concerns for ₦30.2tr monthly e-payments.' <https://guardian.ng/news/> accessed 30 November 2022

[40] 'Obiwanne Invictus Obi Okeke gets 10-year jail term for fraud'.< https://guardian.ng/news/ > accessed 23 February 2022

[41] John Culhane. 'Defamation's 15 Minutes of Defame' <https://slate.com/news-and-politics/> accessed 30 April 2022

tarnishes the reputation of the targeted person, would have legal implication. Cyber defamation therefore can be categorized under two factors; (1) where the originator of the statement is considered liable; (2) where an Internet service provider whose duty is to regulate materials, published the defamatory report on their web page.

Internet trolls whose identities are unknown also post false statements about another person. An Internet troll refers to a person who intentionally posts provocative and abusive comments to cause offence and distress. However, the fact that the defamer is unknown cannot stop the victim from seeking justice.[42] A victim can seek monetary damages for alleged libel from the defamer especially where the use of social media negatively impacts on the person's human rights, mental health and general wellbeing.

Case Studies

a. ***State of Tami Naldu v. Suhas Katti***[43] – The case related to the posting of obscene defamatory and annoying message about a divorcee woman in the yahoo message group. Emails of the obscene message were also forwarded to the victim. The case was filed by the victim on the basis that she was being harassed after getting obscene messages on various groups with the intention of offending her since it was sent by the man who was very keen in marrying her but whom she rejected. The Court held that the woman deserves to be protected from various unhealthy remarks because sending obscene messages has harmed the reputation and character of the woman.
b. ***Kalandi Charan Lenka v. State of Odisha***[44] - the petitioner was tracked online and a fraudulent account was created in her name to denigrate her character. The perpetrator also sent vulgar texts to friends with the objective of defaming the petitioner. The High Court concluded that the accused person's actions constituted cyber defamation.
c. ***Defteros v. Google LLC***[45] – The plaintiff a solicitor who practiced in criminal law represented persons who were well known as criminals although their charges were later withdrawn. Google then published this

[42] *Hegglin* v. *Person(s) Unknown & Google Inc.* (2014) EWHC 3798
[43] (2004) C No. 4680 – 5/11/2004
[44] 2017 SCC Online Ori 52
[45] (2022) HCA 27

news and included a webpage with a hyperlink which published an article relating to the plaintiff imputing that the plaintiff had become a friend and confidant of criminal elements. The trial Court held that Google had published the defamatory material despite the fact that another webpage published it. On appeal, It was held that Google did not approve the writing of defamatory matter because it did not contribute to the publication of the article written by another webpage publisher provided in the hyperlink as Google was only assisting persons searching the web to find certain information and to access it, but not to entice or encourage the searcher to click on the hyperlink.

d. ***Julius v. FRN***[46] - the Court of Appeal convicted the Appellant under Section 13 of the Cybercrime Act 2015 for disseminating unverified information on his Facebook platform with the intent that the unsuspecting public would believe and act on same as if it was authentic or genuine.

e. ***Nicholas Okoye v. Ladun Liadi, Google Inc & Google Nigeria***[47]
In a landmark case on Internet libel and publication/transmission of libelous statements, a Lagos State High Court awarded damages against the defendant blogger on GOOGLE blogging platform for defaming the claimant in the article which elicited vile, adverse and derogatory comments against the claimant. The Court referred to the provision governing Defamation under the Laws of Lagos State and held that GOOGLE Inc. were mere Internet intermediaries who had put frameworks in place for bloggers to moderate comments on their blogs and they could not have known that the alleged publication was defamatory.

A professor of criminal law in Syria has warned that offences punishable under the cybercrime law do not only cover serious matters but also extend to humour and that any electronic slander in a WhatsApp group whose members know each other falls under the offence of non-public defamation of which penalty is a fine even if the impugned conduct is a joke. This is because slander covers not only serious matters but also jokes.[48]

---

[46](2021) LPELR-54201 (CA) ; See the article titled 'Cybercrime, Criminal Defamation and Social Media' written by Thomas O. Okaba <https://barristerng.com > accessed 10 March 2022

[47] LD/170/2012

[48]SAWT AL-ASIMA. 'Cybercrime Law Punishes Humour, Even on WhatsApp Groups' <https://syrianobserver.com/news/75013/> accessed 10 April 2023

How do we prove Cyber Defamation?

A lie circulates faster than the truth on the Internet. This is especially what happens when you post defamatory words on social media or when you instigate comments that are menacing or hurtful in nature. A social media publication containing offensive words, malicious and false words against someone could be held defamatory and punishable under Section 24(1)(b) of the Cybercrimes (Prohibition, Prevention Act, etc.) 2015. In Nigeria, Section 373 of the Criminal Code provides that defamatory matter is likely to injure the reputation of any person when you expose him to hatred, contempt, or ridicule, or likely to damage him in his profession or trade by an injury to his reputation. In practice, defamed victims usually consult their lawyers to put up a demand letter of retraction (cease and desist letter) and apology and if the defamer refuses to apologise upon the expiration of the letters, then victims may commence a libel suit against those responsible. Online publishers are therefore mandated to verify their facts before publishing.

An extension of defamation applicable mostly for minor transgressions is called 'Internet pillory' which is an act of public shaming against others on the Internet. This is when people use the social media tools to publicly humiliate others for anti-social behaviour. Acts like filming racist behaviour on public transport, showing footage of a person urinating in public places or when citizens upload their shame files into digital space for people to laugh at. Where victims may find this acceptable and if the content is deemed inappropriate, a website can remove the video while the footage will be handed over to the Police for identification where such case may end in litigation.[49]

A photo posted on social media by someone else can also amount to defamation, if the image would be damaging to the reputation of another person or if the photos provide the wrong impression of the person. Defamation occurs when an individual or company utilizes a photograph or video to make it appear as if you committed a crime when you did not, but making you or your business to suffer.[50]

---

[49]Kristy Hess and Lisa Waller. 'Media as Pillory: The Power to name and shame in digital times' <https://theconversation.com/media-as-pillory-/> accessed 20 November 2022

[50] Vanya Verma. 'What to do if someone posted a picture of you without your permission' <https://blog.ipleaders.in/> accessed 28 August 2022

5. CYBERBULLYING

Bullying itself is the state of being mean or cruel repeatedly to another person. Bullying usually involves repeated incidents or a pattern of behaviour that is intended to intimidate, offend or degrade or humiliate a particular person or a group of persons. It has also been described as the assertion of power through aggression.[51] Bullying can take place physically or on the Internet. Virtually, it is an act of bullying taking place by means of Internet technology or the use of electronic communication to bully people by sending messages of an intimidating or threatening nature. Cyber bullying takes place on social media platforms such as Instagram, X, Facebook, etc. Examples of cyberbullying are sending threatening messages through email or cell phone, posting hurtful messages on social networks that depicts the victim in negative ways, creating a fake online personality to bully others, sexting, removing someone out of online groups, harassing the victim during a live chat, spreading rumours and defamatory messages, posting embarrassing photos or secrets and spreading them, recording unauthorized video and uploading them, sending viruses by email, hacking into accounts and posting damaging messages; sending text-speech attacks and stealing identity of persons. Victims can also be harassed when perpetrators send unusual and vulgar messages or asking for sexual favours via mobile phones.

Globally, 85% of women have experienced or witnessed digital violence according to the Economist Intelligence Unit. The abuse takes on many ugly forms such as non-consensual sharing of intimate images (revenge porn), cyberstalking, sextortion, doxxing (revealing a person's personal details online) and deepfake porn (in which a woman's head is attached to someone else's body in sexually explicit scenarios). A cyberbullying action is prevalent, persistent, repetitive, widespread and perpetrated by an anonymous aggressor from any part of the world.[52] In ***Buturuga v. Romania,***[53] the ECtHR pointed out that cyberbullying was currently a recognised aspect of violence against women and girls which could take on a variety of forms, including breaches of privacy, intrusions into the victim's computer and the capture, sharing and manipulation of data and images.

---

[51] 'Internet Harassment or Cyberbullying' <htpps://www.cchos.ca/oshanweres/> accessed 14 August 2023

[52] Ms. Buster. 'My Ex Shared My Naked Photos Online. So I took Him To Court. <https:// www. elle. com/culture/> accessed 10 December 2021

[53] ECHR 056 (2020)

Where cyberbullying issues are not addressed, it would affect women's participation in digital decision-making and their right to live in a safe cyberspace would be negatively impacted. Cyberbullying has extreme damaging consequences on victims as it can be a continuous abuse unlike an in-person bullying; therefore we all need to be aware about the need for security and privacy to keep ourselves protected. Be mindful that a person who causes extreme fear or threatens any person by means of a letter, e-mail, SMS telephone call or any other means of communication will be held liable for cyberbullying.

Prevention

Be aware that criminals have predefined intentions while sheltering themselves behind a concealed identity. In view of this, cybersecurity is everyone's business. We can protect ourselves against cybercrime if we: Don't respond to a bully; Don't retaliate; Block the bully; Talk to a trusted adult; Save the evidence (the conversation history) and be civil; Don't be a bully yourself; Use a strong password; Never open attachments in spam e-mails; Don't give out personal information unless secure; Think twice before posting anything online; Check your privacy settings; Limit those who can contact you on your social media platforms; Never reveal your personal details; Do not share your password with anyone; Check antivirus and firewalls and be vigilant. Keep a log of any harassing activity, save all offending communications for evidence, both electronically and in hard print and report the incident to the Police if the cyberbullying is getting serious. Do not edit offending messages sent by the bully in any way.

Health Impact of Cyber Bullying

The offline consequences of cyberbullying are brutal and long-lasting. Even if the acts of cyberbullying are passive and non-threatening, the bully can become aggressive. Victims can experience feelings of loneliness and isolation, alarm, distress, self-harm, suicidal thoughts and suicide,[54] alcohol dependency, depression and violence. Victims may also need to undergo therapy to handle the constant bullying they faced online. The psychological impacts are worry, restlessness, irritability, sadness, hopelessness, anger, guilt

[54] 'Amsterdam Court needs more Canadian detail before Sentence in Cyberbullying case' <https://bcta.ctvnews.ca/local/britis-columbia/> accessed 30 July 2023

and withdrawal symptoms. All these negative factors can also worsen mental, physical and emotional well-being thus increasing the prevalence of depression and anxiety.

6. CYBER STALKING

Stalking is defined as an unwanted communication, following or watching a person with the purpose of inducing fear or causing emotional distress to that person.[55] Section 58 of the Cybercrimes Act, 2015 defines cyberstalking as a source of conduct directed at a specific person that would cause a reasonable person to feel fear. The examples of cyberstalking includes using the Internet to send repeated depraved texts and unwanted emails or instant messages; sending the victim's online photos to sexual oriented sites; sending viruses; passing offensive messages on social media; secretly tracking a person's Internet activity; intentionally circulating false information on audio telephone, via social media handles for the purpose of causing insult.[56] Threatening to upload nude pictures of a woman on social media or having a woman's image taken, manipulated and shared without her permission is a violation of privacy, dignity and autonomy of the victim. An individual can be prosecuted for felony or aggravated stalking and violation of privacy when he uses a tracking device and smartphone app to keep tabs in order to know the location of his ex-partner or places a tracking device on his partner's vehicle. Bugging an ex-partner's car, listening to her conversations, tracking her movements and taking her phone without permission are all acts of stalking. Cyberstalking is an offence under Section 24 of the Cybercrimes Act 2015 and can also be held to be a disorderly conduct likely to cause breach of peace under Section 168(d) of the Criminal Law of Lagos State 2015.[57] In Lagos State, distributing sex video of some school pupils through an accused person's Twitter handle was charged as an offence contrary to Section 23(2) of the Lagos State Domestic and Sexual Violence Agency Law 2021.

Types of Stalkers – These could be rejected stalkers, resentful stalkers, intimacy stalkers and predatory stalkers. The perpetrators could be former

---

[55] See the ICCS 2015 Framework of UNODC

[56] ***AGF* v. *Olanrewaju Suraj*** (FHC/ABJ/CS/370/2021

[57] 'Broadcaster docked for sharing Chrisland student sex tape' < https://www.vanguardngr.com/2022/05 > accessed 09 May 2022

or current cohabiting spouses.[58] The perpetrator could also be known or unknown to the victim.

Types of Victims – These are likely to be previous intimates, former romantic partners, casual acquaintances, friends, workplace contacts and strangers. A husband can also become a cyber-stalker if he uploads vulgar photographs of his ex-wife just to defame her on social media. A person who posts nude pictures of someone online can be charged with extortion so far he uses any two-way communication device to facilitate the felony. Sextortion is an arm of extortion as well as a form of blackmail in which sexual information or images are used on the victim in order to extort sexual favours or financial gain from the victim. In other words, sextortion is when someone blackmails a victim by threatening to release or upload his or her sexually explicit material – ranging from nude photos to sexual acts that are caught on camera. Sextortion can be triggered by either sexual or financial desires. It is either the blackmailer demands additional sexual acts or the blackmailer demands for money. Even minors have become a favourite target of sextortionists.[59] Nowadays, it is common to read of male partners electronically stalking their victims by threatening to upload nude pictures of their former lovers on social media or kill them if they refused to re-friend them.[60] Your partner is also a cyber-stalker if he installs spyware on your phone to monitor your calls. In U.K, a stalker was handed a 12-month community order, restraining order and damages for following the victim on Instagram and sending her unwanted emails.[61]

Kalandi Charan Lenka* v. *State of Odisha - The victim petitioner was continuously being stalked, and a fake account of her was created and obscene messages were sent to the friends of the victim petitioner by the culprit. A morphed nature picture was also posted on the walls of the hostel

[58] Sam Corbishley. 'Ex-cop who filmed wife having sex with lover outside Screwfix guilty of Stalking'< https://metro.co.uk/2024/> accessed 30 April 2024

[59] Bri Michele. 'The Escalation of Sextortion' <https://medium.com/counterarts/> accessed 03 August 2023

[60] Sheila Stogsdill . 'OK man pleads guilty to strangling woman for refusing to friend him on Facebook' <https://www.fourstateshomepage.com> accessed 16 August 2022

[61] See the online report titled: 'UK Court sentences Nigerian man 12-month community service for stalking a woman' <https://www.vanguardngr.com/2022/05/ > accessed 27 May 2022

where the victim petitioner stayed. The Court held the culprit liable for his offence,[62]

AGF* v. *Ayan Olubunmi[63] - A Federal High Court sitting in Ekiti State, South West Nigeria, sentenced the defendant to two years imprisonment with an option of fine for committing a cybercrime of breaching Section 23(2) of the Cybercrimes Act 2015 after releasing his girlfriend's nude picture on Facebook.

In another Nigerian case, The defendant blackmailer was arraigned before the Federal High Court, Yenagoa on a one-count charge of cyber-stalking by circulating the picture of a man's nude picture on a WhatsApp Group, after she tried to blackmail the victim into paying N15 million. The defendant allegedly shot the video after having an intercourse with the victim at a hotel. Ruling on the admissibility of the printout of the electronic evidence, the trial Judge while admitting that the evidence was relevant, said the evidence could not be admitted because of the disparity in models of the phone because the man's mobile phone was a Samsung Galaxy A5, but the certificate of compliance accompanying the printout read Samsung Galaxy A7. The Judge therefore ruled that the evidence did not meet the criteria for admissibility for computer-generated electronic evidence as stipulated under Section 84 of the Evidence Act 2011.[64]

In view of the criminality of stalking, a software stalkerware has been developed as a technological solution deployed to actively monitor an individual through a mobile device with stalkerware apps that can be used to track spouses, ex-partners, children and even employees. This means that you can track their location and movement through GPS, eavesdrops on their calls and social media conversations, stealer logs, and monitoring browser activity using a device camera to listen or take photos. Some people install stalkerware apps to check when the victim even visits the bathroom or prepares a meal. Note that stalkerware are installed on smartphones but

---

[62] 'Sukriti Mathur. 'Cyber Defamation in the Indian Context' <https://www.sbhambriadvocates.com > accessed 22 January 022

[63] *FHC/AD/17c/2017*

[64] Court rejects WhatsApp messages as evidence in trial of Bayelsa teenager'. The Nation Newspaper of 09 November 2021

more common on Android handsets but once installed, these apps run quietly in the background and can be extremely difficult to detect.[65]

Cybersecurity in Shared Nude Pictures

A number of women experience cyber-violence in various ways across social media platforms. The circulation of their nude photos on the Internet for public dissemination threatens their dignity and infringes their right to privacy as well as their bodily integrity. In the Indian case of ***State of West Bengal v. Animesh Boxi***,[66] the defendant was found guilty of uploading the intimate pictures and videos of his former girlfriend on pornography websites. Victims are thus advised to take the following steps if a stalker threatens them with their nude pictures or videos:[67]

a. Do not delete the picture because it is a source of evidence otherwise you are destroying evidence;
b. Take a screenshot as soon as you receive the picture before the stalker deletes the picture;
c. Get expert help;
d. Do not give in to the blackmailer's demand;
e. Contact the Police.

Case Study

UK Citizen Extradited and Pleads Guilty to Cybercrime Offences

A UK citizen pleaded guilty to his role in cyber-stalking and multiple schemes that involve computer hacking including the hack of Twitter (X). His criminal activities were flagrant and malicious, and his conduct impacted multiple people's lives. Like many criminals online, the defendant tried to stay anonymous by using his sophisticated abilities and a computer to hide behind stealth accounts and aliases from outside. He harassed, threatened and extorted his victims, causing substantial emotional harm.[68] The case serves as a warning that the Internet keeps tabs, history and records of where we are and what we have been up to. There is also a clear message to cyberstalkers

---

[65] Charlie Osbourne. 'How tech is a weapon in modern domestic abuse-and how to protect yourself'. <https://www.zdnet.com/article>/ accessed 14 February 2022

[66] CRM No. 11806 (2017)

[67] Rachiyta Jain. '5 Steps to Immediately take if your nudes are being used to Blackmail You' <https://cybeblogindia.in/> accessed 14 February 2022

[68] Department of Justice Press Release <htpps://www.justice/gov.opa./pr/> accessed 09 May 2023

that the reach of the law is long, and criminals anywhere who use computers to commit crimes will get caught and end up facing the consequences of their actions in places they did not anticipate.

7. ONLINE SEXUAL EXPLOITATION AND ABUSE (OSEA)

Women are invariably the targets regarding OSEA. This abuse includes heinous acts such as online grooming, live-streaming of sexual abuse, child sexual abuse material (CSAM), online sexual coercion, online trafficking, online hate speech, doxxing, bullying, image-based sexual abuse and non-consensual intimate images such as upskirting, cyber-flashing and deepfake pornography.[69] On 20th May 2022, the UN's foremost policymaking body on crime prevention and criminal justice issues known as the Congress of Crime Prevention and Criminal Justice (CCPCJ) at its 31st session stakeholders 'meeting, placed special focus on the use of digital evidence in criminal justice and countering cybercrime as well as the abuse and exploitation of minors in illegal activities via the Internet.[70]

Image-Based Sexual Abuse

Sometimes, when sex videos or sexually explicit images of individuals get into the wrong hands, they are uploaded on the Internet and this comes with terrible consequences and becomes a scandal. Sadly, majority of the victims are women and girls who experience revenge porn – a non-consensual involuntary pornography or sexually explicit images uploaded online without obtaining consent from the parties in the videos or pictures without a legitimate purpose. Digital voyeurism is also a subset of non-consensual intimate image abuse in which perpetrators take non-consensual photographs or videos of women's private areas and share them online (i.e. upskirting, creepshots and downblousing). Another example is cyber-flashing. This is when someone sends sexually explicit images of himself to the victim despite the fact that the images were not requested for. During Police investigation, these images can be used as evidence against perpetrators to seek for justice.

---

[69] UNFPA Newsletter <https://wwwunfpa.org/news/women-and-girls/>accessed 14 December 2022

[70]<https://www.undoc.org/undoc/frontage/2022/31st-session-of-the-ccpcj-addressing-global-challenges-through-international-cooperation-on-crime-prevention-and-justice.html> accessed 21 May 2022.

Using the tool of AI, anyone with high-powered computer, a graphics processing unit can create realistic fake videos known as deepfake. Cybercriminals use the AI tool to assess which facial images of a person will be most sellable as a face swap in a pornographic video. These are known as *parasite porn* or *morph porn.* To morph means to change the form or character of someone or something. Parasite porn is when your picture is stolen and downloaded from your social media account like Facebook and used on pornography websites. Although all social media users have privacy rights,[71] notwithstanding, your face could be cropped out and photo-shopped as sexually explicit images in porn sites. In India, the father of a minor girl filed a complaint that some boys had allegedly morphed a picture of his daughter to make it look vulgar and had posted it on a social media website.[72] The implication is that when pictures are uploaded on the Internet for all to see, then that will fall under the realm of cyber-stalking or cyber-harassment of which causes could be traceable to failed intimate relationships, scorned ex-lovers, hacking, theft by a phone repair technician. Their motive is always to use for blackmail, extortion or simply for private amusement. Its distribution may also be as a result of the victim's carelessness, negligence or mistake.

Romance scammers also blackmail their victims with private pictures they must have shared with the scammers. Uploading sexual act or nudity is a form of sexual violence against women in the cyber world and the consequences are numerous. It is an emotional, psychological abuse and infringement of human rights. Such victims suffer depression, distress, psychiatric injury, public humiliation and this may sometimes drive them to commit suicide. Others may succumb to the blackmail and have to continuously pay in cash or kind in order to silence the blackmailer while others may lose their job, friends and family. It is clearly an invasion of privacy that can ruin the victim's life, career and reputation for the rest of her life if she does not brace up. The harm is perpetual because the Internet never forgets. In Nigeria, the legal frameworks to protect victims are

[71] Nicola Henry, Anastasia Powell and Asher Flynn. 'AI can now create fake porn, making revenge porn even more complicated' <https://phys.org/news/2018-03/> accessed 12 February 2022

[72]Express News Service. 'Three minor boys booked for allegedly posting 'morphed photo' of girl' <https://indiaexpress.com/article/delhi/> accessed 07 August 2022

derivable from the (1) Constitution – right to privacy; (2) the Criminal Law – distribution of obscene images; and the (3) Cybercrimes Act.[73]

Prevention

Anonymise yourself on the Internet. Build and always update your security knowledge. Practice basic cybersecurity hygiene. Do not click links in emails or download software. Install updates and use security software. Lock down access to your core systems. Get an IT support service. Fortify your password security. Configure your email settings to block suspicious attachment from being shared. Report any offender to their Internet service provider. Do not share all your photographs and activities on social media. Be suspicious of some 'funny' e-mails you're not sure of. Conduct a reverse Google image search of your stolen photos to see where it was published online. Educate others about cyber abuse. Do not trust anyone with your phone. Consider everyone a suspect. Never allow your partners to take your intimate pictures even while your relationship is smooth and always remember that any relationship can go wrong. Delete your private photos before you hand over your phone to the phone technician. Consult your lawyer for legal advice as quickly as possible. Report the blackmailer to the Police for proper investigation so that the perpetrator can be apprehended and charged for unlawful dissemination of intimate images.

8. ONLINE GROOMING

Crimes involving sexual exploitation of minors are very common to read on the social media. It is not restricted to adults alone. In this ICT age, many kids have access to the Internet in their homes. This could be through their home computers, mobile devices and other interactive video chat technologies that their parents bought for them, especially in the wake of COVID-19 pandemic lockdown when children were not in schools which greatly exposed them to online predators. It is a known fact that children are very vulnerable and can be so trusting even of strangers. Consequently, these online predators work on the weaknesses of children. For instance, some vulnerable girls with mental health issues usually want to seek for validation

[73] Maame Efua Addadzi-Koom. Revenge pornography as a form of sexual and gender-based violence in Ghana- Emerging judicial issues. In Gender, Judging And The Courts in Africa- Selected Studies (World Bank Publication. Edited by J. Jarpa Dawuni (2021) DOI:10.4324/9780429327865

or solidarity from their online male friends. In such circumstances, they are likely to fall to the ploy used overtime by Internet predators to sexually exploit these children.

The United Nations Economic and Social Commission for Asia and the Pacific define child sexual abuse as 'contacts or interactions between a child or adult when the child is being used as an object for the adult's sexual needs. As a crime involving online child grooming, this is when an adult uses the computer or social media in a predatory fashion to try to lower children's inhibitions, or heighten their curiosity about sex with the aim of eventually meeting them in person for the purposes of engaging in physical sexual activity with them. Online sexual abuse is when the predator coerces or entices a minor to produce child pornography or gets the child to perform sexual acts or take sexually explicit photos and send them to the predator or when a predator gets the child to engage in similar acts through a webcam.[74] These predators hide behind their computers to harm children. As computer predators and paedophiles, they establish online relationships with young girls by taking advantage of the Internet to abuse, exploit or entice children to commit sexual misconduct. The interactions become sexual when predators get to these children through video-game chats and portray themselves as responsible and trustworthy adults in a place of their parents. Other common tactics that predators use are, falsely identifying themselves online as a child, flattering or complimenting children, promising them gifts and exchanging of sexual pictures to make the victim comfortable in sending sexual pictures or videos in return.[75]These groomers screenshot or film these innocent children and sexualize them.[76] They go as far as sharing the contents of the video recordings on darknet forums and even encourage children to do more. Any content produced as a result of grooming can then be used to threaten and blackmail the child victim into performing more acts.

Every year the number of photos and videos containing child pornography or child sexual abuse materials (CSAM) found online keeps increasing. Victims are predominantly under-aged girls. CSAM is defined as

---

[74] 'Everything you Need To Know About Online Grooming' <https://www. innocentlivesfoundation.org > accessed 16 February 2022

[76] 'Five jailed In Horrific German Child Abuse Case' <https://www. channelstv.com/ 2021/07/06/> accessed 16 February 2022

imagery or videos which show a child engaging in or is depicted as being engaged in explicit sexual activity, involving a minor that is under 18 years. CSAM depict images and videos of rape and criminal assault, affording sex predators, sex traffickers to profit from their crimes while remaining less visible to law enforcement. CSAM is illegal because it is the filming of an actual crime of children that are sexually abused while their videos are shared across the Internet.[77]

Case Study (1)

A 31-year old man in California is facing federal charges on sexual exploitation and attempted sexual exploitation of a child for the purpose of producing a sexually explicit visual depiction, enticement and attempted enticement of a minor to engage in criminal sexual activity, and receipt of child pornography. The prosecutors alleged the perpetrator enticed young girls suffering from mental health issues he met on the Internet and encouraged them to engage in masochist practices.[78]

Case Study (2)

The Central Bureau of Investigation (CBI) in India lodged a First Information Report (FIR) after they received report from Google that a man was allegedly involved in creating objectionable text or digital images, collecting, seeking, browsing, downloading, advertising, promoting, exchanging or distributing material in electronic form that depicts children in an obscene or indecent or sexually explicit manner by using various social media platforms to upload the materials. Consequently, a team of CBI visited the house of the accused along with forensic experts to lift evidence. At the 90th Interpol General Assembly hosted by India in 2023, a resolution was passed towards supporting member countries in their efforts to identify and investigate cases regarding the protection of children on the Internet and exposing online child predators.[79]

---

[77] 'Overview of CSAM' <https://www.missingkids.org> accessed 16 February 2022

[78] 'SoCal man allegedly groomed young girls to become his 'slave,' encouraged them to self-harm' <https://truecrimedaily.com/2022/02/24/> accessed 26 February 2022

[79] Mahender Singh Manral. 'Alerted by Interpol, CBI arrests man for sexually abusing four minors, uploading their videos online' <https://indianexpress.com/article/cities/> accessed 14 July 2023

Case Study (3)

In 2023, a Nigerian who arrived in United Kingdom to study was arrested for investigation and possible prosecution for attempting to date children under the age of 15 after multiple children between the ages of 14 and 15 reported him with evidence of the perpetrator grooming and sexually harassing them. Evidence showed the text messages he had with some of the victims and unsolicited indecent pictures the perpetrator sent to the victims, asking them for their house addresses, sex invitation amongst other disturbing messages.[80]

Statutorily, Section 23 of the Nigeria Cybercrimes Prevention Act 2015 provides that a person who intentionally uses any computer system to produce, procure child pornography, to transmit or distribute child pornography, sends pornographic images commits an offence. While Section 23(2) of the same law criminalises the act of child grooming when a person uses a computer network for the purpose of having sexual activities with a child by coercion, inducement, force or threats; or causing a child to participate in pornographic performances in a sexually explicit conduct.

Recommendations for Help

Sharing knowledge and engaging more in parental control for online safety helps to reduce the burden. The Police should also be alerted while efforts should be made to report to the concerned social media network where the abuse took place.[81] In Germany, the law gives the Police broader powers to monitor online communication of suspects. In any event, the Courts have always pronounced that sexual abuse of children is unquestionably an abhorrent type of wrongdoing which leaves debilitating effects on its victims. Children and other vulnerable individuals are therefore entitled to State protection in the form of effective deterrence from such grave types of interference with essential aspects of their private lives. The child's safety comes first and freedom of expression on the Internet can be legitimately limited to protect children.[82]

---

[80]Adekunle Sulaimon. 'Nigerian Student arrested in UK over sexual harassment of minors' <https://punchng.com/> accessed 08 June 2023

[81]James, Thorn Staff. 'Online grooming: what it is, how it happens, and how to defend children' https://www.thorn.org/blog/ accessed 04 February 2022

[82] European Court of Human Rights. Research Report. Child Sexual Abuse and Child Pornography in the Court's Case-Law. (2011) <www.echr.coe.int > accessed 16 February 2022

9. CYBER EXTORTION

This cybercrime occur when cybercriminals threaten to disable the operations of a target business or compromise its confidential data unless they receive a payment. The two most common types of cyber extortion are Ransomware and Distributed Denial of Service (DD0S) attacks. Ransomware is a type of malware or malicious software distributed via emails, infected websites or fraudulent networks. Stealing sensitive data has become a common part of ransomware attacks which is on the rise. When recipients of such emails and visitors to the websites download the malicious software immediately they click on the link provided, the software then proceeds to encrypt the victim's files rendering their computers and networks unusable. The cybercriminals will thereafter contact the victims, offering to decrypt their files for a fee or threaten to release their data to the public or sell their data to the dark web.

Ransomware attacks on public institutions such as cities, schools and hospitals have risen sharply in recent years. Cyber-attackers know that government computer networks contain troves of sensitive data and often have weak points than those of major companies. During a ransomware attack, hackers steal or block access to key files or data, then demand payment in exchange for returning or restoring them. Such attacks can also involve threats that expose sensitive information, such as Social Security and credit card numbers, if the victim doesn't pay.[83]

A global security firm has said that 71% Nigerian businesses it surveyed were hit with ransomware in 2021, up from 22% in 2020. According to the report on ransomware 2022, it revealed that $706, 452 was paid as ransom to the cybercriminals by Nigeria businesses in the year.[84] In the United States of America, research has indicated that ransomware attacks are common. For example, when a cyber-attack crippled a County Sheriff's Department computer system early this year, the ransomware attack forced the department to temporarily shut down some of its computer systems, e-mails, car computers and some law enforcement databases until millions of

---

[83] Laura Nelson & Richard Winton. 'Hackers extorts $1.1M in Cyberattack on Calif. Sheriff's Website' <https://www.police1.com/ransomware/article/> accessed 09 May 2023

[84] Samson Akintayo. '71% of Nigerian businesses were hit by cyber-attacks in 2021-Report.' <https://nairametrics.com> accessed 03 May 2022

dollars were paid.[85] To this end, the government has employed four lines of effort to counter the threat: (1) Leveraging international cooperation to disrupt the ransomware ecosystem and isolate those countries that provide safe havens for criminals; (2) Investigating ransomware crimes and using law enforcement to disrupt ransomware infrastructure and threat actors; (3) Bolstering critical infrastructure resilience to withstand ransomware attacks; and (4) Addressing the abuse of virtual currency to launder ransom payments.[86] By so doing, the government will shift the burden of defending US cyberspace away from small organisations and cyberspace and individuals.

The summary is that in DDoS attacks, cybercriminals often threaten businesses claiming that the attack will occur if a fee is not paid to stop it and threatening to go further and publish sensitive or confidential data which could lead to lawsuits.[87] Cybersecurity experts have therefore advised that these criminals are not to be trusted because even after victims of ransomware attacks pay to restore access to their network, some cyber criminals may not hold up their end of the deal.[88]

In a recent cybercrime attack, a threat actor convinced a victim phone carrier to transfer a phone number to his SIM card. After accessing the number, the threat actor contacted the victim's friends impersonating the victim and started obtaining money from other unsuspecting victims. The threat actor also locked the victim out of her accounts and sent her messages demanding a ransom for returning control of her account, threatening to further release her personal videos and photos. The threat actor has since pleaded guilty to perpetrating multiple cybercrime schemes using SIM swapping.[89]

10. CYBER TRAFFICKING

Human trafficking is commonly operated offline. This is where individuals trafficked to other countries are forced to perform sex or labour work or

[85]Laura Nelson & Richard Winton. 'Hackers extorts $1.1M in Cyberattack on Calif. Sheriff's Website' <https://www.police1.com/ransomware/article/> accessed 09 May 2023

[86]Dan Goodin, 'Biden Administration wants to hold companies liable for bad 'cybersecurity; https://arstechnica.com/infortation-technology/> accessed 03 March 2028

[87]Embroker Team. 'Understanding Cyber Extortion and How to Protect Your Business' <https://www.embroker.com/blog/> accessed 04 February 2022

[88]Danny Palmer. 'This company paid a ransom demand. Hackers leaked its data anyway' <https://www.zdnet.com/article/> accessed 25 August 2022

[89]Ionut Arghire. 'Los Angeles SIM Swapper Pleads Guilty to Cybercrime Charges' <https://www.securityweek.com> accessed 25 July 2023

even sold as slaves despite being promised enticing offers of bounties. Human trafficking occurs across international borders. It is an extreme form of irregular migration involving coercion and exploitation.[90] The UN Protocol to Prevent, Suppress and Punish Trafficking in Persons, especially Women and Children defines trafficking as the recruitment, transportation, transfer, harbouring by means of threat or coercion to achieve the consent of a person for the purpose of exploitation. In this digital age, there are many ways physical human trafficking can transform into cyber trafficking. For example, social media is the fastest means of human trafficking which accounts to why traffickers are making use of online technology to recruit victims. This is human trafficking that is driven by computer network, especially on chat forums and social media platforms. Although, technology helps us accomplish our objectives with communication devices such as .phones, laptops as well as other electronic devices, sadly, traffickers leverage this same technology for online trafficking. They may use online chatrooms, social media, online employment agencies, or forged immigration assistance websites to recruit potential victims and connect them to syndicates. The trafficking services range from forced prostitution, child pornography, mail-order brides, vending of babies and selling of human organs. Cyber or digital trafficking could also be propelled by scammers who fake romantic relationships with victims on social media. For example traffickers may initiate cyber trafficking victims are told to perform sexual acts through webcams or persuaded to send their nude pictures or videos as a bait to traffick them to foreign lands. When the victims agree to perform the acts, these traffickers may resort in using GPS software in their phones to track or monitor the movement of victims through video surveillance.[91] The National Agency for the Prohibition of Trafficking in Persons (NAPTIP) had once arrested a young boy who trades these nude photos of a young lady online.[92] Traffickers lure unsuspecting victims through sham or deceptive social media advertorials claiming to be offering various employment opportunities. They lure footballers. They create websites or post advertisements on payment for illicit services with cryptocurrencies or

---

[90] Felix Chadhary. 'Fiji woman lured to Egypt on promise of a job; falls victim to human trafficking scam' <https://buff.ly/42LsGRV> accessed 12 April 2023

[91] 'Human Trafficking and Technology' <https://icat.un.org/> accessed 28 July 2022

[92] Stephen Angbulu. 'NAPTIP records 70,000 inline trafficking reports in 10-month'<https://punchng.com/naptip/> accessed 28 July 2022

bitcoin while controlling the victims with cell phones or webcams.[93] In 2021, experts from around the world met online to discuss strategies to combat human trafficking and how to make the best use of technology to prevent human trafficking and conduct investigation on the issue since victims were mostly hired on social media.

In 2022, NAPTIP disclosed the tricks used by Traffickers in Persons (TIP) who leverage on social media to lure the victims with technology used as a tool for displaying phoney job adverts or opportunities for victims to leave their environment for purposes of surrogacy, sports, and orphanage, among others.[94] In the face of glaring challenges, NAPTIP in collaboration with relevant foreign governments and donor agencies have procured the latest version of digital evidence-gathering devices and their software to assist with the prosecution and law enforcement regarding human trafficking.[95] NAPTIP has further partnered with Facebook, Instagram and WhatsApp to enhance diligent investigation of cyber trafficking. It is interesting to note that law enforcements officers have infiltrated the dark web to survey, track, identify and block illegal trafficking activities.

In the illegal body organ trade business, the Internet has largely become a powerful tool for cybercriminals and for those willing to let go of their body organs for a price. There are syndicates who facilitate the illegal buying, selling and transplanting of organs. There are equally scammers who demand money from the seller of body organs up front so they can have their blood type tested but once the money is paid, the scammer disappears into thin air.[96] According to the Protocol to Prevent, Suppress and Punish Trafficking in Persons, especially Women and Children, Trafficking in Persons for the Removal of Organs (TPRO) also include the removal of organs as an end purpose of trafficking.[97] In view of the need to inform future anti-trafficking prevention efforts, the Police around the world have resorted to fighting

---

[93] Nula Frei. "On 'cyber trafficking' and the protection of its victims' <https://voelkerrechtsblog.org/de/> doi: 10.17176/ 20170731-180154. accessed 17 December 2021

[94] Bukola Adetoye. 'How human traffickers find their victims- NAPTIP' <https://nnn.ng/> accessed 09 June 2022

[95] See the National Action Plan on Human Trafficking in Nigeria 2022-2026

[96] Shaun Swingler. 'The dark world of Internet kidney trafficking' <https://www.news24.com /health24/medical/> accessed 30 May 2022

[97] See The United Nations Trust Fund for Victims of Human Trafficking

human trafficking with advanced technology such as facial recognition, open-source intelligence, mobile and digital forensics.[98]

11. CYBER TERRORISM

Terrorists are using the Internet for terrorist purposes. Terrorists rely on the Internet to recruit members, fund operations, indoctrinate target audiences and garner attention on a global scale in order to cause broad damages.[99] Terrorism can be authored by those who perpetrate targeted act of violence through written and spoken communication on social media, cell phone videos, online forums and personal websites. A person can therefore be charged with terroristic threats or acts and dissemination of information relating to terroristic acts via computer.[100] Terrorism could be motivated by extreme ideologies, personal grievances, race and ethnicity, anti-government stance, jihad, vengeance and hate, misanthropy and other terrorism-related reasons.[101] Section 2 of the Terrorism (Prevention and Prohibition) Act 2022 define terrorism as an act wilfully performed with the intention of furthering an ideology, whether political, religious, racial or ethnic which may seriously harm or damage a country or an international organisation; unduly compels a government to perform or abstain from performing any act; seriously intimidates a population; destruction of public facilities, propagates and disseminates information materials calculated to cause panic, evoke violence intimidate government or group of persons and all acts that endanger government and public properties as specified under this Section.

One of the primary uses of the Internet by a terrorist organisation is for circulating propaganda through recorded videos, music and computer games. These are terroristic threats made via electronic communication or the unlawful attacks and threats of attacks against computers, networks and the information stored therein when done to intimidate or coerce a government or its people in furtherance of their political or social objectives. They can use the Internet for recruiting new members for the organisation. The

---

[98]Joshua Lee. 'How technology can help law enforcement fight human trafficking' <https://www.police1.com/investigations/articles/> accessed 26 May 2023

[99]Ruth M. Eglash, 'Hamas Cyber terror is a test case for other non-state players, report say' <https://www.foxnews.com/world/> accessed 23 November 2022

[100] 'Bulloch County 17 year old behind bars, facing felony charges for what he posted on TikTok' <https://www.wjcl.com/article/savalas-harden-/> accessed 25 July 2023

[101] Julia Kupper. 'Preventing Attacks Using Targeted Violence Manifestos' <https://leb.fbi.gov/articles/featured-article/> accessed 30 May 2022

Internet can also be used for a training ground for terrorists or used for setting up virtual training camps to share specific methods and techniques required to carry out terrorist attacks, as well as financing terrorist organisations.[102]

Experts have thus identified five main types of cyber terrorism attack which are: incursion, destruction, disinformation, denial of service attack and defacement of websites.[103] Section 18(1) of the Cybercrimes Act 2015 provides that a person who accesses or causes to be accessed any computer network for purposes of terrorism, commits an offence and is liable on conviction to life imprisonment. Examples are hacking into computer systems, introducing viruses to vulnerable networks, unleashing website defacing and launching DDoS attacks. For the purpose of emphasis, cyber terrorists are digital terrorists who target military forces, government cyber and physical infrastructures, private industries and entities. Their motive are usually social, cultural, religion and political. Cyber terrorism can lead to extensive monetary loss, breaches of national security secrets, failure of military equipment, theft of valuable and sensitive data such as medical records. Cyber terrorists paralyse or disrupt telephone and computer networks making data unavailable.[104] Terrorist use of the Internet is a transnational problem, requiring an integrated response across borders and among national criminal justice systems. In ***Public Prosecutor v. Hicheur***,[105] a French Court sentenced an Algerian-born French national to jail for participation in a criminal conspiracy and preparation of a terrorist act after he sent an e-mail communication containing Jihadist content to the website of the French Republic which was traced back to a member of Al-Qaida in the Islamic Maghreb with dozens of decrypted e-mail communications being presented at trial.[106] Note that accessing highly radicalised *jihadi* material from the web world does not demonstrate committing or planning any

[102] Apoorva Iyer. 'The Expansion of ISIS from Terrorism to Cyber-Terrorism <https://dras.in/use-of-the-Internet-by-isis> accessed 02 January 2022

[103] Jordan J, Plotnek. 'Cyber terrorism: A homogenized taxonomy and definition' <https://doi.org/10.1016/j.cose2020.102145> accessed 04 February 2022

[104] See The Tallinn Manual & the Application of International Law Principles to Cyberspace 2003 which applies international law principles to cyber operations

[105] Case No. 0926639036 (2012)-<http://www.undoc.org/documents/ frontpage/ Use_of_ Internet+for _Terrorist_Purposes.pdf>

[106] See 'The Use of the Internet for Terrorist Purposes' – United Nations Office on Drugs and Crime Publication (2012)

terrorist act.[107] In the case of ***Foundation of Media Professionals* v. *Union Territory of Jammu & Kashmir***[108] also known as the *4G Landmark Case,* the Supreme Court of India examined the conflict between national security and right to freedom of speech and expression because the case was filed against the government for restraining the speed of Internet in the territory and for reducing the speed to 2G when the country is supposed to be heading towards 5G Internet services. The petitioner wanted the Court to order the restoration of the 4G Internet services while the government contended that it could not do so based on the grounds of national security and that the restriction of Internet speed will stop online circulation of terror provoking materials. The Court upheld the justification of the government by saying that people can still send and receive messages even if the Internet service is slow, noting that the slow Internet will mostly affect only the people promoting terror activities.

12. CYBER-ESPIONAGE

This is also called cyber spying that is carried out through digital channels. It is a form of cyber-attack that steals classified, sensitive data, money, intelligence or intellectual property to gain an advantage over a competitive company or government entity. Cyber-espionage allows cyber criminals and nation state-backed hackers to steal information and conduct their activity with little chance of being detected. Cyber-espionage is a mixture of spying and stealing. The main goal is to disrupt businesses and disseminate fear. Cyber-espionage groups could be sponsored by government in one country against the other. For example, suspected Russian criminals defaced Ukraine's website domains which disrupted their IT systems and took down their power grids in 2015. Any government or organisation hit by a cyber-attack would result in breach. Cyber-espionage is of three types: *corporate espionage* - where domestic trade secrets of businesses in the same country are the target; *economic espionage* - businesses in two different countries; *nation-state espionage* - where governments attempt to steal the sensitive nuclear or military data of another country. Cyber-espionage, when

[107] Anand Mohan J. 'UAPA Case: Possessing Jihadi literature not offence, there must be material about executing terror acts, Delhi Court tells NIA' <https:// indianexpress.com/article/cites/delhi/ > accessed 03 November 2033

[108] (2020 SCC Online SC 453)

successful can create problems ranging from financial loss, compromised data, to loss of reputation or loss of competitive advantage.[109] In recent times, it has been reported that a hacking and cyber-espionage campaign is abusing legitimate cloud services as part of a covert operation to steal sensitive information from high-profile targets. The group is widely believed to be linked to the Russian Foreign Intelligence Service responsible for several major cyber-attacks. The attacks begin first with phishing emails which are sent out to targets at European Embassies, posing as invites to meetings with ambassadors and completed with a supposed agenda attached as a PDF. The PDF is malicious and the intention is to use malware to create a backdoor onto an infected network and steal sensitive information, either for use in further attacks or to be exploited in other ways.[110]

Case Study - In 2014, a grand jury in Pennsylvania indicted five Chinese military hackers for computer hacking and economic espionage. The indictment alleged that the defendants conspired to hack into American entities, to maintain unauthorised access to their computers and to steal information from those entities that would be useful to their competitors in China.[111] However in 2024, the U.S. House of Representatives is considering whether to approve the *Protecting Americans Data From Foreign Adversaries Act in* order to prevent companies from selling the American people's data to rogue nations like China and Korea, over concerns based on foreign espionage and data mining.[112]

---

[109] Beth Hendricks. 'Espionage in Digital Crime: Definition & Types' <https://study.com/academy/lesson/> accessed 26 February 2022.

[110] Danny Palmer. 'Hackers turn to cloud storage services in attempt to hide attacks' <https://www.zdnet.com/article/> accessed 20 July 2022

[111] Press Release – 'U.S. Charges Five Chinese Military Hackers for Cyber Espionage Against U.S. Corporations and a Labour Organisation for Commercial Advantage' <https://www.justice.gov/opa/pr/> accessed 19 December 2022

[112] Reynold Schweicckhardt, 'Congress should address recurring cases of cyber espionage at home' <https://www.fedealtimes.com/opinion/2024/> accessed 16 April 2024

Chapter 5

OTHER ACTS OF CYBER THREAT

Threat is a statement of the intent to harm or punish someone or a thing that presents an eminent danger or harm to someone. When the threat is carried out on the Internet, this enable threat actors to perform malicious activities online and it then transform into a cybercrime especially if it emanates as a possible act of malicious attack that seeks to access data unlawfully, disrupt digital operations, or damage information. Some of the types of cyber threats are social engineering, malware, man in-the-middle attacks and injection attacks, web/page jacking, ransomware and DDoS attacks. According to Section 58 of the Cybercrimes Act, damage means any impairment to a computer or the integrity or availability of data, programme, system or information that causes financial loss, modifies or impairs any activities from physical injury and threatens public safety to death. Cyber threat is carried out by corporate spies, hacktivists, terrorist groups, hostile nation states, criminal organisations, lone hackers and disgruntled employees. What interventions exist to curtail cyber-threat? Two bodies have been established by the General Assembly of the United Nations. These are (i) the Group of Governmental Experts focused on advancing responsible State behaviour in the cyberspace in the context of international security, and (2) the Open-Ended Working Group on developments in the field of information and telecommunications in the context of international security. Both bodies have affirmed that international law and the Charter of the United Nations are applicable and essential in maintaining peace, security and stability in the ICT environment.[1]

Apart from individuals that are making positive steps to be personally cybersecurity-conscious, there is need to exhaust countermeasures and

[1] Press Release of the Security Council on 'Explosive Growth of Digital Technologies of Creating New Potential for Conflict, Disarmament Chief Tells Security Council in First-Ever Debate on Cyber threats' <https://www.un.org/press/en/2021/sc14563.doc> accessed 23 February 2022

other cybersecurity strategy to implement best practices to protect our businesses and data from internal and external threats while continuously adapting to emerging threats and risks.

I. CYBER THREATS DISCUSSED IN ACADEMIC LITERATURE

Cyber threats could take the following forms and these are acts of flaming, trolling and doxxing as discussed in academic literature.[2]

a. **Flaming –** Flaming, also known as *Roasting* is the act that involve insulting messages or flames between Internet users. Flaming is synonymous with cyberbullying and cyber harassment. It is a form of aggressive, hostile, profanity-laced online discussion which is always expressed by insults, swearing vulgar and angry words which could be expressed in typography to elicit a response from another online user.[3] Flaming is fuelled by the Internet's inherent lack of personal interaction and anonymity especially if the online discussions focus on controversial issues that could be of political, social, cultural, religious and other trivial differences.[4] Often targeted at women, flaming is misogynous in nature and a clear violation of netiquette or Internet etiquette. In order to avoid flaming, you need to exercise restraint and be composed.

b. **Doxxing –** Doxxing is a form of online harassment that targets specific individuals or organizations. It is an act of compiling and revealing publicly the peculiar identifying information about someone on the Internet with malicious intent. For example, when you search, collect and publicly share the personal identifiable information (PII) consisting of a person's personal details and sensitive data against his will, such as his name, online alias, home address, photographs, and details of his family members as well as his criminal history and personal health information. Such details are used in campaigns of harassment and digital threats which could also be a precursor for violence in the physical world. The aim of doxxing attacks is to humiliate, bully, harass, or otherwise harm a person Doxxers can be

---

[2] See the: European Institute for Gender Equality Report on Combating Cyber Violence against Women and Girls 2022

[3] In typography, text or font contains capital letters without any lowercase letters. Writing this way is interpreted as shouting while highlighting exclamations convey or emphasise strong emotions.

[4] Margaret Rouse. 'Flaming' <https://www.techopedia.com/definition/5356/> accessed 27 December 2022

charged for cyber stalking, harassment, identity theft or incitement to violence.[5]

c. **Trolling -** An Internet troll refers to a person who intentionally posts provocative and abusive online comments to cause offence and distress to a person. He could also be someone who anonymously stirs up discontent or out-rightly harasses another person online just for the fun of it. Oftentimes this takes the form of fat shaming, slut shaming or racism. Recently, there has also been an upsurge of 'Concern Trolling'. A concern troll is someone who is on one side of the discussion, but pretends to be a supporter of the other side with concern. His aim is to cause discord while pretending he is saying what he is saying out of concern.[6] However, Internet trolls whose identities are unknown could also be indicted under the law depending on how severe the trolling is.[7]

d. **Down Blousing –** This is an inappropriate act of taking a photograph down a woman's top (breasts or cleavage) without her knowledge or consent. Clearly the woman is absolutely unaware of being photographed. This act is not illegal in some countries.[8]

e. **Upskirting –** This is an act of taking photographs of a woman in which her underwear is showing. This act also includes indecent filming of anyone without their knowledge or taking photos of topless female bathers at a public beach, placing a camera under a staircase where women in dresses or skirts are likely to pass by.[9]

f. **Cyber-Flashing** –This is an act of indecent exposure when someone sends a picture of his genitals or image of his naked body to another person, usually the opposite sex in order to upset or scare the person who has not asked for such pictures.[10]

---

[5] Nica Latto. 'What is Doxxing, Is Doxxing Illegal, and How Do You Prevent or Report It?' <https://www.avast.com/> accessed 10 July 2023

[6] Eliza Castile. 'Watch Out For This Kind of Troll' <https://www.bustle.com/articles/144447/> accessed 27 December 2022

[7] *Hegglin v. Person(s) unknown & Google Inc (2013) EWHC 3798*

[8] Emmie Harrison-West. It's obvious 'downblousing' should be illegal-but I'll believe it when I see it' <https://metro.co.uk/2022/07/11/ > accessed 27 December 2022

[9] Rick Sarre. 'What is Upskirting and what are your rights to privacy under the Law?' <https://the conversation.com> accessed 20 November 2022

[10] See <https://dictionary.cambridge.org/> accessed 20 November 2022

g. **Creepshots –** This is a photograph taken discreetly of women in public by men. The act is particularly focused on women's clothed bodies done to highlight her sexualised areas such as her breast, buttocks and groin.

h. **Catfishing –** This is a scam where the scammer called a catfish creates a fictitious online identity and seeks out online relationship, especially romantic ones or to solicit donations. Most catfish just want to see if they can get away with being someone else online, but some have more fraudulent intent. The classic sign of being a catfish is if the scammer is not known in town or if the job he is posting about on the Internet cannot be verified.[11]

i. **Non-Consensual AI Deepfakes** – This is the dissemination of disgusting and abusive content depicting deepfake sexualised images of women without their consent. It can also be defined as the circulation of sexually explicit AI-generated images that predominantly exploit women. These could come in form of videos, photos or audio that seem real but have been manipulated. However, there have been debates over whether there should be real consequences for those who post these offending images or those who allow them to proliferate on social media.[12]

j. Cyber-Mobbing - Cyber-Mobbing is similar to cyber bullying except that it generally involves coming more from one person or one online aggressor. Cyber mobbing is defined as a group of people ganging up on someone using tactics of rumour, innuendo, discrediting, isolating, intimidating, and above all, making it look as if the targeted person is responsible (victim blaming). In cyber bulling, you know the bully but in cyber mobbing, you don't know the ringleader instigating the attack.[13]

Note that women are invariably the targets in these denigrating photos that go viral after they are uploaded on social media platforms by men who think the acts are harmless or it could just be their way of showing admiration for women. Also note that creepshots are not illegal in some

[11] KSchang. 'How to Catch a Catfish Scammer: A Step-by-Step Guide' <https://discover.hubpages.com/technology/> accessed 20 May 2022

[12] Noir AL-Sibai. 'Will There Be Any Consequences For All This Disgusting AI Taylor Swift Porn?' <https://futurism.com > accessed 27 January 2024

[13] 'Cyber Mobbing' <https://www.amayda.com/au/cyber-mobbing/> accessed 10 March 2023

countries because the reasonable expectation to privacy does not include public spaces.

2. INFRASTRUCTURE SECURITY

Infrastructure security begins with physical and human security. This is the security provided to protect infrastructure, such as network communications, banks, hospitals, highways, airports and all IT infrastructures in physical places. The aim of infrastructure security is to prevent vulnerabilities in the events of sabotage, intrusion and disruptions. Infrastructure security helps protect enterprise IT infrastructure, data, servers and platforms, network and perimeter, and cloud infrastructure against external and internal threats.[14] Lapses in physical security can negatively impact cybersecurity. It could also be referred to as the human aspects of cybersecurity. This is when human beings determine the way they perform their tasks or when their errors lead to security threat, many of which could be mitigated. In other words, when your behaviour on the Internet exposes you or your business to cybersecurity threat. For example, when you share password with another person or click on unsafe links, this has far-reaching consequences. Instances of the vulnerabilities can occur through:

a. **Employee's Carelessness** – When an employee accidentally forgets his flash drive in a public place and it gets stolen or another employee throws stacks of old company bank records into a trash bin where a criminal later finds them.[15]

b. **Tailgating** - when an unauthorized person without a proper identification follows an authorised person unto a secure area, such as a bank. This can lead to theft of sensitive information or even physical theft.

c. **Shoulder Surfing** -when someone looks over the shoulder of an individual who is using his ATM card to transact or typing in a password to a computer system to steal that information.

---

[14] 'Technology Q&A.' <https://www.hcltech.com/technology-qa/> accessed 20 May 2022
[15] 'Cybersecurity Basics for Small Businesses' <http://FTC.gov/SmallBusiness> accessed 23 July 2023

d. **Piggybacking** -when an unauthorised person enters a secure area by closely following an authorised person, without proper identification or authentication.

e. **Criminal Identity Theft –** This is when a criminal uses your stolen information in dealing with law enforcement or misuse your personal information for a fraudulent purpose, especially to mislead law enforcement agencies.

f. **Physical Theft -** When a burglar steals the files and computers from your office after entering through an unlocked window. Generally, computers and other devices could be lost or stolen. Take note that the smaller our devices are, the more they attract thieves and the easier for them to steal.

g. **Fake re-KYC Fraud** - when scammers pretend to be from a legitimate organization, asking customers for up-to-date KYC (*Know Your Customer*) information such as passport information.

h. **Baiting –** An attacker for instance can leave a malware-infected flash drive or a CD in a public place or a targeted organization's premises with the hope that someone will pick the harmful flash drive/CD up, out of curiosity.[16]

Appropriate security measures against these threats can be significantly reduced by raising awareness about the importance of cyber security through installation of cameras and access control systems to prevent unauthorised access and protect customers' sensitive information. Restrict those who do not need physical access from coming into contact with security devices. Store paper files or devices securely. Limit physical access only to those who need it and send reminders to employees to put their paper files in locked-file cabinets. Organisations should regularly track, review and update their security policies and procedures, conduct regular

[16] 'What is a Baiting Attack, and How to Prevent it' <https://powerdmarc.com/> accessed 15 August 2023

security audit/testing and invest in employee training, awareness programmes and AI as well as respond effectively to evolving physical security threats.[17]

3. CRIME OF VIRTUAL REALITY

Virtual humans or digital humans are simulations of human beings on computers that are enabled by AI which is just a piece of software. There are people who are convinced that that these digital avatars are also real in life since they are controlled by human beings. Historically, the term *metaverse* was coined by Neal Stephenson in his 1992 science fiction novel where he programmed humans as avatars. In the tech world, an avatar is a graphic identity that users select to represent themselves either in a virtual world or gaming session. An avatar can also be a computer-representation or realistic photo-like image mildly resembling the person.[18]

It then follows that these virtual humans can be a tool of virtual crime because they are created by AI to mimic human behaviour for many reasons. Virtual crime or in-game crime refers to a virtual criminal act that takes place in the metaverse. The metaverse itself is a new virtual world that is based on Virtual Reality (VR), Augmented Reality (AR), Artificial Intelligence (AI) and other advanced technologies - a combination of digital worlds in which people will gather to work, play or hang out.[19] Others may want to call the metaverse an alternate universe or the 'next Internet' - a replication of the physical or real world where criminal activities such as scams, phishing, malware, assets laundering, child sexual abuse and sexual violence can take place.[20] So, when we log on to the Internet, it could be for the purpose of networking with friends and information sourcing, just like metaverse participants who also want to engage in video games to escape from reality such that when a participant puts on the virtual reality headset, he can see himself participating in different sport games that are displayed on the helmet screen in the virtual world. This is enabled by AI and computer vision which uses TV imagery and sensors embedded in the helmets creating a digital replica of game scenarios in a virtual environment. For example, some games

---

[17] Infrastructure Security. Compiled by Asuman Lukwago (Cybersecurity Forum Initiative) April 29,2023

[18] See the definition in <https://techterms.com> accessed 20 August 2023

[19] Erick Massey. 'Will A Metaverse-Ready Smartphone Be Just Another Gimmick?' <https://www.outlookindia.com/business/> accessed 20 July 2022

[20] Harsh Kumar. 'All You Need To Know About Crimes In Metaverse World' <https://www.outlookindia.com/business/> accessed 20 July 2022

like, walking on a tight rope, flying over cities or playing football with celebrities. Although the games are only illusion, it could also be regarded as real in the physical world because the technology is such that the simulation will make it appear like it had happened in real life. Objectively speaking however, the software is not real but the individual involved experiences a first-person perspective because he is actually participating in the virtual game happening in a virtual arena. The question then arises and that is now that we know cybercrime has gone to the next level, can we control virtual crime in the metaverse especially if the game has to do with avatars involving themselves in murder, robbery operation or molesting children? Can forensic evidence connect a metaverse crime and the criminal in a virtual world? And do metaverse crimes have real-world ramifications?[21] As the metaverse becomes more popular, the implication is that it will also become vulnerable to new experimentation of crime such as virtual theft, virtual fraud, virtual extortion, virtual harassment, amongst many emerging crimes. A psychotherapist had complained that she was virtually gang raped in Facebook's metaverse after three to four avatars attacked her. Similarly, a woman complained of groping on Horizon Worlds.[22]

Recall that this software is created by an individual and distributed to interested participants who buy them and play the game without been forced to do so. Moreover, these simulations are not yet known to exist in law since they are still considered a science or fantasy fiction but these unethical games could be a subject of litigation in the future.[23] According to an author, for decades these ideas have been limited to science fiction and video games but they are now poised to revolutionise every industry and function from finance and healthcare to education, consumer products, city planning, dating and well beyond.[24] In view of the challenges related to the regulation, administration and governance of virtual environments and virtual reality applications, it has been suggested that the existing laws and ethics, such as

---

[21] JerryBui.eith. 'Calling all Forensic and Fraud Investigators into the Metaverse' <https:// medium.co, /digital-forensics-future/ > accessed 14 August 2022

[22] Arab News. ' Woman describes 'horrible' ordeal of being gang raped in virtual reality world' <https://www.aarabnews.com/node/2017706> accessed 24 July 2022

[23] HG. Org Legal Resources. 'When Virtual Crimes Become Crimes IRL. <https://www.hg.org/legal-article/> accessed 12 February 2022

[24] Matthew Ball. 'The Metaverse and How it will Revolutionize Everything' <https://wwnorton.com/ books/> accessed 23 July 2022

those governing intellectual property, fraud, money laundering data breach, jurisdiction and cybercrime can apply to crimes committed in the metaverse and law enforcement agencies should punish anyone who violates them.[25]

Robots' Vulnerabilities

It is common knowledge that we live in an AI-driven world. The term 'Artificial Intelligence' (AI) was coined at a conference in Dartmouth in 1956 by John McCarthy, an American Computer Scientist, who defined AI as the science and engineering behind what gives machines their intelligence. Others have defined AI as a branch of science that gives machines the capacity to execute tasks involving planning, learning, reasoning, logic and perception than humans.[26] The goal of AI research is sometimes described as the developing machines that can think and act rationally like a human.[27]

While humans are real users of the Internet, the automated users are the Internet robots powered by AI and created to harness the ability of machines to learn and perform cognitive functions similar to that of the human brain. By making use of intelligent chatbots, this simply means the process is automated.[28] It should be noted that robots have come a long way since Czech writer Karel Carpek (1890-1938) best known for science fiction used the word 'robot' to describe an artificial automata or artificial person. Once largely confined to factories, robots are found everywhere from the field of military and medicine to education. People have created humanlike robots that can make art, plant trees, attend to patients, and complete many tasks we can design a machine to do.[29] Some Robots can scan for undesirable social behaviours or unlawful activities in public places. Robots are also going into the outer space to build structures. Robo-umpires have made appearances in sporting events. There are robot vacuum cleaners, bomb disposal bots, feeding robots assisting people living with tetraplegia,[30] factory

---

[25] 'Exploring crimes in the metaverse' <https://integrity-asia.com/blog/> accessed 23 February 2023

[26] Kizito Ogedi Alakwe. 'Human Dignity in the Era of Artificial Intelligence and Robotics: Issues and Prospects,' *Journal of Humanities and Social Sciences Studies.* <ISSN:2663-7197. DOI: 10.32996/jhsss> accessed 17 June 2023

[27] Mark Robert Anderson.. 'After 75 years, Issac Asimov's Three Laws of Robotics nee updating' <https://theconversation.com/amp > accessed 25 February 2022

[28] Marion Cook. 'Artificial Intelligence in Government' <accessed via Linkedin on 20 December 2022

[29] Emma Hart. 'Meet the robots that can reproduce, learn and evolve all by themselves' <https://www.newscientist.com/article/mg2533375 > accessed 25 February 2022

[30] Matthew Sparkles. 'Robot that learns social cues could feed people with tetraplegia' <https://www.newscientist.com/article/2330657/> accessed 27 July 2022

robots and academic robots that can help research. There are also computer generated virtual influencers which are artificial celebrities that promote consumer products. A physical device such as Google's driverless car has the potential to kill or harm or damage property. These robots have a manufacturer or designer and they can be held culpable because manufacturers are humans who are controlling them.[31] In other words, robots are deployed for security use cameras, sensors, broadband communication, navigation equipment and electric motors-all packed into its body with a big rechargeable battery and computer. The robots use Wi-Fi or a wireless data network to communicate with their manufacturers who remotely monitor the robots' cameras, microphones and other sources of data.[32] Robots deployed for bombs, use chemical munitions fully equipped to deliver a flash-bang grenade or explosives to disorient suspects. Currently, we also have the open artificial intelligence (OpenAI) bot called the ChatGPT – a chatbot system which can chat and write essays and computer programmes for humans.[33]

This makes us to ask whether robots can be held culpable under the law just in case their acts of omission/commission leads to a physical crime because if a human person or corporate organization committed a crime, they can be prosecuted for the crime. But what if it is a robot which is not a legal person though created humanoid to think, look and talk like humans? Obviously, the robots are electronic controlled devices but they also have human creators. In criminal law, what happens when robots fail to complete a task or if their failure leads to catastrophic impacts? In law, liability rises whenever harm is caused by a certain act while an accused is culpable for his actions.[34] Being connected to networks and run via software, it is possible that hackers can hijack robots to steal trade secrets, damage equipment, cause bodily harm and insert potentially malicious code into the assembly

[31]Jeffrey Wale & David Yuratich. 'Robot law: what happens if intelligent machines commit crimes? https://theconversation.com/> accessed 12 February 2022

[32] Rachel Metz. Rise of the Robot Security Guards' https://www.technologyreview.com/ > accessed 15 February 2022

[33]Stephen Shankland. 'ChatGPT: Why Everyone is Obsessed this Mind-Blowing AI Chatbot' <https://www.cnet.com/tech/computing> accessed 14 December 2022

[34]Christopher Markou. 'Even robots can commit crimes; we might soon need a law' <https://www.business-standard.com/article/ > accessed 13 February 2022.

process in robots.[35] For example, a robocop software has also once being accused of racial discrimination.[36]

Having stated that an Internet bot or web robot is a software application which runs automated tasks over the Internet usually to emulate human activity on the Internet that are able to perform simple and repetitive tasks faster than a person could ever do. Before you access a website, the system may actually want you to establish your identity as to whether you are a robot or human and that is why you might be required to fill in the CAPTCHA, a short form for 'Completely Automated Public Turing test to tell Computers and Humans Apart' and the message goes like this: *("We're sorry about this, but it's getting harder and harder to tell the difference between humans and bots these days")*. You will then be required to fill in the CAPTCHA random numbers or letters before you are granted access. CAPTCHA verification is a security measure known as challenge-response authentication which helps protect you from spam and password decryption/ All it does is to ask us to complete a simple test that proves us human and not a computer malware trying to break into a password protected account. To pass the test and prove we are truly human, simply type the characters provided in the image into the text box and you will be granted access.[37]

In today's digital world, many are convinced that robots will take over the world and invariably, our jobs. This concept is called the AI-Takeover which is a hypothetical scenario in which an AI becomes the dominant form of intelligence on Earth. This simply means that technology will eventually surpass human capabilities and take over because of the belief that the computational power of machines out-performs the human brain.[38] In view of this development, a group of industry leaders have warned that the AI technology they were building might one day pose an existential threat to humanity and should be considered a societal risk on a par with pandemics

---

[35]Brandon Barborka. '3 Ways That Hackers Can Hijack Your Industrial Robots' <https//www .staffmanagement.com> accessed 13 February 2022

[36] Maggie Harrison. 'Man sues City of Chicago Claiming its AI Wrongly imprisoned him' <https:// futurism.com/the-byte/> accessed 26 July 2022

[37] 'What is CAPTCHA' <https://support.google.com/a/answer/1217728> accessed 13 February 2022

[38] 'Will technology take over humans' <https://www.dediscourse.com/article/technology/> accessed 23 February 2023

and nuclear wars.[39] Clearly, this is evident as we can see the impact of technology in AI, robotics and machine learning.

While we marvel at the capabilities of AI, it is pertinent to ask whether a robot controlled by computer software, enabled by AI can come alive and be classified as a human being just because it speaks, or rather whether machines can replicate a complex system of human biology, psychology and lived experience. In other words, AI, once a matter of science fiction, has now become our everyday reality.[40] That is why there have been reports about people who have tried to seduce a computer robot. There are chatbot apps that help users prepare for death or chatbots who are fighting sex trade. There are robot lawyers that could predict the outcome of cases.[41] In fact the creators of the *Loebner Prize* had organised an annual test of artificial conversation with robots in which computers try to fool humans into thinking that they too, are human.[42]

The founding origin of this thinking has ever been based on the three law of Robotics which according to American Professor of Biochemistry, Issac Asimov (1920-1992) stipulates that: (1) A robot may not injure a human being or allow a human being to come to harm; (2) a robot must obey orders given it by human beings except if such orders would conflict with the first law; (3) a robot must protect its own existence, to personhood.[43] Scientists have finally refuted the claims that robots are human on the ground that AI is not yet conscious being since it is just a computer science and algorithms assigned technology.[44] Notwithstanding, robots are not perfect as they lack certain human qualities. Being a mere computer that can be manipulated, chatbots can be biased due to their design, development and training because AI learns from the data the

---

[39] Prabha Kannan. 'Another Warning Letter From AI Researchers and Executives' <https://www.newyorker.com/humor/> accessed 12 June 2023

[40] 'Can AI Develop Emotions> The Great Debate of the Digital Era' <https://rev3altechnology.medium.com/> accessed 22 May 2023

[41] Rory Cellan-Jones. ' The robot lawyers are here-and they're winning' <https://www.bbc.com/news/technology/> accessed 13 February 2022

[42] Tim Harford. 'Can a computer fool you into thinking it is human?' <https://www. bcbc.com/news/business/> accessed 13 February 2022

[43] Victor Tangermann. 'Google Suspends Engineer Who Claims the Company's Experimental AI has Become Sentient' <https://futurism.com/google> accessed 14 June 2022

[44] Maggie Harrison. 'Analysis: No, AI Isin't Sentient, You Absolute Morons' <https://futurism.com/> accessed 10 August 2022

trainers provide.[45] Moreover, humans will always have the upper hand when they still have to confirm or deny whether AI robots have accurately labelled things correctly. This is called the process of data annotation or data labelling.[46] Note that there are scam bots that are created by malicious bot programmers who have encouraged AI to commit bot fraud or to perform various forms of cyber-attacks.

4. WEBSITE CRIME

A website is a central site or location of web pages that are accessed by visiting the website's home page while using a browser.[47] In ***Abubakar v. INEC***,[48] the Supreme Court defined a website as a computer connected to the Internet that maintains a series of web pages on the World Wide Web. Website crime is a cybercrime or computer crime. Cybercrime or computer crime is the use of a computer as an instrument to further illegal ends while a cybercriminal is a person who uses his skills in technology to do malicious activities on the Internet.[49] A cybercriminal can tamper with websites in the following ways:

a. **Website Cloning** - To clone means to copy something or to create a product that is very similar to another one. Website cloning is when you copy materials from a website and you post it on another website or you publish it in a newsletter. It is a process of creating a replica of an existing website design or content possibly to create a new website with ease.[50] Stealing a website code means someone else is duplicating your logo or trademarked material. Printing a copy of an image or posting it online without permission is a violation of copyright. Note that all digital content enjoys the same copyright protections just as non-digital offline content because the contents of a website are the same with the contents of a book in terms of copyright protection. Copyright is automatic. The information need not have a copyright notice or symbol associated with it

---

[45] Joshua Lee. Ethical Considerations for using ChatGPT for law enforcement' <https://www.police1.com> accessed 26 May 2023

[46] Gulbahar Karatas. 'Data Annotation: What it is, Why it matters, and Implementations' <https://research.aimultiple.com/data-annotation/> accessed 12 January 2022

[47] <https://www.computerhope.com> accessed14 December2023

[48] (2020_ 12 NWLR (Pt. 1737) 37

[49] Michael A. Dennis. 'Cybercrime' <https://www.britannica.com/topic/cybercrime> accessed 05 June 2023

[50] 'How to Clone a Website like a Pro'< https://www.cloudways.com> accessed 12 January 2022

to be copyrighted.[51] So if you must copy from a website, you have to obtain the author's permission before you can use his content. In ***Land Nordrhein-Westfalen* v. *Dirk Renckhoff***,[52] a student in Germany used a photo taken from a travel website in a school project. The school then put the project on its website. The photographer who had created the photo had not authorised the school to use his work in this way nor was he acknowledged on the school website because his details had not been included on the original travel site. The photographer claimed breach of copyright. The Court of Justice of the European Union (CJEU) held that the posting of the photograph on the school website constituted the communication of the work to a different audience than the audience of the travel portal and that; therefore it was an infringement of the photographer's copyright. It has also been held that an infringer of copyright on the Internet is to be treated the same way as an infringer in the physical world. In ***New Balance Athletics Inc.* v. *Ashok Kumar trading as*** *<www.myshoeshop.in>*,[53] the defendant infringed the trademarks of other brands on his fraudulent website. In ***UTV Software Communication Ltd* v. *1337x***,[54] the Delhi High Court while elaborating on the concept of rogue websites which shares infringing content held that there is no difference between an infringer in the physical world and the one in the online world.

b. **WebJacking** – This is when hackers illegally seek control of a website by taking over a domain in order to deceive owners that a web page is real. A phishing attack by hackers is known to steal user data, login credentials and credit card numbers. Hackers do this to damage someone's reputation or to collect ransom from the real owners.[55]

c. **Pagejacking** – This is when hackers illegally copy the content of original websites (usually in the form of source code) to another website

---

[51] FindLaw. 'Is it Legal to Copy Content from a Website? < https://www.findlaw.com/ smallbusiness/ business/> accessed 22 January 2022

[52] Case C-161/17

[53] CS (Comm) 531/2022

[54] (2019) SCC OnLine Del. 8002

[55] Ajay Ohri. 'Webjacking: A Basic Overview in 3 Points' <https://www.jigsawacademy.com/> accessed 11 November 2022

designed to replicate the original website. The intention of the pagejacker is to illegally direct traffic from the original site to cloned web pages.[56]

d. **Formjacking** – This is when cybercriminals hack a website and embed malicious Javascript code, which hijacks the function of the forms on the site to collect user information. This type of theft is usually intended to steal payment information or personal information often used at at the points of payment where goods are bought.[57]

e. **Cousin Domain Attack** – Here, the attacker creates a website that looks nearly identical to your bank's website but ends with *.com* instead of *.org* or *.net*. The attacker will then proceed to send emails from this fake site and when people click on links in those emails they will be taken to the fake site instead of their real bank's site.[58]

f. **Internationalised Domain Name (IDN) Homograph Attack** – This is an act of mimicking a well-known website in order to lure Internet users to fraudulent sites. Scammers create 'lookalike websites which are websites that mimic legitimate sites to sell counterfeit goods, steal money or credentials, and spread malware.

5. MALICIOUS MALWARE

The intentional creation or dissemination of a computer virus or other destructive programmes no doubt will affect the normal operation of a computer information system. This malicious is a criminal act of sabotaging a computer information system. Malicious Software is a long word for malware. It performs malicious tasks such as corrupting or destroying data. It is software developed by cyber attackers with the intention of gaining access or causing damage to a computer or network. It also threatens a country's computer infrastructure. Often, the victims are oblivious to the fact that there has been a compromise. A common alternative description of malware is computer virus, which was coined by American computer scientist, Professor Leonard M. Adleman. One of the most common forms of

[56] 'Defining Pagejacking.' <https://fraud.net/> accessed 04 June 2023

[57] Irene Park. 'Top identity theft scams to avoid' <https://cyberguy.com/security/top-identity-theft-scams-to-avoid> accessed 04 June 2023

[58] Ahona Rudra. 'What is an Impersonator Attack?' <https://powerdmarc.com> accessed 11 November 2022

malware is the Trojan horse. This is a form of malicious software that often disguises itself as legitimate tool, tricking the user into installing the software so it can carry out its malicious goals.[59] Consequently, a criminal after hacking into a computer can control the computer information system and install destructive malware, For example, hackers embedded info-stealer malware into a fake ChatGPT browser extension, which collected millions of login credentials.[60] Below are other forms of malicious software:

a. **Spyware** – This malware records the activities of the user, such as the password he types into the computer, and transmits this information to the person who wrote the malware. Once infected, the spyware can turn our smartphones into a remote eavesdropping device thus making it easy for the attacker to siphon our data.
b. **Ransomware** – This is a malware that demands payment in order to refrain from doing some harmful action or to undo the effects of the harmful action.
c. **Wiper Malware** – This is a class of malware that destroys data from any storage device which makes information unavailable and irrecoverable.
d. **Computer Worm** – This is a stand-alone malicious programme that can self-replicate and spreads copies of itself from computer to computer, without the help of any human interaction.
e. **Adware** - This is a form of malware that hides on your device and serves you advertisements or monitors your behaviour online in order to target you with specific adverts.
f. **Botnets** - are created by a malware that allows an attacker to control a group of computers and use them to gather personal information or launch attacks against others, such as for sending spam emails or flooding a website with so many content that the server cannot cope with, like a (DDOS) attack.[61]
g. **Cryptocurrency Miner Malware** - This malware easily infect devices through multiple ways from downloads to browsing on a compromised website, just so to mine forms of online currency known as

[59]Danny Palmer. 'What is Malware? Everything you need to know about viruses, Trojans and malicious software' <https://www.zdnet.com/article/> accessed 20 July 2022

[60]Kurt Knutsson 'International crackdown on criminal marketplaces selling stolen data' <https://cybeguy.com/security/> accessed 02 June 2023

[61] The Open University. Introduction to Cybersecurity. <https://www.futurelearn.com/courses/ > accessed 07 September 2022

cryptocurrencies which are digital form of moneys not associated with a central repository.

h. **Fileless Malware** – This malware uses a computer system's built-in tools to execute a cyber-attack due to the vulnerabilities present in the installed software. It does not rely on files and leaves no footprint, making it challenging for computer investigators to detect and remove.
i. **Mobile Malware** - This is a malicious software specifically designed to target mobile devices, such as smartphones and tablets, with the goal of gaining access to private data.
j. **Android Malware** – This is a malicious software that specifically targets Android devices. The intention is to harm the user's device and steal his data.
k. **Internet of Things (IoT) Malware** – This is a type of malware that perform DDoS attacks or brute-force attack in order to gain access to IoT devices.

It is against the law to distribute a virus to others or cause intentional damage using malicious mobile code a criminal act. If you write or distribute rogue code, which causes damage to someone else's computer system, you can be charged with breaking the law. However, the challenge for the security expert is being able to successfully track down who wrote and distributed the code to prove malicious intent. The reality is also that hundreds of new malicious code programmes are being created and spread each month without leading to criminal prosecution.[62]

And how do we protect our computer systems from malware? Malicious malware attack can be prevented from taking over your electronic devices even though it can spread fast. Cyber vigilance and monitoring of any suspicious behaviour is vital because some of these attacks can be sent by text messages with an attachment that carries security vulnerability, allowing the execution of a malicious code. You may also need to update your devices. Avoid clicking on links from unknown or untrusted sources. Exercise caution with attachments and install good antivirus software on your devices.[63]

[62]'Malicious Code and the Law' <https://www.oreilly.com/library/view/> accessed 01 August 2023

[63] Kurt Knutsson. 'A new malicious malware is specifically targeting iPhones' <https:// cyberguy.com/security/> accessed 02 February 2023

6. CYBERCRIME ON SENIOR CITIZENS

In this digital escape age, the Internet has put information in our hands. Thus, it has become a cornerstone for bridging the gaps in our societies. The Internet is both a convenience and necessity for everyone including the elderly ones who are left at the mercy of threat actors or Internet scammers who use computers for criminal activities despite the positive role of the Internet. Cybercrime against the elderly has become a cause for concern. An elderly person is also called a senior citizen. People from ages 65 to 74 years old are usually considered early elderly while those over 75 years old are referred to as late elderly.[64] Evidence has shown that the Internet technology can improve their general well-being of senior citizens, improve their mental and physical health as well as improve their cognition and memory skills. But just like young people, elderly people can become hooked on social media that could put them at risk of serious harm. The elderly ones are not spared by hackers, therefore it is important that we provide a safe cyberspace for the elderly just like in the physical world where family and friends support their elderly siblings.[65] However in reality, the physical space is entirely different from the cyberspace because the elderly ones may not even get the support that they crave for in the physical space since most families nowadays are nuclear families who are not at home to guide their elderly siblings while browsing on the net. Elderly people can sometimes find themselves getting age-crippled and lack direction because as we age, each of us will encounter a number of life changes and circumstances, such as the death of loved ones, which can lead to anxiety, sadness or stress. A void comes in with them resorting to explore the Internet life. The Internet has therefore heightened their need for an emotional connection with others.[66]

Naturally when someone is alone or lonely, he may decide to seek for attention online. Elderly people are faced with isolation. Apart from this, they do not have energy for face-to-face gathering, so they are left alone with their Internet gadgets. That is why they easily become victims of cybercrime which can come in the form of romance scam, debit card fraud, fraudulent

[64] Aaron Sinykin. 'At What Point is Someone Considered Elderly?' <https://devotedguardians.com/> accessed 12 August 2022

[65] Monica Anderson and Andrew Perrin. 'Technology Use among Seniors'< https://www.pew/ research/ org/Internet> accessed 12 August 2022

[66] 'Online Therapy: A Mental Health Guide for Older Adults' <https://ncoa.org/artice/> accessed 05 May 2023

text message, delivery scam or healthcare scam, among several other scams because cyber criminals know it is easier for the elderly ones to transfer funds from their mobile phones. In other words, senior citizens are targeted majority of them are not that tech savvy. Cybercriminals know that majority of the elderly ones are lonely yet they have extra money to look after themselves. The implication is that older citizens are vulnerable or susceptible to social engineering attacks such that when they are duped, they are less likely to inform the Police about it. Elderly men also become victims of property crimes, holiday scams or emotional crimes while elderly women fall victim to romance scams, sympathy scams, crowd funding or donations and identity theft. In romance scams, male perpetrators generally create fictitious online personas to develop online romance relationships with these old women mostly in foreign lands, and then leverage those relationships to obtain money and property.[67] Senior citizens may also fall victims to a scam called 'pig butchering' which is a type of crypto investment fraud, which combines romance scam and crypto investment spin. In Nigeria, pig-butchering scam is defined as a type of fraud in which criminals lure victims into digital relationships to build trust before convincing them to invest in cryptocurrency platforms.[68] In this scenario, the scammer creates a fake profile to reach out to potential victims on social media, WhatsApp, and other dating sites. He pretends to be an old friend and initiates a cordial discussion with the victim, attempting to be a new friend or lover. While building trust with the victim, the scammer slowly introduces the idea of project investment.[69] Older citizens may also need to guide against falling for 'brushing scams' The term 'brushing' comes from the idea of brushing aside suspicion. A brushing scam is a fraudulent activity that involves an e-commerce seller sending unsolicited packages to people.[70] Other types of scams that elderly people are likely to fall for, are, funeral and cemetery scams, fraudulent anti-ageing scams, fake product reviews, telemarketing

---

[67] Press Release. 'Nigerian Man Sentenced for Online Fraud Schemes' < https://www.justice.gov/usao-ma/pr/> accessed 11 May 2023

[68] 'Crypto trader convicted of cyber 'pig-butchering' scam' <htpps://thenationonlineng.net/> accessed 10 October 2023

[69] Michigan Department of Attorney General. 'Cryptocurrency Scam-Pig Butchering' <https://www. michigan.gov/ag/consumer-protection/> accessed 24 December 2022

[70] Kurt Knutsson. ' How to guard against brushing scams' <https://cybeguy.com/security/ > accessed 09 August 2023

scams, counterfeit prescription drugs scam and grandparent scam, among others.[71]

Cybercriminals usually want to deprive the elderly ones out of their property, money and inheritance. Some hackers deliberately target to even go as far as stealing the phones of senior citizens so they can use their phone numbers to spoof calls pretending to be them or to access their online social media and banking accounts. Unfortunately, when the elderly ones become victims of cybercrime, they are very reluctant to go to the Police to report. Through cyber intelligence and open intelligence, the Police can track those victimizing the elderly. For family members, they may need to sensitise their elderly ones about cyber vigilance and cybercrime preventive measures. Note that, improving safe digital access in Africa particularly among vulnerable groups should be of utmost priority to all relevant stakeholders.

7. WHY CYBERCRIMINALS SOMETIMES EVADE JUSTICE

No doubt, the invention of the Internet brought advantages to the world but sadly has its downsides which enabled cybercrime making it easier for people to commit criminal activities while hiding behind their screens. Notwithstanding this, why do some of these cybercriminals continue to evade detection? The reasons could be attributed to the following vulnerabilities that can be exploited by attackers:

a. Human error. Even with the best security measures in place, employees or customers may still make mistakes such as leaving their access card or ID badge unattended, or sharing passwords wlth others.
b. The evolving nature of cyber threats where security systems may not always be able to keep up with sophisticated AI. New technologies create new criminal opportunities and hacker lexicons that only cybercriminals themselves know about. Such lexicons include: pig butchering scam, dumpster diving,[72] leapfrog attack,[73] phreaker,[74] phracker,[75]

[71] Georgia Attorney General's Consumer Protection Division. 'Top 10 Scams Targeting Seniors' <https://consumer.georgia.gov/? accessed 09 August 2023

[72] This is an act of looking through trash for access codes or other sensitive information.

[73] This is an act of using a password or user ID obtained in one attack to commit another attack.

[74] A person who hacks telephone systems usually for the purpose of making free phone calls.

[75] A person who combines phone phreaking with computer hacking

steganography,[76] pretexting,[77] grandparent scam,[78] cryptocurrency and blockchain attacks.

c. Online fraud yield better results and less risk for cybercriminals with significantly less chance of being caught, making it very difficult for local law enforcement officers to investigate.
d. The Internet is still not safe. With sophisticated tactics and tools, these criminal elements use secure software to remain anonymous,[79] while some officers have scant experience in cybercrime investigations.
e. The social psychology concept of 'De-individuation 'which explains that many people exhibit certain behaviours in a group. This consequently resonates that some people thrive better on anonymity in a place which they can conveniently hide without being singled out. In this instance, the Internet offers criminals multiple hiding places. That is why they misbehave because they believe they are in a large group, which does not focus on one individual.
f. Cybercrime is non-local in character such that cybercriminals are located in other jurisdictions than their victim's countries. They also move around a lot and that is why victims do not have face-to-face interaction with hackers.
g. They conceal their locations by using online pseudonyms on the dark web. They use other people's pictures to defraud and deceive others. Other technologies like ToR and the security mechanism of encryption enable them to hide their identity. The Internet hacker therefore commits hundreds of these crimes and almost never gets caught.[80]
h. Gathering electronic evidence and investigation of Internet crimes is time-consuming, complex and more technical than traditional criminal activities. Forensically identifying, preserving, retrieving, analysing and presenting digital evidence in Court takes a lot of time and expenses.

---

[76] The practice of hiding information inside something that appears normal and is not secret.

[77] The attacker fabricates a situation, or a pretext to deceive the victim into giving away information or carry out a certain action.

[78] Scammers use emotional pleas, panic and urgency to pressure grandparents into acting without verifying information.

[79] NortonLifeLock Employee. 'How Do Cybercriminals Get Caught?' <https://us.norton. com/blog/ emerging-threats/> accessed 28 September 2022

[80] Roger A. Grimes. 'Why Internet Crime Goes Unpunished' <https://www.csoonline.com/ article/ 2618598/> accessed 28 September 2022

i. Cross-national boundaries and the inter-state nature make Internet crime especially difficult to track and prosecute.
j. Countermeasures to fight computer systems vulnerability are not tight. The Police may need to do extensive follow-up and consulting experts. Understanding crime patterns vary and collecting diverse data sources are major handicaps.
k. When governments fail to develop stringent regulations and international frameworks to monitor and control the development or deployment of technologies.
l. Cybercriminals still prey on many Internet users because apart from being vigilant or failing to follow good online practices and safety habits, users sometimes don't want to report suspicious cyber-activities they encounter.
m. Risk of insider threats, where employees or other insiders with access to sensitive information or assets intentionally or unintentionally cause a security breach.
n. Lack of proper maintenance and oversight of security systems. Without regular maintenance and testing, security systems may become outdated or ineffective, and potential vulnerabilities may go undetected.[81]

[81] Infrastructure Security. Compiled by Asuman Lukwago. (Cybersecurity Forum Initiative) April 29,2023

Chapter 6

CYBERSECURITY TOOLS AND DATA PROTECTION

I. ACCESS CONTROL

When someone does not give you access to use a thing or place, in the layman's explanation, that means you will be denied access or that you do not have the right to enter a place. In the cybersecurity context, when you are granted access, it means you have been given authority or permission to use a computer data or programme. You can even be given access to a computer system from another location (remote access). You may also be allowed partial access to a file, but not allowed to edit or delete the file. Even transacting offline banking through the Unstructured Supplementary Service Data (USSD) authentication pin gives you access to use mobile banking. The essence is to prevent a random person from gaining 'entrance 'into a device except you are registered on the device.

In cybersecurity, employees that have access to application networks or information can decide to use this access with bad intent or they can even make mistakes, causing security breach. The employees involved in this act are called 'insider actors gone rogue'. As a matter of fact, many Chief Information Security Officers (CISOs) believe that employees leaving an organisation contribute to loss of sensitive information and data loss incidences.[1]Access restricts the use and distribution of information, settings and the general use of a system.[2] When a user is given the control to access a system, it simply means he has the authority or permission of the system regulator or the system administrator to view or use the system resources in a computing environment. This aligns with the ability to ensure those

---

[1] „Proofpoint"s 2023 Voice of the CISO Report Reveals Nearly Two-Thirds of CISOs have had to Deal with the Loss of Sensitive Data in the Past 12 Months" <https//www.proofpoint.com.us/newsroom/> accessed 10 May 2023

[2] „What does Access mean?"< https://www.techopedia.com> accessed 12 May 2022

networks' data system services are accessed by authorised parties,[3] which enables us to know who owns the information on a computer and who should have access to such information. Section 58 of the Cybercrimes Act 2015 defines an authorised access as a means of gaining entry into, instructing or communicating with the logical, arithmetical or memory function resources of a computer system or network. Any authorised access has an access device which gives the user the right of admittance. Section 58 of the Cybercrimes Act 2015 defines Access Device to include electronic cards in the form of debit cards, credit cards, passwords, electronic plate, code number, electronic serial number, smart chip based cards, charge cards, loyalty cards, mobile identification number, personal identification number (PIN), automated teller machines (ATM), point of sales (POS) terminals and other vending machines.

Note that the person in charge of the control access will always be the owner of the computer system itself as the goal of access control is to minimize the security risk from other persons getting unauthorised access to physical and logical systems[4] considering the fact it is a serious security vulnerability when hackers gain access to a user's computer network, including his personal information and private messages. Identity access management therefore provides an opportunity to detect malicious or unauthorised intrusions before they happen, because even if the cyber-attacker has the correct password, the user has to confirm that it is a legitimate login attempt to prevent illegal access.[5] Any unwarranted interference is illegal access to computer and examples of these are, computer hacking, illegal interception, data and system interference, unauthorised use of hardware, theft of software, the use of computers to commit fraud, the phenomenon of hacking and data theft, sabotage in the form of viruses, making false claims for computers and degradation of work.[6] Illegal access also has to do with someone that is granted access by the owner but uses the opportunity to pursue illegal activity such as to divert funds or to corrupt a computer-stored information or to hack by gaining

[3] Danny Palmer. „ Why cloud security matters and why you can't ignore it" <https://www.zdnet.cfom/article/> accessed 01 June 2022

[4] Ben Lutkevich. „„Access Control" <https://www.techtarget.com/searchsecurity> accessed 21 April 2022

[5] Danny Palmer. „ Why cloud security matters and why you can't ignore it" <https://www.zdnet.cfom/article/> accessed 01 June 2022

[6] Lou Berzai. „„Ethical Problems in Computing" <https://www.compta.org/blog/ > accessed 21 April 2022

unauthorised access to a computer system with the intention of committing theft, or it could even be by an act of 'piggyback' when someone gains an unauthorised access into your computer system through another user's legitimate connection. Piggybacking could also occur when you steal or borrow your neighbour's WIFI network just because his network is not secured.

In line with the Section 58 of the Cybercrimes Act 2015, authorised access means a person has unrestricted access to any programme or data held in computer if (a) the person is entitled to control access to the programme or data in question; or (b) the person has consent to access such programme or data from a person who is charged with granting such consent.

It is therefore of key importance that those who are entrusted with this responsibility to access should not abuse it. In other words, data should not be altered without proper authorization. In Nigeria, the Economic and Financial Crimes Commission (EFCC) secured the conviction of a software consultant/developer contracted by a petroleum company to develop and manage its billing software payment system. Unfortunately the consultant without given any authorized access took advantage of his office to carry out a fraud.[7] In ***R v. Thompson,***[8] a dishonest programmer used the access to his employer's computer to perpetrate a theft. In ***United States v. Van Buren,***[9] the Supreme Court held that there are two ways of committing the crime of improperly accessing a protected computer: (1) obtaining access without authorization, and (2) obtaining access with authorisation, but using that access improperly." Therefore an individual "exceeds authorised access under the Computer Fraud and Abuse Act 1986 if he accesses his employer's computer with authorisation but then obtains information located in particular areas of the computer that are off-limits to him." However, it is not a crime when a computer science professor instructs his students to hack into the university's system for the purpose of exhibiting their skills and knowledge of computer systems. Access control systems perform the following functions for users:

---

[7]Soonest Nathaniel. „EFCC Secures Conviction of Software Engineer, Forfeits Over N100m Properties" <https://www.channelstv.com/2022/02/24/> accessed 25 February 2022

[8] (1984) 3 All ER 565

[9] 940 F.3d 1192 (11th Cir. 2019)

1. **Authentication** – the process of verifying the identity of a person or device;
2. **Identification** – the process of ascribing a user identifier (ID) to person or to a computer;
3. **Authorisation** – The process of not exceeding authorised access to files or information that is off-limits to you on a computer system. ***United States v. Van Buren***;[10]
4. **Accountability** - the principle that you are entrusted to safeguard and control the computer system such that if anything goes wrong, you are answerable for the loss or misuse of the system or information;
5. **Policy Procedure** – the minimum standards of behaviour expected for activities connected to the computer system and apps, setting out rules for using email encryption, providing guidelines for creating passwords and rules on social media;[11]
6. **Training** – provides information pertaining to specify what users are permitted to do, the resources they are allowed to access and what operations they are able to perform on a system.[12]

Regarding unlawful access to a computer, Section 6(1) of the Cybercrimes Act 2015 provides that a person who, without authorisation, intentionally accesses, in whole or in part, and unlawful accesses computer system or network for fraudulent purposes and obtains data that are vital to national security, commits an offence and is liable on conviction five years imprisonment or to a fine of not more than ₦5,000,000 or both. Similarly securing access to any programme, commercial or industrial secrets or classified information; using a device to avoid detection; trafficking in any password to access a computer without lawful authority are all punishable under section 6 of the Cybercrimes Act. On computer and electronic data misuse offences, Section 387 of the Criminal Law of Lagos State 2015 provides that any person who intentionally causes a computer to perform any function with intent to secure unauthorised access to any programme or data in any computer commits a misdemeanour and is liable on conviction to imprisonment for two (2) years. Section 388-390 of the same Criminal law

---

[10] *supra*

[11] <https://www.trellix.com/en-us/security-awareness/cybersecurity/cybersecurity-policies.html> accessed 12 May 2022

[12] <https://www.coursera.org/learn/access-control-sscp?isNewUser=true&showOnboardingModal=1> accessed 12 May 2022

also criminalises the act of unauthorized access with intent to facilitate crime and unauthorised modification of computer data.

2. MULTI-FACTOR AUTHENTICATION (MFA)

The two-factor authentication (2FA), is both a cybersecurity tool and solution. It is regarded as the gold standard of data security. This is a security measure that requires the user to provide two or more proofs of identity to gain access to digital services. Here, you may need to prove your identity whether by physical key, a fingerprint, face or retina scan.[13] MFA typically requires a combination of something the user knows (pin, secret question); something you have (card, token); or something you are (fingerprint or other biometric).[14] Online threats are constantly evolving such just like cyber-attackers are constantly looking for sophisticated ways to hack into our devices at any slightest opportunity they get. There is no doubt that passwords can be stolen when attackers try to guess passwords using common combinations of letters and numbers through a criminal tactic called credential stuffing where lists of stolen passwords from one breach are matched to potential usernames in order to attempt another breach. Other breaches include exploiting the browser vulnerabilities to extract passwords, and phishing emails that trick individuals into revealing their personal information or account credentials.[15] So, if someone steals your password using a phishing message or website, no matter how complicated your password is, the attacker only has to copy and paste it into the login page and logs in successfully. And what if your email is spoofed or hacked? Turn on the 2FA and change your email password. Staying on top of cybersecurity best practices means we have to be proactive and reactive. With MFA, you can use a password in addition with a unique code/numbers which will be sent to your mobile device to authenticate yourself.[16] MFA or the 2FA verification system falls into the protective category thus serving a basic security measure. Unlike password length which helps protect users to an

---

[13] Cybersecurity Forum Initiative on Linkedin. Accessed on 29 April 2023

[14] J.J. Jeong. A. Nanda & S.W. Ali Shah. „What is Multi-Factor Authentication and Should You Use it?" <https://computer.howstuffworks.com> accessed 07 October 2022

[15] Anthony Lansing. „Multi-Factor Authentication Is Critical To Law Firm Data Security" <https:// afinety.com/multi-factor..> accessed 24 February 2022

[16] Emily McKeown „What is Multi-Factor (MFA)?" <https://www.pingidentity.com/en/resources/blog/> accessed 24 February 2022

extent, MFA goes an extra step further to protect against phishing attacks and computer hacking. It is a security key to enter a second authentication process in addition to your password which has overtime been widely regarded as one of the most effective ways to mitigate phishing and other forms of account hijacking. And truly, research says this has greatly reduced account hacking and hijacking in the cyber world. Unfortunately attackers are also getting technologically advanced at leveraging techniques that circumvent MFA by intercepting verification codes through stolen text messages or by stealing cookies from users' browsers after they have already completed their verification process. However, experts have cautioned that we should not rely solely on MFA for protection because attackers have developed techniques to bypass MFA codes, such as SIM swapping and phishing attacks targeting MFA codes. Nonetheless, MFA is still regarded as an effective defence to counter account hijacking and other cyber threats posed by trapdoor virus or backdoor trojans as well as generally making the web a safer place for us all.[17] To this end, organisations must therefore adopt a defence-in-depth approach, combining MFA with other security measures such as behaviour analytics, user monitoring, and adaptive access controls.[18]

3. PASSWORD

Every account needs a strong, hard-to-crack and unique password. Be aware that cyber attackers deploy many sophisticated tools to crack passwords if you do not use a strong password. For example, our email addresses provide a gateway into our personal information, financial data and potential account. Hackers use various criminal techniques to gain access if you do not have a strong password.[19] A strong password secures your system for maintaining security against any unwanted prying. This requires that we must have secured our accounts to prevent cybercriminals from gaining access to our security details. Passwords are important when it comes to privacy, online security and protecting our data. With the assistance of the password

[17] Josephine Wolff. Is Multifactor Authentication Less Effective Than It Used To Be? <https:// slate.com/technology/2022 > accessed 23 February 2022

[18] Sarmad Hassan." 7 Key Takeaways From Verizon's Data Breach Investigation Report 2023" <https://antidos.com/blog/verizons-data-breach/> accessed 30 July 2023

[19] Kurt Knuttsson. „What happens when a Cybercriminal Gets Access to your Email Address?"<https://cyberguy.com/security/ > accessed 27 April 2024

manager[20] which helps us to generate and remember the passwords we have chosen to use, we are guided to use a unique password for information security and as a digital protection tool.[21] Data is said to be the currency of the modern world because if we allow hackers to get access into our Internet account, they can impersonate us, steal our data and money. Typically in order for us to access our online account, we enter our passwords when logging in to check our e-mails, to open our electronic devices, to conduct banking transactions, to purchase online items and to secure other information. Generally, password is an e-mail security check service that helps to protect the privacy of the owner of an account from cybercriminals. Recent statistics have however shown that the number of password–stealing malware attacks in Nigeria doubled in 2022 when compared to year 2021. Unfortunately many websites also allow weak or common passwords such as *123456* and *P@44w0rd*.[22] These attacks enable hackers to steal passwords and account information, giving them access to the sensitive information of individuals and corporate networks.[23] Essentially the rules of passwords are:

a) Do not use weak passwords, or easy-to-guess passwords like your name, birthday, marriage anniversaries or pet's name;
b) To avoid password spraying attack, do not re-use passwords; or the infamous password 12345;
c) Do not use preselected library of commonly used words and phrases. For two or more users who have similar passwords, you may try password salting to make your passwords unique. Password salting is a technique to protect passwords stored in databases by adding a string of 32 or more characters and then hashing them.[24] Salting and hashing prevent hackers from stealing your passwords and slows down brute-force and dictionary

[20] Kurt Knutsson. „Best Password managers expert reviewed for 2023" <https://cyberguy.com/security/best-password/> accessed 03 May 2023

[21] Partner Content From TotalAV. „How to Protect Your Privacy Online" <https://computer.howstuffworks.com > accessed 13 May 2022

[22] Jeremy Hsu. „75per cent of the world"s top websites allow bad passwords" <https://newscientist.com/article/> assessed 25 June 2022

[23] Sami Tunji. „Password-Stealing Malware attacks Rise by 145.65% in Nigeria- Report" <https://punchng.com> accessed 01 June 2022

[24] "654234accH5551aghb29714g6dd72z4y91"

attacks. This adds additional layer of security to thwart hackers who look for consistent words and phrases;[25]

d) Use the two-factor authentication to secure your account because if a cybercriminal gets one password right, he could get into all your accounts.

Note that poor password choices are susceptible to vulnerabilities because hackers can use credential stuffing to decode password. Credential stuffing is a type of cyber-attack in which a cyber-criminal uses stolen usernames and passwords from one organisation to access user accounts of another organisation. This is based on the presumption that people often use the same user ID and password across multiple accounts.[26] Hackers also use brute force method – a trial and error method to get plain-text passwords from encrypted data. Here, the hackers try many possible combinations of characters, letters and numbers in sequence. Hackers may use social engineering techniques based on the information they get from your e-mail address, mother's maiden name, and date of birth. Other known illegal acts associated with password attack are perpetrated through dictionary attacks,[27] brute-force attacks,[28] rainbow attacks,[29] keylogger, password sealing or buying, password sniffer and cryptanalysis.[30] It follows those intelligent criminal elements that are close to you or know you, your habits and personalities can randomly guess your password, and so are persons who peep into your saved password or your computer repairer who helps you solve your computer problems.

So, how do we observe good password hygiene?[31] Keep your password private. You can write your passwords in a safe place in your notebook if you think you may forget them. Don't use the same passwords for the many online accounts you have. Although to remember many passwords is difficult

---

[25] Rahul Awati. „Password Salting" <https://www.techtarget.com/searchsecurity/> accessed 05 May 2022

[26] What is Credential Stuffing <https://www.imperva.com/learn/application-security/> accessed 05 May 2022

[27] Attempt to use the most common password.

[28] Attempt to guess every possible password combination and then run these combinations through a hashing algorithm.

[29] Attempt to use rainbow tables to crack unsalted hashes. A rainbow table is a password hacking tool that uses a precomputed table of reversed password hashes to crack passwords in a database,

[30] This is the process of studying cryptographic systems to look for weaknesses or leaks of information in order to gain access to the contents of encrypted messages.

[31] Victoria Woollaston. How DID hackers steal celebrities" private iCloud photos? Tech experts suggest wide range of security flaws for data theft. <https://www.dailymail.co.uk/sciencetech/article/> accessed 05 May 2022

but notwithstanding, you must have a complex and strong password to keep hackers off.[32] It is usually easier for hackers to crack short password. Choose a hard to crack password. If you need to change your password, do so. Using a Multi-Factor Authentication (MFA), the anti-spam measure CAPTCHA can reduce the effectiveness of credential stuffing. By following the rules, you and your networks and systems will be safe from security challenges and threats. Interestingly, every 5th day of May is observed as the day to celebrate strong passwords, so that our private information will not be compromised. Perhaps this could be why the UK government recently enacted a law titled *'the Product and Telecommunications Infrastructure Act (PSTI) 2022,* which has banned connected devices from having weak default passwords. This law is aimed at protecting consumers from hackers and also ensure manufacturers of the devices must meet minimum security standards.[33]

4. ENCRYPTION

Encryption is a crucial tool to protect our information from prying eyes. It is the process of encoding messages or information so that only the intended users can read it. End-to-end encryption (E2EE) therefore makes our messages, phone calls and video chats secure and unintelligible to outsiders everywhere except on the devices involved in the conversations, so that online snoops and interlopers will not be able to access what we are saying or writing – and neither can the network provider company that offers the communication platform.[34] As a protection for digital communications, encryption is used in three different ways:

1. **Encryption-in-Transit**: For example, when you download or upload files to a cloud storage provider, the data is encrypted during the transmission for protection. In Https for instance, the letter 'S' stands for security;
2. **Encryption-at-Rest:** This type of encryption protects stored data when it is not being used;
3. **End-to-End Encryption:** In E2EE, data or information is encrypted at one end and transmitted in the form of ciphertext to reach the other

[32] „World Password Day 2022: How safe are password managers" <https://m.timesofindia.com/gadgets-news/ > accessed 05 May 2022

[33] Dev Kundaliya. „UK bans devices with weak passwords"< https://www.computing.co.uk/news/> accessed 30 April 2024

[34] Lily Hay Newman. „End-to-End Encryptions" Central role in Modern Self-Defense" <https://www. wired. com/story> accessed 05 July 2022

end, where it is decrypted. That is when you trust only the website or network such as WhatsApp which is not a public place. Consequently, hackers or any third party cannot read your data or information while it is transmitted from one end to another or resting on the server. In ***Nivrutti v. State of Maharashtra & Pooja,***[35] the Court considered the WhatsApp policy of end-to-end encryption which provides the security to the users where the messages, photos, videos, voice messages, calls and documents can be seen, heard or read only by the sender and the receiver. Thus communication is secured such that not even WhatsApp has the power to go through any user's messages.

E2EE is a method of securing communication which prevents third parties from accessing data while it is transferred from one end system or device to another. It is a system of communication where only the communicating users can read the messages. It is regarded as safer because it reduces the number of parties who might want to interfere or break the encryption. It ensures that only you and the person you are communicating with can read or listen to what is sent, and nobody in between, not even WhatsApp. The messages are secured with locks and only the recipient has the special key to unlock and read the messages.[36] For e-mails, it has to be encrypted in order to protect your communications since we do not really want any third party to get hold of our sensitive information and use it for criminal purposes. Encryption is a enabled by 'Code Obfuscation – a process of encrypting and complicating lines of code, data and communication loops, that gives hackers immense difficulty in interpreting and changing existing information.[37] This goes to show that encryption is a vital means to advance and respect the human rights of privacy between a sender and recipient of a message. The secured communication protects human rights in the society where everyone needs privacy and security. To this end, a company called Business for Social Responsibility (BSR) has published a report about the human rights impact of end-to-end encryption which found out that end-to-end encryption is overwhelmingly positive and crucial for protecting human rights and as a mechanism for checking digital abuse. This is in tandem with the United States (US) government and the Federal Bureau of Investigation

---

[35] (2020) 2 AIR Bom R (Cri) 762

[36] „What is end-end encryption? <https://www.ibm.com/topics/ > accessed 08 April 2022

[37] Does Obfuscation Affect Code Performance" <https://www.premptive.com/> accessed 17 February 2023

(FBI) which has long argued that comprehensive encryption will make criminal investigation difficult to apprehend criminal suspects thus endangering the public and national security. To address this concern, BSR recommended that *Meta* should explore other mechanisms like providing safe and responsive reporting channels for users plus the analysis of unencrypted metadata to curtail potentially problematic activities without bothering to have a direct communication access. New research keeps developing daily about encryption tools that will protect our private and sensitive data from quantum computers. For example, in the United States, the Department of Commerce's NIST has chosen four designed encryption algorithms to withstand the hacking of a future quantum computer and protect digital information.[38] A quantum computer is a type of computer that is 158 million times faster than the most sophisticated supercomputer we have in the world today and can perform in four minutes what it would take a traditional supercomputer 10,000 years to accomplish.[39] In recent times, a group of researchers have however claimed that this same quantum computer is capable of cracking the encryption we use to protect emails, bank accounts and other sensitive data. This claim has been debunked by security experts.[40] Nonetheless, the essence of E2EE is to assure users of social media platforms that they have a trusted space where they can communicate freely without encountering interactions they don't want.[41]

Sometimes, sometimes standard encryption like the two methods of encryption mentioned above is not always good enough to secure our private data. Even WhatsApp has advised its users to add an extra layer of security to the two-step verification by setting up a pin to our WhatsApp account more secure. That is where zero-knowledge proof (ZKP) and zero-knowledge encryption comes in, which both offers superior privacy and data protection because your data is always secured due to the fact that the decryption key lies with the user, so that only you can access the encrypted data. Equally, a ZKP allows the verification of information without disclosing

---

[38] Esther Shein. „NIST selects four encryption algorithms to thwart future quantum computer attacks" <https://www.techrepublic.com/article/ > accessed 05 July 2022

[39] Mark Smith. „Quantum Computing: Definition, facts & uses" <https://www.livescience.com> accessed 05 July 2022

[40] Matthew Sparkes. „Quantum computers break major encryption method, researchers claim" <https://www. newscientist.com/article/2353376/> accessed 05 January 2023

[41] Lily Hay Newman, „Meta Tries to Break the End-to-End Encryption Deadlock" <https:// www.wired.com/story/ > accessed 08 April 2022

the underlying data, thereby offering a higher degree of security and privacy to sensitive information.[42]

5. OBSCURITY ON THE INTERNET

Obscurity is the deliberate act of insignificantly hiding oneself. It is the state of being unknown to many people or it could be something that is difficult to see. In the context of cybersecurity, a company can hide its security systems just to reduce the probability of it being attacked or stolen. That means you must take the normal digital security measures to avoid catastrophic scenarios and data leaks from attacks. These include authentication methods, encryption, application security, data security, antivirus software, cryptography and other intrusion prevention systems that have earlier been discussed in this book. However security by obscurity is quite different from the regular digital security methods because it consists of hiding your files in a non-visible place. Thus security by obscurity is defined as the processes and methods to hide some data or system. Secrecy is a vital factor of this method. By this, the systems do not openly disclose some information. The effect is that only those who know where to search will find it. For example, when you use a non-indexed link to share data on the Internet, then you are practicing security by obscurity. The disadvantage of this obscurity method is that the secrecy to protect your data may end up dangerous if you are the only one privy to it, and so what happens if other co-workers including your trusted ones have no idea? Won't the secrecy die with you? No wonder, cybersecurity professionals have criticised the security by obscurity method because it cannot prevent damages when attacks occur. However they have suggested that if a company can use security by obscurity as an extra layer and combined with other security methods, then security by obscurity will become a powerful method to reduce the chances of cyber-attack.[43]

6. DATA PRIVACY

The right to privacy is guaranteed and protected by Section 37 of the 1999 Constitution of Nigeria which provides that the privacy of citizens, their

---

[42] Sandeep Babu. „What is a Zero-Knowledge Proof in Cybersecurity and How Does it Work?" <https://www.makeuseof.com/> accessed 10 June 2023

[43] Vinicius Fulber-Garcia. „Understanding Security by Obscurity" <https://www.baeldung.com/cs/> accessed 25 December 2022

homes, correspondence, telephone conversations and telegraphic communications is guaranteed and protected. This right includes the right of an individual to exercise control over his personal data. In a simple sense, privacy has to do with the power you have over your information on the Internet because only you can control or limit what you want others to see your digital footprints you leave behind. In ***K.S. Puttaswamy* v. *Union of India*,**[44] the Court ruled that the ability of a person to control his own life would also encompass his right to control his existence on the Internet because the right to privacy is a fundamental right under the Constitution,

As companies, organisations and Internet users are increasingly being targeted daily; data privacy too is equally under attack. For instance, Google uses our data that we post on the Internet, to personalize our searches and post advertisements of their services. This demonstrates that Internet users' data are collected, stored, and used without their express consent. While using these data, their identities, preferences, habits and activities are tracked, analysed and may be sold for profit or power. This can bring undue attention or exposure of data to threat actors.[45] However, this data is stored remotely via the Internet instead of on-site, giving us little control over the use of our personal information. That is why it is generally believed that once we are on the Internet, it is beyond our power to control our privacy or limit our exposure since the Internet cuts across boundaries. This is however an erroneous impression.

a. What is Data?

Data is the representation of information or concepts that are being prepared in a form which is suitable for us in a computer.[46] It is a type of information security that deals with how the facts about us are being properly handled. In other words, the consumer wants to know how their personal information is collected, used, stored and shared. Data can come in the form of statistics, figures, observations, graphs, observations and other collection of information. According to the Nigerian Data Protection Regulation (NDPR) 2019, there are two categories of data which consists of Sensitive Data and Personal Data. The new Nigerian Data Protection Act

---

[44] (2017) 10 SCC 1

[45] Sammy Nathaniels. „The Sketchy Pathway of Data Protection: How to Navigate It" <https://hackernoon.com/> accessed 19 May 2023

[46] Section 58 of The Cybercrimes Act 2015

(NDPA) 2023 under Section 30 defines sensitive personal data as the personal data relating to an individual's genetic and biometric data, to uniquely identify a natural person, race or ethnic origin, religious or similar beliefs, such as those reflecting conscience or philosophy, health status, sex life, political opinions or affiliations, trade union memberships and other information prescribed by the Data Commission.

Regarding the safeguards applicable to protect sensitive information, Article 2.6 of the NDPR on data security provides that 'Anyone involved in data processing or the control of data shall develop security measures to protect data; such measures include but not limited to protecting systems from hackers, setting up firewalls, storing data securely with access to specific authorized individuals, employing data encryption technologies, developing organizational policy for handling personal data (and other sensitive or confidential data), protection of emailing systems and continuous capacity building for staff.

Across the globe, there has been frequency of violations to data privacy especially when non-users who have not subscribed to any software service suddenly could get to see their details published on a software database. In other words, our data is not safe, even if we don't use a app.[47] A man once filed an application against Truecaller claiming he is not a registered user of Truecaller, yet the software listed and published his name and phone numbers as a user without his consent. However, the High Court of Lagos State dismissed the matter on jurisdictional grounds.[48] So, which organizations are collecting or processing our personal data? In the first place, it is only fair that consumers must give their consent to companies that collect and capture their data before their personal information are given out. Thus privacy statement needing our consent goes like this: '*I would like xxxxx to share my information with select partners so I can receive relevant information about their products and services.*' We must also know why our data is being collected because such information can be misused to create dangerous situations or threat to peoples' lives. In ***ACLU & Ors v. Clearview AI***,[49] the plaintiffs filed a lawsuit against the defendant alleging

[47]Jenna Roach. „Don"t use Tik Tok? The China-owned social network may still have your data"< https://cyberguy.com/security/> accessed 30 June 2023

[48] Wole Olayinka. „The People v Big Tech: Nigerian takes Truecaller to court for alleged violation of privacy rights" <https://techcabal.com/2019/09/30/ > accessed 09 May 2022

[49] 2020 CH 04353 (Cir. Ct. Cook City, Ill

violation of their privacy rights under the Illinois Biometric Information Privacy Act (BIPA), after it was revealed that the defendant had offered the data of residents enabling private companies and government to have access to the database of those residents. The plaintiffs asked the Court to order the defendant to delete their faceprints from the data and cease capturing new faceprints unless they comply with BIPA consent procedures. The plaintiffs also claimed that the defendant's violations of their privacy has posed a disastrous threat and affront to their human rights.[50] The United Kingdom (UK) has become the fourth country to take enforcement action against the firm of the defendant following France, Italy and Australia after it was revealed that the firm takes publicly uploaded pictures from Facebook, Instagram and other sources without the knowledge of the platforms or any permission to create a global facial recognition database. Consequently, the UK's privacy watchdog has ordered the firm to pay the sum of 7.5 million pounds and delete the data of UK residents.[51] However, this may not necessarily be the position in the data obtained from public websites. In ***HiQ Labs Inc. v. Linkedin Corp,***[52] the US Court held that unauthorized data scraping (copying data or information of users from public websites) is legal. This means that the law does not criminalise scraping publicly available Internet information.

If there is a need for consumers to mobilise a class action against companies that are involved in data breach, they must have the *locus standi.* The Ally data Breach class action lawsuit is a good example where the Court in the case of ***De Medicis et al. v. Ally Bank et al.***[53] held that the consumer behind the proposed class action lawsuit had not shown that their credentials were misused and thus did not have the standing to file the complaint.

It should be emphasised that our data is valuable because we can use it anywhere. Since the aim of cyber-attacks is to get at our data and use it for criminal purposes, we can can prevent this data breach by keeping our data safe, by deleting old data and using strong passwords. In ***R v. Gold,***[54] a

---

[50] <https://www.aclu.org/cases/aclu-v-clearview-ai> accessed 09 May 2022

[51] Monica Freitas. „Clearview AI Fined in UK for Illegally Storing Facial Images" <https:// hackernoon.com/clearview-ai-fined-in-uk > accessed 12 June 2022

[52] D.C. No. 3:17-cv-03301-EMC of the United States Court of Appeals for the Ninth Circuit

[53] (Case No. 7: 21-cv-06799)

[54] (1988) 1 AC 1063

hacker was able to easily memorise the password details which consisted of the letter 'A' repeated several times. So, what do we do? We need to update our security software, train our employees and ourselves on data encryption; be vigilant of the warning signs of cybersecurity attack; monitor unusual behaviour or irregularities; Investigate suspicious files; run anti-virus scans or anti-malware programme;' and review system communication.[55]

It should be noted that Internet users do not expect Internet service providers (ISPs) to expose or sell their web browsing history and habits, geo-location data, app usage, health information and the content of their communications without their consent or share their sensitive and personal information to advertisers, otherwise hackers, identity thieves and foreign governments can take advantage of the information. Consent is a fundamental and established principle in law. Article 2:1 9(d) of the NDPR provides that personal data must be secured against all foreseeable hazards and breaches such as theft, cyber-attack, viral attack, and dissemination, manipulations of any kind, damage by rain, fire or exposure to other natural elements. However free sources on the Internet can give anybody access to our name, home address, e-mail address, phone number, birthday and even the names and information of our siblings. In May 2022, the Spanish Data Protection Agency imposed a penalty on Google for transferring data to third parties without a legal basis to do so and for hindering citizens' right to erasure, access and modify data contrary to Articles 6 and 7 of the European General Data Protection Regulation.[56]

Note that data privacy does not mean you will be invisible to the world or that it can hide us from the government, after all we all leave digital footprints on the Internet. When you visit a website, it collects information about you, your location, your browsing habits and preferences which determines what type of newsfeed and advertisements you will receive. So, one way or the other, we have an online identity however we also have the right to remove ourselves from people-search websites and if we do this it makes us feel more secure when we know we can get our privacy back especially from online users who may have potential criminal intent against us. In this context, "privacy means the right to be free from public attention

---

[55] Cybersecurity vs. Data Privacy <https://amtrustfinancial.com/blog/ > accessed 02 February 2022

[56]. „Spain fines Google 10 million for giving data without permission" <https:thesaxon.org/spain> accessed 19 May 2022

or the right not to have others intrude into one's private space uninvited or without one's approval. Privacy means we are able to stay away or apart from others without observation or intrusion. It also includes the protection of our personal information from others. The right to privacy extends to anything that is private and personal to him including communication and personal data."[57] However, it is interesting to note that there are some privacy companies that can remove our data from the Internet or search sites especially where there is a Court other to that effect.[58] Article 3:9 of NDPR provides that:

> The Data Subject shall have the right to request the Controller to delete Personal Data without delay, and the Controller shall delete Personal Data where one of the following grounds applies: (a) the Personal Data are no longer necessary in relation to the purposes for which they were collected or processed; (b) the Data Subject withdraws consent on which the processing is based; (c) the Data Subject objects to the processing and there are no overriding legitimate grounds for the processing; (d) the Personal Data have been unlawfully processed; and (e) the Personal Data must be erased for compliance with a legal obligation in Nigeria.

Is data privacy regulated under the law? Yes because if privacy rights are violated, it can pose greater risks to an individual's security, privacy and safety. In 2022, the U.S. Internal Revenue Service (IRS) accidentally released thousands of taxpayer data records on its website because of a technical issue which was caused by a third-party contractor who was hired to handle a database. The records leaked both private and sensitive information, Even though the IRS apologized for the error and the contractor was sacked, some victims still filed a suit against the IRS, alleging the agency violated their right to privacy.[59]

---

[57] See ***Incorporated Trustees of Digital Rights Initiative* v. *NIMC*** Suit No. AB/83/2020. See also SERAP 2020 Report titled „We are all Vulnerable: Crackdown on Data and Digital Rights in Nigeria"

[58] Cindy Coleman. „How LEOs can reclaim personal privacy online" <https://www.police1.com/police-products/ > accessed 02 February 2022

[59] Larry Lease. „IRS Mistakenly Releases Taxpayer Data Due to Technical Glitch" <https:// original. newsbreak.com/@larry-lease-1591168/2865533080604/ > accessed 28 December 2022

For a start and before the data protection laws were enacted in Nigeria, the right to privacy can only be enforced under Section 37 of the 1999 Constitution which provides that the privacy of citizens, telephone conversations and telegraphic communications is hereby guaranteed and protected. Thus Internet service providers should respect a customer's right to privacy under this law by not sending unsolicited text messages.[60] Privacy regulations in Nigeria are governed by the Nigeria Data Protection Act 2023, Nigeria Data Protection Regulation (NDPR) 2019 and its Implementation Framework of 2020. However, the NDPR does not apply to the use of data in the advancement of national security, safety, public health and order by Federal agencies, State, or Local government, persons/organisations expressly appointed to carry out such duties, the investigation of criminal offence and tax offences. Aside from Section 37 of the 1999 Constitution of Nigeria, other regulatory frameworks are Cybercrimes (Prohibition, Prevention) Act 2015, the Nigeria Communications (Registration of Telephone Subscribers) 2016, the Central Bank of Nigeria Protection Framework 2016, the Freedom of Information Act which protects data in records of public institutions and the Credit Reporting Act 2017. [61]

Rights of data consumers or subjects are constitutional rights. People have the rights to be secure in their homes. In Nigeria, Section 37 of the Constitution provides that that the privacy of citizens, telephone conversations and telegraphic communications is hereby guaranteed and protected. The components of these rights means that nobody including the government can spy on you or place you under surveillance, without any just cause. It means nobody can use your personal data without your consent and if your data is misused or stolen, such criminals would be sanctioned. Everyone maintains their social boundaries in a democracy. You are assured that your personal information is confidential and that you have control over your data. You are entitled to your freedom of speech and thought which are protected. It gives you a right to protect your reputation and finances online as well.[62] Personally, to protect your data privacy, you may insist you

[60] ***Ezugwu Anene* v. *Airtel Nigeria Ltd,*** Suit No. FCT/HC/CV/545/2015 (Unreported). See also ***Godfrey Eneye* v. *MTN Nigeria Communication Ltd.,*** Appeal No: CA/A/689/2013 (Unreported)

[61] AbdulKareem Abu. „A Comparative Analysis of the Nigeria Data Protection Regulations (NDPR) 2019 and the Illinois Data Transparency and Privacy Act (SB2330) 2020

[62] Emmaline Soken-Huberty. „10 Reasons Why Privacy Rights are Important" <https://www.humanrightscareers.com> accessed 09 May 2022

do not wish to be recorded when you are attending an online programme, although some apps do indicate they are not collecting your data except you wish to provide your data willingly. Their privacy notices may openly declare that your data is not shared with unaffiliated third parties or companies so that those companies won't need to market their products to you.

So, how then can you protect your data? Privacy expectations are higher. Be mindful when you are sharing vulnerable or risky details that may reveal private aspects of your life which could be susceptible to abuse.[63] Reject computer prompts demanding that you link your accounts to different profiles and other accounts. Manage your identities on your own and resist apps and services that may want to consolidate and connect all of your accounts and services together.[64] In ***ACLU & Ors v. Clearview AI,*** the parties in the suit submitted a settlement agreement to the Court to the effect that the defendant firm will be permanently banned nationwide from making their faceprints' database available to most businesses and other private entities while the firm will also be barred from selling the access to their faceprints' database to any entity including the state and the Police for five years. Note that X (Twitter) was sanctioned for misuse of public information concerning the users of X (Twitter) when it was alleged that X (Twitter) was using their information to help companies send targeted advertisements to consumers.[65]

Public advocacy and awareness on the rights of data consumers is important. Article 15 of the NDPR Implementation Framework 2020 provides that NITDA shall organise or facilitate seminars, workshops, conferences and other information dissemination programmes periodically, to improve public awareness, acceptance and compliance with applicable data protection laws. However, when an individual voluntarily gives information to a third party such as banks, the privacy interest in that information is forfeited. Thus in ***United States v. Miller,***[66] the Court held that a defendant had no right to privacy in his banking records as they were business records belonging to the bank. Every January 28, the world celebrates the World

---

[63] *United States* v. *Jones* 565 U.S. 400 (2012)

[64] Cindy Frenkel. „How to Set Healthy Boundaries Around What You Share Online" <https://www.wired .com/story/> accessed 09 May 2022

[65] TCR Staff, „Twitter to Pay $150 M Civil Penalty for Misuse of Public Information" <https:// thecrimereport .org/2022/05/27/ > accessed 31 May 2022

[66] 425 U.S. 435 (1976)

Data Privacy Day to create awareness about the importance of respecting privacy, safeguarding data, ensuring data trust and data protection best practices.[67]

It should be noted that not all data breaches are criminal in action. For example if I mistakenly share classified information with a colleague in my office or if I leave my computer unattended to and my e-mail inbox open with my personal information exposed to my colleague, that is not a criminal data breach so far as the colleague does not forward it to another person for malicious use.[68]

b. Case Study on Zoom Terms of Service

Zoom is a videoconferencing app or a video communication platform that many of us rely upon to host training workshops and webinars. In March 2023, Zoom changed its terms of Service when Zoom claimed the right to use their customer's video, audio and chat data for its artificial intelligence (AI) programmes. The new terms specifically gave Zoom the rights to any "data content, files, documents, or other materials (collectively, Customer Input) in accessing or using the Services or software, and Zoom may provide, create or make available to you, in its sole discretion or as part of the Services, certain derivatives, transcripts, analytics, outputs, visual displays, or data sets resulting from the Customer Input (together with Customer Input, "Customer Content)". These Customer Content rights will give Zoom the right to redistribute, publish, import, access, use, store, transmit, review, disclose, preserve, extract, modify, reproduce, share, use, display, copy, distribute, translate, transcribe, create derivative works, and process Customer Content." Zoom also has a perpetual, worldwide, non-exclusive, royalty-free, sub-licensable, and transferable licence to carry out the Customer Content rights. The implication of these terms of service is that people's data and content would be used to train AI language models without the user's consent. Expectedly, this generated a lot of controversy and criticism from the public. Thereafter, in July 2023, Zoom updated its Terms of Service to read: "Notwithstanding the above, Zoom will not use audio, video or chat Customer Content to train our AI models without your consent." A lawyer has said despite this change of Terms of Service, Zoom

---

[67] The awareness day addresses significant privacy issues for data consumers or data subjects

[68] Auger G., Scott J., Helmus J., Nguyen K., *'Cybersecurity Career Master Plan'* (2021 Packt Publishing)

can still use the data derived from our conferences and materials, without our consent."[69] This calls for vigilance on our part.

c. Data Highlights

i. **Privacy** - Our personal information includes our names, numbers, location, gender, cell phone habits, purchase history, photographs, online credentials, etc. Just like we do not want somebody to snoop into our bedroom from the window, similarly that is how we do not want people to pry into our online data. No one should therefore compromise our personal identity. Our privacy should be protected. This means it is not advisable to record and share all our personal information online because privacy violation can happen anytime we reveal our own information and so, when we post our information, we cannot control what will happen to the information.

ii. **Data Protection** - is the safeguarding of data and sensitive/personal information from abuse, tampering, damage or loss. It involves the relationship between the collection and determination of data, the public perception and expectation of privacy and the political and legal underpinnings surrounding that data, Data protection is important because data is a valuable asset for businesses and individuals, hence it needs to be safeguarded from unauthorized access, misuse or theft.[70] Most importantly, data protection is a fundamental right.[71]

iii. **Data Protection Laws –** are laws that control how control how people, businesses and governments gather, use, keep and exchange personal data. These laws are vital for preserving user rights, privacy, and personal information. Weak or outdated data protection laws usual makes companies not to comply with the data regulation law. In this digital era, data protection rules must adhere to global norms and standards.[72] In Nigeria, the foremost law on data protection is the Nigeria Data Protection Act, 2023.

---

[69] Elizabeth Napolitano. „Zoom"s terms of service changes spark worries over AI uses. Here"s what to know" <https://www.cbsnews.com/news/zoom/> accessed 10 August 2023

[70] Sammy Nathaniels. „The Sketchy Pathway of Data Protection: How to Navigate It" <https:// hackernoon. com/> accessed 19 May 2023

[71] *European Commission v. The Bavarian Larger Co. Ltd* (Case C-28/08) ECJ

[72] Ibid.

iv. **Data Harvesting** – Most online companies and organizations engage in data harvesting when they use the videos we watch, or the online questionnaire we fill and the links we open, to send adverts and newsfeed to us. This arises through frequent collation and processing of enormous volumes of personal data done without the knowledge or agreement of the data subjects because of the unexpected and rapid expansion of data-driven technologies like artificial intelligence, biometrics, blockchain and clod computing. Through these tools, they can access our profiles; predict our likes, our purchases, our interests and intentions. Our data is therefore valuable to these companies and this largely creates risks and vulnerabilities. See the 2010s Facebook Data Privacy scandal which focussed on the collection of personally identifiable information (PII) of up to 87 million users by a British political consulting communication firm. In 2021, the personal data pertaining to 533 million Facebook users was made public on an online forum.[73]

v. **Data Breach** - This is when records of people are exposed and their confidentiality is violated. Exposed data contains our names, dates of birth, social security numbers, physical addresses, gender, information assets and other personal information that could lead to identity theft and fraud committed by hackers. Information asset is the data about people and their financial records. In Nigeria, some banks were sanctioned by NDPB after proper investigation on data privacy and protection was carried out on them. For Data privacy breaches and other violation of peoples' rights, companies risk fines, jail term, and remediation course as consequences.[74]

vi **Challenges on Data Subjects** – Loss of independence and control over personal data; Privacy and dignity violation; Exposure to different risks and consequences, including discrimination, fraud and identity theft;

[73]Michael X. Heiligenstein. „Facebook Data Breaches: Full Timeline Through 2023" <https://firewalltimes.com/> accessed12 May 2023

[74]Emma Okonji. „NDPB to Sanction More Banks, Telcos. Schools over Data Privacy Breach" <https://www.thisdaylive.com/index.php/2023/06/> accessed 29 June 2023

Absence of appropriate redress procedures or remedies; Decreased faith and confidence in data processing agents and actions.[75]

Vii Philosophy of Dataism – This concept was introduced in 2013 by an American political commentator, David Brooks who interrogated the increasing influence of data and its interpretation in various aspects of society. In his words, "dataism is the belief system that regards AI as the most fundamental and powerful force driving human progress that is capable of reducing human biases."[76]

viii. Software Privacy Day – The awareness day every January 28, encourage users to spare a thought about where their data actually goes when it is posted on the Internet, because software data privacy is built to protect the privacy of its users. Internet users must ensure that their online communications are secure. There must be verification of the identity of the users (authentication). Users themselves should not deny that they sent their messages out, at some later point in time (non-repudiation).

7. THE RIGHT TO BE FORGOTTEN

Under the Nigerian Data Protection Act 2023 and the Nigerian Data Protection Regulation 2019, data subjects or owners have the right to right to request the Data Controller to delete their personal data if their personal data is no longer necessary for the purposes for which they were collected; if the data subject withdraws consent on which the processing is based; if the data subject objects to the processing and there are no overriding legitimate grounds for the processing; if the personal data has been unlawfully processed and if the personal data must be erased for compliance with a legal obligation in Nigeria.

In some other jurisdictions, the right to erase one's details from the Internet is called the 'right to be forgotten'.[77] This right is founded on the notion that criminal convictions should be blotted out or forgotten when

---

[75] Michael X. Heiligenstein. „Facebook Data Breaches: Full Timeline Through 2023" <https:// firewalltimes.com/> accessed12 May 2023

[76] Skellos Maloudakis. „Dataism: Idea or Ideology" <https://hackernoon.com > accessed 25 August 2023

[77] „Everything you need to know about the "Right to be forgotten" <https://gdpr.eu/rigt-to-be-forgotten/> accessed 12 April 2022

those individuals seek employment, insurance or other opportunities. In some countries' data protection laws, individuals have the right to ask organisations or data controllers to delete their personal data from the Internet especially if there is a legal ruling to that effect.[78] The Supreme Court in Argentina held that search engines are not responsible for any content they index. That, is search engines are not responsible for the content they have not created except they take other actions to alter the content or take other defamatory steps.[79] In ***Rodriguez v. Google LLC***,[80] the claimant filed a complaint accusing Google and Yahoo of inappropriate use of her personal image, linking her with pornographic websites. She also wanted her name to be removed from two search engines which were responsible for causing harm to her reputation, privacy and image rights. She claimed that by including copies of her photographs in their search results, the defendant had violated her right to control her image under the Argentine Copyright laws based on the law which says 'Any person who is negatively affected by the content can file a request with the search engine to remove the offending content.' However, these requests can be filed in cases where a person is linked to child pornography, genocide, racism, and photomontage or photo manipulation while an injunction can be granted when the issues affect minors. In a similar vein, the European Court of Justice enshrined the right to be erased if the information is no longer necessary or if it directly causes damage to a person's reputation. For the right to be admissible, the victim must precisely identify the offensive content and prove how the offensive content causes damage.[81]

Case Study

Delhi HC restrains 9 YouTube channels from sharing content on Aaradhya Bachchan's health: 'Every child has right to be treated with honour and respect.'[82]

Certain miscreants merely for the sake of publicity over a period of time have been circulating videos on YouTube that the daughter of a

---

[78] *Google Spain SL & Google Inc.* v. *AEPD & Mario Gonzalez* Case C-131/12. ECLI:EU:C:2014:317

[79] See also *Nicholas Okoye* v. *Ladun Liadi, Google Inc & Others LD/170/2012*

[80] 3.20 CV-04688

[81] „Google victory in Argentina: search engines are not responsible for content they index" <https://en.mercopress.com/2014/10/31/ > accessed 12 April 2022

[82] Written by Malavika Prasad and posted 20 April 2023 < https://indianexpress.com/article/cities/delhi/>

Bollywood actor has been critically ill or that she was dead. The application for interim relief sought to temporarily restrain nine (9) entities from sharing videos which breaches the privacy of the plaintiff's family. The Delhi High Court completely restrained nine (9) entities running YouTube channels from sharing on platforms across the Internet any content related to the health or physical condition of the said daughter of the Bollywood actor. The Court therefore restrained the nine (9) entities from creating, publishing, uploading, sharing, disseminating, or transmitting the images and videos relating to the state of health or physical condition of the child mentioned in the application. In the words of the Judge, "every child is to be treated with honour and respect be it a child of a celebrity or a commoner" and dissemination of misleading information to a child especially as regards the physical and mental health is completely intolerable in law. Issuing notice on the interim application to all the defendants, the Court directed Google LLC which runs YouTube, to reveal to the plaintiffs as well as place on affidavit the "identity and all contact details" of the 9 entities. It further directed the ministry of electronics and information technology to ensure they block access to all such content uploaded by defendant YouTube channels as well as any other similar videos or clips containing similar content on the child. The Court further castigated Google for providing a platform where misinformation is being circulated to the public. Thus it is crucial with many less reputable websites containing malicious software that can compromise security.

8. GENOMIC DATA

It is commonly known that hackers are always after passwords, emails or credit card information. Beyond these, hackers also want to have access to our genealogical data or genetic information. Genomic data are central to basic science research, pharmaceutical drug and vaccine development, disease diagnosis and prediction, ancestry tracing and forensic investigations. These applications require information fidelity and appropriate availability as cybercriminals may want to misuse the genomic data to invade our privacy, gain an unfair competitive advantage, or inflict harm that causes devastating effects on individuals, companies and nations.[83] No doubt, users of DNA

[83] „NCCoE Virtual Workshop on the Cybersecurity of Genomic Data" <https://www.nist.gov/news-events/events/2022 > accessed 26 May 2022

database have to give permission before they release their profiles because if there is any hacking or breach to their privacy settings, their profiles will be visible to all other users, including law enforcement agents who use the ancestry or DNA-related sites for solving criminal cases. Where user data is compromised or downloaded during the breach, the breach is likely to erode users' trust in the database which contains a wealth of extremely personal information like family relationships, ancestry and potential health risks.[84] Sensitive data stolen from genetic data could also be used for blackmail or corporate espionage if it gets into wrong hands. These genetic data privacy companies usually have to increase their cybersecurity protocols to eliminate the possibility of attacks or vulnerabilities through genetic encryption.

Notably, some scientists are collecting genetic material and data of patients with ailments such as cancer, diabetes and sickle cell anaemia in Nigerian hospitals. However for genetic research, two essential values of any scientific research should be borne in mind: (1) the need to share data broadly to maximize its use for on-going scientific exploration; (2) the need to protect research participants' privacy.[85] This aligns with the Nagoya Protocol on Access to Genetic Resources and the Fair and Equitable Sharing of Benefits 2014 which establish a framework that helps researchers' to access genetic resources for biotechnology research and any other related activities. It sets out obligations for the contracting parties to take measures in relation to access genetic resources, benefit sharing and compliance.[86]

9. RISKS OF PUBLIC WI-FI

Public Wi-Fi networks can be found in popular public places like hotels, airports, shopping centres, parks and university campuses, among other places. A public network gives access to the public to connect to the Internet. Unlike a private network which is restricted, many people connect to the public network when they are not at home. Though it is usually free, it is your choice to avoid risky activities because with public WI-FI, others are likely to see everything you are downloading, your traffic and may even inject

[84] Emily Mulin. „The Era of DNA Database Hacks is Here" <https://onezero.medium.com/> accessed 27 May 2022

[85] En Espanol. „Privacy in Genomics" <https://www.genome.gov/about-genome-policy/> accessed 27 May 2022

[86] For further research on how organizations can protect genomic data, see the Cybersecurity Framework (CSF) Profile for Genomic Data, 2023, available at <https://crsc.nist.gov>

false information into your device. A hacker can snoop on data transmitted by victim through his home router WI-FI that is not password protected. As a user, you weigh the risks and opt to take them. Here are some of the possible risks associated with a public Wi-Fi where bad actors have figured out ways to use public USB ports to introduce malware and monitoring software onto devices:

a. **Fake Connection** – a fake Wi-Fi hotspot set up by a hacker or cybercriminal which mimics a legitimate hotspot provided by a business which is nearby (hotel, shop);
b. **Packet Sniffing** - a piece of hardware or software to monitor network traffic. Hackers may use this for criminal purposes;
c. **Session Hijacking** - when someone takes over your Internet session. This could be active hijacking or passive hijacking;
d. **Juice Jacking** – this is when public power outlets at free charging stations are being illegally modified to steal your phone's data;
e. **Shoulder Surfing** – when someone watches over your shoulder so as to nab valuable information such as your password, ATM pin or credit card number, at the moment you key it into an electronic device.

Malicious users tend to infiltrate the Internet systems of unsuspecting users by stealing their information. It is always better to be safe than to be sorry, since hackers can set their own Wi-Fi hotspot under the name of an innocent wireless hotspot provider and if the users chose to connect to a free Wi-Fi network. Many company secrets have been stolen from business executives who use their laptops in hotels or restaurants with public Wi-Fi.[87] So, if you suspect someone wants to hack your device using Wi-Fi, cybersecurity experts advise that we should use a Virtual Private Network (VPN), a tool for ensuring that our Internet privacy is intact because the main reason why people prefer to use VPNs is the need to stay private while online. Also use Secure Sockets Layer (SSL) connections, unplug the Wi-Fi and turn off the Wi-Fi. Factory reset and every device you have that connect to the Wi-Fi. Learn how to change your Service Set Identifier (SSID). That is your network's name listed with a check mark. Then hide it and keep it from broadcasting. The Wi-Fi owner can consider whitelisting those he wishes to grant access to his Internet connection. A whitelist is a cybersecurity

[87] „What Does Public Network Mean" <https://www.techpedia.com/definition/26424/ > accessed 02 May 2022

strategy that approves a list of e-mail addresses, domain names or applications, while denying all others. The goal is to protect computers and networks from potentially harmful applications.[88]

Be careful about public Wi-Fi networks and when you share your Wi-Fi password in your neighbourhood because it may implicate you in a crime you don't know anything about. In ***United States v. Sandell,***[89] the defendant moved into a new area and asked his neighbour's for permission to use their Wi-Fi so he could access the Internet and register his sex offender status. The neighbours agreed. Subsequently, investigators knocked on the neighbour's door, questioning them and searching their home. One of the residents then told the officers about sharing their Wi-Fi password with the defendant. Over the course of conversation with Police officers, the defendant admitted that he downloaded child pornography. The officers immediately obtained a search warrant and collected the defendant's laptop, thumb drives and DVDs. Based on the evidence gotten from his devices' search, the defendant was thereafter charged with distribution, receipt and possession of child pornography.[90]

In ***Tobias McFadden v. Sony Music Entertainment Germany GmBH,***[91] a business in Germany operated an unprotected wireless network which could be accessed freely and anonymously by customers and passers-by. The intention of the business owner was to increase traffic to the business website and to promote the business. A user used the network to upload music to the Internet which was in breach of copyright law. The copyright owner immediately notified the owner of the business that his copyright had been infringed. The European Court of Justice held that making an unprotected wireless network available to the general public fell within the scope of the 'mere conduit' defence[92] since the Wi-Fi service was provided free to users and consequently, there was no infringement by the business owner.

---

[88]Brien Posey, Peter Loshin. „Application Whitelisting" <https://ww.techtarget.com/searchsecurity/definition/> accessed 19 April 2022

[89] 2022 WL 619156 (8th Cir. 2022)

[90] Ken Wallentine. „Don't loan your Wi-Fi to sex offenders" <https://www.lexipol.com/resources/blog/ > accessed 19 April 2022

[91] Case C-484/14 < https://www.icaew.com/library/subject-gateways...> accessed 20 April 2022

[92] That is the business owner has not initiated the transmission of the infringing data; did not select who is to receive the transmission and did not modify the information in transmission.

On the lighter side, the World Wi-Fi Day is observed every 20th June to celebrate the great contribution and innovation that Wi-Fi brings to our daily lives. acting as a charter to connect the unconnected. It is also a day to recognize and celebrate the significant role Wi-Fi is playing in cities and communities around the world and understand how Wi-Fi is helping to reduce digital poverty as well as helping to bridge the digital divide globally.[93]

93 <https://wballiance.com/world-wi-fi-day-home/> accessed 20 June 2022

Chapter 7

CYBERCRIME INVESTIGATION AND EVIDENCE

Technology has become an indispensable tool of communication, which has contributed to the growth of cyber-dependent and cyber-enabled crimes. Cyber-dependent crimes are crimes carried out against computers and any other related devices, such as hacking into a computer and undermining the security of networks; while cyber-enabled crimes are crimes committed that use computers and other devices to carry out other crimes. For example, cyber bullying, trolling, making malicious and offensive communications online, etc.,[1] unfortunately, technology has also become a tool that that cyber criminals use for covering their tracks but what they don't know is that people leave digital footprints on their communication devices and social media as evidence. Where a computer has been compromised for example, the indicators of compromise (IoC) will be used as evidence left behind by a cybercriminal or malicious software to identify a the perpetrator or security incident. This aligns with the Locard's Exchange Theory which says there is always a record left behind in any activity we do. Basically, the Evidence Act 2011 and the Evidence (Amendment) Act 2023 governs the admissibility of evidence in Nigeria. Evidence is the available body of facts or information indicating whether a belief or proposition is true or valid. Evidence can be direct or indirect. Direct evidence is first-hand evidence which consists of eyewitness account, confessions and videos or camera. Indirect evidence is circumstantial evidence which could be biological or physical and useful for implying a proof of fact to link a perpetrator to a crime. Direct and indirect evidence can apply to cyber-dependent and cyber-enabled crimes depending on how the perpetrator commits the crime because perpetrators of crime

[1]Thames Valley Police. „Protect Your World-the risks of cybercrime" <https://www. thames valley police. uk/> accessed 20 June 2022

use the Internet through their websites, personal social handles, computers, phones and other devices to engage in crime. The sources of digital evidence are evidence extracted from smartphones, laptops, social media, open source, cryptocurrency, CCTV, drones, and citizen-shared digital evidence while on the inside of a computer are components such as hard drives, external drives and other electronic devices and the information they contain.[2] In the words of David Williams of Microsoft, "90 per cent of crime has some type of digital evidence tied to it."

Note that all actions taken by computers are carried out by human beings and not the computer by itself. Computer actions are therefore human-enabled and so if a computer-enabled crime happens, digital detectives and investigators will be needed to utilise their technology expertise to trace the IoCs of the digital identities or assets and link it to the perpetrator in the cyberspace.

Trace evidence enables an investigator to identify the evidence stored in computer systems that we cannot see at face value or be explained with the naked eye except with the aid of experts. Clearly, cyber attackers may not be able to totally conceal themselves without leaving their digital footprints on the Internet. The reality is that whenever we visit a website, send an e-mail, download an image or do online transaction, we leave digital footprints which means leaving a trail of our activities on the Internet.[3] A digital footprint, sometimes called a digital shadow or an electronic footprint refers to the trail of data we leave when using the Internet. According to the National Institute of Standards and Technology (NIST), there are hardly any major crimes that do not have connections to digital technology since criminals use cellphones and computers to perpetrate their criminal activities even offline while some of the data on their phone or other device might be relevant to an investigation.[4] For Internet users, it is what you reveal on the Internet that will become public information. Notwithstanding the falsehood you post on the Internet, your digital footprints will prove otherwise, through observation, investigation and analysis. In this digital age and the

---

[2] A.K. Gupta, G.S. Sodhi. V., Rarh *et al.* „Digital Forensics" <6317_et_6317_et_et.pdf> accessed 20 June 2022

[3] Vincent Tabora. „Digital Footprints-Leaving Trails Behind For Cyber Forensics" <https:// medium.com/the-infosec-journal/> accessed 20 May 2022

[4] NIST Update to Software Reference Library Will Aid in Criminal Investigations. <https://www.forensicmsg.com/> accessed 01 July 2022

advancement of computers, forensic science has become the standard in modern investigation. This has raised the following concerns:

a. The need to develop sound digital forensic processes and practices;
b. The need to generate acceptance of digital forensics evidence in Courtrooms built upon sound evidence which starts right from evidence-gathering process and how law enforcement officers or forensic investigators carry out their tasks;
c. The accreditation and audits of experts and agency managed by a global organisation and supported by internal boards. Accreditation means that the evidence cannot enter into the Court system more smoothly and without as many questions;
d. The need for experts to know what needs to be examined while identifying and collecting items with potential evidentiary value and what does not need to be examined because there are some evidence that is not critical to building a case;
e. The need to share critical skills/knowledge in forensic expertise and exchange programme with other professionals in the tech industry so as to increase their ability to successfully process and document digital crime scenes.

Nonetheless, time is of the essence in any investigation exercise. If timely victim identification is slow, perpetrators will continue to commit crimes leaving all of us vulnerable to crime. Consequently, victims of crime will become frustrated while offenders will escape justice.

1. COMPUTER-PROCESSED EVIDENCE

Evidence is the means by which facts relevant to the guilt or innocence of an individual at trial is established. In Nigeria, the general admissibility of evidence is governed by Section 6 of the Evidence Act 2011(as amended in 2023). A piece of evidence is admissible once it is found relevant and irrespective of how it was obtained. Cybercrimes are computer crimes. Section 418 of the Criminal Law of Lagos State 2015 defines a computer as a device that computes, especially a programmable electronic machine that performs high-speed mathematical or logical operation or that assembles, stores, correlates or otherwise processes information. When you use computer or any e-device to perform a function, the evidence emanating from it is considered an electronic document. Electronic evidence is all such materials that exist in electronic or digital form which can exists in the form of computer files, logs and metadata or network data.[5] Text messages generated from Global Satellite Mobile (GSM) system into mobile phones are also computers when the message so generated is printed out as the printed copies thus become primary documented evidence.

Section 258(1)(d) of the Evidence Act 2011 defines a document to include any device by means of which information is stored, recorded or retrievable including computer output. A GSM gadget with useful information can therefore be tendered in evidence together with the message or information stored by it. For example, an online trail of incriminatory statements is sufficient proof and once tendered and admitted in evidence, it becomes documentary evidence.[6]

During the course of criminal investigation involving computers or security incidents, intelligence is required as a tool for effective identification mechanism. Ordinarily, intelligence is all about assessing a range of information to help in the process of identifying, apprehending and convicting criminals.[7] These ranges of information in physical intelligence are usually backed by proper investigation and evidence on the Internet. In the same vein, digital intelligence is the data collected and preserved from digital sources and data types – such as smartphones, computers, and the cloud – and the process by which agencies collect, review, analyse, manage and obtain insights from the collected data to run their investigations more efficiently. Acquisition of relevant knowledge and skill is crucial as well as the need to deploy science and technology in evidence-gathering.

However, sharing and copying evidence obtained from devices could be damaged or when altered could be problematic while trying to save the evidence. This affects the ability to use the data to bring suspects to justice and protect citizens. So how can investigators maintain the integrity of the chain of evidence? This can be achieved through careful documentation, handling practices and technology. Note that the original version of the data that is extracted from a digital device is called the Gold Copy – (a version

---

[5] See the United Nations Office on Drugs and Crime Vienna Comprehensive Study on Cybercrime Draft. February 2013

[6] *Orogun & Anor.* v. *Fidelity Bank PLC (2018) LPELR-46601 (CA)* See also*: Emerging Markets Telecommunications* v. *Etisalat & Adoyi (2021) LCN/14954(CA)*

[7] Patrick Coleman. „Detectives & Spies: the worlds of investigation and intelligence" <https://www.visitnesm.org.uk/post/ > accessed 30 April 2022

that must stay in its original position) before it is acceptable by the Courts. This Gold Copy needs to be carefully stored and tracked with several duplicate copies made as it is shared, so that the original data remains golden – in its original state. The Gold Copy has to be in its original state otherwise it may affect the investigation exercise. It is also advisable for investigators to set up special data repositories where the original data can reside while forensic investigators can work with the duplicate copies even as they are documenting the sharing of data and taking photographs of the labels that are attached to the devices.[8]

In light of this, the International Organisation of Computer Evidence (IOCE) defines digital evidence as information stored or transmitted in binary form that may be relied upon in Court.[9] Information that is stored electronically whether from the Internet or web activity is digital evidence as long as it has been broken down into digits, binary units of ones and zeros that are saved and retrieved using a set of instruction called software, code or stored data and transmitted by electronic devices which takes or processes input and then calculate the results from the input. An input is any information or instructions that are fed into a computer. Therefore, any evidence discovered through a "trove of electronic communications detailing online information or videos" or through any digitized platform about a particular crime will qualify as digital evidence.[10] Digital media is a lot different from traditional media (e.g., conventional radio, television and newspaper). As a rule, digital evidence usually comes in hard and soft copies and is admissible under Section 84(1) and (2) of the Evidence Act of 2011. The Section provides that 'in any proceeding, a statement contained in document produced by a computer shall be admissible as evidence of any fact stated in it of which direct oral evidence would be admissible, if it is shown that the conditions in subsection (2) are satisfied in relation to the statement and computer in question…' In ***Anyaebosi* v. *RT Briscoe***[11] the

---

[8] Heather Mahalik and Stephanie Kurtz. „Computer Forensics: Best Practices for Sharing Digital Data" <www.forensicmag.com> accessed 23 July 2021

[9] Read more from Shahzed Saleem. „Protecting the Integrity of Digital Evidence and Basic Human Rights During the Process of Digital Forensics". <www.diva-portal.org> accessed 02 December 2020

[10] See the United Nations Conventions on the Use of Electronic Communications in International Contracts 2007

[11] (1987)3 NWLR (Pt. 59) 84. See also *Nuba Commercial Farms Ltd* v. *NAL Merchant Bank (2001)16 NWLR (Pt.740) 510; Kubor* v. *Dickson (2013)4 NWLR (Pt. 1345) 538* – According to the Supreme Court, the correct interpretation to be given to Section 84 of the Evidence Act where electronically

decision was that once evidence originates from computers, it is secondary evidence. Computer in this context is defined in Section 258(1) of the Evidence Act 2011 as a device for storing and processing information and any reference to information being derived from other information is a reference to its being derived from it by calculation, comparison or any other process. In ***GTB v. Bendu Peter Services (Nig) Ltd***,[12] the Court held that information in the documents that are downloaded from the Internet or websites of private organisations must still comply with requirements of Section 84 of the Evidence Act which ascertains the authenticity of the device from where the document was produced in consonance with with Section 34(1)(b) of the Evidence Act before according it as probative, credible and capable of being believed.[13] Section 41 of the Evidence Act takes into cognizance, electronic devices in the ordinary course of business. In the same vein, Section 10(4) of the Administration of Criminal Justice of Lagos State (ACJL) 2011 defines 'record of arrest of suspect' to include pictures, fingerprints, sample and biometric details. Section 15(4) Administration of Criminal Justice Act (ACJA) 2015 provides that statement of suspect shall be recorded electronically or a retrievable video, compact disc or such audio visual map, while Section 232(3)(a) of ACJA 2015 also provides that the Court may receive evidence by video link where it is necessary to protect the identity of the victim or a witness.

What is the position of the law as regards electronically generated evidence? In ***Okpu v. Trust Bond Mortgage Bank PLC,***[14] the Court of Appeal held that it is no longer the law that a party must produce a certificate of computer generated document in all circumstances before any computer generated document can be admitted in evidence. Rather the law now is that a party who intends to use a computer generated document having filed and frontloaded it, must at trial, either produce the required

---

generated document is sought to be demonstrated is that such electronically generated evidence must be certified and must comply with the preconditions laid down.

[12] (2022) LPELR- 57064 (CA)

[13] Section 34(1)(b) provides that " in the case of a statement contained in a document produced by a computer, the question whether or not the information which the statement contained, reproduces or is derived from , was supplied to it, contemporaneously with the occurrence or existence of the facts dealt with in that information; and the question whether or not any person concerned with the supply of information to that computer or with the operation of that computer or any equipment by means of which the document containing the statement was produced by it, had any incentive to conceal or misrepresent facts"

[14] (2021) LPELR-54554(CA)

certificate or give oral testimony as to the use of the computer in producing the said document, both of which method is permissible. However, where any evidence emanating from digital or scientific evidence is wrongly admitted by a trial Court contrary to Section 84 of the Evidence Act 2011, the Appellate Court can expunge the evidence.[15]

As technology changes, cyber threats will also respond to the changes. To address growing cybersecurity threats, digital forensics plays a central role in helping businesses protect their most valuable digital assets. Having described digital forensics as the recovery and investigation of digital devices and digital materials often related to crimes,[16] sometimes when recordings are not clearly visible to the ordinary eye, a digital forensics expert who specializes in searching electronic devices for evidence is called upon to utilize his digital investigation tools to detect and filter relevant evidence because digital issues require a certain level of expertise and specialised knowledge. That is why it is very important that victims should retain and preserve material evidence that may be required for disclosure and interpretation in the future. Once a message is posted online or through any electronic device, the Police can use it as evidence but the victim must endeavour to preserve the chain of custody of the evidence. For example, in case of defamatory posts or messages sent on social medial platforms such as WhatsApp, Twitter, Facebook, Instagram, Snapchat and several others, a victim should not delete the messages of the perpetrator. He must take screenshots of the messages or make multiple copies (if it is a video) including having a cloud-based backup and secure it. In ***R v. Noble & Johnson,***[17] a text message from a girlfriend of a defendant was admitted into evidence as the text message suggested that the defendant was in a certain place with a firearm. However, where social media messages are deleted, they can be retrievable by using various forensic recovery software methods and tools which can be handled by forensic experts. Such messages can be cited as direct evidence or circumstantial evidence, depending on the circumstances of the case. For large scale offences involve terrorism, child pornography and drug cases that may have to depend on getting material evidence from the perpetrator's device and in the absence of perpetrator,

---

[15] *Emmanuel* v. *FRN* (2018) LPELR-45235 (CA)
[16] How Well Do You Know Digital Forensics. <eccouncil.org> accessed 02 October 2020
[17] (2016) EWSCA Crim 2219

his password, the Police may apply to the Court for a warrant to unlock the phone or break into its command devices.[18] Section 46(5) of the Nigerian Data Protection Act 2023 provides that where any material to which an investigation relates or consists of information stored in an electronic device, the Data Protection Commission may require the person named to produce such material or give access to the Commission to conduct an inspection on the material. There is therefore the need to make a strong investment in digital forensics tools and incident response technology to safeguard all evidence relating to cyber communications and dealings.[19]

2. EVIDENCE IN AUDIO RECORDING OF VIOLENCE

When an individual misuses technology to harass, intimidate and threaten others, the receiving smartphones can collect evidence of abuse. Digital violence starts when you are harassed through your phone which has audio a recording app. An audio recording is a recording of a conversation between people. Audio recording applications built in your device allow you to record edit, share, save and delete the recording. Therefore, maintaining the record of events is important in criminal and civil proceedings because any recording that is being video-graphed or audio-graphed dispels doubt until it is proved otherwise. Moreover they are classified under electronic evidence which has statutory backing and could be admissible if the rules of condition that is laid down under the Evidence Act are met. In audio recordings, the information is automatically stored in phone records which are invaluable source of evidence for criminal Court cases. This enables you to strengthen your case by providing proof in domestic violence incidents. So what does this involve? Protect yourself first. If it is an intimate-partner violence, do not let the perpetrator have access to your phone so that he does not delete the evidence right in front of you. Do not let him know you are capturing evidence in the first place, because you can place the devices anywhere without it being visible. Consider your phone password safety. For preservation, use the video screen or audio recorder built in your phone. Make a transcript of the recording or get someone else to do that for you or

---

[18] Nicola Antoniou & Eleanor Scarlett. „Social Media in Court: Your Tweets could be used as Evidence against you." <https://theconservation.com> accessed 12 December 2020

[19]Magnet Forensics Survey: Digital Forensics to Increase to Combat Cyber Threat" <http://www. forensic mag.com/584624/> accessed 28 March 2022

use online transcription tools, so that the Court can easily listen to it when the recording gets to them. Ensure there are no background noises in the audio. That could serve as a distraction. Document the abusive voice or behaviour. This helps the Court to have first-hand knowledge of the cyber abuse. Print out your call history or call logs if the abuser repeatedly keeps calling you. Take the screenshots of the phone log. It is legal to record a conversation that you are part of. You can tell the Court why you have done so even without the perpetrator's consent particularly if it is an on-going violence. Do not edit the audio recording in any way or criminally merge other recordings that are not part of the abuse. Keep a copy of the recording in its original form. Document the time and date of the recording. Ensure the volume control is high so that investigators can hear any whispered utterances. You can transfer the audio file to another device. But if the authenticity is contested, you will need to produce the original copy. You might also need to prove the identity of the criminal or abuser because the perpetrator can deny his voice. But if it is a phone, the phone number will always be associated with the owner of the phone (Truecaller app).[20] Evidence of in-person surveillance of the perpetrator could also strengthen your case. Enlist the help of a digital forensics scientist who possesses a formal scientific qualification and with his verification tools, he can help you secure the digital evidence. or can equally advise you on how evidence on devices are likely to get wiped away or compromised in any way, because securing and protecting digital evidence has always been a problem where law enforcement officers and detectives fear that their stored digital evidence may become lost or broken.[21] Note that the advantages of recorded cases are: It provides valuable insight into the violence. It gathers evidence against the suspect or exonerates him and provides closure.

Court's Evaluation of Digital Evidence

Realise that digital evidence is generated by technological and other communicative devices from where digital information can take many forms -

---

[20]BC Society of Transition Houses. „How to Preserve an Audio Recording as Evidence" <https:// bcsth.ca/ digitalevidencetoolkit/ > accessed 24 December 2021

[21]Sergeant Joshua Lee. „5 reasons digital recordings are valuable for suspect interviews" <https://www. police1.com > accessed 11 April 2022

metadata,[22] recorded video,[23] e-mail, conversation history[24] and a person's post on social media. Communication devices are any equipment that aids the analogue, digital or wireless transmission of data, including mobile phones, tablets, laptops or Bluetooth devices.[25] These devices can provide convincing evidence for critical incident data collection. This is because online conversations, emails and social media posts have been used successfully in a variety of Court cases as long as the authors have been authenticated. For example, the person making the chat should agree that it is his voice and the evidence must connect that person to his mobile phone.[26] In ***Katz v. United States***,[27] acting on a suspicion that Katz was transmitting gambling information over the phone to clients in other states, Federal agents attached an eavesdropping device to the outside of a public phone booth used by Katz. Based on the recordings of his conversations, Katz was convicted for illegal transmission of the gambling information. On appeal, Katz challenged his conviction arguing that the recordings could not be used as evidence against him. The Court of Appeals rejected his contention, noting that there was no physical intrusion into the phone booth itself.

In the International Criminal Court (ICC) for example, evidence has shifted from physical witness testimony to digital evidence and it is now relied upon during international trials. Prosecutors and defence counsel can use digital tools in building their cases on international war crimes, genocide, survivors and victims, human right offenders and violations. However, the evidence must meet evidentiary standards when relevant and reliable footage that can stand the test required in the Criminal Court are captured. See the decision of the Court in the Democratic Republic of Congo 2018 incident where photo and video evidence were admitted in the *'Affaire Castro et Kizito'* case, using the *eyeWitness app*, a ready-for-Court technology developed to

[22] This is a data that provides information about other data. For example, author, date created, date modified and file size.

[23] A video tape recording, video clips or a motion picture of a television production.

[24] This is your text conversations that are organized by your contact name and date.

[25] See Section 46 of the Nigerian Correctional Service Act 2019

[26] „Can Online Chats Be Used as Evidence in Court?" <https://www.azizilaw.com/> accessed 20 March 2022

[27] 389 US 347 (1967)

streamline the documentation of international crimes.[28] In Rwanda, photo evidence/eye evidence with contra capture technology was recognised as a specific technology and accepted by the ICC.

As a defence counsel, what do you take into consideration in digital evidence? Sometimes, prosecution may try to rely on social media evidence which can include uploaded photographs, videos, profiles, wall posts, list of friends and status updates. In ***Campbell v. Texas***,[29] a defendant was charged with aggravated assault following a domestic dispute with his girlfriend. At the trial, the prosecution presented Facebook messages sent from the defendant's Facebook account in which he regretted striking his girlfriend and asked for her forgiveness. The defendant later denied sending the Facebook messages, contending that both he and his girlfriend had access to each other's Facebook accounts. The Court agreed that though electronic communications are susceptible to fabrication and manipulation, it will nonetheless admit the evidence based on circumstantial evidence because the messages were sent directly from the defendant's Facebook account.

Social media evidence can corroborate other types of evidence such as witness statements, physical evidence or contents of documents. Equally, the identification of the defendant's voice is admissible under the Evidence Act. But the voice has to be audible before it can be deemed accurate and admissible.[30] The audio must be discernible because if the sound is of low quality, it may affect the admissibility of the evidence. Generally the Court should be mindful of the fact that electronic evidence in this digital era and apps, could be susceptible to tampering, alteration and transposition when recordings on mobile phones are copied from the hard disc of the computer to a pen drive before it is being handed over to the prosecution. In a case where the accused person contended that he had nothing to do with the conversations of the intercepted mobile phones copied from the hard disc of the computer to a pen drive, the Court held that the electronic evidence in the form of the intercepted conversations and the call detail records is inadmissible because it does not satisfy the requirement of the law under

[28] C. Gabrielle, K.Matheson and RV Liorente. „Incorporating Digital Technology in the Investigation of International Crimes: Lessons from the DRC" <https://www.justsecurity.org/76780/ > accessed 20 March 2022

[29] No. 03-11-00834-CR,2012 BL.225712 See also, Justin P Murphy and Adrian Fontecilla. „Social Media Evidence in Criminal Proceedings: An Uncertain Frontier" (Digital Discovery & e-Evidence 2013)

[30] Alaba Omolaye-Ajileye. „*Electronic Evidence*' (Jurist Publications Series 2019)

Section 65 B of the Evidence Act of India. The Court also observed that cases involving calls that required using a software application for investigation should not be done manually to avoid tampering.[31] Since general notion is that scientific evidence hardly lies, the investigator must be able to link the defendant's voice conversations to the crime while the prosecutor must substantiate the evidence before bringing the case to Court. However in the recent case of ***Mahani Prasad Ram Tripathi@ MPR Tripathi v. State of UP,***[32] the High Court of India held that a telephone conversation between two accused persons cannot be excluded from evidence on the ground that it had been obtained illegally, regardless of whether it was intercepted. The Court also noted that the telephone conversation recorded in the digital voice recorder was not the solitary evidence relied upon by the prosecution since the prosecution proposed to produce additional evidence during the trial.

In Court settings, it is possible that the expert witness may want to present his evidence through a reconstructive graphic illustration by virtual media such as computer-generated visualisations, digital displays or three-dimension virtual simulations to get his message across to the Court especially where the specific details are complicated or scientific. In many instances, these forms of visual media are demonstrative as it helps explain theories better and can potentially help make the evidence more relevant and easier to understand.[33] This would not however affect the admissibility of evidence.[34] The expert may also want to explore the e-discovery evidence that could be presented during civil or criminal litigation.[35]

In any case, aiming to utilize technology in crime investigation, the Supreme Court has directed that a mobile app used by the Delhi Police for videography and photography of crime scenes be tested by experts. In the words of the Court, "if the mobile app so developed is found to be fool-

---

[31] See *Jagdeo Singh @ Jagga* v. *The State* on 11 February 2015 available at <https://indiankanoon .org/doc/ 35565129/> accessed 20 September 2022

[32] (No.935 of 2023) See also <https://legalvidhiya.com/allahabad-high-court-rules-recorded-phone-conversations-admissible-as-evidence-regardless-of-illegall-obtained/> accessed 01 September 2023

[33] Damian Schofield, „The Use of Computer Generated Imagery in Legal Proceedings" <https://www. academia.edu/resource/work/29669331> accessed 01 August 2022

[34] *Commonwealth* v. *Serge 586 Pa. 671, 896 A .2d 1170 (2006)*

[35] „What is E-Discovery?" <https://www.proofpoint.com/us/threat-reference/> accessed 04 March 2023

proof and reliable by the experts, their report will be of great assistance to the Court before any directions are passed."[36]

3. VOICE IDENTIFICATION

Research scientists on voice technology have claimed that the word we say and how we say them can be used to identify us and even build our profile.[37] Voice can be used as a form of identification to nail a perpetrator of crime or verify his identity. Voiceprint identification is based upon spectrographic voice analysis and in the United States; the law varies from jurisdiction to jurisdiction. Voice spectrographic is founded on the scientific assumption that no two human voices are alike. The spectrograph is an electromagnetic instrument which analyses sound and disperses it on paper in a graphic array of time. The spectrograph operator compares a known voice with an unknown voice by pairing spectrograms of similar words and phrases from each voice to determine whether they were uttered by the same speaker. In ***State v. Williams***,[38] the Ohio Supreme Court held that expert testimony and exhibits based on voice spectrography analysis are admissible if they are relevant and will assist the Court to assess the level of threat or violence. In reaching its decision, the Supreme Court examined three analytic models for assessing admissibility of scientific evidence which hinges on reproducibility and standardization. They are (a) the general acceptance standard as set forth in ***Frye v. United States***[39] (b) the reliability standard and (c) the testimony by experts under Evidence Rule 702.

In accordance with the Frye rule, the experts must be experts in speech, hearing and related fields or experts who have worked with voice spectrograph. The reliability standard means that the method must have gained some measure of acceptance and credibility to be meaningful in the forensic process. Note that the voice spectrograph expert will not just come to the Court to give a conclusion or verbal descriptions alone, rather he must be able to show some demonstrations through digital visual display. If the evidence has to do with voice identification, the expert must present his

[36] PTI. „SC directs testing of mobile app for videography/photography of crime scene by experts" <https://m.economictimes.com/news/india/> accessed 03 June 2022

[37] Matt Burgess. „The Race to Hide Your Voice" <https://www.wired.com/story/voice/> accessed 03 June 2022

[38] Ohio St. 3d 53, 446 N.E. 2d 444 (1983)

[39] 293 F. 1013 (D.C.Cir.1923)

tapes and spectrograms to authenticate the identity of the person's voice.[40] Essentially, in this ever-evolving criminal landscape, the investigator must be able to link the defendant's voice conversations to the crime while the prosecutor must substantiate the evidence before bringing the case to Court.[41]

Limitations

Although technology can accelerate investigative skills, evidence relating to synthetic content and voice examination could be limited by: low quality standards affecting the audible part of the recording, ethical dilemma, poor oversight and accountability, evidence interpretation and professional credentials, passive intelligence or lack of proper guidelines for the collection of digital evidence; Police may be unable to keep pace with the technology required in digital forensics to deal with voice clones and other deepfake technologies; lack of competent and trained digital media investigators to recover or retrieve evidence from mobile phones, especially where criminals deliberately damage their phones, submerge them in water, smash and even shoot their phones in an attempt to destroy evidence; no clear understanding of digital forensics to complement police investigation and good practices.[42]

In addition, limitations could also arise when transcripts of questioned and specimen voice recordings are not provided; or if an incomplete transcript is provided; or if there is a computer breakdown during the operation of transfer from the hard drive to the pen drive. Where a person uses AI to spoof another person's voice, voice spoofing verification tools could be vulnerable to a variety of voice spoofing attacks during replays, voice conversions and speech synthesis. A defendant can also claim his voice was mimicked by somebody else.[43] In this digital age, there are various voices changing hardware that allow anyone to quickly change the sound of their

---

[40] Ashar, Linda C. (1984) "Admissibility of Scientific Evidence: Voice Spectrography." Akron Law Review: Vol. 17: Iss. 4, Article 12. < https://ideaexchange.uakron.edu/akronlawreview/vol17/iss4/12 > accessed 24 December 2021

[41] Kelvin Pope. „6 ways Digital Investigations Will Change in 2024" <www.forensicmag.com> accessed 28 February 2024

[42] „NIST Tests Forensic Methods for Getting Data from Damaged Mobile Phones <„https://www.nist.gov> accessed 12 December 2022

[43] See *Jagdeo Singh @ Jagga* v. *The State* on 11 February 2015 available at < https://indiankanoon.org/doc/35565129/> accessed 20 September 2022

voice to a new voice. This voice anonymisation technology and deep fake voice cloning involve passing someone's voice through experimental software that will change or alter some of the parameters in the voice signal to make it sound different. Android phones for instance, have audio lab apps where users can edit, convert and compress audio recording including other inbuilt features such as split audio, reverse audio, voice change, karaoke effect, video trim, channel manipulation to create noise and wave generator. Spoofed voice samples can be produced by changing the original audio signal using recording, manipulating or mimicking.[44] Where evidence has been accessed by unauthorized people or tampered with, it may be difficult to build a case against a suspect. If hackers access the location where your voice data is stored and use it to impersonate you in payment scams, it could affect voice identification evidence. Some companies also collect voice prints and with the assistance of AI-generated technology, online behaviour attitude and emotion can be subjected and analysed into a summative data to develop a profile.[45]

4. INVESTIGATION AND MANAGEMENT OF A CYBERCRIME SCENE

Getting bad guys off the Internet could be tougher than getting bad guys off the street. For investigators, a cybercrime scene or a digital crime scene can be a more challenging process to manage than a physical crime scene. The perpetrator needs to be traced. Such tracing is a process that enables the criminal to be identified. You have to learn what it takes to be a cyber-investigator because evidence will be gathered digitally as they are digital exhibits from computer documents, e-mails, Internet histories, images and other electronic devices. It requires taking a painstaking investigative exercise because of certain challenges where the access is obtained remotely. For instance, most times cybercriminals get access to computer systems from their own homes and this holds true when the computer or smartphone belongs to a suspected hacker or a paedophile suspected of storing or sharing child pornography. The offender may also want to erase the data

---

[44] Hussain Dawood, Sajid Saleem *et al.* „A robust voice spoofing detection system using novel CLS-LBP features and LSTM" <https://doi.org/10.1016/j-jksuci.2022.02,024 > accessed 03 June 2022

[45] Matt Burgess. „The Race to Hide Your Voice" <https://www.wired.com/story/voice/> accessed 03 June 2022

thereby destroying the evidence.[46] Witnesses to the crime, usually the recipient of the offender's information may have evidence on their phones but the evidence needs to be extracted and correlated with the data from other phones owned by other witnesses. Notwithstanding this, the perpetrator leaves behind a cyber-trail. You must be a digital forensics investigator and expert in cyber operations in order to discover the traces in digital files such as deleted e-mails, chat transcripts, encrypted files, password protected files, formatted hard disks and even in messages hidden inside pictures, so that you do not destroy any evidence as soon you press a single key on the computer.

Addressing computer security or developing a cybersecurity plan is a process of coordinating all of the known vulnerabilities and being proactive about the unknown until the overall risk level is within a specified range. Design a network that hackers cannot break into. Computer security specialists use a procedure called Octave to assess the vulnerability of an information network. The first step in Octave is to identify all the vulnerabilities of a network. That is to find out, the ways in which an attacker could penetrate a system. The second step is to identify the risks of each vulnerability. That is to examine the potential damage that could be caused by exploiting it.[47]

Without any doubt, hackers are getting smarter by the day with the various techniques they are deploying. Digital forensics investigators usually want to detect the indicators of compromise or attack such as the mode of hacking, the identity of the hackers and advice on how to prevent future attacks. The unique skills needed by these experts are the knowledge they possess about log analysis, endpoints, understanding the cloud, dark web, malware analysis and forensic intelligence including the basics of phone networks, proficiency in forensic tools, curious and analytical mind, connecting the dots, communication skills and abiding by ethics.[48] To the layman, data is just an imaginary junk except it is interpreted by experts. In this vein, the goal of digital forensics is to collect, define and analyse the data to solve crimes by following digital footprints and reconstructing past events.

---

[46] Chalie Osbourne. „How to delete yourself from Internet search results and hide your identity online" <https://www.zdnet.com/article/ > accessed 11 May 2022

[47] Bruce Berkowitz. „Secrecy and National Security" <https://www.hoover.org/research/ > accessed 22 May 2022

[48] EC-Council

In order to maintain the chain of evidence custody, investigators use digital investigation software for better results as strong corroborating evidence. The chain of custody is the logical sequence that records the sequence of custody, control, treatment, analysis and disposition of physical or electronic evidence in legal cases.

The tool that allows investigators to analyse digital evidence in their environment are categorized as follows:

(1) **Call Detail Records (CDRs)** – Records of incoming and outgoing calls are the most impartial and reliable source of digital evidence today as this can reveal the date and time calls are placed. Printouts of CDRs can be taken from the computers/servers by a mechanical process and certified by a responsible official of the service provider.

(2) **Mobile Extractions** – the collection of a device's contents like pictures, e-mails, texts, videos, Internet navigation history, etc., from wireless carriers if the user and sender are both communicating through text messages.

(3) **Cell Site Analysis** - provides information of where telecommunication towers spread their signal and coverage.[49] These data obtained from service providers provide reliable evidence better than individual or personal social media data. Prosecution can rely on the evidence listed above. What if the perpetrator's computer or device is found? Modern phones track our physical location. The phone knows which cells are communicating. Our devices retain our Google search history such that numerous sites and services can use that data to personalize advertisements and other types of recommendations. A map app and location on our phone can tell us where a user of the phone is. The search history can reveal what the perpetrator has been up to, except he deletes his Google search cache.[50]

Digital intelligence in this context is the data collected and preserved from digital sources and data types – such as smartphones, computers, and the cloud – and the process by which agencies collect, review, analyse, manage and obtain insights from this data to more efficiently run their

[49] <https://securcube.net/phonelog/?gclid=CjwKC> accessed 01 April 2022

[50] Jack Wallen. „How to clear Google search cache on Android and why you should do it" https://www.zdnet.com/article/ > accessed 06 <April 2022

investigations.[51] Time is critical for the forensics investigator who must ensure the computer is not powered down so that he does not lose essential information when the power is up again or when he logs in. Take a snapshot of the computer first and the unencrypted passwords and the proofs of links that is displayed for forensic work. Follow the protocols for digital forensic analysis which can be found within the guidelines provided by your investigative institution. If you come across potential computer exhibits that are already powered down, they need to be seized as evidence and then investigated by experts. It is important to preserve the chain of custody by recreating the computer in a clean, sterile and forensic environment letting you access the evidence. This is called making a virtual replica of the suspect's computer.[52]

Digital forensics scientific process encompasses data collection, examination and analysis, reporting phase, expert testimony, basics of network forensics, computer forensics and mobile devices. The investigator must be able to properly handle policies, guidelines, and procedures; preserve and maintain evidence; observe best practices, and ensure evidence is not compromised with the overall aim of bringing cybercriminals to justice.

Law enforcement officers and digital forensics lab technicians, including analysts and examiners who are experienced in detecting cyber-attacks have to be careful with phishing emails that lead to files infected with malware so they don't infect other digital tools in the lab. If the investigator wants to extract a data from a computer device, the malware scan should be done first when the computer is running. Look for signs of malware activity. To a trained eye, a mobile device infected by malware may exhibit unusual behaviour. If the evidence you're looking for, appears to be missing, search for the back-up files that could confirm whether the data on the device has been altered. The report on the state of digital evidence must contain the potential impact of malware on the digital evidence and whether the critical data was affected by the malware. In his digital evidence report, the digital forensics investigator must state the following:

a. What type of malware is detected?

---

[51] Heather Mahalik & Jean-Phillipe Noat. „How Digital Analysts Manage the Impact of Malware" <http://www.forensicmag.com/3425?> accessed 04 February 2022

[52] Ron LaPedis. „Key steps to managing a cybercrime scene" <https://www.police1.com> accessed 30/11/2021

b. How does the malware attack device' functions like messaging?
c. Is it more of a human activity or malware activity?
d. What apps were operating on the device when the forensics investigator took over the computer investigation?

If the digital evidence is not secured against malware, the defence counsel at Court trial can argue that any investigation coming out from a malware-infested system is not to be regarded as legitimate evidence or that proper protocol has not been followed to maintain the chain of custody. So an investigator must stay on top of cybersecurity training to strengthen his case in Court.[53]

If there is no need to decrypt a phone, a search warrant can be obtained by Law enforcement agencies to conduct searches on a phone just as it is physically done in homes or workplaces in the course of crime investigation. This could also happen where crimes are committed electronically. Digital forensics investigators can issue warrants to cloud service providers such as Google and social media apps like Facebook and Twitter, to request for subscriber information such as phone numbers, Google accounts, and email addresses, although this may cause delay in criminal investigation because service providers are aware of the implication of infringing their user's right to privacy of their information since users have constitutional expectation of privacy.[54] In ***Carpenter v. United States,***[55] the Supreme Court held that a warrant is required by the Police to access the cell-site location information (CSLI) from a cell phone company (the detailed geo-location information generated by a cellphone's communication with cell towers).

In order to identify the mobile devices near the US Capitol riot, FBI once requested Google to identify all active devices in the area at a given time and date, when users were not able to erase their digital trails. FBI had to obtain a *Geofence* Search warrant which is a warrant that would be served on Google or any Internet networks to assist FBI to locate anyone in a given area using digital services. Geofence warrant is also called reverse location warrant. It means your devices has shown up near a crime scene or indicate

[53]Heather Mahalik & Jean-Phillipe Noat. „How Digital Analysts Manage the Impact of Malware" <http://www.forensicmag.com/3425?> accessed 04 February 2022

[54] Stephanie Kurtz. „How to Access Digital Evidence that Doesn't Demand Decryption" <https://www.forensicmag.com/3425-Featured-Article/ > accessed 17 June 2022

[55] *585 U.S No. 16-402 (2018)*

certain geographic area at a specific time. This is because Google's location history system is both powerful and widely used, as it leverages GPS, Wi-Fi and Bluetooth signals to pinpoint a phone within a few yards. Location history also works in a plane mode where phones can continue to receive GPS satellite signals. It can further show when users move their phones. The Geofence evidence can be admissible in Court if there is no security camera footage, no eyewitness account and no forensic evidence to show whether a person is at a crime scene. Despite the warrant, Google still strives to protect the privacy of their users even while supporting the work of law enforcement. The Police request is not automatic for Google would still consider the request for validity and constitutional concerns. Sometimes these investigators may object to producing any information at all, since users have constitutional expectation of privacy.[56]

Nevertheless, there are limitations that may become a barrier. Digital evidence stored in USB flash drives could be lost, damaged or stolen easily.[57] Strong encryption can make investigation harder for forensics examiners who want to solve crimes because images, messages and emails can remain hidden from a face-value view without a passcode or sophisticated technology to lawfully decode data and sometimes by the time they obtain the data, it may not present the full forensic picture that will build a convincing case.[58] The use of anonymising technologies can make it challenging for law enforcement to investigate cybercrime forums, especially when an encrypted browser commonly used to circumvent local Internet censorship. This is called The Onion Router (ToR) which is privacy and security tool or technique for engaging anonymous communication over a computer network. For digital investigation concerning a suspect website or webpage, the ToR network is a special network of computers on the Internet used to hide browsing activity, designed to conceal the true IP addresses and identities of its users. Many have reasoned that ToR is for those who are engaged in criminal activities.[59] Despite this characterization,

---

[56] „A Peek Inside the FBI"s Unprecedented January 6 Geofence Dragnet" <https://www.wired.com /story/fbi/> accessed 03 December 2022

[57] Ryan Parthermore, Saas Evangelist. „Why strong Evidence in the Cloud is safer, Faster and Better" <https://www.forensicmag.com/3425-Featured-Article/> accessed 28 October 2022

[58] Stephanie Kurtz. „How to Access Digital Evidence that Doesn"t Demand Decryption" https://www. forensicmag.com/3425-Featured-Article/ > accessed 17 June 2022

[59] Deborah Brown. „When Digital Rights and Cybercrime Collide" <https://www.hrw.org/news/2021/11/10 > accessed 04 February 2022

the ToR is still not considered anonymous because Internet service providers can trace and log connections between computers due to our browsers which can reveal our IP addresses, login details and private messages as well as the browsers we are using and its version. In line with the Locard's Exchange Theory, there is always a record left behind in any activity we do.[60] Locard's principle applies to the world of digital footprint because physical and logical evidence are hardly wrong. The evidence is there and the Internet never forgets. An investigator may also want to explore all the stages of the e-discovery solution that could be presented during civil or criminal litigation. E-Discovery is a form of digital investigation that attempts to find evidence in all electronically stored information (ESI) such as emails, and other forms of data.[61]

In May 2022, the National Institute of Standards and Technology (NIST) published a draft report titled *'Digital Investigation Techniques: A NIST Scientific Foundation Review'* which has reviewed the methods of how digital forensics experts extract data to analyse evidence from computers, mobile phones and other electronic devices. According to NIST, copying data, searching for text strings, finding timestamps on files, reading call logs on a phone are basic elements of a digital investigation which all rely on fundamental computer operations that needs to be properly understood.[62] Similarly in February 2024, the NIST released the official 2.0 version of the Cybersecurity Framework (CSF) which is a series of guidelines and best practices to reduce cyber risk and improve security posture.[63]

In the digital world, the preventive solution is playing a vital role in the area of raising cyber awareness to justify why prevention is always better than cure, because it is better to nip cybercrime in the bud than go through a cyber-attack.

5. MEMORY FORENSICS

Memory Forensics is a vital form of cyber investigation which allows an investigator to identify unauthorised and anomalous activity on a target

---

[60] <https://www.sciencedirect.com/topics/computer-science/onion-router> accessed 04 February 2022

[61] „What is E-Discovery?" <https://www.proofpoint.com/us/threat-reference/> accessed 04 March 2023

[62] „NIST Review Evaluates Digital Forensic Methods" <https://www.forensicmag.com/586019/ > accessed 12 May 2022

[63] Available in <https://www.nist.gov.cyberframework>

computer or server.[64] It is the process of capturing the running memory of a device and analysing the captured output for evidence of malicious software or computer virus. In other words, the actual programmes were running on a device when the memory dump was captured by the investigator. The memory dump is the snapshot of the memory you have captured to do the memory analysis. It means you are responding to a current or suspicious threat unlike in a hard drive forensics where you are responding to a malware or virus that had already taken place. Note that the memory of a device is known as Random Access Memory (RAM). To check the size of your hard disk and the amount of RAM on your laptop, open an application on your device. You will see the certain amount of RAM that is allocated to that application so it can run. The more applications you open, the more RAM will need to be allocated by the device. So when a device is being compromised, your first reaction will be to want to turn the device off to contain the threat. This approach is not considered the best because any malware that is running on the device is equally running on the memory at the same time, so if you turn it off, you will likely lose the network connection and the running process. This means by powering the device down, you will destroy valuable evidence as well. The preferred option is always to go for network containment. In other words, you isolate the device from the rest of the network to contain the volatile data or information in the memory. Note that memory forensics enables you to commence an investigation after you must have truly confirmed that your device has a malware running on it. As an investigative tool for first responders, you should capture the system data for later scrutiny. Experts also use several memory forensics specialist tools to respond to cybersecurity incident in order to identify potential malware and other compromised devices.[65] According to experts, the capability to perform memory and volatile data analysis is the backbone of any cybercrime investigative unit.[66]

---

[64] Graeme Messina. „Computer Forensics: Memory Forensics" <https://resources.infosecinstitute.com/> accessed 12 May 2022

[65] Neil Fox. „Memory Forensics For Incident Response" <https://www.varonis.com/blog/> accessed 10 December 2021

[66] „Researchers Use AI to Track Cybercrime in Louisiana and Beyond" <https://www.forensicmag .com/ 591799/> accessed 10 November 2022

6. SOCIAL MEDIA INVESTIGATION (SMI)

We are all enjoined to be careful of our social media footprints so we do not get into trouble. An officer once claimed that social media is one of the best means of tracking gang members because they are not only narcissistic but they also like to show off and that is why they can be easily identified on the Internet as questionable characters.[67] There is also the belief that people with faces depicting threatening expressions or muscular bodies on the Internet are likely to be seen as potential criminals.[68] These false assumptions portend danger as it can mislead us to stereotype these individuals as people who do bad things online. Whatever the case may be, social media sites have been a great source of gathering intelligence-led report about an individual's personality and data regarding his address, activities, schools, social circles, family, employers, professional associations and other raw information, for the purpose of evidence collection, collation, analysis and dissemination. Law enforcement agents as undercover agents can also use social media innovative tactics to collect evidence from our Internet pages and even from those we have online interactions with. Where a person is suspected as a cybercriminal, law enforcement officers can take on assumed identities by creating usernames to infiltrate or access the suspect's online networks by sending him friend requests to interact with him or pose as customers depending on the type of unlawful transaction the suspect is involved with on the Internet.[69] These law enforcement officers are Internet detectives who use the Internet as an investigative tool to track suspects. An Internet detective is someone who spends his time looking all over the Internet to prove someone's claim false.[70] Forensic tracing and tracking is important in online investigation which require such investigators to sift out what matters or what does not matter and detect Internet scams and the perpetrators. With this, law enforcement can use the evidence gathered against such suspect and they may go to the extent of asking social media

[67] Book excerpt: Called to Serve: The Inspiring, Untold Stories of America"s First Responders" <https://www.police1.com>

[68] McElvarney, T.J., Osman, M & Mareschal I, Identifying criminals: No biasing effect of criminal context on recalled threat" Men Cogn (2022) https://doi.org/10.3758/s13758/s13421-021-01268-w > accessed 12 April 2022

[69] ***United States of America* v. *Ross Ulbricht*** (No. 15-1815-cr (2d Cir. May 31. 2017)

[70] See:< https://www.urbandictionary.com/define.php?term=Internet%20detectice&amp=true> accessed 02 May 2022

platforms to surrender the suspect's data to them if there is a probable cause of suspicion.

According to history, the first social media platform known as Six Degrees was launched by Andrew Weinreich in 1997, followed by Friendster in 2002, Linkedin in 2003, Orkut, MySpace, Facebook in 2004, YouTube in 2005, Twitter (now X) in 2006, WhatsApp in 2009, Instagram 2010 and Snapchat in 2011including others which are used worldwide.[71] Much as social media platforms are useful for global communication, information and business connection, it has also been used as a process for finding and making a detailed analysis of an individual or organisations social media accounts for the purpose of providing assistance in criminal or civil investigation and adjudication of cases on fraudulent activities, data theft, background checks, or to establish defence of alibi.[72] Social media investigation provides a platform to collect evidence from social media posts, photographs/pictures, direct messages, group conversations and message IP addresses. This means, a social media platform's user account can be tracked together with a recorded time/date a user logs onto a social media app and his activities particularly when a user posts content on their social media network. Other data is also collected like a user's comments, likes, tags, reply to a friend's post, follows and other engagement data that third parties will find useful, to establish a person's character. In an Indian case, the Court held that the social media posts/blogs of a woman reflected she had reservations about the institution of marriage and live-in relationships.[73]

Essentially, our location can be tracked by Google, to help investigators provide more useful information about our whereabouts because Google records the things we have done and places we have been, based on location history.[74] The record thus leads to a possible identification, apprehension and prosecution of a perpetrator. Social Media Investigation (SMI) has therefore become a standard part of many investigations that may arise in case of any

---

[71] „Social Media Day 2022. Here"s all you need to know" <https://www.livemint.com/news/> accessed 30 June 2022

[72] Corporate Forensic Investigations. Social Media Investigation." <https://cyfor.co.uk/ > accessed 14 May 2022

[73] Express News Service. "Man accused of raping woman he met on Tinder granted bail, Delhi HC takes her social media posts into consideration" <https://indianexpress.com/article/cities/delhi/> accessed 27 October 2022

[74] Vincent Tabora. „Digital Footprints-Leaving Trails Behind For Cyber Forensics" <https://medium. com/the-infosec-journal/> accessed 20 May 2022

suspicious activity from alleged intellectual property theft, online defamation, drug use, insurance fraud, custody, divorce and criminal cases. In doing so, a social media investigator will search for key terms and posts relevant information to where and what he is looking for, based on the assumption that the data of the person wanted would likely be on Facebook, Twitter(X), Linkedin, Instagram, Wikipedia, YouTube and other social media platforms.

So, if you find yourself facing criminal charges, what you post on social media could play a role in the prosecution's case against you as prosecutors can use the information they gather on social media to connect you to a criminal activity. If you frequently troll others, sharing violence-related posts to abuse people or make threats against other users online, this could pass a message to investigators. The kind of language that you use, your public posts and photographs can equally show where you were or what you did around the time of the alleged crime.[75]

Case Study

A suspect tried to mislead investigation after making a Twitter (X) post containing picture and words allegedly against a particular religious community. The tweet was enough to incite feelings of hatred among people and detrimental to public tranquillity. After, another Twitter user verified the post was made from suspect's personal handle, the matter was subjected to investigation The suspect remained non-cooperative during the investigation. The suspect thereafter instructed his family to dispose of his mobile phone and laptop which he used for tweeting the alleged post in case he was apprehended. The Police eventually recovered the phone, laptop, invoices and the hard disk used for perpetrating the religious incitement. The Police subsequently deposited the exhibits at the forensic Science Institute to retrieve the tweets.[76]

Challenges

The challenges in online investigations often connect to the following issues:

[75] „How social media posts can be used as evidence against you" <https://www.mingledorfflaw.com> accessed 14 May 2022

[76] Express News Service. „Mohammed Zubair Posts Content that Triggers Religions Sentiment to remain trending on Social Media: Delhi Police to High Court" <https://indianexpress.com/article/cities/delhi/> accessed 31 October 2022

a. Cyber investigation is laborious and enormous without advanced technology tools. Gathering evidence online can be time-consuming especially if it is done manually. An investigator can therefore spend a lot of hours on social media because he may need to take screenshots of posts, photos and comments on many other social media accounts particularly if the suspect has multiple social media sites. Sometimes, online photographs can be misleading with today's AI technology which affords us the opportunity to edit or manipulate unwanted elements from our photos and replace them;[77]
b. Reasonable expectation of Privacy – In ***BC & Others* v. *Chief Constable Police Service of Scotland,***[78] a Police Force conducted a criminal investigation into a sexual offence alleged to have been committed by one of its officers. The Police Force seized the officer's phone and came across a WhatsApp group chat in which several other officers in their service have posted offensive messages. The claimants contended that in using WhatsApp messages to bring misconduct proceedings, the Police force had violated their privacy rights;
c. Social Media Investigation tools are relevant for collection, collation, analysis and sharing of information. On this basis, social media information widely reported against a suspect are not to be ignored as rumour, rather they are considered as sources of intelligence and information where cause and origin of facts can be inferred. Such preservation of social media evidence and other online content require the investigator to be armed with a sophisticated technology to help him search and monitor the activity of a targeted suspect These forensic preservation tools can quickly expand content from long collapsed posts, comment threads and replies on websites or social media accounts whether hidden or lesser-known platforms.[79] With Open Source Intelligence (OSINT) tools, a SMI can get information from publicly available sources by means of artificial intelligence to obtain possible matches to subject target. A social media investigator also looks into the social media posts, status, updates, photos and conversations of an individual. When conducting investigations, the

---

[77] Magic Erazer on Google is available to all Android phone users to transform photos.
[78] (2018) CSOH 104
[79] Peter Callghan.;5 Social Media Investigation Tools that Save You Time & Reduce Frustration" <https://blog.pagefreezer.com/ > accessed24 August 2021

investigator will be required to document such activities by compiling a report. Social media evidence has its place in Court as was evident in ***Zimmerman v. Weils Markets, Inc.***[80] In this case; the plaintiff suffered an injury while operating a forklift in the course of his employment at defendant's warehouse. The plaintiff later filed a suit claiming that he lost wages and was now burdened with an emotionally traumatic scar that prevented him from wearing shorts in public. The defendant thereafter took a look at the plaintiff's public social media profiles (Facebook & MySpace profiles) and discovered the plaintiff enjoyed bike stunts alongside photos of him with a motorcycle and facial injuries around the time of his alleged forklift accident. The defence also found pictures of the plaintiff's public Facebook profile directly contradicting his claim. The Court called for the plaintiff to turn over his social media login credentials and not to alter existing information on those accounts. The lesson is that what we post on social media can find its way to the Courtroom.

Can screenshots evidence taken by an investigator from defendant's laptop/chat logs suffice as valid? Surely, this could shed more light on the type of offence the defendant is being charged for. If someone has posted incriminating information that could help your case and the investigator takes a screenshot. But later the person deletes the post. How do you prove the deleted evidence because the challenge is when you transform a social media post into a simple JPEG, it strips it of metadata and makes it impossible to authenticate. Metadata provides information about digital data. When it comes to a social media post, it would include information about the author of the post, the message type, post date and time, versions, links, locations, likes and comments. Without this metadata, there is no way to prove that your JPEG copy accurately represents what was originally posted on the social media platform. All you have is just an image that could have been photoshopped or manipulated while the Court may not be satisfied with your evidence because screenshots are viewed with suspicion. In ***Moroccanoli Inc v. Marc Anthony Cosmetics,***[81] the defendant submitted screenshots of a Facebook page that illustrated how customers used some words. The Court ruled that there was no way to prove that the screenshots were an exact copy of what existed on the live Facebook site

[80] 2011 WL Keller, No. CV 12-72-M-DLC-JCL

[81] 57 F.Supp.3d 1203 (C.D. Cal. 2014)

because there was no way to authenticate the screenshots. In ***United States v. Vayner***,[82] the U.S. Court of Appeals held that the mere fact that a page with the defendant's name and photograph happened to exist on the Internet at the time of the investigator's testimony does not permit a reasonable conclusion that this page was created by the defendant or on his behalf.

Note that Police investigators can access People-Search Websites to look for wanted people. These website operators are data brokers who collect and sell personal information. Google, the search engine for example is a data broker. The sources of their information could be publicly available information downloaded from real estate transaction, voter registration, marriage licenses, divorce decrees, unsealed lawsuits and sex offender registrations. People-Search sites collect information or buy users data from Facebook, Linkedin and other popular online platforms. They also buy information from small companies that collect personal data from research surveys, mailing lists and business listings, but these are collected without the knowledge of the data subject.[83]

7. INTERNET SEARCH HISTORY

Internet users cannot be arrested for every topic they Google no matter how bad it is because you can be in the confines of your room and Google how to murder a person or how you can be a hacker. In fact, very few us expect these search results to be used against us in a Court of law. But the reality is our Internet service provider tracks all the websites we visit, the date that we logged in, the hours we spent on the website, what device we used to log in. whether we have bookmarked the topics and our specific location.[84] When you install a mobile app or you sign for any online service, you can be tracked on the app or online platform. When we visit a website, the page can capture our IP address. From there, you can be tracked based on your IP address that you used for accessing the Internet. It leaves a trail that can be checked as proof that a user visited a site. This can be implemented with site cookies which record your IP address, a timestamp

[82] 769 F.3d 125 (2d Cir. 2014)

[83] Dave Roos. „CanYou Remove Your Personal Info From People-Finder Websites?" <https:// computer. howstuffworks.com/> accessed 17 June 2022

[84] Law Offices of Christopher J. Cherreta. „Your Internet Browsing History and Its Use in Court" <https://www.wicriminaldefense.com> accessed 30 April 2022

and your device's name.[85] Search engines are built on preferences of the Internet user. Every time you search for information on the website, it tells the algorithm what you are interested in. As you keep searching, the algorithm gives you more similar feedback relating to any news you read on the net, except you take a stealth approach just for a change and do your research incognito mode to get a different result.[86] Even when you attend zoom meetings, there is record of the history of your recent meetings on your device because it is always indicated that the meeting is being recorded by the host or participant and that by staying in the zoom meeting, you have consented to being recorded although you have the option to leave or agree to stay, or we might even have a website that we so trust which tells us to log in using our Google or Facebook account, instead of logging in with our password. This is called Open Authorisation (OAuth).[87]

Your Internet search history is a component of your digital footprint. A digital footprint is your electronic footprint which can either be passive or active. An active digital footprint is when you share information about yourself on the social media. For example, when you post, comment, complete an online form, subscribe to a newsletter or agree to accept cookies on your browser. While a passive digital footprint is when information is collected about you without being aware. For example, when websites or advertisers collect your information based on the networking sites you have visited.[88]

Note that when you become a suspect or you are charged to Court, your search history can be considered as incriminating evidence or be used to support further charges against you. In other words, your search history record is corroborating evidence that can be made against a suspect with experts using their forensic tools that can acquire, extract and analyse evidence from a wide range of sources including mobile phones, tablets,

---

85 Vincent Tabora. „Digital Footprints-Leaving Trails Behind For Cyber Forensics" <https://medium.com/the-infosec-journal/> accessed20 May 2022

86 Megha Satyanarayana. „Critically Evaluating Claims". < www.theopennotebook.com> accessed 20June 2022

87 Roger Grimes, Josh Fruhlinger. „What is OAuth? How the open authorization framework works" <https://www.csoonline.com/article/3216404/> accessed 30 April 2022

88 „What is a digital footprint? And how to protect it from hackers"<https://www.kaperski.com/resource-centre/> accessed 28 August 2023

computers and other cloud memory files.[89] According to a criminal defence lawyer, "it is now a common occurrence for computers to be analysed along with telephones and for all social media to be interrogated. If we intend to get involved in crime or if we have been involved in crime, then beware of your Internet search history."[90] In order to decode your Internet history, a computer forensics analyst can check your laptop and investigate your search history even if you have deleted your topic or videos or go incognito on the net. Timing is also important. What you Googled yesterday may be a factor to consider in the recent crime you committed today. A one-time search is enough. It does not have to be a hundred searches. Investigators can go as far as recovering your deleted searches and the fact that you deleted your search history could also mean you have something to hide. During criminal trial, prosecution may file a subpoena to have your search history presented as evidence especially if the crime has to do with any acts of cybercrime, because deleted search information remains stored in the computer in unallocated space on the hard drive. Investigators can recover the history record while tracing the process, enables the criminal to be identified. Google is storing all our email if you are using a *gmail* account. But they cannot disclose the contents of your email to any government agency except there is a court order to that effect. The prosecution can get a court judgment to order your Internet provider to access your records. They can also subpoena your own computer to view the records themselves.[91]

Internet history evidence must however meet the following standards in a Court trial for admissibility purposes. (1) The information must be relevant to the case and to the accusation being prosecuted; (2) The information must be obtained legally and properly and it must be proven that it was so done; and (3) The information must comply with all applicable rules of evidence in the offender's jurisdiction.[92] In ***Hegglin v. Persons Unknown & Google,***[93] the applicant claimed he became the victim of abusive and

[89] „Browser Forensics and the Case of Casey Anthony" <https://belkasoft.com/case_of_casey_anthony/ > accessed 30 April 2022

[90] Amelia Tait. „How your Google searches can be used against you in Court" <https://www.newstatesman.com/science> accessed 30 April 2022

[91] Stladman. „Can Google Search History Be Used as Evidence" <https://www.steventituslaw.com/blog> accessed 30 April 2022

[92] Law Offices of Christopher J. Cherreta. „ Your Internet Browsing History and Its Use in Court" <https://www.wicriminaldefense.com> accessed 30 April 2022

[93] (2014) EWHC 3798

defamatory allegations contained on websites that could be reached through a Google search. The defamatory statements alleged that the applicant was "a murderer, a Nazi, a KKK sympathizer, a paedophile, a corrupt businessman, an insider trader and a member of the mafia." The applicant sought a wide range of reliefs among which is to remove any such defamatory results from Google user's search query. Consequently, Google reached an out-of-court settlement with the applicant and agreed to remove the defamatory material from its hosted websites and search result.

Case Study on Search History

Internet evidence apart from being a fact-seeking process is very important to modern investigations and prosecutions.

1. ***The Nancy Crampton Brophy case*** - She was convicted for her husband's murder and sentenced to life in prison. She once published an essay titled "How to Murder your Husband." Her browser history revealed that she first began her Internet research by searching for information and videos on ghost guns and even logged into a website to find out where guns are sold and how to clean and assemble a gun. Investigators were tasked to analyse her computers, phones and other devices to see if digital evidence on her devices would confirm or dismiss their theory that Nancy killed her husband. Investigators later discovered Nancy had three laptops. One in her closet. Another on her bed and the final computer was recovered from a storage unit. Her location tower data recovered from her cellphone confirmed she was at the crime scene area at the time of the murder.[94]
2. ***Someone using Casey Anthony's*** family desktop computer before the death of her two-year-old daughter surfed the web for information on chloroform, neck-breaking and making weapons for five times in 2008. Witnesses testified they found evidence of large quantity of chloroform and residue from a decomposing human body in Casey Anthony's car trunk. An expert testified that someone deleted the record of search. At the trial computer expert who created the forensic software for recovering deleted information testified that the search history was deleted intentionally rather than by an automatic function of the

[94] Magnet Forensics. „Internet History helped Portland Investigator crack the "How to Murder your Husband" case" <https://www.police1.com/investigations/article/> accessed 02 March 2023

computer and further that the computer user also looked at information often in Wikipedia on alcohol, inhalation, death, head injuries and self-defence. Through the computer search history, expert testified that the user spent a total of 3 minutes and 11 seconds on 5 websites relating to chloroform. It was also revealed that she searched for chloroform 84 times for five days.[95]

3. ***Jacob Greer***

Mr. Greer who was charged with child pornography and exploitation tried to conceal evidence by using Internet platforms instead of using his own electronic devices and he would sometimes delete files. For several years, Mr. Greer received, possessed, and distributed child pornography on the Internet. However in 2015, the law enforcement authorities executed a search warrant in his home and seized his numerous electronic devices containing child pornography,[96]

What are the possible Implications? Anyone can exploit your digital footprints including cybercriminal and law enforcement agencies, A case built around photographs, text messages and Internet evidence is not perfect just like any other human activity. Criminals usually want to clean their digital footprints by erasing their browsing history and browser's cache. Computer examination and search history can be faulty which could be very prejudicial if there are mistakes or errors on the part of the computer examiner.

8. DIGITAL FIELD FORENSICS

Digital evidence is defined as the information and data which is stored on, received or transmitted by an electronic device, such as computers, mobile phones and the Internet. Oftentimes in a physical crime scene, the investigator cannot make any investigative assumptions based on what is visible to him and as a result, the investigator cannot reasonably classify persons or items he can see at the spot.[97] Equally, the Court will always want to rely on visual aids to break down complex incidents, when necessary.

---

[95] Barbara Liston. „Casey Anthony"s Computer Used for Chloroform Search" <https://www. reuters. com/articles/us> accessed 22 May 2022

[96] „Jowa survivalist who faked his own death to avoid child porn charges sentenced to 2 decades" <https://truecrimedaily.com/2923/01/31/> accessed 25 June 2023

[97] Roy Gehl & Darryl Plecas. „Introduction to Criminal Investigation: Processes, Practices and Thinking" <https://www.academia.edu/resource/work/71849358 > accessed 22 May 2022

When Police officers are the first responders at a crime scene, digital evidence like phones and computers are treated the same way as biological evidence. That is, the phones, tablets and computers are kept secured in the investigating officer's safe hands until they are handed over to the digital forensics experts.[98] But before the arrival of forensic investigators, Police officers can conduct digital field forensics by doing a manual forensic analysis of the phones and electronic devices found in a suspect's possession, since there could be an offending content inside the devices. This visual inspection is an 'on-the-spot digital collection and viewing of the electronic devices in order to make very quick decisions about a person at risk, or about preventing future crimes. The advantage is that this field forensics can reduce the backlogs at forensic laboratories. Depending on the nature and urgency of the crime such as kidnapping or child pornography, Police investigators can use a field solution device to examine a registered sex offender's phone and check whether the perpetrator has indecent images of children on his laptop or computer. At other times when investigators seize computers or cellphones from a perpetrator, they may need to filter out irrelevant data so they can focus attention on finding relevant evidence. In the words of NIST; "let's say you've got a computer that might contain incriminating photos or financial records, but it also has few video games. Games often come with a lot of graphic files. An officer will want to run his investigation as quickly and efficiently as possible, so what he needs is a way to get rid of all the video game images. Then he can run your computationally expensive analysis on the files that remain."[99]

Here, investigating officers may be called upon to collect evidence using their field technology knowledge that can preserve the chain of evidence while lawfully collecting actionable intelligence in accordance with local Standard Operating Procedures (SOP)[100] and international Organisation for

[98] See generally „ INTERPOL Guidelines For Digital Forensics – First Responders: Best Practices For Search and Seizure of Electronic and Digital Evidence" 2021

[99] NIST Update to Software Reference Library Will Aid in Criminal Investigations. https://www.forensicmsg.com/ accessed 01 July 2022

[100] SOP in digital forensics is the standard operating procedures are agency unique documents describing the methods and procedures to be followed in performing routine operations. SOPs are essential to improve the quality and to implement uniform processes for conducting digital evidence and forensic tasks in a precise, accurate manner. See the" Scientific Working Groups on Digital Evidence and Imaging Technology" <https://www crime-scene-investigator.net > accessed 16 April 2022

Standardization (ISO)[101] requirements. So, instead of sending an exhibit extracted from the data into the Lab straight off, the frontline officer can do an extraction of data before the highly trained digital forensics staff can dig into the information.[102] Note that field forensics should be practiced only by Police officers who have been trained in best practices for lawful accessing and collection of digital data. These Police officers as basic forensic examiners can use handy technology to quickly examine digital devices, although field forensics does not mean just picking up a phone at a crime scene and scrolling through texts or getting the consent from witnesses to check their text messages or browse the photos on their phones as this can cause evidence to be lost or lower the value of evidence. The ethical practice is always to follow the best rules in digital field forensics. These are:

a. If a witness suggests he would want to text the evidence on his phone to an officers' phone. Know that the officer's phone will also become part of the chain of evidence which means the evidence could also be deleted or altered while it is on the officer's phone. Unfortunately, this could negatively affect the admissibility of the evidence in Court;
b. An officer should not take the photos of a suspect's phone screen showing text messages or images because the screen recording would not include data such as the date and time the original image or when the text was recorded. Rather, it is forensically sound to use apps that safely capture the evidence and upload it to third-party servers. Witnesses can then scan the Quick Response (QR) code that allows specific files to be sent wirelessly to the officer's device. Your QR code is a machine scan-able image that can instantly be read using a smartphone camera. When your smartphone scans the code, it translates information into something that can be easily understood by humans;[103]
c. An officer does not have to take physical possession of devices. Just obtain the consent of the witness during the process of sharing digital

---

[101] This covers the standardization and guidance in the field of forensic science. This includes the development of standards that pertain to laboratory and field based forensic science techniques and methodology in broad general areas such as the detection and collection of physical evidence, the analysis and interpretation of evidence and the reporting of results and findings. <https://www. iso.org/committee/4395817.html > accessed 16 April 2022

[102] Adam Riley. „Push Tech to the Frontlines to Solve Cases Faster"< https://www.forensicmag.com/3425-featured-article/> accessed 12 December 2022

[103] Michael Antonelli. „How to scan a QR codes on an Android device using the default camera app or the Google Lens app" <https://africa.businessinsider.com > accessed 16 April 2022

evidence as it would take few minutes. If an officer needs other pieces of evidence, he should use any portable device that can extract a fuller range of data;

d. Note that if a device is damaged or locked, this requires the attention of skilled digital forensics investigators who have the knowledge and technology to bypass locked devices or extract data from damaged devices. In this instance, field forensics is not the solution;
e. Documentation is also required in field forensics. Officers must do a report and write what they have done with the devices or evidenced as soon as they are collected. In any event the laboratory would need to know what the officer has done to the device;[104]
f. Whether digital field forensics investigation or findings will prove to be enough to convince law enforcement officers to help determine cases that will be prosecuted depends on the evidence collected by forensic experts who must have considered the admissibility, standardisation and accuracy of the evidence in view.

9. FORENSICS IN PERSONAL DATA PROTECTION

Cybercrime Investigation must be conducted in a coordinated manner just as it is done in a non-computer environment. Pairing forensic data analysis with cybersecurity is vital to law enforcement and lawyers who have to rely on the interpretation given by digital forensics investigators who possess the skill specifically for that purpose. This is critical to helping law enforcement officers and the Court to draw scientific and legal conclusions about what actually happened and enables them to make informed decisions to help advance their understanding because forensics seeks to improve investigative efficiency, leveraging technology and best practices to solve crimes and improve case closure. The results will have broad implications for criminal justice response and future research.[105]

A forensic investigator goes beyond the visible layer. When managing a digital scene, he takes a closer inspection with his scientific tools to detect elements of cybercrime. This has many dimensions guiding him:

---

[104] Heather Mahalik. & Andy Martin „Conducting Digital Forensics in the Field" <https://www.forensicmag.com/585159 > accessed 16 April 2022

[105] Noor AL-Sibri. „NASA has assembled an Expert UFO-Hunting Team" <https://futurism.com/the-byte/> accessed 22 December 2022

a. The four data protection principles are accuracy, storage limitation, integrity and confidentiality (security) and accountability;[106]
b. Digital evidence examination and understanding how data works rests on a firm foundation of computer science,[107] much so, that data is said to be the language of scientists and makes the 'unexplainable explainable;
c. Forensic science supports data protection. At the same time there is also conflict. That is, as a forensic scientist is digging for truth, he does not also want get involved in data breach because he has to protect disclosure;
d. Who invokes forensic investigation? It could be from an internal source - the victim or from suspected or actual data. It could also be external if the Police call for criminal investigation;
e. What is privacy? It is a human right concept. It is a right to ensure that an individual is left alone. Unfortunately law cannot protect the mental state of all the citizens and hence has redefined the right to privacy as right to exercise a choice of control on his personal information;
f. Files and programmes that are unused on our personal computers can clog the memory of computers and cause confusion during retrieval and slow down the computer making it initially difficult during investigation;
g. Instrument of Privacy Protection**:** It is a contract of offer and acceptance provided by the data principal to a data fiduciary who determines the purpose and means of processing the information;
h. Data is passed on to the data processor by the data fiduciary;
i. It is consent-driven. Consent can be provided only for the personal information known and provided by the data principal;
j. Data processors may discover new users for which they try to take fresh consent. But where someone mistakenly publishes another person's data online, that is data breach;[108]

---

[106] <https://ico.org.uk/for-organisations/guide-to-the-general-data-protection-regulation-gdpr/principles/> accessed 16 April 2022

[107] „NIST Publishes Review of Digital Forensic Methods" <https://www.nist.gov/news-events/news/> accessed 10 May 2022

[108] „UK Government fined 500,000 pounds after revealing home addresses in New Year honours data breach" <https://wwwtheguardian.com > accessed 02 January 2022 ; See Tim Sandler. Five cyber security myths that need to be busted <https://www.digitaljournal.com> accessed 30 April 2022; Further insights from The 11th Cybercrime Security International Conference India – 27/11/2021

k. In data forensics, there are complexities. A professional should know the tools and limitations of the tools as well as the law. There should be no mis-steps.

10. ISOLATING DEVICES TO PRESERVE EVIDENCE

When collating the chain of evidence, time is of the essence. Every step is critical, right from finding a device, finding an online account with digital data to presenting digital evidence in Court. There is need to gather critical information that will enhance the true understanding of the situation on ground. But how do you cut off a device from its cellular access or data without changing the evidence or deleting older data or wiping off data from a phone, so that if an investigator is given a device, he must make sure the data remains intact otherwise he may lose the evidence at the beginning. A digital forensic investigator must not do anything that will trigger operations altering the device's data or go near a location with Wi-Fi. Be mindful of the best practices in isolation methods to preserve evidence are:

1. Certain computer forensic test procedures of electronic systems require an isolated environment free of electromagnetic interference. This is known as Faraday Cage;[109]
2. Put the device in a faraday bag or box which has a device charging port. The device will keep on charging. If there is no faraday bag, wrap the phone carefully in several layers of foil and get the device to forensic investigators as soon as possible;
3. Ensure there is no loss of power because any mobile devices may lose data or initiate additionally security measures once powered off;
4. Switch the phone into airplane mode so that the phone won't be able to receive messages or calls or won't be reporting locations or won't receive wipe commands. Investigators will then have the opportunity to extract data from the device after using After First Unlock (AFU);
5. Remove the Sim Card to disable connections to cellular data;
6. Turn off device to isolate it from available connections.

It is important for the investigator to document all evidence of the methods used, including the limitations they face with each method they

[109] „New Faraday Cage. Research Facility to Help Combat Digital Crimes" <https://www.forensicmag.com/ 592380/> accessed 01 December 2022

try.[110] When the Universal Forensic Extraction Device (UFED) is used and connected to your phone, all the contents on your phone can be downloaded, for example, contacts list, call history, text messages, social networking files, downloads, browser history, pictures, video, and even your ringtones. With this, the Police do not need your password or biometric data before they access your phone. The Police can also use a Cellebrite UFED to extract data from a suspect's phone. In ***Riley v. California,***[111] the Supreme Court held that the Police must get a warrant before they search a cellphone.

However, digital evidence techniques are not perfect. To address issues that may crop up, it is recommended that there should be more information-sharing among computer information technology experts, adopt a more structured approach to testing forensic tools that can eliminate the data you need and isolate the evidence that needs preservation, have access to high-quality reference datasets, sharing of high-quality forensic reference data that can be used for education, training and research in order to move the field forward.[112] Advancements in technology in Digital forensics surely plays a huge part in phones and computer investigation as well as in mixed data.

11. SCIENCE & EVIDENCE OF DIGITAL FORENSICS

The use of digital computer to launch attacks on information about individuals, corporations or governments is usually very technical. It highlights the centrality of networked computers, hence the prefix 'cyber'. An important aspect of digital forensics is that it involves the investigation of disk, network, wireless, database, malware, email, memory and mobile phones because cybercriminals leave clues as to their identity and location in an effort to cover up their crime. This is where digital forensics experts are relevant. Investigators concerned can use the expertise of mobile and digital forensic tools to analyse text messages, emails and social media posts between criminals and victims in order to build strong links required for prosecution.[113] An expert will need to explain the processes of preservation,

[110] Heather Mahalik & Ian Whiffin. „Isolating Devices to Preserve Evidence" <http://www.forensicmag.com/3425-Featured-Article> accessed 18 February 2022

[111] 573 U.S. 373 (2014)

[112] „NIST Review Evaluates Digital Forensic Methods" <https://www.forensicmag.com/586019/ > accessed 12 May 2022

[113] Joshua Lee. „How technology can help law enforcement fight human trafficking" <https://www.police1.com/investigations/articles/> accessed 26 May 2023

identification, extraction and documentation of any evidence generated from electronic items to the Court as it relates to the main components of digital evidence which are:

a. Evidence collection;
b. Evidence ingestion;
c. Evidence case management;
d. Evidence sharing;
e. Evidence storage and archiving;
f. Evidence purging.[114]

Similarly, the concept of what is called the Electronic discovery also known as e-Discovery solution is relevant in cybercrime investigation, while trying to identify, protect, detect, respond and recover what caused the cyber breach. E-Discovery is the electronic aspect of identifying, collecting and producing electronically stored information (ESI) in emails, voicemail, databases, social media, presentations, websites and documents, in response to a request for production in a law suit or investigation. Large organisations use the e-Discovery solutions to gather and review electronic information. They preserve such information to be used as evidence in a legal case. Both e-Discovery and digital forensics have a role to play in legal matters. While e-Discovery involves organizing, analysing and producing ESI as part of an investigation, e-Discovery often can only take place after digital forensics ensures that legal teams have all of the relevant ESI.[115]

It is instructive to note that digital forensics and investigation rests on the discipline and foundation of forensic science. This scientific foundation is useful to knowledge in several ways. First, it can help establish trust in methods that rest on solid scientific foundations when properly applied. Second, it can help forensic practitioners, investigators, Courts and others to understand the capabilities and limitations of forensic methods and ensure they are used appropriately. Third, by identifying knowledge gaps, the knowledge can help provide strategic direction for future research because the research will guide our justice system in its effort to ensure accuracy and fairness especially where the evidence relates to new technologies.[116] It is

---

[114] Lawrence Williams. „What is Digital Forensics? History, Process, Types, Challenges?" <https://www.guru99.cpm/digital-forensics.html/ > accessed 26 December 2022

[115] „What is E-Discovery?" <https://www.proofpoint.com/us/threat-reference/> accessed 04 March 2023

[116] „NIST"s Researchers Look Ahead to High-Tech Trends in 2023 and Beyond" <https:// www.forensicmag.com/593287/> accessed 29 December 2022

not surprising that law enforcement agencies in some Western jurisdictions have gone a step higher to reconstruct and analyse digital evidence to solve crimes by using a simplified high-tech toolkit.[117]

12. CCTV FOOTAGE ETHICS AND FRAMEWORK[118]

a. Introduction

Gone are the days when we depended solely on human photographers to document events into pictorial evidence or we employ spies to monitor events and share the captured information with us. Unfortunately, these methods were not totally error-free until the advent of Closed Circuit Television (CCTV) which is a form of visual representation that serves as a piece of visual evidence of an event that took place. It is simply a digital video recorder or a television system in which signals are not publicly distributed but are monitored, primarily for surveillance and security purposes. The footage plays a key role as a part of digital forensics evidence in the criminal justice system. CCTV is designed for both internal and external use while the purpose is to improve public safety, security of life and property As a crime detection and prevention tool with a network video recorder (NVS), the surveillance camera enabled by its data driven built-in computing sensors to store, receive, transmit, process sights and sounds for audio-visual analysis and comparison. Historically, CCTV was invented by an electrical engineer and pioneer of German television Walter Bruch such that in 1942, which invention made it easy for German military operators during the World War II to use this early form of CCTV simply as a wartime technology to watch live, close-up images of their rocket power bombs in private, over a closed circuit. Thereafter CCTV became commercially available in 1949 till it landed on the British shores in 1960.

b. Legal Framework

Generally, the switch from analogue to digital has brought a dramatic change to the way the Courts look at video evidence.[119] CCTV is a source of evidence. By virtue of Sections 84 and 258 (1) of the Evidence Act 2011,

---

117 „Purdue Simplifies Digital Evidence Toolkit for Police" <https://www.forensicmag.com/596547/> accessed 02 May 2023

118 Uploaded on Academia „Closed Circuit Television Evidence" <https://www. academia. edu/ resource/ work/76240013> (April 2022)

119 Grant Fredericks. „Can Video Evidence be Trusted?" <https://www.police1.com/police-products/ radios/> accessed 20 December 2022

CCTV video meets the requirement for admissibility of computer generated evidence, since it produces electronic/digital information that is useful for collection of evidence and identification of suspect. Thus, videos are considered strong trial exhibits, as long the video is founded on reliable and relevant facts which must show no gap or error in the chain of custody process before the admissibility of the video is considered. In criminal trials, the prosecution still has to prove its case beyond reasonable doubt and that all evidence was collected, handled and analysed during the investigation of the case. In a decided case, the Court held that CCTV footage is the best piece evidence to prove the presence of an accused person at the scene of a crime. Where the image in the CCTV video is complex or controversial, an expert using his specialized skill must be called upon by the court to forensically interpret or analyse any forensic elements attached to the video, taking into consideration the quality of the video, the storage of the video, the playback of the video and the transfer/export of the video. In this regard, the court may want to evaluate the video with the assistance of an expert, to determine whether the images shown on the CCTV video are good enough for present and future visual reference. In line with Section 68 of the Evidence Act which expressly provides that expert witness should have some special skill or knowledge in the field required, the court would want to inquire the following; is the expert qualified to form a better opinion in the subject matter at hand? Has the video been safeguarded to prevent unauthorized viewing or manipulation of the footage? Has the expert replayed the video in order to confirm the authenticity of the video or was it recorded by another device? Is the CCTV video compatible and integrated with other third-party cameras? In this context, a forensic audio/video analysis expert is likely to be the expert the court needs to verify the authenticity of video footage in contention. The expert in this field should vast knowledge in computer engineering, electronics/electrical engineering, digital media, IP, telecommunications, wireless technology and other forms of media equipment.

It should be noted however that a video does not automatically prove guilt for several reasons because expert opinion could be subjective or biased. The video could have been edited when transferring the video from the hard drive to another device, just to show that the person being recorded is a criminal and that is why the video analysis of the expert must be done in a way to describe the gadgets and the process used in order to give the case the strength of evidence especially if it is a video clip that is alleged to have captured the perpetrator making criminal utterances or committing crime. The Court has to be mindful that in this age of digital distrust and with challenges emanating from Internet Protocol (IP) address conflict, IP spoofing, and deepfake, a user can manipulate images and audio in real time such that it can make another person say things he never said. An age-old proverb says every coin has two sides and same is the case of CCTV evidence which may portray two conflicting interpretations. However, some forensic experts have also contended that CCTV footage can hardly be manipulated because of a watermark which gets broken immediately the footage is tampered with. The purpose of a watermark is to make it more difficult for the original image to be copied, or used without consent or be tampered with. In this regard, a judge should therefore take account of all these factors into consideration before coming to a definitive decision. On the whole all we can say is that CCTV may be admissible subject to the discretion of the trial judge.to exclude it.

c. Ethical Use of CCTV Cameras

When CCTV monitoring equipment is installed, it is important for the CCTV owner to be aware of the rules which are placed at the heart of human rights and law. For instance, if the CCTV is in a public place, there is no privacy concern. This demonstrate that the deployment of CCTV on the highways, streets, shopping centres, markets, estates, airports, hotels, office buildings, banks, car parks, schools, etc., should be conspicuous enough to everyone entering such public facilities. Data Protection laws must be complied with. If the CCTV is for your personal use, your camera placement is important as it should not extend into other people's property neither should it be used for monitoring your neighbours and their visitors' activities on their premises because recording them without their consent is illegal. A CCTV owner should therefore not position his camera in such a way that it will infringe on other people's privacy because surveillance of your neighbour's residence is deemed intrusive. In Nigeria, the right to privacy is guaranteed under Section 37 of the Constitution which provides that the privacy of citizens and their homes is guaranteed and protected. Hence, there is a reasonable expectation of privacy in toilets, bathrooms, dressing rooms, hotel rooms, rented rooms, otherwise; the CCTV owner would be held liable for a criminal act of voyeurism, including a breach of trust and privacy. In business or commercial settings, your staff must be aware that they are being recorded. See the Nigeria Data Protection Regulation and its Implementation Framework. Essentially, CCTV owners must comply with data privacy laws and data protection laws. In most jurisdictions, the government is fully supportive of the use of overt surveillance cameras in public places whenever the use is in pursuit of legitimate aim or when it is necessary to meet a pressing need. If a criminal activity has taken place in your house, premises or workplace, the Police may request you to hand over the footage to them so as to get to the root of the crime unlike the CCTV installed in public places which can easily be accessed by the police without needing anyone's permission.

d. Evaluation of CCTV Footage

The handling, interpretation and presentation of CCTV footage is vital to the criminal justice system. Evaluation has to do with using the CCTV footage to scrutinize the behaviour or character of anyone – victim, suspect or witness to an offence. It is a tool for viewing and gathering evidence to help determine whether a defendant is guilty or innocent, In this digital age where cameral tell lies, CCTV footage requires careful interpretation and evaluation because it can be misleading and lead to miscarriage of justice especially in today's CCTV market – where no standards exist for image reliability, video can no longer be accepted at face value nor can it be expected to accurately represent what it purports to show, when compression, motion prediction and enhancement technology may inadvertently change and alter the events captured by the camera.[120] This implies that different interpretations can be obtained from the same footage. Yet the justice system often relies upon digital evidence to support investigations and prosecutions and CCTV is one of the most relied upon forms. CCTV also provides many benefits to investigators, as earlier stated, it can help identify suspects and witnesses, and implicate or eliminate suspects. It can help to corroborate or refute accounts provided by suspects and witnesses. However, the evaluators should note the shortcomings: CCTV is sometimes inaccessible or lost

---

[120] Grant Fredericks. „Can Video Evidence be Trusted?" <https://www.police1.com/police-products/radios/> accessed 20 December 2022

because the detective who is sent to retrieve the footage lacks the skills, training, or equipment to recover the evidence in a timely manner; CCTV is often deleted within some weeks of being recorded; Owners are unable to access systems or cannot manage the volume of CCTV requested; important footage which could exonerate a suspect may not be disclosed to the defence which could mean innocent people are imprisoned; when experts are left out to interpret the footage; and when there are blurry images.[121]

Video Evidence – Digital videos are valuable sources of investigating crimes, but gone are the days when it was common for people to say that video evidence speaks for itself or that the video doesn't lie. Unfortunately, many officers and investigators may not receive training on collecting, handling or analysing digital video evidence. This lack of knowledge can lead to legal challenges regarding the validity and authenticity as well as improper interpretations of digitally produced visual information. What about the capabilities of the recording device and the subjective and potentially error-prone interpretation of viewers? The impact of 'perspective bias' and the techniques to manipulate the attention and perception of viewers just like it is done on television are also issues to consider. The reality is charges against an accused person can be dismissed by the Court if the evidence was founded on a faulty interpretation and analysis of the video evidence presented by the prosecution.[122] In ***State v. Matthews,***[123] the trial Court convicted the respondent of murder based on a video footage obtained from a nearby home security camera. His face was indiscernible in the video. The Police sought for expert evidence in order to determine the height of the person in the video footage. The Court of Appeals reversed the conviction partly because the uncertainty surrounding the video evidence was based on several variables such as camera distance, resolution of the imagery, unevenness of the landscape and body position of the subject,

---

[121] Helen Jones & Fiona Brookman. „The Challenges, Risks of CCTV in Murder Investigations" <https://www.forensicmag.com/595687/> accessed 29 March 2023

[122] David Blake and Robert Mcfarlane. „Digital media evidence and force investigations: 5 methods to assist in writing accurate reports and conducting thorough investigations" <https://www.police1.com/ > accessed 10 October 2023

[123] 479 Md.278 (Md 2022)

e. Conclusion

If your property is under 24-hour surveillance, you can have peace of mind. The merits of CCTV cannot be underestimated in every contemporary society, hence the law allows the use of CCTV for the purpose of securing public facilities, Section 28(1) of the Nigerian Correctional Service Act 2019 provides that there shall be provided monitoring devices to protect, control and safeguarded correctional activities including CCTV and other instruments of restraint. CCTV is also useful for recognition and tracing of suspects. It is obvious that the traditional methods of investigation have improved with CCTV being a first step for law enforcement officers investigating a crime. Based on the information gathered from CCTV, this tool sheds more light on criminal investigation, intelligence gathering and prosecution of crime. In the first place, it is always better to deter crime than us trying to investigate them. CCTV is useful as corroborating evidence in Court particularly where there are no eye witnesses to establish the identity of an accused person. Some people refer to CCTV as the unseen witness or the eye of God. In other words, deploying CCTV camera whether indoor or outdoor, can uncover other potential crimes and be held sufficient to support a conviction. It serves as exculpatory, inculpatory and corroborative evidence which has a probative value. It improves community safety, deters crime, prevents crime, reduces crime and helps provide closure thus strengthening crime research data and in turn the criminal justice system.[124] In the face of rising criminality and insecurity in Nigeria, it brings to bear that criminals should not be made to have a field day and that is why we must continue to encourage the installation of CCTV cameras in public places. Nigeria is yet to pass into law what is called a' Bill to compel compulsory Installation of CCTV on private and public organisations. However, in as much as it is advisable for the Police to review surveillance footages in the area where a crime takes place, it is also necessary that the Police should interview anyone who may have witnessed any unusual occurrence.

---

[124] In the case of *Tomaso Bruno & Anor v. State of UP*, S.L.P (Crl.) N0. 1156/2013 the Court held that CCTV footage was the best piece of evidence to prove the presence of the accused at the scene of crime and it was for the prosecution to have produced such evidence/

CYBER THREAT TO CCTV: "Like any technology, CCTV systems can equally be vulnerable to hacking and cyber-attacks. It is therefore important to ensure that your CCTV systems are up-to-date with the latest software and firmware and that it is configured securely."

13. RING DOORBELL AND CAMERAS

Ring is a smart security device company whose video doorbell product allows users to see and record people who approach their doorsteps, deterring theft and allowing them to monitor around their homes.[125]Thus, ring doorbell and cameras are audio and video recording/surveillance devices which are deterrent against criminals but the devices can also break data laws and contribute to harassment, especially where the Ring doorbell camera capture images of a neighbour's house and garden. A judge has ruled that security cameras and a Ring doorbell installed in a house unjustifiably invaded the privacy of a neighbour. The Judge opined that audio data that could capture conversations is even more problematic and detrimental than video data.[126]

Ring cameras also come-in handy as Police cameras because the Police can get warrantless access to the devices if there is an emergency.[127] A report published of a home-surveillance company which handed videos over to law enforcement officers was captured by the owner of 20 Ring cameras[128] against his will. Earlier the said law enforcement officers sought a warrant for camera footage – including from inside the owner's house – while investigating his neighbour. According to the report, after the owner willingly provided the video which showed the street outside his home, the Police then used the courts to access more footage against his will. The supports the fact that while law enforcement often seeks warrants for digital data, those warrants typically pertain to the subject of a particular investigation. However, as networked home surveillance cameras have become increasingly popular, law enforcement is likewise turning to

[125]Stacy Liberatore. „Amazon"s Ring doorbell cam is set to force cops to make requests for footage on its public Neighbors app" <https://www.dailymail.co.uk/sciencetech/> accessed 10 August 2023

[126]Jane Wakefield. „Neighbour wins privacy row over smart doorbell and cameras" <https://www.bbc.co.uk/news/technology/> accessed 15 December 2022

[127]„Can you use Ring camera footage in Court?" < https://www.thehealthyjournal.com> accessed 15 December 2022

[128] All ring inside cameras has the ability to automatically record audio, noises and conversations whenever motion is detected.

individuals who are completely unaffiliated with a case to provide data and so, the lack of legal controls on what the Police can ask for, opens the door for a bystander's indoor home footage to be lawfully acquired by the Police.[129]

[129] Lily Hay Newman. „Security news This Week: How a Catholic Group Doxed Gay Priests" <https://www.wired.com/story/> accessed 11 March 2023

Chapter 8

LEGAL FRAMEWORK AND POLICIES

1. NIGERIA'S CYBERSECURITY LEGAL REGIME

As technology continues to evolve, many people hold the impression that the Internet is largely unregulated or unsupervised due to the fact that anyone with a phone or computer can easily connect to the Internet without been cross-checked. This is a wrong impression, regardless of the ubiquitous feature of the Internet. Ubiquitous connectivity describes a state where devices are able to create, share and process information on the Internet. According to the United Nations Office on Drugs and Crime (UNODC), cybercrime or computer crime is an evolving transnational crime which takes place in the border-less realm of cyberspace and bound by every country unique laws, regulations and policies. These laws and policies are regulatory frameworks and guidelines which play a keynote in developing the technology industry, enable increased access to digital services and reveal a new vista of research areas for scholars. These guidelines provide the administrative rules, legal procedures and best practices on how an industry activity ought to be regulated.

Cybercrime occur when a person uses the Internet and technology to facilitate crime or when a person is committing a crime through the computer or any electronic device. As of July 2022, the active telecom subscribers have grown significantly to 212.2 million while basic Internet subscriptions have grown to 152.7 million.[1] With this massive development in the telecom industry, some criminals continue to take undue advantage to commit crime on the Internet. For example, the Financial Institutions Training Centre (FITC) in their 2023 Reports of Fraud and Forgeries in Nigerian Banks disclosed that mobile fraud, computer/web fraud and POS fraud cases made Nigerian banks to record 24, 232 fraud cases in the first six

[1]Ogunsakin Mustapha. „Telecom policies enhancing digital access, knowledge production – Danbatta" <https://thegavel.com.ng> accessed 05 December 2022

months of 2023. So, what is the prosecution and punishment of perpetrators like? Are there laws and remedies that victims can look up to? Who investigates cybercrime and regulates our cyber activities? In Nigeria, the law enforcement authorities must have established and substantiated their case against the suspected perpetrators before the Court pronounces them guilty. Which Court prosecutes cybercrime? In State High Courts, the punishment ranges from imprisonment, fines and forfeiture of property and tools of crime. In Lagos State, Magistrate Courts adjudicate on cybercrime matters.[2] The Federal High Court also has jurisdiction to try cybercrime offences. The Evidence Act 2011 is equally important in this vein, where Sections 84 and 258 deals with admissibility of electronic evidence. The new Evidence (Amendment) Act 2023 has further expanded the scope of computer generated evidence by recognising electronic oath, digital signatures, electronic gazette, authentication of electronic records that are stored in optical, magnetic media or cloud computing database which are admissible as documents.

Regulation is a legally binding rule or requirement that is created and enforced by a government agency. Regulations are used to control and govern industries to protect public health, safety and welfare. Regulations specify functions or activities that required or prohibited and sanctions for non-compliance. Compliance with statutory and regulatory framework is vital. Hence the role of regulation entails protecting consumers' personal and sensitive data; obligations of network operators who share our data; safeguarding financial transactions; enforcing compliance; promoting capacity building and awareness on cybersecurity measures like encryption, two or multi-factor authentication, fraud detection; as well as encouraging innovation and protecting ideas. This ensures justice for the victim and against the perpetrator.

2. THE CYBERCRIMES (PROHIBITION AND PREVENTION, ETC) ACT, 2015 AS FURTHER AMENDED IN 2024

This is the apex law regulating cybercrime in Nigeria. The law was passed following a high rate of online crimes in the country. The objectives of the Act under Section 1 are:

---

[2] „Lagos Bizman Circulating Ex-Lovers" Nude Photos Arraigned, Gets Bail" <https://newswirelaw andevents. com/> accessed 13 July 2022

a. To promote cyber security and the protection of computer systems, electronic communications, data and computer programs, intellectual and privacy rights.
b. To provide an effective and unified legal, regulatory and institutional framework for the prohibition, prevention, detection, prosecution and punishment of cybercrimes in Nigeria.
c. The Act also provides that where there are reasonable grounds to suspect that the content of any electronic communication is reasonably required for the purpose of criminal investigation or proceedings, a Judge may require a service provider to intercept, collect, record, permit or assist competent authorities with the collection or recording of content data and/or traffic data associated with specified communications transmitted by means of a computer system. The Judge may also authorize a law enforcement agent to collect or record electronic communications through application of technical means. A service provider is required to comply with the Judge's order and to generally assist with the identification, apprehension and prosecution of offenders.

Some of the cybercrime offences outlined under the law are: unlawful access to a computer, system interference, intercepting electronic message, emails and electronic money transfers, wilful misdirection of electronic messages, computer-related forgery or fraud, cyber terrorism, cyber threats, identity theft, child pornography, cyberstalking, cybersquatting, phishing, spamming and spreading of computer virus.

In ***Solomon Okedara v. Attorney General,***[3] the appellant contended that the provision of Section 24(1) of the Cybercrimes Act 2015 was vague, overbroad and ambiguous which threatened his rights to freedom of expression under Section 39 of the 1999 Constitution. The Federal High Court held that Section 24(1) was not vague and that the Section is necessary in a democratic society as it relates to the interests of defence, public safety, public order, public morality or public health pursuant to Section 45 of the 1999 Constitution. Dissatisfied, with the judgment, the Appellant appealed to the Court of Appeal which also held that the Legislature has the power to enact laws that are reasonably justifiable in a democratic society; and therefore that Section 24(1) of the Cybercrimes Act

[3] (2019) LCN 127/12768(CA)

does not conflict with constitutional right to privacy rights of the citizens. However in the case of ***SERAP v. Federal Republic of Nigeria,***[4] the ECOWAS Court of Justice held that the Nigerian Government should amend Section 24 of the Cybercrimes Act 2015 because Section 24 does not conform with Article 9 of the African Charter on Human and Peoples' Rights (ACHPR) and Article 19(2) of the International Covenant on Civil and Political Rights (ICCPR) both of which promotes free speech and which Nigeria is signatory. The ECOWAS Court expressed the view that the modification would meet the obligations under Article 9 *(Every individual shall have the right to receive information)* of the ACHPR and Article 19(2) of the ICCPR which provides that everyone shall have the right to freedom of expression.[5]

Note: In 2024, the Cybercrimes (Prohibition, Prevention, Etc) Amendment Act, 2024 has amended the 2015 Act to insert some consequential words that were inadvertently omitted in the 2015 Act. For example, *Section 24(1) of the 2015 Act is amended by substituting for paragraphs (a) and (b), with new paragraphs "(a)" and "(b)"* as follows *–"(a)…is pornographic; or (b)... he knows to be false, for the purpose of causing a breakdown of law and order, posing a threat to life, or causing such message to be sent."*

3. THE NIGERIA DATA PROTECTION ACT, 2023

The objectives of the law are set out in Section 1 to:

a. safeguard the fundamental rights and freedoms and the interests of data subjects as guaranteed under the 1999 Constitution;
b. provide for the regulation of processing of personal data;
c. promote data processing practices that safeguard the security of personal data and privacy of data subjects;
d. ensure that personal data is processed in a fair, lawful and accountable manner;
e. protect data subjects' rights and provide means of recourse and remedies in the event of the breach of data subject's rights;

[4] ECW/CCJ/APP/09/19 (unreported)

[5] See „ECOWAS COURT orders Nigeria to amend Cybercrime Law" <https://therecord.media/> accessed 30 April 2022

f. ensure that data controllers and data processors fulfil their obligations to data subjects;
g. establish an impartial, independent and effective regulatory commission to superintend over data protection and privacy issues and supervise data controllers and data subject's rights; and
h. strengthen the legal foundation of the national digital economy and guarantee the participation of Nigeria in the regional and global economies.

4. NATIONAL CYBERSECURITY POLICY AND STRATEGY (NCPS) 2021

This is a framework that is aimed at providing a safe and secure digital community and provides opportunities for its citizens to thrive in an enabling environment that will strengthen cybersecurity governance and coordination; foster a trusted cyber environment that optimizes Nigeria's cybersecurity readiness and capacity geared towards addressing the nations' cyber risk exposure.

Sanctions or punishment for cybercrime offenders under the legal frameworks in many jurisdictions are:

- arraignment before a Court of law;
- monetary damages;
- imprisonment;
- Detention ranging from 5 days but less than 10 days in prison. This is common in China if the nature of the crime is minor;
- Community Service Order. An Internet fraudster was ordered to cut grasses around the Court premises from 10 am to 12 noon for two days under the supervision of a non-custodian correctional officer;[6]
- Restraining order or Cease and Desist order.[7];
- Electronic Curfew – temporary ban imposed on the accused person from using electronic devices;
- Restitution – Perpetrator will turn over his computer to the victim; or pay a specified amount to the victim;

---

[6] Victor E. „Internet Fraud: Court orders man to cut grasses around court premises" <https:// barristerng. com/> accessed 11 July 2023

[7] Ben Kuchera. „Sony granted temporary restraining order against PS3 hacker" <https:// arstechnica. com/ gaming/2011/01/> accessed 24 January 2022

- Forfeiture of items which was used to perpetrate the crime to the Federal Government;
- Extradition;[8]
- Content restriction;
- Destruction. The Court ordered the iPhone being the instrument of cybercrime, be burnt in front of the Court in the presence of the EFCC prosecutor, the defence counsel, the convict, Police orderly and the Court Registrar. However the evidence of destruction must be forwarded to the EFCC Legal Department and the Court;[9]
- Seizure of computers, hard drives, mobile phones and software - In ***Trabajo Rueda* v. *Spain*,**[10] the applicant contended that the police seizure and inspection of his computer which contained child pornography materials had amounted to an interference with his right to respect for his private life and correspondence. The ECtHR held that it had been a violation of Article 8 (right to respect for private life). That although the Police pursued the legitimate aim of prevention of crime and protection of the rights of others, the Police seizure of the computer and inspection without prior judicial authorisation had not been proportionate to the legitimate aims pursued as required in a democratic society;
- Offender can be put under limited incarceration or surveillance in addition to being fined;[11]
- Offender's house could be sealed for collection of further evidence.[12]
- Offender could be registered as a sex offender.

5. CYBER REGULATORS AND INSTITUTIONS

The rise in cybercrimes has no doubt given rise to pro-active control measures set in motion by cybersecurity regulatory bodies. Cybersecurity technology covers three primary control types – preventive, detective and

---

[8]Press Release. „Defendant extradited from the United Kingdom" <https://www.justice.gov/usao-ma/pr/> accessed 11 May 2023

[9] Victor E. „Internet Fraud: Court orders man to cut grasses around court premises" <https:// barristerng. com/> accessed 11 July 2023

[10] 32600/12 (2017) ECHR 487

[11] See China"s Cybersecurity Law

[12] Mahender Singh Manral. „Alerted by Interpol, CBI arrests man for sexually abusing four minors, uploading their videos online" <https://indianexpress.com/article/cities/> accessed 14 July 2023

corrective. This means the regulatory agencies and policies governing the cyber framework are to ensure the primary control functions are strictly adhered to.[13] It follows that if there is need arises to regulate an activity, then there must be institutions or agencies set out to regulate the working process or the policies that would coordinate the activity for better performance in line with global best practices. According to the National Digital Economy Policy and Strategy (NDEPS), although, regulation is usually negatively perceived as something that tends to stifle development and innovation, regulation is still considered a key tool for achieving the social, economic and environmental policy objectives of government for ensuring that proper regulatory instruments are in place, and essential for operators, data consumers and the regulators in the cybersecurity industry to mitigate critical cyber threats. Who are the regulators? These are relevant security agencies that have the competence to investigate and prosecute cybercrimes as stipulated by law. They include:

a. The President of the Federal Republic of Nigeria - Under the Cybercrimes (Prohibition, Prevention, Etc.) Act 2015, Sections 3, 58 and 59 of the Act provides that the president of Nigeria through an executive order can declare any computer, website system or data as vital and critical national information infrastructure;
b. The Data Protection Commission - Under the Nigeria Data Protection Act, 2023, Section 46 provides that a data subject who is aggrieved by the action of a data controller or processor may lodge a complaint with the Data Protection Commission which can investigate all complaints and order the violator to appear before it. The Commission can make compliance orders, cease and desist orders, penalty orders or enforcement orders to remedy the violation;
c. The Federal Ministry of Communications, Innovations and Digital Economy; was created to facilitate ICT as a key tool in the transformation agenda for Nigeria in the areas of job creation, economic growth and transparency of government that enhances national security,
d. The Nigerian Communications Commission (NCC) - The NCC is the regulator of the telecommunication industry, which provides an enabling environment for the development of ICT that seeks to promote

[13] Security Technologies. „<https://www.javapoint.com/cyber-security-tech.../> accessed 22 May 2022

competition for the purpose of setting performance standards for telephone services in Nigeria. The major players in the telecommunications market are the telcos (GSM) operators, Internet Service Providers (ISPs) and other market participants such as infrastructure providers;

e. NCC Internet Code of Practice – to protect the right of Internet users to an open Internet and outline the obligations of Internet access providers in the handling of offensive and potentially harmful content as well as the protection of minors and vulnerable audiences online while ensuring adequate safeguards are put in place;
f. The NCC 'Lawful Interception of Communications Regulations, 2019 legalises the interception of certain communications by authorized agencies in Nigeria. The NCC also established the Digital Bridge Institute (DBI) as a tertiary institution to promote the development of human resources capacity by training personnel in the telecoms and ICT-related sectors of the economy, and to generate a rounded understanding of the policy, law and technical ramifications of Telecom and ICT worlds.[14] This is a good development because it will encourage disseminating of ICT and cybersecurity research, gaps and needs as well as encourage collaboration among IT professionals and policy makers;
g. Nigeria Data Protection Bureau (NDPB) – focuses on data protection and privacy for the country. The bureau will consolidate the gains of the Nigeria Data Protection Regulation (NDPR) and support the development of primary legislation for data protection and privacy. See ***Incorporated Trustees of Digital Lawyers Initiative & Ors v. National Identity Management Commission.***[15]
h. Nigeria Computer Emergency Response Team (ngCert) - gives security advisory;
i. Computer Security Incident Response Team (CSIRT) under NCC – gives security advisory;
j. National Digital Economy Policy and Strategy (NDEPS) – ensure the datafication of our society.

---

[14] < https://ncc.gov.ng/accessible/the-ncc/stakeholders/projects/73-digital-bridge-institute-dbi> accessed 12 June 2022

[15] CA/IB/291/2020

k. National Information Technology Development Agency (NITDA) – to standardize, coordinate and develop regulatory frameworks for all IT practices in Nigeria;
l. the NITDA Code of Practice for Interactive Computer Service Platforms/Internet Intermediaries 2022 - to protect fundamental human rights of Nigerians and define the guidelines for interacting on the digital ecosystem in line with international best practices as obtainable in democratic nations. Also to protect Nigerians against online harms, such as hate speech, cyber bullying as well as disinformation and misinformation;[16]
m. The Wireless Telegraphy Act (WTA) sets out the framework for regulating the use of wireless telegraphy;
n. Law Enforcement Agencies - The Terrorism Prevention Act 2022 provides that law enforcement agencies have the power to apply for a Court order to compel communication service providers to intercept specified communications, provided they obtain the requisite approvals of the Attorney-General of the Federation (AGF) and the National Security Advisor (NSA);[17]
o. Nigerian Broadcasting Corporation (NBC) is to licence social media platforms;
p. The Central Bank of Nigeria (CBN) - In 2018, the CBN wrote all the mobile money operators and other payment service providers in Nigeria to comply with Section 44 of the Cybercrimes Act which says they must pay levies to the National Cybersecurity Fund which is administered by the CBN and the office of the NSA;
q. Banks' Initiative through the Committee of Chief Information Security Officers of Nigerian Financial Institutions (CCISONFI), in partnership with Cybersafe Foundation and the CBN;
r. Nigerian Electronic Fraud Forum (NeFF) – This was set up in 2012 to check e-fraud incidences in the country. It consists of all relevant stakeholders to actively and proactively put a check on fraud and safeguard integrity of e-payment channels;

---

[16] <https://nitda.gov.ng/wp-content/uploads/2022/06/Code-of-Practice.pdf> accessed 13 November 2022
[17] Nigeria: Telecoms, Media and Internet Laws and Regulations 2022. < https://iclg.com/practice-areas/ > accessed 27 February 2022

s. The CBN Risk-Based Framework Cybersecurity Framework and Guidelines for Other Financial Institutions (OFIs) which will take effect in January 2023. The framework comprises six parts namely, cybersecurity governance and oversight, cybersecurity risk management system, cyber resilience assessment, cybersecurity operational resilience, cyber-threat intelligence as well as the metrics, monitoring and reporting. With this guideline, it has become mandatory for institutions to strengthen their cyber defences to remain safe and sound;
t. The Nigeria Police Force, EFCC, ICPC, DSS – Pursuant to Article 10.1.5 under the NDPR Implementation Framework 2020, where the NITDA has determined that a party is in breach of the provisions of the NDPR, especially where such breach affects national security, sovereignty and cohesion, it may seek to prosecute officers of the organization as provided for in section 17(1) and (3) of the NITDA Act 2007. The NITDA shall seek a fiat of the AGF or may file a petition with any authority in Nigeria, this may include; the EFCC, DSS,[18] the Nigeria Police Force, the ICPC and the Office of the NSA. Note that there is an arm of the Nigeria Police called the Nigeria Police Force National Cybersecurity Centre domiciled at the Force Criminal Investigations Department, Abuja;
u. The National Intelligence Agency (NIA) and Defence Intelligence Agency (DIA) can intercept and monitor calls, messages and social media accounts, if found likely to endanger lives. In 2021, the Federal Government increased the capacity of these intelligence services to tackle cybercrime and counter terrorism;[19]
v. NCC (Registration of Telephone Subscribers) Regulations 2011;
w. NCC's Mobile Number Portability Regulations 2014;
x. National Digital Economy Policy and Strategy (NDEPS) 2020-2030 provided 8 pillars of the digital roadmap required to accelerate the development of the Nigerian Digital Economy which are; Developmental Regulation, Digital Literacy & Skills, Solid Infrastructure, Service

[18] See the Online Report made by Rayyan Alhassan that was published „inin <https://dailynigerian.com/> dated 23 June 2023 and titled "SSS has powers to prosecute cyberstalking, court rules" where a Federal High Court in Yenagoa dismissed a prelimnary objection filed by a defence counsel challenging the prosecution powers of the State Security Service (SSS), to prosecute cybercrimes under the Cybercrimes Act. 2015

[19] Queen Esther Iroanusi. „Nigeria government moves to control media, allocates N4.8bn to monitor WhatsApp, phone calls" <https://www.premiumtimesng.com > accessed 27 February 2022

Infrastructure, Digital Services Development & Promotion, Soft Infrastructure. Digital Society & Emerging Technology, and Indigenous Content Development & Adoption;

y. Nigeria Data Protection Regulation 2019;

z. Nigeria Data Protection Regulation Implementation Framework 2020;

aa. National Information and Technology Development Agency Act 2007;

bb. The 1999 Constitution. Section 39 provides that every person shall be entitled to freedom of expression, freedom to hold opinion, freedom to receive and impart ideas and information without interference. By this, digital rights could qualify as inexplicit rights;

cc. Section 8 of the Child's Right Act 2003 - Every child is entitled to his privacy, family life, home, correspondence, telephone conversation and telegraphic communication. See also Section 31 of the NDPA 2023 which provides that where data subject is a child lacking the legal capacity to consent, a data controller shall obtain the consent of his parent or legal guardian;

dd. The National Health Act 2014;

ee. The Criminal Code, Laws of the Federation 2004;

ff. The Penal Code Act, Laws of the Federation Nigeria 2004;

gg. Freedom of Information Act 2011;

hh. The Money Laundering (Prohibition) Act 2011;

ii. The National Identity Management Commission Act 2007;

jj. Advance Fee Fraud and Other Fraud Related Offences Act 2006. Sections 3 and 22 provides that any person that knowingly permits or allows his property to be used for Internet scam is guilty of an offence and punishable for not less than 5 years and not more than 15 years without an option of fine;

kk. the Credit Reporting Act 2017;

ll. NITDA Guidelines for the Management of Personal Data by Public Institution in Nigeria 2020;

mm. The Framework and Guidelines for Public Internet Access 2019;

nn. The Central Bank of Nigeria Consumer Protection Framework 2016;

oo. National Cybersecurity Policy and Strategy 2021;

pp. The HIV and AIDS (Anti-Discrimination) Act 2014;

qq. The Cybercrime Advisory Council headed by the Chairman of National Security Adviser;

rr. National Digital Forensic Laboratory;

ss. Guidelines for the Provision of Internet Service, ISP's licensed by the NCC have the precautionary obligation to protect their users, who may be content users;

tt. Decisions of the NCC/ NBC/FCCPA can be filed at the Federal High Court. By virtue of Section 50 of the Cybercrimes Act 2015, the jurisdiction to hear the case is vested in the Federal High Court;

uu. The FG Ministerial Standing Committee on Advisory Role for the Protection of Nigerian Cyberspace and ICT Infrastructure, which was inaugurated as a build-up to the 2023 presidential elections in Nigeria.

6. INTERNATIONAL LEGISLATION ON CYBERSECURITY

The fight for a safe cyberspace is global. Across the globe, there is a fundamental need to safeguard the cyberspace and ensure we keep to the rules. In doing so, States also have a positive obligation to protect their citizens from cybercrime.[20] They must not fail in this obligation while criminal investigation on reported cases of cyber violence must be promptly attended to, otherwise States can be made to pay compensation to the victims.[21] As we know, cybercrime does not have territorial limits. It is trans-boundary. That explains why terrorists are desperate to unleash crime in the cyberspace with the way technology has brought people and nations together although bedevilled with challenges. It should be noted that there is no international cybersecurity law in place. However there are general international regulation and framework enforcement instruments on cybersecurity which includes 'The African Union Convention on Cybersecurity and Personal Data Protection (the Malabo Convention) 2014. The framework governs the various aspects of information technology such as electronic transactions, personal data protection, cybersecurity and cybercrimes. Among other functions, it sets forth security rules essential for establishing a credible digital space while each Member State is expected to establish a domestic legal framework to strengthen fundamental rights and public freedoms, protection of physical data, and punishment of violation of

---

[20] ***K.U.* v. *Finland*** (2009) 48EHRR 52

[21] See ***Buturuga* v. *Romania*** ECHR 056 (2020); ***Volodina* v. *Russia*** (Application No. 40419/19)

privacy without prejudice to the free flow of personal data.[22] In Nigeria, Article 16 of the NDPR Implementation Framework 2020 provides that where the NDPR Framework does not provide for a data protection principle or process, the African Union Convention on Cyber Security and Personal Data Protection (Malabo Convention) 2000 and European Union General Data Protection Regulation (EU GDPR) and its judicial interpretations shall have a persuasive effect in Nigeria.

Beyond this, what are the regulatory regimes at the regional and international level considering the need for safety and security in the cyberspace? Note that the coalition of law enforcement and Interpol are partners in combating cybercrime while the partnership aims to strengthen and enhance digital connectivity with a view to creating a safe cyberspace.

a. The Convention on Cybercrime also known as the Budapest Convention on Cybercrime 2004 is a treaty-based international convention which seeks to address Internet and computer crime issues by harmonizing national laws, improving investigative techniques and increasing cooperation among nations.
b. The Council of Europe Convention on Preventing and Combating Violence Against Women and Domestic Violence 2011 better known as The Istanbul Convention.
c. The Lanzarote Convention on Protection of Children against Sexual Exploitation and Sexual Abuse 2007.
d. United Nations Security Council Group of Governmental Experts and the Open-Ended Working Group.
e. United Nations Office on Drugs and Crime Vienna Comprehensive Study on Cybercrime Draft 2013.
f. Common Thread Network – For Commonwealth Countries.
g. African Joint Operation against Cybercrime (AFJOC).
h. Network of African Data Protection. – The Round Table of African Data Protection Authorities (RADPA).
i. AU, EU and ITU Policy and Regulatory Initiative for Digital Africa (PRIDA)
j. 2001 European Cybercrime on Convention.

[22] Challenges and Prospects of the AU Convention on Cybersecurity and Personal Data Protection - Africa Data Security Conclave

k. INTERPOL Cybercrime Advisory Board - Google informed Interpol about a man who uploaded nude photos and videos of children in his Google account.[23]

l. The Economic Community of West African States (ECOWAS) Directive on fighting Cybercrime 2011 – that there should be a regional legislation in the face of the increasing level of cybercrime in the region.

m. The UN Economic and Social Council (ECOSOC) Resolution 2019 urges Member States to encourage the training of law enforcement officers, investigative authorities, prosecutors and Judges in the field of cybercrime, including relevant skills in evidence collection and information technology, and to equip them to effectively carry out their respective roles in investigating, prosecuting and adjudicating cybercrime offences.[24]

n. The UN Strategy and Plan of Action on Hate Speech 2019 is guided by one of the principles which states that in the digital age, the UN should support a new generation of digital citizens, empowered to recognizes, reject and stand up to hate speech. This calls for a coordinated data collection and research on the root causes, and conditions conducive to hate speech, while using technology to encourage more research on the relationship between the misuse of the Internet and what factors generate hate speech.

o. The Coalition for Digital Environmental Sustainability (CODES) 'Action Plan for a Sustainable Planet in the Digital Age' 2022. CODES is a global engagement platform for governments, businesses and civil society established under the UN Secretary-General's Roadmap for Digital Cooperation. The CODES stakeholders' sets out nine global impact initiatives that require taken collective actions and engage multi-stakeholder collaboration which seeks to address digital competencies, connecting transformations, digital divide, rights violations, governance breakthroughs and digital sustainable innovations.[25]

p. The e-Commerce Protocol to the African Continental Free Trade Area (AfCFTA) 2021, harmonises digital economy regulations and leverage the benefits of digital trade negotiations and agreements.

---

[23] Mahender Singh Manral. „Alerted by Interpol, CBI arrests man for sexually abusing four minors, uploading their videos online" <https://indianexpress.com/article/cities/> accessed 14 July 2023

[24] <https://www.unodc.org/rddb/document/crime/resolution/2019>

[25] <http://sdg.iisd.orgnews/global-coalition-launches-plan-for-sustainable-digital-transformation/?utm> accessed 28 July 2022

7. THE UNITED NATIONS CYBERCRIME DEBATE

The United Nations has recognized the importance of encryption, pseudonymisation and anonymity for ensuring the enjoyment of human rights to the Internet while governments should not interfere with their use. To this end, UN had to establish the 'Ad Hoc Committee to Elaborate a Comprehensive International Convention on Countering the Use of Information and Communication Technologies for Criminal Purposes' in 2020. The goal is to develop a global agreement that will comprehensively facilitate international cooperation and coordination to tackle cybercrime, identify cyber-enabled crimes and counter the misuse of ICT for criminal purposes. The Committee has thus recognized that cybercrime poses significant threat or risk and have security implications on human rights. In recent years, the UN General Assembly and various human rights organisations have expressed concerns over the fact that cybercrime laws are being misused by some countries to gag freedoms of expression in their domains. In response to this, some human rights organisations and experts from 56 countries sent a letter to the Ad Hoc Committee in 2021 calling for member states to ensure that any proposed convention on cybercrime incorporates clear and robust human rights safeguards; that purporting to combat fake news should not be used to imprison bloggers, journalists, Internet activists, whistle-blowers and digital security researchers who should be allowed to do their work without fear of prosecution, while at all times, there must be respect for international human rights standards.[26]

In 2024, while recognising the growing dangers of cybercrime, tht UN has set about drafting a legally-binding international treaty to counter the threat.[27]

Generally, these frameworks emphasise that member States/countries should adopt strategies that would improve cyber resilience and enable them to share information on vulnerabilities and capacity building. States must therefore comply with their international law obligations, respect human rights and promote trust in their domain. The right of all countries to independent Internet development must also be respected with regards to

---

[26] „Letter to the United Nations to include human rights safeguards in proposed cybercrime treaty" <https://www.hrw.org/news/2022/01/13/ > accessed 30 April 2022

[27] „Global Cybercrime Treaty: A delicate balance between security and human rights" <https://news.un.org/en/interview/2024/> accessed 10 March 2024

peaceful use of cyberspace.[28] However, the position of customary international law is that every treaty in force is binding upon the contracting states to it and must be performed by them in good faith. This principle is known as *Pacta Sunt Servanda*" - that agreements are to be respected is a fundamental tenet of customary international law.[29] Note that if a country does not subscribe to the primary cyber conventions, the treaty will still be binding on the country under the rules of customary international law. In the United States of America, the Internet Crime Complaint (IC3) is designated as the proper complaints website for all Internet crimes, computer-assisted crimes and reporting of suspected or real Internet animal abuse as long as the abuse occurred in the US. The website will usually direct the complainant to the page where victims can file their complaint.

8. UNITED STATES CISA GUIDELINES ON CYBERSECURITY

It is well known that a cybercriminal exploiting computer vulnerability can perform malicious actions in many ways such as installing malicious malware, running malicious code, network scanning, e-mail spamming and stealing sensitive data. The US has taking many proactive steps on cybersecurity one of which is the establishment of their federal agency called the Cybersecurity and Infrastructural Security Agency (CISA) - the government's cybersecurity agency that monitors, manage and reduce risk to the country's critical infrastructure. It also issue alerts relating to high-profile data breaches and vulnerability disclosures. As part of its continuing mission to reduce cybersecurity threats across the US and territorial governments, CISA has compiled a list of free cybersecurity tools and services to help organisations to further advance their security capabilities. According to CISA, all organisations should take certain foundational measures to implement a strong cybersecurity program such as fixing known security flaws in software; implement multifactor and authentication (MFA); halt bad practices and sign up for CISA's Cyber Hygiene Vulnerability Scanning. Organisations are also requested to use the free services and tools provided by CISA to reduce the likelihood of a damaging cyber incident, detect malicious activity

[28] Press Release of the Security Council on „Explosive Growth of Digital Technologies of Creating New Potential for Conflict, Disarmament Chief Tells Security Council in First-Ever Debate on Cyber threats" <https://www.un.org/press/en/2021/sc14563.doc.htm> accessed 23 February 2023

[29] See the Vienna Convention on the Law of Treaties 1969

quickly, respond effectively to confirmed incidents and maximize resilience.[30] In 2004, National Cybersecurity Awareness month was created through a partnership between CISA and the National Cybersecurity Alliance (NCSA) where individuals come together in the month of October of every year to pursue their passion for online protection based on the belief that cybersecurity is everyone's job. According to CISA, the many ways to observe the cybersecurity awareness month includes being cyber vigilant, changing passwords, becoming a cybersecurity champion, running antivirus scans on all devices, providing Endpoint Detection and Response (EDR) and Network Detection and Response (NDR) solutions which can help organisations stay ahead of cyber threats.[31]

In recent times, CISA has expanded its Known Exploited Vulnerabilities (KEV) catalogue for the purpose of curbing vulnerabilities and malicious actions in the cyber space. KEV are types of vulnerabilities that are frequent attack vectors for malicious cyber actors that pose significant risks to the federal enterprise.[32] In other words, these are vulnerabilities that have been explicitly discovered through scanning and testing.[33]

In 2023, the Joe Biden administration released the implementation plan for its National Cybersecurity Strategy – officially setting in motion its ambitious initiative to shore up vulnerable cyber defences and improve preparedness nationwide. The plan established five plans which are:

- defend critical infrastructure;
- disrupt and dismantle threat actors;
- shape market forces to drive security and resilience;
- invest in long-term cybersecurity internationally.[34]

9. GLOBAL CONSENSUS ON DIGITAL COOPERATION

Digital cooperation is the act of enhancing global collaboration in multiple forms to address the societal, ethical, legal and economic impacts of digital technologies, aiming to maximise the benefits to society and minimise harms.

---

[30] <https://www.cisa.gov/free-cybersecurity-services-and-tools> accessed 22 February 2022

[31] Danika Veilkamp. „The History of National Cybersecurity Awareness Month" <https:// infosystems. biz/ cybersecurity/ > accessed 10 November 2021

[32] Ionut Arghire. „CISA Tells US Agencies to Patch Exploited Roundcube, VMware Flaws" <https:// www.securityweek.com/> accessed 26 June 2023

[33] Check the CISA Website for the KEV catalog <https://www.cisa.gov/known-exploited-vulnerabilities/>

[34] Tom McKay. „The National Cybersecurity Strategy is now officially in motion" <https://www. itbrew.com/stories/2023/7> accessed 20 July 2023.

The purpose is to provide a vision and steerage for a digitally interdependent world. It lays out actions for the global community to connect, respect and protect people in the digital age.[35]

Tracing the history of digital cooperation, it will be recalled that in 1998, the International Telecommunications Union (ITU) passed a resolution calling on the UN to convene a summit of world leaders to develop the emerging information society and utilize ICT to bridge in the global development divide. Consequently in 2003 and 2005, a World Summit on the Information Society (WSIS) took place in Geneva, Switzerland and Tunisia to define the issues, policies and frameworks to tackle ICT to foster development which became a critical moment in the history of the Internet. Thereafter in 2018, a high-level on Digital Cooperation was convened to introduce proposals that will strengthen cooperation in the digital space among state, non-state actors and other relevant stakeholders who issued a report titled '*The Age of Digital Interdependence*' offering five sets of recommendations for the international community with a view to optimizing the use of technologies and mitigate risks. In 2020, following a multi-stakeholder consultative process with Member States, another report titled '*Roadmap for Digital Cooperation*' was published to envisage action points to connect, respect and protect the online world. In 2021, the SG appointed a *Special Envoy on Technology* to help facilitate a multi-stakeholder policy dialogue on emerging technologies and guide the UN's strategy on technology trends. In 2023, another attempt was made to codify international digital cooperation in a report titled *Policy Brief on a Global Digital Compact.*

It should be noted that the UN does not lack platforms on digital cooperation because currently, there are over 20 UN intergovernmental and multi-stakeholder digital cooperation bodies and forums working on digital-related issues and innovation.

The UN published a report leading to the Summit of the Future in 2024 where a new consensus on the future of humanity is expected to be forged. In so doing, the SG set up a vast multi-stakeholder consultation on digital cooperation track of which outcome will address current gaps in digital governance. The UN observed that in 1991, the world was on the verge of a

---

[35] See the Report of the Secretary-General Roadmap for Digital Cooperation. <https://unicri.it/news/report-secretary-general> accessed 01 June 2023

digital revolution when Internet technologies previously accessible only to governments and research institutions were about to be accessible to everyone with the aim of empowering them with digital access to information. The UN having recognized that although States have continued to drive the pace of commercial interests as it relates to technology in the physical world, sadly it is not replicated in the digital space which still remains insufficiently governed, prompting urgent social, ethical, economic and regulatory questions.

As underscored by the UN Secretary-General, the digital domain is a global public good that should benefit everyone everywhere while Internet access should become a basic human right. In the 2023 *Policy Brief on a Global Digital Compact*, the SG outlined a multi-stakeholder approach to ensure "open free and secure digital future for all that is anchored in universal human rights positively driving the attainment of the Sustainable Development Goals (SDGs)." Some of the outlined interventions will address:

- digital connectivity and capacity building;
- digital cooperation to accelerate progress on the SDGs;
- upholding human rights;
- an inclusive, open, secure and shared Internet;
- digital trust and security;
- data protection and empowerment;
- agile governance of AI and other emerging technologies;
- global digital commons.[36]

10. LAW AND TECHNOLOGY

Internet technologies is a technical field that covers the necessary skills to develop applications on the Internet or Internet based systems, harnessing e-commerce, cloud, mobile and Web based technologies.[37]The laws play a supporting role in science and technology while the intersection of law and information technology helps improve the cyber world in addressing challenges. As we implement and incorporate technologies into the justice system through the introduction of electronic justice services and integrating

[36]Evgeniya Altukhova. „Connecting the World Through Digital Cooperation" <http://sdg.iisd.org/commentary/policy-brief/> accessed 03 June 2023

[37] „Overview of Computer Internet Technology"<https://learn.org/artcles/> accessed 30 June 2023

ICTs such as video conferencing, holographic evidence presentation technology, the nexus between technology and law continues to grow.[38] Obviously, we are in a stage where almost every field requires technology to adequately function. Technology requires expertise and training which in turn offers the opportunity to use digital information and infuse law into the *techie* field while sharing it appropriately with the public. Despite the fact that technology is advancing, it is subject to regulation especially when it comes to complying with local, state and federal government requirements. Instances are legal framework on regulating technological products using (both hardware and software) to improve productivity and get results; selling technologies to create revenue; regulating companies which creates technology and participation in technology events; and regulation of those who work in tech companies, etc. This in effect means that law governs the use of technology as it pertains to cybersecurity. It covers all of the ways that modern devices and methods of communication impact on society. It seeks to answer the rights and obligations of individuals or private corporations relating to the information in the technology space. In view of this, technology law is a subset of information technology law, regulating the legal aspects of cybersecurity governing cybersecurity protocols, data privacy, data risks, data security, digital rights, digital forensics, darknet, quantum computing and edge computing issues, cloud, blockchain, IOTs, Police investigations, preventive forensics, intellectual property and all cyber-related activities and transactions. Technology related law intervenes when technological issues or disputes arise, thus developing the field for electronic governance and monitoring the use of electronic data interchange and other forms of electronic communication transactions. In criminal investigation, technology proves useful in crime scene analysis and evidence gathering. High technology crime refers to those crimes that are conducted using electronic and digitally based technology like the Internet through the help of a computer. These crimes are called cybercrimes, computer crimes or technological crimes. There are two categories:

a. Computer-assisted crimes such as Internet fraud, distribution of child pornography, laundering money, committing online slander and defamation, etc.;

[38] Mayki Hovhannesyan. „Emojis & the Law." <https://www.linkedin.com> accessed 24 October 2022. Also see: ***South West Terminal Ltd* v. *Achter Land*** (2023) SKKB 116

b. Crimes that are directed toward a computer or computer network such as hacking and distribution of computer viruses. This shows that every field has a tech presence.[39]

A lawyer therefore has a role to play in advising technology companies involved in provision of technical solutions/services or to individuals who use software and hardware. The lawyer must understand some basic knowledge in technology,[40] thus provoking the following points to ponder:

- Technology is human controlled. Any human controlled activity is subject to law;
- How has law embraced technology or merge the two fields together?
- Are justice systems digitized? Digitisation of case law unlike the physical congestion of cases that we are traditionally used to;
- Using telecommunications with our clients through email, voicemail, web conferencing and zoom webinars instead of physical attendance and travel;
- Digitising legal documents effectively and efficiently. Digital case management enable lawyers to share files with other colleagues through electronic law platforms;
- Leveraging technology analytics helps understand the context of complex statements in legal documents;
- With the intervention of AI, a work that can take longer time can be quickly attended to and dispensed with. It can help with complex research better than physical record searches and personal knowledge alone;
- Creating online legal communities to collaborate and network;
- **Cyber Law -** also called the Law of the Internet, deals with the legal issues of cyberspace. Internet law seeks to explore and determine how law and legal principles govern the use of the Internet. These laws help businesses to prevent any kind of identities and data theft, privacy violation and fraud. It also include laws related to e-commerce, e-contracts, digital signatures, intellectual property rights and cybersecurity and various categories of cybercrimes. To become a cyber-law professional, you must get certificated and acquire skills or training in knowledge of IOTs, cybersecurity, network identity, access management,

[39] <https://definitions.uslegal.com/h/high-technology> accessed 20 May 2022

[40] Joshua Omale. „What Exactly is a Tech Job" <https/hackernoon.com/> accessed 31 May 2022

malware analysis and cybercrime, the practices, the standards, procedures and methodologies related to cybercrime and law.[41]

- **Cyber Justice** – this field connects to a larger set of issues which requires an accessible justice system. This is the act of protecting and promoting human rights on the Internet or the cyberspace and the regulation of the interaction between providers and Internet users. For instance, when you integrate ICTs into online dispute resolution processes, filing of writs to the writing of judgment; introduction of IT in the traditional justice system to serve its various stakeholders (Training Judges, Lawyers, Court administrators and parties to understand AI and to apply it). The goal is to ease the justice system and make it more affordable, accessible and efficient through technology.[42] Furthermore, in accordance with the Nigerian Judiciary Information Technology Policy Document, stakeholders must be exposed to adjudication of online disputes, online identity, digital rights and other emerging field of telecommunications. Similarly, the new Judicial Information Technology Policy provides guidance for acceptable use of systems, services and technological as well as provisions for secure storage of judicial data and recovery processes in the event of emergencies or distress. This applies to all Courts handling information that is generated received, stored, transmitted or printed including other supporting mechanisms and technology.
- Cyber justice recognises that there should be rules in place to guide digital practice in remote proceedings, electronic recordings / electronic filings/ transcript and translation function / data management / paperless Court / training Judges to understand technology and practical application of it. Cyber justice will also seek ways to balance the interest of users of technology while not hindering cutting-edge advancements in science.
- **Cyber Forensics** – This is the maintenance of the tread of evidence and documentation to find out who committed a crime digitally. It is a field involving cyber forensics investigation tools, e-discovery, digital evidence collection and preservation, e-mail investigation, tracking and recovery,

[41] Anshuman Singh. „What is Cyber Law? All You Need to Know" <naukri.com> accepted 20 August 2022

[42] Kenny Benyekhlef. „Cyberjustice" <https://www.academic-foresights.com/> accessed 15 April 2022

search and seizure of computers, recovery of deleted evidence, password cracking as well as encryption and decryption.

- The UNODC ECOSOC Resolution 2019 urges Member States to encourage the training of law enforcement officers, investigative authorities, prosecutors and Judges in the field of cybercrime, including in relevant skills pertaining to evidence collection and information technology, and to equip them to effectively carry out their respective roles in investigating, prosecuting and adjudicating cybercrime offences.[43]
- National Office for Technology Acquisition and Promotion (NOTAP) – an agency under the aegis of the Federal Ministry of Science & Technology. The body has structured departments like technology innovation, technology transfer and research coordination, for the purpose of correcting certain imperfections in the acquisition of foreign technology when they are brought into the country.
- Technology skills are practical skills which improve lives. To celebrate the positive impact of technology, every January 6 of every year, the National Technology Day is observed as an awareness day to discuss how technology has changed the world for good and how we can relate with the future of technology. For example, we embrace technology in agriculture, healthcare, education, security, entertainment and other areas that impact our daily lives. In the area of communications, we use various tools to communicate with people as well. Anything that advances productivity is driven by technology.[44] In other jurisdictions, technology day is observed every year on May 11 as a day to recognize technical advancements that have aided in nation building.[45] No doubt, technology surely improves productivity and gives us an insight into how the world works.

---

[43] <https://www.unodc.org/rddb/document/crime/resolution/2019> accessed 12 November 2022

[44] „National Technology Day – January 6" <https://nationaldaycalendar.com> accessed 13 December 2022

[45] Sudeshna Dutta. „National Technology Day 2023: Date, Theme, History, facts, Ouotes, Theme" <https://www.edudwar.com/> accessed 05 January 2023

Chapter 9

CYBER VIOLENCE AGAINST WOMEN IN NIGERIA

I. ABSTRACT[1]

Historically, women have always been at the receiving end of various forms of violence. This violence has been extended to the digital space in recent years. Cyber violence is indeed real and it is often used interchangeably with 'online violence', 'e-violence', 'digital violence' or 'techie violence' which evolved with the advent of information communications technology (ICT). The major forms of cyber violence against women includes cyber(sexual) harassment and bullying, cyber stalking, online gender-based hate speech, flaming, image-based sexual abuse/non-consensual pornography revenge porn and doxing.[2] According to the survey carried out by the Economic Intelligence Unit, 85% of women globally have experienced or witnessed digital violence. In Nigeria, there is a growing concern over perpetrators who are making criminal use of technology to attack women in the cyberspace. These perpetrators with vast majority of them being male abusers hide behind the Internet as a shield to protect their online identity or digital footprint. A general assumption that people want to believe is that online violence against women is not as dangerous like the conventional forms of physical violence. In view of the fact women are invariably the target of online violence, this chapter will examine the correlation between women and online violence as well as the forms of online violence, the protection mechanisms derived from the existing international and Nigeria's legal framework towards ensuring that the same 'offline' rights and legal

[1] This is an updated version of my paper that was earlier published in the Ekiti State University Law Journal and cited as (2017) 8 EKSU-LJ.

2 See World Bank Group Global Briefs No. 18 Report on „Protecting Women and Girls from Cyber Harassment: A Global Assessment of Existing Laws" (June 2023)

protection that women enjoy in physical life does apply to female Internet users.

2. INTRODUCTION

The cyber space is a product of the information and communications technology (ICT) age which are technologies that provide access to Internet-enabled information through any computer device that store, retrieve, manipulate, transmit or receive information electronically. Connection to the Internet is done via the technology of modem and a telephone line. Section 418 of the Criminal Law of Lagos State 2015 defines a computer as a device that computes, especially a programmable electronic machine that performs high-speed mathematical or logical operation or that assembles, stores, correlates or otherwise processes information. These functions are generated for example through computers, laptops, digital television, Internet, email, wireless networks, cell phones and other communication mediums.[3] The technological or Internet revolution is enabled by the growing surfing of popular social media networks such as *Instagram*, *Facebook* and X (formerly *Twitter)*, etc., as they constitute integral online platforms in the global world.[4] As a matter of fact, statistics say, there are more than 6.5 billion smartphone users all over the world.[5] Out of Nigeria's estimated population of over 200 million people,[6] 36.24 million Nigerians are said to visit *Facebook* daily as at March 2022 and according to NCC, Nigeria's connected mobile lines hit 301.5 million in May 2022.[7] No wonder Nigeria has been ranked number one in Africa and eight in the world in terms of Internet usage.[8]

---

[3]<http://www.thelawyerschronicle.com/ict-and-the-advancement-of-legal-studies-and-practice-in-nigeria/> accessed 30 August 2016

[4]Jeff Hearn. „The implications of Information and Communication Technologies for Sexualities and Sexualised Violence: Contradiction of Sexual Citizenship" – Political Geography, Volume 25, Issue 8, November 2006

[5] „National Cell Phone Courtesy Month" <https://www.daysoftheyear.com/> accessed 16 July 2023

[6] „Nigeria: Population Forecast 2025-2050- Statista" <https://www.statista.com> accessed 12 December 2022

[7] Samson Akintaro. „Nigeria's connected mobile lines hit 301.5 million in May 2022, over 97 million not in use" <https://nairametrics.com/2022/06/27/> accessed 30 July 2022

[8] < www.vanguardngr.com/nigeria-ranks-no-1-Internet-usage-africa/> dated 16 November 2016

Globally, while men are still more intense users of the Internet, women are said to be almost at par with men and even stay longer on the Internet.[9] In 2015, 51% of *Instagram* users were said to be male while 49% were female. 56% of *Linkedin* users were male while 44% were female.[10] Currently, *Facebook* and *Instagram* have a larger female user base as 77% of women globally use *Facebook* compared with two-thirds of men. 31% of women use *Instagram* compared with 24% of men[11] while the youths occupy the remaining space. In February 2022, the global *Facebook* user distribution by gender in 2022 showed that 43.4% of female users were women while 56.6% were male. As at February 2022, there were 326 million female users and 430 million male subscribers on *Linkedin.*

Due to the rise in the use of digital technology, the participation of Nigerian women in the online space has improved considerably overtime especially with the Federal Government initiatives that were focussed on ICT gender-friendly schemes such as the *Smart Woman Program, 1000 ICT Girls Training, Digitals Girls Club* and *Young Innovators Competition.* These schemes align with Goal 5 of the 17 UN 2015 Sustainable Development Goals (SDGs) which advocated that one way of achieving gender equality and empowerment for all women[12] is not only by giving free and easy access for women to have unhindered public information but also by ensuring that they enjoy provision of education and representation in decision-making process. All these initiatives are information-driven and thus in agreement with Section 39(1) of the 1999 Constitution of Nigeria which provides that every person is entitled to freedom of expression, including freedom to hold opinions and to receive and impart ideas and information. Therefore, free speech being a fundamental human right means it is important for Nigerian women to be positively informed and take advantage of information (whether offline or online) through the use of technology to set sustainable goals for their future in order to enhance their self-development,

Nonetheless, women's interaction with the cyberspace has become an enabling platform and a voice to share information in an easier, flexible,

---

[9]Anunobi CV, Mbagwu FC. „Prevalence of Gender Discrepancy in Internet Use in Nigeria: Implication for Women Empowerment." African Research Review Vol.3 (1) 2009, 259-274

[10] The Guardian Newspaper of December 21, 2015

[11] Statistics from Pew Research Centre of May 2016

[12] Gender equality is one of the 17 Global Goals that make up the 2030 Agenda for Sustainable Development. Available at: <www undp org/content/...sdgoverview/..> accessed 28 August 2016

fastest and efficient way.[13] For instance, any news concerning the plight of abused women and other gender hashtags usually attract global attention during the yearly observance of the International Women's Day and the United Nations 16 day-activism on elimination of violence against women. The yearly awareness objectives are focused on promoting respect for women's rights as human rights and the total elimination of all forms of gender-based violence. By sharing information, we correct wrong impressions and amplify that women's rights are human rights.

Whilst it is common knowledge that the growth of technology in modernised digitization process have created a trans-boundary world of 'positives' for the female gender, the rebound is that it has equally created an opportunity for perpetrators to infringe on the rights of women online. This is usually referred to as 'technology-related violence against women (otherwise shortened to '*tech-related VAW*') which the 1979 *Convention on the Elimination of all forms of Discrimination against Women* (CEDAW) insist it should still fall under the realm of general violence against women having been redefined as acts that inflict physical, mental or sexual harm or suffering, threats or such acts, coercion and other deprivations of liberty.[14]

This evolving process of social media has predisposed women to various forms of online violence such as sharing of negative gossips or wicked rumours, spreading demeaning pictures/videos and hate messages, Internet stalking, sexual and non-sexual harassment,[15] romance fraud and extortion, cyber bullying, identity theft, public shaming, and other indecent acts that are classified under psychological or mental violence[16] that have subjected her to emotional distress, depression, damage to reputation, physical harm, suicidal ideation and even death. In 2022, the UNFPA revealed that 57% of

---

[13] Snapchat is a photo and messaging application where the videos only be seen briefly for 10 seconds and after that, the pictures and videos disappear forever, while the story exist only for 24 hours. In India, Snapchat has been used as a proficient tool by women (who had previously been silenced) to open up about their harrowing experience about sexual assaults on video. The Snapchat filters obscure the survivors" identities although viewers can still capture their facial expressions. However their anonymity is protected. Available at: <http.qz.com/762880/> accessed 16 September 2016

[14]APC Women"s Rights Programme. Briefing Paper on VAW of June 2015. Available at: <www.apc.org/en/system/files/HRC%2029%VAW%20a%20briefing%20paper_FINAL_June%202015.pdf> accessed 28 August 2016

[8] The United Kingdom Equal Opportunities Commission (EOC) defines sexual harassment as "actions which are unacceptable to the people on the receiving end and which may include unwelcome comments, or suggestions such as requests for sexual favours"

[16] Obiamaka G. Araka. „Family Violence and Child Abuse" in *Law of Domestic Violence in Nigeria.* Azinge E and Uche L (eds) (NIALS Press Abuja 2012) pp 410 - 442

women have had their videos or images online, abused or misused while 96% of online deepfake videos are pornography images of women. UNPFA further stated that violence against women remains the world's most chronic, most devastating and most overlooked violation of human rights.[17]

Similarly, a UNESCO study of Journalists found that 73% of women surveyed online had experienced cyber violence, while 20% said that they had experienced physical attacks or had been abused offline in connection to online abuse.[18] The threat of online violence also affects professional women with high ranking public profile and in these groups are women in the entertainment industry and women that are political office holders. Every age group is at risk. This has raised growing concerns that women need to be reassured that they need to be safe in the cyberspace just like in the real world.

Basically, there are specific legislations which seek to address the challenges posed by cyber violence against women, with the apex law being the Nigeria's Cybercrimes (Prohibition, Prevention, Etc.) Act 2015 and other protective frameworks set out to prosecute cybercrime of all sorts. In light of these challenges, this chapter will examine the issues and implications of the impact of cyber world on women as victims of online violence. It will clarify key concepts, explore case studies and consider the available international and national protective framework with its limitations and offer recommendations with a view to achieving right-based solutions for female victims or survivors in Nigeria.

3. CLARIFICATION OF CONCEPTS

With virtually everyone having a computer and Internet access, perpetrators of cybercrime continue to commit cyber violence in privacy, concealment and anonymity against women online,.

i. Cyberspace

Cyberspace is common to all, for it does not have a geographical barrier. Other terms ascribed to the cyberspace are web, Internet, online world, social networks and social media. The term 'cyberspace' was first used by

[17] UNPFA Newsletter <unpfa.org/press/statement/> accessed 28 June 2022

[18] Gina Neff. „The Internet is at Risk of Driving Women Away" <https://www.wired.co.uk> accessed 24 December 2022

the American-Canadian author William Gibson in his science-fiction novel where he defined cyberspace as the creation of a computer network in a world filled with artificially intelligent beings.[19] The *Merriam-Webster Dictionary* also defined the cyberspace as the online world of computer networks and Internet while the Law Dictionary Online describes the cyberspace as the realm where computer communication and simulations are used on the Internet. Based on the above perspectives, cyberspace encompasses a digitally loose platform for interaction, exchange of ideas, sharing of information, provision of social support to conduct business, play games, and engage in political discussions among several activities. In other words, the web could either be an open unrestricted platform or a hidden web that is indexed by search engine. Note that it is possible for a person to be on the cyberspace without leaving the confines of his room. All he needs do is just to log on to a portal or other social networks with the tools of the Internet. According to a *Forensic Magazine*, "some people do not only go online, they are living online where they are trying to find someone to accept them."[20]

ii. Information and Communications Technology (ICT)

ICT is an electronic communication channel for disseminating good and bad information. Under the Nigerian framework, Section 58 of the Cybercrimes (Prohibition, Prevention, Etc.) Act 2015 categorised the forms of electronic communications into format instant messages, short message service (SMS), email, voice mails, multimedia message service (MMS), fax and pager.[21] ICT has compressed the world into a global village making it easier for users to transmit and share whatever messages they like at any given time although the web also provides a fertile ground for cyber criminals to hide in places

[19] Jennifer Bussell. „Cyberspace" <https://www.britanicca.com/topic/> accessed 10 March 2022

[20] Available at: www.forensicmag.com/news/2017/02/social-media-age-more-suicides-violent-acts-streamed-live?et_cid=5812642&et_rid> accessed 01 February 2017

[21] See Section 153 of the Evidence Act 2011 which provides for the presumption of telegraphic and electronic messages. With this, the Court may presume that any message you feed into your computer originated from your email, so far it is delivered from your email address. The Court will deem it as proved unless it is disproved by superior evidence.

where the long arm of the law cannot easily reach them. The implication of ICT was expressed thus by Lord Hoffman in **R v. *Brown*:**[22]

> One of the less consequences of ICT revolution has been the ease with which it has become possible to invade the privacy of the individual. No longer is it necessary to peep through the keyholes or listen under the eaves. The right to keep oneself to oneself to tell other people that certain things are none of their business is under technological threat.

ICT therefore has implications for women's rights to privacy guaranteed by Section 37 of the 1999 Constitution which applies even to one's telephone conversation and telegraphic communication.

iii. Cyber Violence

Violence is generally associated with physical force. However, where a person uses computer systems or a computer network to facilitate criminal activity, it becomes a cyber-assisted crime and this extends farther than the 'yahoo boy' somewhere in the cyber café perpetrating online fraud.[23] It is worthy to note that the definition of cyber violence relates to a form of attack or assault that occur by electronic technology committed with the help of phones, computers and tablets or through communication platforms such as social media sites, text messages, chat platforms and websites, so that when a person sends abusive text messages or emails or post false information, share embarrassing pictures or videos and fake profiles via social networking sites like *X(Twitter)* , *Facebook, Instagram, WhatsApp,* or *Snapchat* right from the convenience of his room to molest, threaten or create fear to another, through the computer, then such a person is indulging in online or cyber violence. Examples of cyber violence are cyber bullying and cyber stalking which the National Crime Prevention Council defined as the process of using the Internet, cell phones, or other devices to send or post text or

---

[22] (1996) 1 ALL E R 545 at 555 - For example, a paedophile can easily and sometimes convincingly masquerade as a 16 year-old boy or girl. Also see Ian J. Lloyd, *Information Technology Law* (Oxford University Press 2011)

[23] Ikenga K.E. Oraegbunam „ Draft Paper on Cyber Criminality and Socio-Economic Development in Nigeria Today: Examining the Possible Impact of Cybercrime Act of 2015" Available at <www.altng.org/wp content/uploads/2016/06/04.pdf> accessed 08 September 2016

images intended to hurt or embarrass another person.[24] Bullying on the Internet platform include posting negative comments, abusive remarks, sending repeated insults on a user's wall or using pictures or videos to harass another user.[25] However these actions must cause panic attacks and threaten the victim's life or create fear and disrespect the dignity of the victim. Closely associated with cyber violence perpetrators are Internet trolls who intentionally try to provoke or offend others online in order to elicit a reaction.[26] Suffice it to say that Article I of *The Protocol to the African Charter on Human and Peoples' Rights on the Rights of Women in Africa* defines 'Violence against women' as all acts perpetrated against women which cause or could cause them physical, sexual, psychological, and economic harm.'[27] Sadly, women have mostly become victims of cyber violence while its consequences have led to actual suicide, suicidal tendencies, physical or emotional harm, depression, mental illness and death.[28]

iv. Protective Framework

It is generally known that the Internet gives greater freedom to users but without a baseline or structured ethics of what sort of information should be posted online. It is therefore not surprising that stories concerning women make viral headlines on social networks where the circulation does a lot of damage to their psyche. For instance, a study conducted by Columbia University and the French National Institute revealed that up to six in 10 *Facebook* users share links without even opening them - meaning some stories spread without knowing whether the details are actually true.[29] Any protective framework is majorly law-driven that guarantees the online safety, privacy and digital well-being of all especially women who are regarded as vulnerable. In fact, women whose rights are being infringed online can use the protective framework in the 1999 Constitution to enforce their

[24] <www.ncpc.org/> accessed 22 November 2016

[25] See Section 56(1) of the Criminal Law of Lagos State where the punishment is 3 years imprisonment. Section 57(4) of the Law provides that an electronically generated image is a form of pictorial representation.

[26] NC Asthana „Inside the Minds of Internet Trolls: A Psychological Analysi < https://m.thewire.in > accessed 28 April 2020

[27] UNGA Article 1 of the Declaration on the Elimination of Violence against Women 1993 defines violence to women as any act of gender-based violence…whether occurring in public or in private life.

[28] See Nigerian Tribune, 19 August 2016. "Cyber-bullying: Celebrities as endangered Species" pp. 20-21

[29] Caitlin Dewey. „6 in 10 of you will share this link without reading it, a new, depressing study says" <https://www.washingtonpost.com > accessed 16 November 2016

fundamental human rights. The rights are constitutionally guaranteed so that if there is a breach, an aggrieved woman may proceed to Court to enforce her rights pursuant to Section 46 of the 1999 Constitution where she may be entitled to compensatory remedies. A protective framework also includes the actions of the law enforcement agencies and other stakeholders who take accelerated actions and initiatives to ensure a safer and more secure Internet for present and future generations. For instance in the United Kingdom, the establishment of the *Office of Cyber Security and Information Assurance* in 2009, the 2008 *Report on Safer Children in a Digital World*, the *UK Internet Watch Foundation* and the *Safer Internet Programme* are established protection initiatives designed to protect female ICT users because women are considered most vulnerable to online violence. In Nigeria, initiatives such as the establishment of *Nigerian Cybercrime Working Group*, the 2008 *Child Online Protection* (COP), the 2013 *Child Helpline Steering Group*, the *EFCC 2009 Project Eagle Claw* and *West African Internet Fraud Summit* have all collectively helped to achieve a safe online space to an extent. The role of intermediaries or digital gate-keepers such as Internet/content service providers, Internet entrepreneurs of social media networks and search engines are also very important in ensuring online respect and a secured online space for Internet users.[30] The overall objective is to ensure a safe online space with safety controls where technology will not threaten the survival of women and impede their progress.. Member States under international law are therefore under obligation to protect women from harmful online activities.[31]

---

[30] At a time, the website „*Megaupload'* was shut down by the US government for allowing illegal sharing of files. <Forensicmag.com> online reports that the creator of a dark web child pornography site known as "Playpen"was sentenced to 30 years in prison and lifetime supervision. He was also ordered to forfeit his residential home and other property related to his crimes. Concerning Facebook, for instance, if a Facebook friend"s comment is annoying or insulting on your post, Facebook allows you to mark such comment as spam and gives you the option to block the friend so you will not see the commenter and his future posts. An aggrieved person can also report to Facebook and demand that any malicious content be taken down. Facebook administrators can help to send a message to the commenter that his comment is annoying. In regard to violent graphic content, Facebook can remove the graphic images which glorify violence or disable access to any content that is maliciously reported. The Social Network has also started to attach warning labels to made-up stories as it did recently in Germany. Facebook has equally agreed to hire more staff to stamp out violence.

[31] United Nations is on the verge of making a new law that prevents children from accessing pornographic websites. See The Daily Mail Newspaper, July 12, 2017. Page 28

4.LINK BETWEEN CYBERVIOLENCE AND WOMEN

Women encounter all sorts of characters online and so become frequent targets of cyber violence. The easier accessibility to the Internet has made it easy for cyber-abusers to connect seamlessly with women and exploit them. Sadly, this endangers their physical, mental and emotional well-being. The linkage comes in different ways such as:

1. Risk of young girls and women chatting with evil-minded and pretentious adults who fraudulently set up meetings to abuse their victims. In some countries, threats from social media accounts of men posing as innocent individuals are on the increase. For example, a 13 year-old girl was arrested and charged with one count of threatening to kill by electronic message after she contacted an online clown to help her murder her teacher;[32]
2. As women and girls continue to seek for love or companionship on social media dating apps/sites, scammers come up with bad intention to defraud the female victims, Lonely women seeking harmless fun or genuine relationships online sometimes fall into the wrong hands of these perpetrators who extort them. Sometimes these men illegally use the online details of women to trick them into releasing funds. For example, some Nigerians were arrested in Malaysia for defrauding women they met on dating sites through what they call cyber-dating. Those involved in the various *China Telecomm Fraud* cases also targeted elderly women, single mothers, female college students and unemployed women and what it entailed is just a scammer posing as some kind of government official. There is also a new scam called 'pig butchering' which is a combination of romance scam with an investment spin. The scammer here creates a fake profile to reach out to potential victims on social media, WhatsApp, and other dating sites. He pretends to be an old friend and initiates a cordial discussion with the victim, attempting to be a new friend or lover. While building trust with the victim, the scammer slowly introduce the idea of making investment.[33] Another instance is when online male friends and strangers engage in sexual messaging (sexting) or phone sex with women;

---

[32] <https://truecrimedaily.com/2016/10/94 > accessed 27 August 2018

[33] Michigan Department of Attorney General. „Cryptocurrency Scam-Pig Butchering" <https://www.michigan.gov/ag/consumer-protection/> accessed 24 December 2022

although it may be seen as a consensual act, sexting mostly require a level of coercion from men;

3. Advertised online movies, online games, uncensored porn sites are disguised in a deceitful manner to purposely draw web traffic of women towards certain websites where they meet violent sexual predators. In fact, some AI dating apps have been created deliberately to harass women.[34] This play a critical role in negatively influencing and shaping the psyche of affected female users. For example, there are celebrity porn websites where naked pictures are taken from female participants without their consent. Exposure to some dangerous sites has also led some women to kill themselves, when they are being blackmailed;
4. Online methods of inflicting violence can also be exhibited through trafficking of innocent female undergraduates into cult or prostitution groups (runs girls)[35] all have turned into hunting grounds for vulnerable victims masquerading as closed or secret groups on social media platforms. Some of these groups are also used as channels to recruit or conscript young ladies and women as terrorists but displayed under the guise of religion;[36]
5. A lot of web-gender based information consists of junk and misleading information which lacks authority, accuracy and objectivity. Issues relating to content in spam and illegal/ harmful content on some Internet sites are programmed to extract database of potential female victims to perpetrate criminal activities and to exploit these women;
6. There is an ever growing addiction to the Internet by these women who have encountered cyber scams in business investments, scholarships, jobs, lotteries, grants, loans and medical emergency schemes;[37]
7. The endless webcam streaming and sharing of sexual activities on social media platforms relayed live through video apps.[38]

---

[34] Frank Landymore. „Meet Cupidbots, The Horrifying Dating App Using AI To Harrass Women"<https://futurism.com/the-byte/ > accessed 17 March 2023

[35] Data from the International Organisation for Migration (IOM) reports that about 12,000 Nigerian women arrived in Italy by sea in 2015 and 2016 – a six fold increase on the previous two years. See Sunday Vanguard of 27 November 2016.

[36] The Hate Preacher and Internet celebrity, Anjem Choudary was jailed for five years and six months in London for radicalizing and promoting the ISIS terror group online to his 32,000 Twitter followers. < http://metro.co.uk/2016/09/06> accessed 09 September 2016

[37] Example: Medical emergency scams concerning disabled women and medical-challenged children have been shared on WhatsApp inviting them to come for free surgeries at a certain date.

In summary, online perpetrators usually target the female gender especially young women who are mostly adventurous in nature or vulnerable women who are disproportionately affected by poverty due to prevailing economic difficulties, discrimination, health challenges and other factors that limit their access to getting employment, educational, migration and other viable opportunities.[39] However, it has also been revealed that online information available on search engines sometime ruin some women's future prospect when employers conduct background checks on them or when men who are in search of future partners decide to use a damaged online report against women.[40] Such discredited reports have exposed women to psychological violence.

5. CASES INDICATIVE OF ONLINE VIOLENCE

Cyber violence is an extension of physical violence. The inability to handle incessant online violence makes women endure the trauma while the intimidation and loss of self-esteem experienced from such violence creates psychological effect on the victims' state of mind. The below-outlined case studies constitute threats to their online freedom of expression online because with time, they become survivors causing torture, emotional, psychological and physical injury to the victims. Such instances manifest through these case studies when criminals are using technology to commit crimes:

i. The alleged slanderous story and picture of a young lady flooded the social media in September 2016 where she was described on *WhatsApp* as an armed robber, although it was later discovered she offended someone who then decided to blackmail her on social media. The online report was shared as follows:

   i. Z.A., a full Hausa Fulani from Katsina State, well educated in both Western and Islamic education, but leader of a gang specialised in kidnapping, armed robbery and many notorious things. Very pretty, tall elegant, always dressed expensive and beautiful. She operates in Kaduna, Abuja. She pretends her car is having

---

[38] Charlie Parker. „Gang Rape on Facebook Live" <https.//www.the scottishsun.co.uk/> accessed 22 January 2017

[39] Okike Ajanwachukwu „Trafficking in Women and Young Girls: The Nigerian Situation" -NIALS Journal of Law and Gender (Maiden Edition) 2013. pp 85 - 95

[40] What Lies Have Been Written About You Online?" <howlifeworks.com/> accessed 28 August 2016

problems. If you stop to assist her you become a victim. She is always with a pistol in her bag and her trouser.[41]

ii. a Nigerian actor became a hot topic on the Internet when her "supposed" support towards raising funds on the online for a sick fan earned her hate messages and online insults after it was alleged at some point that she was trying to scam a sick fan's family and Nigerians. The Police were later called in to investigate the matter. Reports confirmed she was distraught and had to take time off social media and public life to regain her composure;[42]

iii. The trial of 4 accused persons alleged in 2012 to have jointly murdered their young female *Facebook* friend after she was lured to a hotel in Lagos. The defendants have since been sentenced to death by hanging;[43]

iv. On dating websites, the worst hits are matured single, divorced, widowed and disabled women who are contacted online by men with fake online profiles and picture display pictures on their social networks. These men later turn malicious by demanding for money from the women for variety of reasons while the private chats, photos, numbers of these women re-directed to another website and published where the victims will be threatened to pay certain money if they want their information removed from the website;[44]

v. The uncontrollable nude pictures of married women exposed online and used for blackmail by aggrieved male friends/ex-lovers. Many popular celebrity entertainers have been victims of this crime.[45] In September 2016, the Nigerian Tribune reported that a 31 year-old man was arrested by the Nigeria Police in Ibadan for allegedly drugging, raping and recording

---

[41] Story of a beautiful lady armed robber on Abuja highway is another Internet scam. <https://,politicalnigeria.wordpress.com/2016/> accessed 11 September 2016

[42] Nigerian Tribune, 19 August 2016. "Cyber-bullying: Celebrities as endangered Species" pp. 20-21

[43] Nicholas Ibekwe. „Killers of Cynthia Osokogu sentenced to death" <https://www.premiumtimesng.com> accessed 23 March 2017

[44] The Metro Lawyer Online of February 6, 2017 reported that a US District Court in East St. Louis has jailed a Nigerian man 27 years Internet romance scam perpetrated from 2007 to 2014. Prosecutors said the accused person drove some women to bankruptcy and at least one to the brink of suicide. He was therefore indicted of mail fraud, wire fraud, conspiracy and interstate extortion. The Court held his act is act was the kind of crimes that leave broken lives, wrecked women, fractured families, devastation, desires to die, humiliation and shame so extreme. The Judge described cyber violence as the most devastating crime one could ever imagine without laying hands or even eyes on another person."

[45] <2000viewsng.com> accessed 10 September 2016. A lesbian sex tape involving a former Nigerian beauty queen was circulated recently on the social media although the lady claimed her face was superimposed via photoshop by her alleged detractors.

the sexual molestation of a 19 year-old girl with the intention to blackmail her;[46]

vi. In December 2016, a United States based lady had complained to *Instagram* that some Nigerians were using her profile pictures for criminal activities. The suspect's *Instagram* handle was placed under investigation and the perpetrator was subsequently apprehended by operatives of the Rapid Response Squad of the Lagos State Police Command.[47] In the United States, two defendants were convicted and sentenced to 4 to 5 years imprisonment for not only sexually assaulting a 16-year-old girl but for also videotaping the attack and sharing it on Snapchat. In fact, the victim's friend testified at the trial that she received the graphic videos of the assault;[48]

vii. A five-strong gang who groomed teenage girls on *Facebook* before administering them with drugs or drinks and raping them were jailed for 42 years for rape, sexual assault and human trafficking. The five men were said to have chatted with the victims online over a period of months before securing a face-to-face meetings to commit havoc on the girls. They were arrested after Police officers sift through their text messages to identify further potential victims and their abusers. They Court however hoped the convictions will give the other women the courage to speak out;[49]

viii. AI-enabled intimate image abuse that combines images to create or generate deepfake, are other weapons for online abuse that disproportionately impact women. Estimates from *Sensity AI security monitor* claims that between 90% to 95% of all online deepfake videos are non-consensual porn and around 90% of those feature women;[50]

---

[46] In United Kingdom, an optician was arrested for installing hidden camera in Ladies Toilet and Changing rooms to film up women"s skirts. When Police raided his home, they saw 24,000 images and 27 videos on his computer. All the women later identified as victims have been left feeling nervous, violated and psychologically disturbed. See *The Daily Mail* of September 23, 2016. Another man was arrested for planting a hidden camera that sent images straight to his iPhone so he could see his female tenants whenever they shower and use the toilet. – *Daily Mail*, January 12, 2017

[47] See: <thenationonlineng.net/undergraduate-disguises-woman-dupe-33-men-instagram/> accessed 24 May 2016

[48] <bostonglobe.com> accessed 16 September 2016

[49] <www.thesun.co.uk/> accessed 26 January 2017

[50] Gina Neff. „The Internet is at Risk of Driving Women Away" <https://www.wired.co.uk> accessed 24 December 2022 Gina Neff. „The Internet is at Risk of Driving Women Away" <https://www.wired.co.uk> accessed 24 December 2022

ix. A broadcaster was arraigned in Court on a two-count charge of cyberstalking and breach of peace for allegedly sharing the sex video of a minor on *Twitter (X)* without the consent of the minor's parents or school;[51]

x. Raking sexually intrusive photographs of ladies without their permission such as down blousing, upskirting and creepshot. Online violence could also be manifested through cyber-flashing.

6. INTERNATIONAL FRAMEWORK

Legal intervention and reforms are global phenomenon. Across the globe, there is a fundamental need to safeguard the cyberspace and ensure we go by the rules governing the Internet. Cyber violence is a global issue which requires the intervention of international instruments and local laws to deter any unlawful online activity. Noteworthy is the fact that Nigeria is signatory to many international instruments all deriving their origin from the *Universal Declaration of Human Rights* (UDHR) 1948 so that women can enjoy their offline and online wrights. The principle of the human rights approach is that Member States have obligations under international human rights law to eliminate violence against women, both in the physical and virtual realm for the purpose of promoting, protecting and fulfilling their human rights aspirations. In ***Buturuga v. Romania,***[52] the ECtHR held that cyberbullying is an aspect of violence against women and girls which should be properly investigated. In ***K.U v. Finland,***[53] the ECtHR ruled that States have a positive obligation to protect their citizens against cybercrime, including sharing of pictures in an advertisement of sexual nature without consent. Similarly in ***Volodina v. Russia,***[54] the ECtHR held that the State had failed in its duty to protect the victim from the acts of cyber violence she suffered and also that the victim should be compensated. States are thus to prevent, protect, prosecute, punish and provide redress and reparation to aggrieved victims in accordance with the applicable instruments such as:

1. The Budapest Convention on Cybercrime of 2001;

---

[51] <https://pmnewsnigeria.com/2022/05/09 > accessed 09 May 2022

[52] ECHR 056 (2020)

[53] (2009) 48 EHRR 52

[54] Application No. 40419/19

2. The Additional Protocol on Acts of Racist and Xenophobic Nature Committed Through Computer 2006;
3. Convention on the Elimination of all forms of Discrimination against Women (CEDAW) 1979;
4. Landmark Declaration for the Elimination of Violence against Women 1993;
5. In 1999, 2008, 2010 and 2013, United Nations adopted various resolutions to eliminate all forms of violence against women;
6. The Council of Europe Convention on Preventing and Combating Violence Against Women and Domestic Violence 2011 better known as The Istanbul Convention;
7. The Lanzarote Convention on Protection of Children against Sexual Exploitation and Sexual Abuse 2007;
8. The Criminal Misuse of ICT on women was addressed in 2013 by the Commission on the Status of Women's Agreed Conclusion at its 57th session where governments and relevant stakeholders were urged to develop mechanisms for ICT and social media-induced violence against women and girls their safety;
9. The African Charter on Human and Peoples Rights (ACHPR) 1989 and the African Charter on the Rights and Welfare of the Child (ACRWC) 1990. In ***Fatma Yildirim (Deceased) v. Austria,***[55] the CEDAW Committee recognized that continuous and repeated threats made over the telephone contributed to the sequence of events leading to the deceased's death;[56]
10. The Broadband Commission for Digital Development was launched in 2015 by the International Telecommunications Union (ITU) – the UN agency for ICT and the United Nations Educational Scientific and Cultural Organisation (UNESCO) in response to the UN Secretary General's call to harness the Internet for global development for the purpose of meeting the objectives of the Sustainable Development Goals;
11. The United Nations agency dedicated to advancing sexual and reproductive health and rights and ending gender-based violence called

---

[55] Communication No.6/2005

[56] In the Daily Mail Newspaper of 16 November, 2016, it was reported that one of the reasons for charging a British comedian to Court for allegedly harassing and stalking a married woman was done through sending her electronic text messages.

the United Nations Population Fund (UNPFA) in 2021 launched its 'bodyright campaign' to demand protection from online violence.

Case Study of the Online Safety Bill Amendment in UK

The reform to the law was passed in June 2023 to address revenge porn victims that are subjected to intimate image abuse. The purpose is to crack down on online abusers who share or manipulate intimate photos in order to hound or humiliate women and girls. This abuse is commonly referred to as revenge porn and is defined as revealing or threatening to share private explicit images or videos without the consent of the person with the aim of provoking distress. It was made a criminal offence in 2015 and perpetrators face jail sentences of up to two years. Now they will no longer have to prove their perpetrators intended to cause distress under a change in the law. It will safeguard victims by overhauling current laws so the prosecution will no longer be forced to prove that explicit images or footage had been posted to trigger distress. The change will make it more straightforward to charge and convict offenders – with those found guilty being hit with a maximum of six months in jail. Where in some cases it is proved that an offender also sought to cause distress, alarm or embarrassment, or shared the material for sexual gratification purposes, they could be given a two-year jail term. Perpetrators who are found to have distributed the image for sexual gratification could also be put on the sex offenders' list. The changes introduced will also criminalise the sharing of deep fakes – defined as explicit images or videos which have been manipulated to look like someone without their consent. The amendments to the Online Safety Bill will make it easier to prosecute perpetrators of intimate image abuse, ensuring justice and better protections for survivors.[57]

7. NIGERIAN LEGAL FRAMEWORK

The foremost extant law protecting Internet users in Nigeria is 'The Cybercrimes (Prohibition, Prevention, Etc.) Act 2015 now amended in 2024. This is a law promulgated to prohibit, prevent, detect and investigate all forms of cybercrimes. On child pornography and related offences, Section 23(1) of the Act provides that a person who intentionally uses any computer

---

[57]Maya Oppenheim. „Revenge porn laws to be overhauled to help victims in new crackdown" <https://www.independent.co.uk/news/uk> accessed 28 June 2023

system or network for producing, transmitting or distributing child pornography is liable on conviction to imprisonment for a term of 10 years or a fine of not more than ₦20,000,000.00 or both. On cyberstalking, Section 24 (1) of the same Act provides that a person who knowingly or intentionally sends a message or any other matter by means of computer systems or network that he knows to be false, for the purpose of *causing annoyance, inconvenience, insult, injury, enmity, hatred, criminal intimidation* to another or causes such message to be sent is liable on conviction to a fine of not more that ₦7,000.000.00 or 3 years imprisonment or both. Section 24(2) of the Act provides that a person who bully, threaten, harass another person through a network and where such communication places another person *in fear of death, violence or bodily* harm is liable on conviction to a term of 10 years or a minimum fine of ₦25,000.000.00. Section 26(1) & (2) of the Act condemns racist and xenophobic attacks perpetrated through a computer or network against a person on political, racist, national, ethnic, cultural, religious or gender grounds while Section 50 provides that the Federal High Court has jurisdiction to try all cybercrimes matter.[58]

Government and stakeholders therefore have a responsibility in law to protect its women from any form of violence. Equally, victims can also obtain justice from the traditional offline provisions:

1. Section 17(3)(f) of the 1999 Constitution - The State shall direct its policy towards ensuring that young persons are protected against any exploitation;
2. Section 37 of the 1999 Constitution – The privacy of citizens, their correspondence, telephone conversations and telegraphic communications is guaranteed and protected;
3. Section 46(1) of the 1999 Constitution - Any person who alleges that any of this chapter on fundamental human rights has been or is likely to be contravened in any state may apply to a High Court in the State for redress;
5. The Violence Against Persons (Prohibition) Act (VAPP) 2015 was passed into law to eliminate all forms of violence in private and public life.

[58] Women who have been victimized by a dating scam or any other online scam are advised to file a complaint with the FBI Internet Crime Complaint Centre (www.ic3.gov). This helps identify the culprits and in so doing, keeps everyone safe. In addition, the Computer Crimes Task Force shares similar concerns with other international organisations in combating cybercrime.

However, stalking is listed under socio-economic violence, although no specific reference is made to technology-related violence;

6. Section 1 of the Defamation Law of Lagos State 2015 provides that for the purpose of libel and slander, the broadcasting of words by means of electronic means will be treated as publication in permanent form. Section 20 of the same law defines broadcasting to include publication for public reception by any electronic device while Section 12 provides that just in case an action is brought against the operator of a website in respect of any statement posted on the website, the operator of the website is not liable if he can show that the defamatory statement was not posted by him;
7. Money Laundering (Prohibition) Act 2022 – Fraud bothering on money laundering; using and taking possession of fund that forms part of proceeds of an unlawful act contrary to Section 21 (a) of the Money Laundering Act;
8. It is apparent that an online violence perpetrator can be indicted using the evidence from his social media page. Such evidence must therefore be preserved by the victim. By virtue of Sections 84, 34(1)(b) and 258 of the Evidence Act 2011, including the Evidence (Amendment) Act 2023 electronic evidence generated from e-documents and e-records are admissible under the law.[59]

8. CHALLENGES

- Cyber violence is still considered a minor problem by the populace, despite the stiff penalties provided in the Cybercrimes Act of 2015. However there is progress. Many women are now coming forward to report sextortion, cyberbullying, cyber blackmail and posting of sex tapes.
- Cybercriminals are not easy to apprehend due to the trans-boundary nature of cybercrime. Jurisdictional challenges and implications of international law are serious limitations to consider.[60]

---

[59] ***Kubor v. Dickson*** (2013) 4 NWLR (pt. 1345) 534

[60] Relevant questions are: Does a person who posts information on the World Wide Web have to comply with the laws of every state from which the website can be accessed? Can the Courts of every State from which information is posted have personal jurisdiction over the creator of the information and the operator of the site? For more scholarly discussion, see: Ikenga K.E. Oraegbunam: „Jurisdictional Challenges In Fighting Cybercrime: Any Panacea From International Law" (2015) 6, NAU JILJ, 57-65

- Victims are sometimes not willing to come forward and lodge a report to the Police, since some online acts of violence against women are still considered an intimate matter.
- Lack of sufficient proof, absence of injury to the victims, and the condition of anonymity of the online perpetrator.
- Cybercrime investigation requires forensic science tools and techniques.

Suffice it to say that the situation has improved with the intervention of technology tools, digital experts and trained law enforcement officers, which raises this question; how do we continue to ensure the safety of women and protect them from online violence? Obviously, one must take cognizance of the following facts: Many criminals have moved from the streets to the web; Women's rights are daily infringed upon in the cyberspace; There is need for regulation of what users post online; Holding digital networks accountable to sanction erring posts; Women and girls are particularly vulnerable victims; Online platforms offer anonymity that criminals take advantage of, because the risk of apprehension of the online offender is low;[61] International Laws and national laws particularly need to keep pace with changing technology; Data collection are pivotal in tackling cyber violence and design effective interventions to enforce the digital rights of women.

9. RECOMMENDATIONS

To ensure a safer online space, it is necessary for us to view online violence as a global problem which requires everyone to take both individual and collective action to protect the victims involved, for it is possible that a pornographic image produced in other countries today may find its way into Nigeria tomorrow. Taking action against online violence and vulnerability is important. Every World Safer Internet Day observed on February 9 of every year, Nigeria joins other countries to highlight how communities can work together to create a harassment-free online environment where women can share information and interact with others without any fear or inhibition. Therefore the government should:

[61] „Ending Online sexual Exploitaion and Abuse of Women and Girls : A call for International Standards" <https://www.equalitynow.org/resource/ > accessed 20 April 2022

(1) Continue to intensify effort on tech-related forms of violence and make special provisions or safeguards for women especially the impunity associated with picture and video sharing on social media;

(2) Provide a special platform template for women to report cyber violence without any fear of stigmatization and establish more supervisory sub-agencies under Nigerian Communications Commission (NCC) to regulate online activities. This is a way of giving victims the public awareness tool and support systems to keep safe from Internet-facilitated criminal activities.

(3) Adopt international benchmarks and best practices for synergy where a dedicated online system can be used to demand for online justice, similar to the data-driven crime prevention initiative called the E-Responder tool developed by the Citizens Crime Commission in the USA whose object is to reduce online violence and encourage positive digital citizenship;

(4) Conduct up-to-date research. Employ strategic efforts to support legislative and civil society actions that promote broad policy recommendations on gender justice and ensure good governance through online ethics;

(5) Human rights approach. Government, policy makers and its relevant stakeholders should be proactive and prioritise women's online security as human rights issue just as it is done in the conventional regulated laws. All these recommendations will collectively boost online vigilantism in gender consciousness.

10. CONCLUSION

Cyber violence against women is a global problem which is also a problem in Nigeria. There is no doubt that cyber violence has made a negative impact on women and it has assumed a worrisome dimension over the years, in spite of the positive side of technology which has made the world a global village and transformed the lives of women by helping them to actualise their advancement in various endeavours. The downside is the potential dangers the cyberspace harbours with respect to proliferation of Internet crimes and violence. As women continue to depend on technology for information and work, the duty imposed on government to promote science and technology according to Section 18(2) of the 1999 Constitution equally comes with a corresponding obligation that nothing should deprive women of their rights to have their privacy protected and their gender respected both in the offline and online world. More proactive investigations, prosecutions and convictions are needed to tackle issues in ICT-facilitated violence in relation with the fundamental human rights of women.

Chapter 10

DIVERSITY, EQUITY AND INCLUSION IN TECHNOLOGY

1.INTERNET GOVERNANCE, CYBER DIPLOMACY AND DIGITAL INCLUSION

The basic functions of technology tools provide access to education in workplaces and homes for communication and entertainment purposes. Irrespective of diverse backgrounds and status, governments across the world must intervene and respond to the quest to promote inclusive growth and sustainable job creation in this age of rapid technological advancements, so that citizens can acquire skills and competencies that meet the present and future needs. In view of these circumstances, taking cognisance of Diversity, Equity and Inclusiveness (DEI) into technology will be advantageous to the society as it will narrow the digital divide between those who have access to technology and those who do not, while striving to promote integral human development and ensuring the fundamental rights of expression by all. When governments deploy the aspect of inclusiveness into technological governance at all levels, citizens feel valued, appreciated and supported. People also feel a sense of belongingness regardless of any form of discrimination or disparities that may want to define the digital landscape and its limited supportive infrastructures, rather everyone is equipped with the little technological tools that is available for them to integrate the impact of what digital technologies and Internet will contribute positively into their lives. Furthermore, deploying the role of equity is essential to advance the dignity of all human persons, providing a level-playing field and a meaningful platform to engage with their broader community. These three synergy factors (Diversity, Equity and Inclusiveness) enables us to recognise that people are different and that regardless of the dynamic human settings lying at the core of digital governance, eliminating the barriers affecting people's access to the benefits of technologies deserves to be prioritised, which will gradually phase out the under-representation of equity deserving groups. This in line with the Principle 2 of the UN Sustainable Development Goals (SDGs) 2030 Agenda which is to leave no one behind.[1] Thus, the object of governance in technology does not only refer to intervention by government regulation and legal mechanisms to protect citizens but also by setting clear guidelines deploying a multitude of institutional and normative mechanisms to enhance, explore and create a pathway for:

a. research, development agenda-setting and public accountability mechanisms;
b. technology assessment, foresight and science advice;
c. public engagement and communication;
d. technical and design standards;
e. legal capabilities;
f. innovative solutions to digital challenges;
g. private sector governance in human resources and self-regulation.[2]

These above-named strategic interventions are inclusive. It does not exclude any group. Rather, it is comprehensive and takes into account all the interests of persons, organizations, the government and other stakeholders, all combining to maintain strong aligned relationships, intensify efforts to implement regulations on cloud-based services with a view to making digital transformation a priority. Inclusion is therefore anchored on equity and community engagement. An aspect of using an inclusive approach in Internet governance is by engaging stakeholders to collaborate and align their resources towards realizing the objectives of existing Internet policy and law for the benefit of the citizenry. According to the United Nations Educational and Scientific Organisation (UNESCO), Internet governance is the complementary development and application between governments, the private sector, civil society and the technical community playing their respective roles regarding shared principles, norms, rules, decision-making procedures and activities that shape the evolution and use of the Internet. UNESCO acknowledges the potential of the Internet in fostering sustainable

---

[1] See the meeting highlights of the 78th session of the UN General Assembly dated the 6th day of October 2023 where a member delegate stressed that digital inequity leaves 2.7 billion people still offline. <https://press.un.org/en/2023.gaef3587.doc.htm> accessed 07 October 2023

[2] OECD. 'Technology Governance' <https://www.oecd.org/sti/science-technology/> accessed 02 January 2022

human development to build inclusive knowledge societies, and also for enhancing the free flow of information and ideas throughout the world.[3] The logic is that if Internet governance functions properly, the Internet can act as a catalyst to drive the future of society in a positive direction and contribute to the social and economic needs of people. In other words, if it is that important to let people have access to the Internet, then they should not be deprived of such. This helps integrate the concepts of inclusion, equity and trust in smart city technology projects. For example, when London City launched a digital inclusion scheme of which the essence is to support thousands of people with upcycled devices[4] after it was discovered that an estimated 270,000 Londoners had no access to the Internet or digital access, with a further 2 million having limited use.[5] In this instance, providing broadband and high-speed Internet for residents is a key factor to bridging the digital divide and enabling smart communities to expand access and services on a broader scale.[6]

In the aspect of cyber diplomacy, Internet governance also has broad implications because cyber-attacks unleashed on critical infrastructures go beyond one country and if this is not handled in a proper manner, affected countries can become enemies. For example, where a major disruption in Country X affects Country Z, technology could be used by proactive governments to boost diplomatic efforts. The foundation of this cyber diplomacy derives its origin from the term diplomacy which is the art of conducting international relations in negotiating treaties, agreements and alliances. The primary framework is the 1961 Vienna Convention on Diplomacy which mandates countries to develop effective diplomacy to address conflicts. On the usage of diplomatic tools to resolve issues involving the cyberspace and the problem of state-sponsored hackers, Internet censorship, cyber espionage and other forms of cyber-attacks could be tackled by cyber diplomacy that leverages Internet governance because both are means to engage with international counterparts to build strategic ties

---

[3] <https://en.unesco.org/themes/> accessed 02 January 2022

[4] These are devices that are no longer in use but to make it functional, you give them a second life. In doing so, the finished product often becomes more practical, valuable and beautiful than what it previously was.

[5] SmartCitiesWorld news team. 'London Launches Digital Inclusion Scheme' <https://www.smartcitieswrld.net> accessed 27 June 2022

[6] NIST Smart Connected Systems Newsletter, July 2022. 'NIST GCTC Effort Focused on Diversity, Equity, Integrity and Technology in Smart Communities.

through digital dialogues and meaningful interventions.[7] Essentially the merger of Internet governance and cyber diplomacy will ensure that the use of ICTs does no potential harm to countries' democracies, political systems, critical infrastructures and citizens. It will ensure that there is a set of rules which define responsible state behaviour in cyberspace. Finally, it will regulate the behaviour of state and non-state actors in cyberspace under the auspices of international law with the purpose of legally harnessing digital technology and mitigating the risks at the same time. Thus, cyber diplomacy is a means of using relevant international organizations, with such cooperation relying on globally-applicable principles on public policy issues that are associated with the coordination and management of critical Internet resources. In so doing, governments can facilitate this development of public policy principles[8] through the applicable regional and international conventions such as the: Budapest Convention, African Convention on Cybercrime and Personal Data (Malabo Convention) and the AU's Digital Transformation Strategy. In the domestic settings, the primary framework is the National Cybersecurity Policy and Strategy 2021 which stands on eight (8) critical pillars namely:

1. Strengthening cybersecurity governance and coordination;
2. Fostering protection of critical national information infrastructure;
3. Enhancing cybersecurity incident management;
4. Strengthening legal and regulatory framework;
5. Enhancing cyber defence capability;
6. Promoting a thriving digital economy;
7. Assurance, monitoring and evaluation;
8. Enhancing international cooperation.

The National Data Protection Regulation (NDPR), Article 2.11 (b) provides that the Attorney-General of the Federation shall take into consideration the legal system of the foreign country particularly in the areas of rule of law, respect for human rights and fundamental freedom, relevant legislation, both general and sectoral, including public security, defence, national security, criminal law and the access of public authorities to personal data. Similarly, Article 4:3 of the same regulation makes reference to local and international cooperation which provides that in relation to foreign

[7] <https://www.indiafuturefoundation.com/cyber-diplomacy/> accessed 23 May 2022

[8] 'An Introduction to the Issues in Internet Governance' <https://cis-india.org/ > accessed 23 May 2022

countries and international organizations, the NDPR Agency and relevant authorities shall take appropriate steps to: (a) Develop international cooperation mechanisms to facilitate the effective enforcement of legislation for the protection of personal data; (b) Provide international mutual assistance in the enforcement of legislation for the protection of personal data, including through notification, complaint referral, investigative assistance and information exchange, subject to appropriate safeguards for the protection of personal data and other fundamental rights and freedoms; (c) Engage relevant stakeholders in discussion and activities aimed at furthering international cooperation in the enforcement of legislation for the protection of personal data; and (d) Promote the exchange and documentation of personal data protection legislation and practice, including on jurisdictional conflicts with other countries. Likewise, Article 16 of the NDPR Implementation Framework 2020 and under its provision on application of international laws provides that where the NDPR Framework do not provide for a data protection principle or process, the African Union Convention on Cyber Security and Personal Data Protection (Malabo Convention) and the European Union General Data Protection Regulation (EU GDPR) and its judicial interpretations shall be of persuasive effect in Nigeria, despite every country having its rules.

In Internet governance, the issue of cyberspace or digital sovereignty has generated heated debates on whether the notion of sovereignty as a fundamental principle of international law could be applicable to the cyberspace especially when offensive cyber operations or cyber warfare are imminent. Basically, cyberspace governance involves countries. It is the effort of a country to create boundaries on a network and then exert a form of control often in the form of law enforcement over such boundaries[9] particularly when concerns regarding Africa's digital sovereignty are threatened by big power rivalries.

To this end, NITDA at the International Conference on Cyber Diplomacy in Bucharest, Romania urged countries to support the development of international cyber norms and establish common grounds on cybersecurity issues. According to the agency, the first step towards promoting the development of international cyber norms is to develop the

[9] J. Obar, A. Clement. 'Internet Surveillance and Boomerang Routing: A Call for Canadian Network Sovereignty' <https://papers.ssrn.com/sol3/papers.cfm?abstract/ > accessed 24 August 2022

capacity of their workforce by increasing awareness among stakeholders and educate them through conferences, seminars, workshops and other enabling platforms. The agency added that another key aspect to promoting the development of international cyber norms, needed to tackle cyber threats is that there should be common grounds on cybersecurity issues which should be widely accepted and followed by all actors in the digital space.[10]

It should be noted that technology is the major component of the Fourth Industrial Revolution (4IR). The 4IR is a combination of cyber-physical systems, capable of transferring digital instructions to the physical world through robotics, IOTs, big data, cloud computing, AI-based systems and several other tools of digital technologies. The key themes of the 4IR are interconnection, information transparency, technical assistance, data governance and access infrastructure.[11]

2. DIGITAL LITERACY AND THE AFRICAN GIRL-CHILD

The annual International Day of the Girl-Child (IDGC) is observed across the world every 11 October. The day usually focuses attention on the need to address the challenges girls face and to promote girls' empowerment and the fulfilment of their human rights. While finding means to close the connectivity gap in technology, the United Nations has always been at the forefront of the need for girls to access technology as one of the solutions to advance gender equality in the world. In year 2021, the highlighted theme was "**Digital Generation, Our Generation**." The day recognized the immeasurable importance of deploying existing and emerging information and communication technologies (ICTs) to drive sustainable human infrastructure growth in capacity building, enabling the girl-child to digitally position herself for future empowerment and positive digital transformation. In year 2022, the theme was "**Our Time is Now – Our Rights, Our Future"** while in 2023, the IDGC's theme focussed on "**Invest in Girls' Rights: Our Leadership, Our Well-Being."**

The underlying factor of all the themes is linked to technology. According to the UN, technology can lift the lives of women and girls around

[10] Blessing Afolabi. 'NITDA urges countries to develop global cyber policies' <https://punchng.com/> accessed 28 April 2023

[11] Klaus Schwab. 'The Fourth Industrial Revolution: What it means, how to respond' <https://www.weforum.org/agenda/> accessed 30 November 2022

the world in myriad ways – from greater access to education, health care, and financial services, to new pathways into business and entrepreneurship.[12] It is important to emphasise that a technology-driven education is always associated with computer, mobile and wireless electronic devices operating through the Internet of Things (IoTs) which are fundamental tools driving the teaching-learning process that young people utilise to improve the quality of their education and disseminate same. IoTs in this vein refers to all devices that can connect to the Internet including sending and receiving information without the intervention of the human factor.[13]

Generally, young persons who are technology-savvy or captured within the circle of Generation Z (Gen Z) are classified as the digital generation. In Africa, the yearly celebrations of the IDGC successfully brings together girls from diverse backgrounds with different perspectives to learn how to leverage technology as a potential tool for collaboration, networking, interaction, evaluation and sharing of positive ideas or displaying their talents and skills from the comfort of their homes down to their various e-communities. Through digital platform, the IDGC also provides opportunity for women mentors to inspire, empower and ensure the online space is safe for the girl-child to express her views while narrowing the widening digital gap to enable her compete intellectually with her peers in other parts of the world as she strives to positively impact her future generation; for it is envisaged that the more a girl-child becomes digitally enlightened, the better her capacity and ability to effectively acquire knowledge and transform her skills to drive sustainable economic growth in her society.

The African girl-child is not left out in the scheme of things particularly on how she can use technology to engage with her peculiar environment. With her digital tools enabled by the use of her mobile devices, the first and best way to find out how to improve herself is to conduct online research in her subject areas. This translates to the fact that the Internet is her companion guide and she is thus able to participate and benefit from the global objectives as set forth in other global observance days related to technology such as 'the Girls in Science Day', the 'Girls in ICT Day', 'STEM

---

[12] Press Release from UN Secretary-General's Office on 8 March 2023 titled: '*DigitAll Innovation and Technology for Gender Equality*' <https://press.un.org/en/2023/sgsm21716.doc.htm./>

[13] VAP ADMIN. 'How IOT Changed Our Lifestyle' <https://www.vapulus.com/en/> accessed 01 July 2022

Appreciation Day', 'Literacy Day', and 'Education Technology Day' which are yearly observances that are focused on youth development and digital interventions, geared towards creating career opportunities in technology-related fields. This aligns with the ICT-driven Goal 5 of the Sustainable Development Goals (SDGs) Agenda 2030 and the African Union Blueprint for Sustainable Development Aspiration 2063, especially in this modern age that promotes virtual learning as a result of the COVID-19 pandemic lockdown in March 2020 which forced everyone to stay indoors. This brought the "new normal" in learning techniques, with the United Nations Children Emergency Fund (UNICEF) successfully unveiling the 'pandemic classroom' after school children worldwide were discovered to have lost about 1.8 trillion hours since the onset of the lockdown. Sadly, only very few African countries replicated such digital schools in their respective domain in spite of the numerous advantages of digital education.

More so, the indigent African girl-child cannot still access the Internet due the following limitations:

- if she is living in a rural community that lacks Internet connectivity;
- If she is living in a desert country with no telephone signal;
- if she is living in a refugee camp;
- if she is out-of-school;
- if she does not have an Internet-enabled phone or a computer laptop/desktop;
- if her parents are financially constrained;
- if she cannot afford the cost of data subscription;[14]
- If the government temporarily shuts down an area Internet network services;
- if she lacks confidence with technology; and
- if there is no electricity to power her computer device.

However, like with every other aspect of life, there are advantages and disadvantages. In as much as the girl-child is expected to relate with other members of the society online,[15] she could also be prone to cyber-violence

[14] This could also be due to the high taxation in the African telecoms industry. See Emmanuel E. Benson. '20 African countries with the most expensive average prices of mobile data' <https://africa. businessinsider. com/local/markets/> accessed 12 May 2022

[15] See Section 18 (2)(h) of the Child's Right Law of Lagos State 2015

especially during the COVID-19 pandemic when most girls spent their quality time on the Internet. The types of online abuse are cyberstalking, cyberbullying, sexting, sexual exploitation, child pornography, identity theft and other forms of online illegalities which are repulsive to girls' rights of privacy. Note that every child's right legislation provides that a child is entitled to his privacy, family life, home, correspondence, telephone conversation and telegraphic communication. Clearly out of ignorance, the girl-child could be a victim of misinformation or dis-information which can harm her self-esteem and well-being.[16] Failure to protect every child from all forms of harm is a clear violations of the fundamental human rights of the girl-child which is guaranteed by domestic legislations, the Convention of the Rights of the Child, the General Comment No. 25 (2021) on Children's Rights in the Digital World as well as the African Charter of the Rights and Welfare of the Child which all provided that governments are under obligation to make provisions not only for the protection of women and children, but also to ensure that the girl-child has the right to live in a space free from violence and discrimination.[17] Furthermore, the girl child is encouraged to report all acts of inappropriate digital threats and behaviour to either her parents, guardian, network regulators or appropriate authorities. In any case, shielding children from online dangers is still a duty largely left to parents, considering the gendered nature of cybercrime.[18]

Digital intervention has nevertheless played a positive and crucial role in the life of the girl-child because the advantages are enormous. She can conveniently use the digital platform for leisure, recreation, cultural and educational activities to enable her speak out whenever her rights are threatened while being mindful that she should not share contents that will make others uncomfortable.[19]

[16] Judith Burns. 'Fake news harms children's self-esteem and trust, say MPs' <https://www.bbc. com/news/ education-444548> accessed 10 July 2022

[17] See the Children's Internet Protection Act of 2020 in America which addressed concerns about children's access to obscene or harmful content over the Internet

[18] Deborah Brown. 'Opening Stages in UN Cybercrime Treaty Talks Reflect Human Rights Risks' <https://www.hrw.org/news/2022/04/28/ > accessed 30 April 2022

[19] Section 11 of the Child's Right Law of Lagos State 2015 provides that every child is entitled to rest and leisure and to engage in play and recreational activities appropriate to the child's age.. The child is also entitled to participate fully in the cultural and artistic activities of her country including African and world communities. See also Section 14 of the Child's Rights Law applicable to education.

In view of the reality that children are spending more time in digital spaces, coupled with their unique vulnerabilities, the UNICEF Office of Research launched a project known as the 'Responsible Innovation in Technology for Children' (RITEC) of 2022 which focused mainly on digital technology and child well-being. On diversity, equity and inclusion matter, the report recognizes that children especially from disadvantaged backgrounds, low or middle–income countries experience a range of barriers to digital engagement ranging from limited Internet access to app costs and culturally inappropriate content.

Digital literacy is all about digital awareness. Digital literacy in this sense is defined as the ability to navigate the online world in an effective and safe way. Proponents of digital literacy have contended that developing digital literacy skills requires that children should have the freedom to learn any information that is worthy of their attention.[20] There are no two-ways about it except to say digitalization will work for the African girl-child only if African governments genuinely commit themselves to change the narrative by taking actionable steps or radical response to provide an awareness platform and technology tools as a solution to eliminate all the inequitable barriers, prioritize digital equity and inclusion, as well as implement sustainable policies or legal frameworks that would enhance digital literacy. In this digital era, African girls should be encouraged to utilize the advancements in technology to increase their productivity while the watchword should be that on no account should any African girl-child irrespective of her age, socioeconomic status, disability or geographical terrain be left behind whether now or in the nearest future. "The right to access information and conduct online research for information, flow from her digital rights while providing our girls with tools and guidance to leverage technology for the purpose of being productive in their respective communities.

In Nigeria, the National Digital Economy Policy and Strategy (NDEPS) 2020-2030 roadmap inaugurated in 2019 particularly Pillar No. 2 strives to integrate digital literacy and skills into the national education curriculum at all levels, in order to create a pool of Nigerians with digital skills and bridge the gap between the academia and the industry as well as lower the access

---

[20] 'Surveillance Technologies and Children' <https://www.priv.gc.ca/en/opc-actions-and-decisions/research/explore-privacy-research/2012/opc_201210/> accessed 23 March 2022

barrier to digital tools by its citizens. To this end, the government shall provide digital training skills, training programmes that incorporate children, women, internally displaced persons and the physically challenged. In March 2022, an online, mobile and offline platform called the Nigerian Passport Learning (NPL) was launched by the Federal Government as an educational model to help bridge the digital divide in early childhood education, primary and secondary education, adolescent skills and technical and vocational education in view of the lack of connectivity affecting low-income countries and rural regions in greater proportions which puts children and youths in these areas at greater risk of missing out on education that continues to perpetuate inequalities.[21]

It is therefore expedient for governments to close the gender gap that exists in digital literacy so that our girls can showcase their tech skills and keep up with the rest of the world. According to UNICEF, the commitment of 'leaving no one behind' is an inclusive approach which lies at the heart of the Education Agenda 2030 and Goal 4 of the UN SDGs.[22] Since perpetuating educational inequity is against the human rights of children, we must be persistent and committed to break the bias and stereotypes so that our girls can excel.

The role of government, parents and stakeholders collectively is important in creating a safe online space for children. This will help to enhance digital literacy in all ramifications. Using the technology inclusivity approach, the human rights-based approach, the gender equality approach as well the principle of leaving no one behind approach meet the UN SDGs and African Union 2063 Goals because having valuable information technology and cyber skills brings wealth of skills and improved education for girls. Not only that, reverse socialisation takes place when the younger generation transfers their acquired knowledge to the older citizens who will in turn use the opportunity to relearn and reacquire skills. Parents should therefore cultivate digital parenting practices while governments should develop and enforce laws against online violence that would minimise cyber risks.

---

[21] Leaving no one behind also means putting in place robust and accessible digital public services for forcibly displaced people. See 'Our Common Agenda Policy Brief 5 of the United Nations'

[22] Resources to Support Marginalized-Caregivers of Children with Disabilities: Guidelines for Implementation (UNICEF 2022)

3. TECHNOLOGY IN LEGAL RESEARCH AND GENDER

This topic rests on a gender-based vantage point where new digital technologies are expected to make research accessible and easier for female legal researchers. It seeks to examine how digital tools in legal research are connected to serve as an inclusion criterion needed by professionals in different fields to reflect diverse variables such as age, gender, disability and access to technology. Gender in the context of this topic will thus focus on female lawyers who work in the academic and non-academic sector as long as they are determined to undertake research writing relating to their respective specialist field. What is expected is that the female lawyer involved in this research activity should clearly exhibit her ability to back up her research findings and submissions with relevant and evidence-based precedents and conclusions. Visualisation is not enough. Prior to her undertaking any purposeful research, the female lawyer needs to identify her area of concern (research problem); decide whether she wants to write a descriptive or analytical essay (research design); clarify whether she wants to go doctrinal or non-doctrinal (methodology) and whether the data she has gathered is capable of being turned into actionable knowledge (research solutions) which of course depends on whether the research topic she has chosen to write about is strictly legal or interdisciplinary. Notwithstanding her selected approach, she would need to embrace technology to boost her knowledge ideas and exchange.

Typically in legal research, a lawyer usually seeks to discover new facts, interrogate and analyse issues as well as proffer new theories as possible solutions for other emerging issues. In doing so, the female lawyer will need to lay a solid foundation by searching for digital copies of case laws, policies, precedents, authorities and related-comparative jurisdictional provisions to support her submissions. Conducting research in an inclusive method means that she must first understand her goal. She should define her audience, choose her research method, analyse and share her result findings to facilitate dissemination of quality information. Prior to the outbreak of COVID-19 pandemic, researchers majorly had to move from one library to the other, looking for books or journals to produce an in-depth and quality research work, while during the pandemic lockdown, researchers relied on electronic sources found on the Internet.

Basically, the COVID-19 pandemic brought to the fore the importance of information science and ICT, which encouraged e-Research, a term applied to the use of advanced ICT to the practice of research. This type of research makes use of Internet-based tools and techniques, assisting a researcher to study topics that could not be researched using traditional methods.[23] Although Google and other search engines have always been with us, the 'new normal' enabled by Artificial Intelligence (AI) and the Internet of Things (IoTs) technologies has opened a gateway for many researchers to participate more actively in remote/virtual work, webinars, podcasts and e-conferences to disseminate their research activities. For legal researchers, scholarly papers, indexed journals, case reporting and analysis in electronic format have become easily available and more accessible where AI-based tools have been of assistance in providing services with respect to, automated language enhancement, correction of punctuation or grammatical errors, proofreading and plagiarism checker tool/software[24] while also tackling issues relating to peer-review, copyright, plagiarism, data fabrication, digitization of written content, online misinformation and disinformation. It should be noted that leveraging technology falls within the ambit of legal informatics which gives the researcher a technical back-up and a digital advantage.

The basic idea is that a gender inclusion factor in technology-aided research will eliminate barriers and disparity in career outcomes and further close the gender discrepancy divide in all fields, including the field of female authorship. By this, the female lawyer is thus advised to invest in technology if she wants her research to be visible to the world.[25] She should enlarge her research career coast and use the tools of Internet technologies to their fullest potentials, while prioritizing her web tools and web access. But let us face it. Technology is human controlled. That is to say we cannot completely eliminate the human element in legal research writing because technology cannot force pens into our hands to write nor implant research topics into our brains or even turn our manuscripts into academic papers overnight. However, the remarkable impact of digital technology has a significant role

[23] 'What is e-Research? <https://www.editage.com/insights/> accessed 10 May 2022

[24] Best Plagiarism Checker Tool for Researchers-Top 4 to Choose from!' <https://www.enago.com/academy/ > (Enago Academy 2021)

[25] DataCite AfLIA webinar. Make your research visible and create more impact using DataCite DOIs' (01 December 2021)

to play in our law-related research writing activities as we continue to gather e-readership and e-visibility, including mentorship and networking opportunities. This transforms research credibility into inclusivity in user research.[26] In other words, if it means we have to configure, install or regularly update computer apps or software that will assist us with our research, let us do so because inclusion in digital technologies depicts that female lawyers should not be left behind in the areas of acquisition of digital tools and keeping to the ethics of cyber-activity. This will help bridge the gap between gender stereotype, female lawyers and legal research.

Key Highlights

- Computerised legal research came into existence in the 1970s, and law firms embraced it. When that capability was made accessible to personal computers in the early 1980s, it boosted the legal tech activities.[27]
- Traditional research in legal methods can be tedious. With the Internet, research became faster and accessible at a shorter cost.
- It is a constitutional right and freedom to practice our profession over the medium of the Internet and to conduct legal business.[28]
- Technology is not going away. Embracing technology ensures an efficient seamless process in legal research. With relevant software, no minor details are hidden and no step is forgotten.
- Apply ICT to improve your legal research. With modern software, you can save your time and be assured of quality work, through panel discussions, practical workshops and experience sharing sessions.
- Regardless of their limited resources and stereotypes that persist, female lawyers have the capacity and the ability to shape the future of legal research, by using technology.
- Using a wide range of technologies to connect with their colleagues all over the world, women have been known to bring unique skills in their research fields. These are tools or technologies that will help them

---

[26] Kelly Erickson. 'How to embrace inclusivity in UX research' < https://dovetaillapp.com> accessed 03 December 2022

[27] 'Why attorneys need to keep up with legal tech advance' <https://legalthomsonreuters.com> accessed 22 December 2022

[28] ***Anuradha Bhasin* v. *Union of India & Ors*** *(2020) 1 MLJ 574*

undertake a diverse range of tasks such as retrieving information, compose texts and refine documents.

- With technology tools at their disposal, women are the crucial part of solutions as they can fit into the growing technology skills shortage.
- There are obstacles and barriers regarding pay gap or disparity, gender bias and inequitable funding opportunities. In ***Ellis & Ors v. Google LLC***,[29] three women filed a class action lawsuit in 2017 on behalf of all women at Google accusing the company of underpaying female workers in violation of California's Equal Pay Act. The complaint also alleged that Google locks women into lower career tracks, leading to less pay and lower bonuses when compared to their male counterparts.[30] Thereafter an amicable settlement was reached after Google agreed to pay $118 million to settle a class-action gender discrimination lawsuit that includes about 15, 500 women. Google is also required to have an independent labour economist evaluate its hiring practices and pay equity studies.
- Building the skills for professional development and female is crucial to ensure that women have equitable access to technology at all times. Gender equality is a key component of technology, forming the basis of UN SDG No. 5, which aims to achieve gender equality and empower women.[31]

Finally, we need to ponder over some questions that offer key clues in personal research development such as: How inclusive are we? Is everyone captured? Are we respecting diverse perspectives in conformity with local and global technology best practices? Do we know the basics and are we armed with top-of-the-line tool and training? Are we determined to remove the obstacles in supporting technology interventions that would help us to access resources? Overall, being inclusive contemplates that we should consider the full range of human diversity that we are different in gender irrespective of our strengths and weaknesses, but that despite the limitations, female lawyers should be determined never to be left behind.

But should the female legal researcher totally embrace AI to conduct her research? Yes, AI tools such as ChatGPT is designed to provide

[29] No. CGC-17-561299

[30] Emma Roth. 'Google to pay $118 million to settle gender discrimination lawsuit' <https://www.theverge.com/2022/6/12/231646/> accessed 21 June 2022

[31] Clare Nadem. 'Women in Science' <https://www.iso.org/news/ref2628.html > accessed 03 December 2022

humanlike responses to user commands. Legal research is tasking and time-consuming. The activity requires us to look for books, journals, laws and case laws to read for analysis and dissemination. This is where the AI technology is relevant, helping us to extract key facts, compare and contrast different sources, generate data and fill important research gaps which improves the quality and accuracy of our research output.[32] With e-discovery tools, legal information is more accessible from all over the world and the researcher is not scared of misplacing her research, more so that the Courts have become technology-compliant. But just like all human activities which are capable of being subjected to abuse, the female researcher should however be cautious because the ChatGPT tool does have a few drawbacks. It tends to have issues with accuracy and credibility due to its propensity to spread misinformation.[33] Likewise for e-Research which may need to be verified by searching for other credible research sources that are free from bias and backed up with evidence.

4.ASSISTIVE TECHNOLOGY IN DISABILITY

Technology education and literacy is critical to the health of democratic societies. Efforts must be made to identify areas where action is needed to improve peoples' right to access information and further overcome inequities that disadvantaged people face in accessing technology services. The tremendous growth in technology knowledge, skills and abilities have translated into research and training opportunities for historically marginalized groups such as people from economically disadvantaged groups, people living with disabilities and those who are diagnosed with learning disabilities. There is no doubt that diversity and inclusion play prominent roles in advancing technology among persons living with disabilities. A technology-inclusive environment gives accessibility to diverse people and considers people living with disabilities so they can enjoy a range of technologies that can assist to improve their functional capabilities with little or no help. With the advent of digital technology, modern technological assistive devices come with a wide range of benefits and limitless

---

[32] 'The value of AI in legal research technology' <https://legalthomsonreuters.com/> accessed 09 August 2023

[33] Dan Milmo. 'Two US Lawyers fined for submitting fake court citations from ChatGPT' <https://www.the guardian.com/technology/2023/ > accessed 10 July 2023

opportunities affording them to stay in close contact with their family and able colleagues especially if the goal is to eliminate barriers and build capacity through technology assistance. Assistive technology (AT) is a form of inclusive technology aiming to resolve inequities and embracing diversity. Digital equity assessment therefore seeks to ensure all citizens thrive with improved access to digital technologies. According to WHO, over one billion people are estimated to experience disability. This corresponds to about 15 per cent of the world's population having significant difficulties in functioning.[34] Assistive Technology is therefore any item, piece of equipment or product system, whether acquired commercially off the shelf, modified or customized that is used to increase, maintain or improve functional capabilities of individuals with disabilities.[35] In other words, assistive technology provides assistive equipment that helps meet the needs of a disabled person.

The United Nations Convention on the Rights of Persons with Disabilities 2006 identify AT as an human rights obligation and provides that countries that have ratified the Convention must ensure the availability of high-quality, affordable assistive products as a right because it is a crucial step towards promoting equal opportunity. AT enables people living with disabilities to compensate for certain impairments which helps them become independent citizens without becoming a liability to the society. The devices range from simple low-technology to complex high-technology devices.[36] This equipment includes mobility products, vision products, hearing products, communication products, cognition products, self-care and environmental products. These technologies make those who depend on this equipment to be more independent so they can perform their tasks easily. In other climes, assistive technology could also refer to adaptive technology or handicap technology. Categories of people in this bracket may include the visual impaired and elderly ones who may have issues with their electronic devices.[37] In 2011, the WHO developed a Model Disability Survey for the purpose of addressing the scarcity and poor quality of information

[34] Disability and Health. ' <https://www.who.int/news-room/fact-sheets/detail/> accessed 20 February 2022

[35] Definition of Assistive Technology' <https://mn.gov/admin/at/services/definition> accessed 20 February 2022

[36] 'What is Assistive Technology' <https://www.physio-pedia.com/ > accessed 20 February 2022

[37] Charlotte West. 'How People in Prison Really Use Technology' <https://slate.com/technology/2023/09/> accessed 28 September 2023

experienced by people living with disability in many countries. Research shows their access to information gets better with different types of assistive technology devices such as adaptive keyboards for those who have motor impairments, vision impairments and mobility impairments. Those who struggle with lingering auditory processing issues are also non-verbal or those living with cerebral palsy use a special device to communicate. A person born with chromosomal disorder that cannot speak or walk will also appreciate the tools of AT. Other e-assistive gadgets include braille note takers that convert information and enable access to Internet, email, and a media player. Dictation software is available for those who have learning difficulties; Electronic magnifiers for people with colour blindness; including software that turns printed documents into digital text for people with low vision and screen magnification software as well as the test to speech software for those who may need them.[38] Other assistive gadgets may include hydraulic lift, wheelchair lifts, handicap elevators and several home/office automation devices. Note that the WIPO-administered Marrakesh Treaty 2013 was adopted to give the blind, visually impaired and print disabled better access to printed material through braille available in large print or screen-reader friendly versions. In Nigeria, the NDEPS 2020-2030 roadmap inaugurated in 2019 particularly Pillar No. 2 strives to integrate digital literacy and skills into the national education curriculum at all levels as well as lower the access barrier to digital tools by its citizens. To this end, the government shall ensure that digital training skills and other training programmes incorporate the physically challenged. Likewise the NCC Internet Code of Practice 2007 which outline the obligations of Internet access providers in the handling of offensive and potentially harmful content and the protection of minors and vulnerable audiences online while ensuring adequate safeguards are put in place. This is a way of breaking barriers for 'no one should be left behind.' Availability and accessibility to assistive devices break the stereotypes associated with disability such that those who have mental and learning disabilities should not be shut out from technology. Where there are no policies on inclusion, aggrieved citizens are encouraged to take advantage of relevant report mechanisms.

---

[38] Holly Tuke. 'Assistive Technology Devices: How Disabled People Use the Web' <https://bighack.org/assistive-technollogy/> accessed 26 May 2022

Interestingly, every April 6 is observed as the National Assistive Technology Awareness Day. Similarly the International Day of Persons with Disabilities observed every 3rd December in line with the 2022 theme stated that in this digital world, efforts should be made to broaden the skills of persons living with disabilities that they require to access the employment they desire in an innovative, rapidly changing technological landscape. They also have the right to be informed as to how assistive technologies can increase accessibility in their employment and be mainstreamed in the workplace in line with SDG 8 *(Promote sustained, inclusive and sustainable economic growth, full and productive employment and decent work for all)* and SDG 10 *(Reduced inequalities within and among countries).*

At all times, we must support innovations that interface technology with human rights to address the realisation of the objectives of the SDGs. The 1999 Constitution of Nigeria also prohibits discrimination of citizens on grounds of disability.

5. GENERAL INTERNET USERS

The law in every legal system and human right conventions supports that everyone has the right to participate in the governance of their countries. Participation can be in different ways. But whatever option we choose, technology makes these possible, giving Internet users the opportunity to participate directly or indirectly. With millions of Internet users of social media across the globe, Internet exists for them to perform many functions with technology providing a platform to share information and experience uniting everyone to build an economy that works for all persons in their diversity.[39] In Nigeria, active telecom subscribers and basic Internet subscriptions keeps soaring daily.[40] So who are Internet Users? These are defined as persons who accessed the Internet in the last 12 months from any device, including mobile phones. These users are involved in Internet usage which is the amount of information transferred over their Internet connection. As they could be doing web browsing, checking their email, downloading and uploading files, streaming audio and video, etc. Internet

---

[39] Jay Aware. 'Social Media: Global Poison' <https://medium.com/illumination/social-media-global-poison-d2d3cc3ab711/> accessed 10 November 2022

[40] Ogunsakin Mustapha. 'Telecom policies enhancing digital access, knowledge production – Danbatta' <https://thegavel.com.ng> accessed 05 December 2022

users can be categorized into four sets – the Geek, the Lurker, the Victim and the Internet Celebrity.[41] Practically everyone online is presumed to be a knowledge worker whether as a researcher, student, trader, professional or a fun-seeker. Irrespective of the age of Internet users, people are classified into different generations. Generation Z (age 5-25), Millennial (age 26-40). Baby Boomers (age 56-75) and the Silent Generation (age 76 - 95).[42] According to the Guide to Human Rights for Internet Users adopted by the Committee of Ministers to Member States of the Council of Europe 2014, the Internet user is any individual who does not have specialized knowledge about the Internet which is based on education or training.[43] Below are news that may interest some of us:

6. The Human Rights Watch states that children from low-income families were more likely to be excluded from online learning because they could not afford sufficient Internet or devices while education systems often failed to provide digital literacy training for students and teachers to ensure they can use these technologies safely and confidently.[44] Due to parents worry over how to keep their kids safe from the Internet's myriad dangers from bullies to predators, a new California bill has proposed ways to force tech companies to take more responsibility to protect kids online, requiring them to consider the best interests of children when designing, developing and providing their products in their sites and apps;[45]

7. An Indian Supreme Court has once held that governments need to look into the provision of necessary software and hardware, computers and the Internet for the benefit of children.[46] In another case, the Indian Supreme Court warned that digital divide caused by online classes will defeat the fundamental right of every poor child to study in mainstream schools and that little children whose parents are too poor to afford laptops, tablets or

---

[41] 'Which of These Four Types Of Internet User Are You?' <https://www.newrisingmedia.com> accessed 1o December 2022

[42] Andre Calilhanna. 'The Reading Habits of Five Generations IInfographic)' https://blog.bookbababy.com/how-to-self-publish/> accessed 10 November 2022

[43] <www.coe,int > accessed 20 July 2022

[44] 'Pandemic's Dire Global Impact on Education' <https://www.hrw.org/news/2021/05/17/> accessed 20 July 2022

[45] Pia Ceres. 'The US May Soon Learn What a 'Kid-Friendly' Internet Looks Like' <https://www.wired.com/ story/california-aadc/ > accessed 02 September 2022

[46] Press Trust of India. 'Use Technology for Welfare of Children: Supreme Court' <https://www.hindustantimes.com/> accessed 23 March 2022

an optimum Internet package at home for online classes during the pandemic have dropped out of school and even run the danger of being drawn into child labour or worse, child trafficking. In the court's observation, "the digital divide produced stark consequences - children belonging to economically weaker sections or disadvantaged groups had to suffer the consequence of not having to fully pursue their education or worse still drop out because of the lack of access to Internet and computer. How can a poor child whose mother is a housemaid and the father a driver afford a laptop or a tablet? These children need them to study."[47]

8. For online activists who desire to engage in Internet media activism, technology can assist them to influence positive social change. Internet activism also known as cyber-activism or digital activism is the use of electronic communication technologies and digital media such as social media, e-mails, text messages and podcasts for various forms of activism to enable faster and more effective communication whether for mass mobilization or political action or for any channel for action to engage protesters or to represent a communal interest. Virtual sit-ins are a form of online demonstration in which a networked community gathers on one or several sites to carry out an act of digital dissent. This could be by clogging a website with a bunch of repetitive requests with protesters' automated 'clickings' slowing down the site which causes it to shut down;[48]

9. We are all impacted by advancements in technology and in order to deliver effective digital transformation, a digital leader must look beyond the IT department. He must hold constructive engagements. He must align with people who will use the technology as part of his transformation journey. He must also encourage best-practice techniques relevant to user experience.[49]

10. Generally, experts believe the use of the Internet enhances and augments human intelligence which has the capability of improving reading,

[47] Krishnadas Rajagopal. 'Supreme Court flags consequences of growing digital divide' <https://www.thehindu.com/news/national> accessed 08 October 2022

[48] Marcella A. Fuentes. 'Digital Activism' <https://www.britannica.com/topic-digital-activism/> accessed 10 June 2022

[49] Matk Samuels. 'Digital transformation strategy: 6 ways to keep your project on track' < https://www.zdnet.com/article/> accessed 08 August 2022

writing and rendering of knowledge.[50]These benefits positively impact our volunteering skills. Volunteerism is often associated with kindness that requires a physical presence. Since technology has come to stay, the Internet affords us the opportunity to also engage in virtual volunteering which is simply an act of service that can be accomplished over the phone or Internet. Those who engage in this act are called Digital volunteers. It presupposes they have basic IT skills and freely offer to help other people get online and use digital technology.[51] However, one should be mindful of cyber criminals.

11. The National Cybersecurity Policy and Strategy 2021 is committed to the advancement of cyber education and workforce thus bridging the gap through ICT. The Policy provides that in order to promote a robust cybersecurity workforce and human resources in the country, cybersecurity education, skills acquisition, professional development, research, development, innovation and indigenous cybersecurity technology should be encouraged while efforts should be made to eliminate quacks from the IT industry;

12. Sending offensive information using any electronic device, stalking and criminally intimidating or threatening someone over the phone are acts of cybercrime.[52] Thus, celebrating the National Technology Day every January 6 annually extends to taking care of our smart devices and digital self;

13. For Authors of e-books, it is important that they safeguard their creative works in today's fast-changing digital landscape where content is easily sold, streamed or available for download online. As the online sharing and distribution of content continue to evolve; authors face new challenges in preserving their intellectual property. Firstly, authors are advised to register their copyright. This legal measure establishes their ownership and gives them an edge in infringement cases. Secondly, an author also has to consistently monitor the usage of his book online. He should employ digital

[50] Lance Whutney. 'The Internet can make you smarter, experts say' <https://www.cnet.com/tech> accessed 25 June 2022

[51] Emma Singer. '24 Virtual Volunteer Opportunities to Make a Real Impact (Without Leaving the Couch)' <https://www.purewpw.com/well/> accessed 20 July 2022

[52] Ademola Olonilua . 'TikToker Bags 3-Year Jail Term For Defaming Eniola Badmus' <https://dailytrust.com/> accessed 02 August 2023

tools and services to detect any unauthorised sharing or use. This is a proactive strategy that will help him to identify any potential violations promptly. Thirdly, upon discovering instances of any unauthorised use, affected authors can send cease-and-desist notices under copyright law. This action prompts the relevant platforms to take down the infringing content. Finally, the author can take legal action if he comes across any intentional reproductions, distribution, and public display without your authorisation. Aggrieved authors should consult lawyers for more intricate situations and advice.[53]

14. ChatGPT can produce text, Images and videos in response to prompts. However in recent times, a number of authors are filing lawsuits against OpenAI and its ChatGPT chatbot on the ground that the 'AI beings' are infringing their copyright either by scanning their works or training its systems with them without their consent.[54] In ***Thomson Reuters Enterprise Centre GmbH v. Ross Intelligence Inc.***[55] the allegation of the plaintiff was that the defendant unlawfully used AI to copy his book and other copyrighted content to train an AI-based platform that competes with it.

15. COMPUTER LITERACY

Computer literacy plays a major role in the society. Literacy is the ability to read, write, speak and listen in a way that lets us communicate effectively and make sense of every word. In today's information age and because information is dynamic, it is important to be computer literate. If people are computer literate, they have enough skill and knowledge to be able to use a computer. A computer is a machine that process information while computer literacy is the knowledge and ability to use computers and existing technologies or applications efficiently with skill levels ranging from elementary use to computer programming and advanced problem solving. Section 108 of the Nigeria Copyright Act 2022 defines a computer programme as a set of statements or instructions that are used in a

---

[53] Credit: BookBaby Newsletter of September 26, 2023.

[54] Victor Tangermann. 'OpenAI may be in Big Legal Trouble' <https://futurism.com/the-byte/> accessed 20 September 2023

[55] 1:2020-cv-00613 (D.Del.2022). See also: 'Open AI hit by another lawsuit over copyright infringement by AI' <https://dig.watch/updates/> accessed 20 September 2023

computer in order to bring about a certain result. To be able to read these instructions is dependent on advanced or proficient computer skills.

The three types of computer literacy are as follows:

i) Basic/foundational computer literacy skills – a beginner knowing how to type, how to turn on or switch off the computer, learning keyboard commands and connecting to the Internet;

ii) Intermediate computer skills – this is a competency beyond the foundational level. The stage falls between a beginner and an expert. Here, you already know the concepts of databases. You can process Internet and email computers, word processing graphics, edit images and spread sheets;

iii) Proficient skills – this is a competency beyond the intermediate level applied in educational and work settings. At this level, your experience and expertise counts here.[56]

The place of computer literacy cannot be over-emphasised in a knowledge economy. Research for instance, leverages computer literacy to respond to the challenges of the present and the future. The knowledge is capacity-building which enables you to perform basic tasks on the computer underpinning education and job opportunities, professionalism, connectivity, communication and other endeavours.[57]

When you are computer literate, it encourages you to get certificated and equipped to transition into the field of cybersecurity, a field within STEM that will help you to protect yourself and your organization. Computer literacy is also a tool of empowerment. In an era where everyone has to earn an income, the knowledge becomes a pathway to economic development.. Governments in Low-and-Medium-Income Countries must therefore ensure people are given computer skills as problem-solving and economic empowerment skills.

A very important point we should also note is the "myth going around that technology comes intuitively to kids that were born into an information age." This is not true because children still have to learn to be computer literate, since computer skill is not an inborn skill. Another assumption tends to contend that just because the Gen Z youths spend a considerable amount of time on technology could mean they are technology savvy. Research says

---

[56] Tom Gerencer. 'Top Computer Skills' <https://zetv.com > accessed 13 December 2022

[57] 'Computer Literacy' <https://www.encyclopedia.com> accessed 12 September 2022

this is a huge misconception because these young adults also go through what is called 'tech shame' – a feeling of personal inadequacy when they cannot handle digital devices or solve their tech problems.[58] However, it is glaring that the young ones are still far more adaptable than older people and will be required to help these older ones who are computer-challenged.[59]

Going further, the UN Educational, Scientific and Cultural Organization (UNESCO) in 2023 published a global education monitoring report titled 'Technology in Education: A Tool on Whose Terms?' The report which relied on SDG 4 on quality education, urges policymakers and educational stakeholders to reflect on whether technology is 1. *Appropriate* – despite the advantage, technology should not be used in excess or made to replace a qualified teacher; 2. *Equitable* – the right to education should be synonymous with the right to meaningful connectivity, even in times of crisis; 3. *Scalable* – there should be robust evidence to prove that digital technology has added value in education; and 4. *Sustainable* – staying focused on basic literacy is critical for digital application.[60] We can thus extend these key factors to encourage and promote women in websites design, development, marketing and maintenance. It is interesting to know that 'webmistress' is now considered a legitimate job title and has entered technology's lexicon

Computer literacy can also expand the field of IT where everyone can learn about:

1. **Website designing** - the process of planning and building the elements of websites, from structure to layout to images, graphics and other designs;
2. **Cascading style sheets** (CSS) reboot – the process of making web pages presentable;
3. **Coding or computer programming** - the process of communicating with computers and other devices through programming languages or manual;
4. **Artificial Intelligence (AI)** – All AI are automation efforts even though they are of different types such as Reactive AI, Explainable AI, Responsible AI, Ethical AI, Limited Memory AI, Theory of Mind AI, Self-Aware AI,

[58] Christina Pavlou. 'Tech shame and remote working: The full story' <https://www.talentlms.com/blog/> accessed 24 February 2023

[59] Victor Tangermann. ' GenZ is Apparently Baffled by Basic Technology' <https://futurism.com/gen-z/> accessed 03 March 2023

[60] 'UNESCO Calls for Appropriate Use of Technology in Education' <http://sdg.iisd.org/news/> accessed 03 August 2023

Artificial General Intelligence (AGI) and Generative AI which seems to be the most popular usable tool. A generative AI is a type of AI that can create high quality text, images, audio and other content depending on the data or models someone is trained on.[61] Notwithstanding the potential misuse of AI, several recommendations have been made about the ethical use of Global AI by world bodies and different countries.[62]

5. **Human Performance Training** focuses on relationships between people and their equipment, systems, procedures and the environment as well as personal relationships between individuals and groups, encompassing the overall performance of different professionals in the computer tech industry;[63]

Overall, computer education addresses the need to drive skills necessary to close gaps so this requires us taking a holistic approach by involving everyone. By this, we would develop research capacity of workers who are committed to advancing and integrating technology into policies and practice. We would strengthen the connection between the government, stakeholders and the citizens for the purpose of prioritizing technology transformation while offering greatest motivation for career advancement.

---

[61]Alexander Gillis & David Peterson. '4 Main Types of Artificial Intelligence Explained' <https://www.techtarget.com/serachenterprise/> accessed 08 August 2023

[62]Oluwatomi Ajayi. 'Understanding the Tool of Artificial Intelligence' <https://thegavel.com.ng/> accessed 25 November 2023

[63] ICAO. 'Human Performance and Cabin Crew' <https://www.icao.int/safety/> accessed 20 April 2023

Chapter 11

PROACTIVE CYBERSECURITY STRATEGIES

Whichever way we may want to look at life, the Internet is playing and will still continue to play a significant role in our day-to-day activities. The Internet is a global communication system that links people together with the rest of the world. We exchange information with others through computers or mobile phones attached to networks. Thus the Internet helps in transferring our messages through e-mail, chat, video and audio conference.[1] Unfortunately, the Internet also has its dark side. Cybercriminals feel so comfortable on the Internet because we cannot easily identify them just as we get hold of perpetrators of crime in the offline world. Cybercriminals have sophisticated tools with which they operate their 'trade'. This in effect means we must devise ways on how to outsmart these Internet criminals because it is so easy to think we cannot fall for scams even when the anonymous scammer seems to have so much of our personal information or that of our organisation. Being proactive on the Internet is all about raising cybersecurity concerns and response mechanisms. The cybercriminal leaves a digital footprint, so he may think he can get away with crime but this is not true. How can we safeguard ourselves from cybercrime? It simply means we have to take deliberate action and not just sit idly by until cybercrime takes place. A proactive person takes action to accomplish a purpose. An action is proactive when we create or control a situation rather than just responding to an event that has happened. In cybersecurity, proactive strategies consist of taking active steps that encompass vulnerability and vendor risk management, incident monitoring and response plan, strong authentication and authorization, cybersecurity training and other protective actions that

[1] 'Internet and WWW.' <https://www.nielit.gov.in> accessed 02 January 2023

will prevent our devices and systems from being compromised by cyber criminals whose attacks can disrupt our life and network.

This chapter therefore complements the legal framework and contains recommendations that aim to reduce cyber risks such as those cybercrimes that are discussed in this book. This is what we generally refer to, as easing our path to cybersecurity. When technology is deployed, we must ensure it lives up to safety benefits. The government's political will must be matched with proactive actions, institutions, capabilities and resources to effectively achieve results so that citizens will be able to access programmes and resources without fear. This will make user experience seamless for all.

1. RESPONSE PLAN TO CYBERSECURITY RISKS

There is need to strengthen cybersecurity and mitigate risks as it is important to address the critical issues confronting data breach and cybercrime. The sad reality is that the Internet offers a window of opportunity for cybercriminals who have escalated fraud, cyber-attacks and other emerging scams which keeps rising daily. Cybercriminals are honing their criminal skills daily, devising illegal methods of breaching or launching cyber-attacks while they continue to evade detection. These attacks are unfortunate by-product of the digital age. Inside the cyberspace, there are different types of hackers with different goals' while 'traditional' cybercriminals attempt to violate systems and applications to steal money, there are hacktivists using hacking as a form of civil disobedience to promote political or social causes, espionage experts looking for industrial secrets or intellectual property who may want to plant incriminating evidence, as well as cyber warriors carrying out digital assaults to attack organizations, nations and governments. These criminals engage in double extortion racket when they steal and encrypt data. They steal data and threaten to leak the contents via a website to pressure victims into paying ransom. Once inside a victim's device, it affords them the opportunity to conduct unlawful surveillance. The Maryland Health Department in the US is reportedly the latest victim of cyber-attacks hitting governments, public bodies and cities. A cyber-attack could potentially disrupt essential critical services, expose personal and financial data, and disable the economy of a city.[2] These have terrible

[2] Gianni Minetti. 'Cybersecurity: a lifelong journey for smart cities' <https://www.smartcitiesworld.net/> accessed 17 December 2022'

implications, No wonder, the sophistication and persistence of threat actors are increasing every day. Individuals are being impersonated in business e-mail compromise attacks, intellectual works being encrypted and exfiltrated through ransomware and the persistent threat of insiders. How do we then protect or defend our organizations? What should the responses be like? and what efforts are organizations, regulatory authorities and investigators making to facilitate the response? Committed efforts and proactive action are required in the field of cybersecurity expertise to mitigate cybercrime and strong national and international legal framework to address cybersecurity challenges because cybercrime is not only organised crime but it is also a transnational or transborder crime. It goes beyond being a lone malicious hacker who sits in a dark room and covers his face, working on his laptop.

One of the ways we can respond to cyber-attacks emanating from cybercriminals who intercept our networks and redirect our information to illegal websites without our consent or hackers who gain unauthorized access to a company's systems or steal a company's data, is by taking swift action to report. The Victim Company should alert their customers, employees and others impacted by the attack about the data breach. However if the attack does not have any negative impact on its operational system, the company should say so. The Company should also notify law enforcement agencies of the attack as well as the Attorney-General of their respective countries. Investigation into the incident will then continue.

The CIA triad is another way of staying proactive on the Internet. Generally, in IT cybersecurity, the CIA triad is the most crucial. Companies and networks should ensure they keep to the tenets of CIA which stands for Confidentiality, Integrity and Availability. It is an information security model which guides an organization's efforts towards ensuring data security as well. The triad is regarded as the cornerstone of a security infrastructure.

Virtual Patching – it is a process of addressing security flaws immediately a cyber-attack happens so as to shield the Victim Company from being exploited and fixing the code later. The aim of virtual patching is to implement temporary security patches in order to prevent further cyberattacks or known vulnerabilities. Patches are software and operating system (OS) updates that addresses vulnerabilities within a programme or product. A patch quickly resolves a bug or security vulnerability.[3]

In addition, a response plan encompasses crime prevention tactics. The National Crime Prevention Institute defines crime prevention as "the anticipation, recognition and appraisal of a crime risk and the initiation of some action to remove or reduce it." This means we should expect that cybercrime is imminent in this digital age. This gives us the opportunity to recognize and evaluate the risk factors and take steps to address those factors.[4] So if companies suffer cyber-attack, then they must develop a plan to protect their company. This process is called an incident response. To avoid cyber-attack, they must follow the cyber incident response plan which organizations utilize to manage cyber-attack. The purpose of incident response is to reduce the damage caused by the cyber-attack and recover as quickly as possible. Companies can set up an incident response team comprising of ICT, IT and physical security experts, to be supported by legal and human resource staff. Because cyber-attacks have severe consequences, the level of response needs to be tailored to the nature and complexity of the offence being investigated. A collective response is needed to develop a safe and secure cyberspace. There are six steps to a response plan:

1. Preparation: develop policies and procedures to follow in the event of a cyber-breach;
2. Identification: detect and assess the breach/threat. and fix a response;
3. Containment: contain the damage and prevent further penetration;
4. Eradication: neutralise the threat and risk and restore internal systems;
5. Recovery: check that all affected systems are no longer compromised and return to working condition;
6. Addressing skills shortage and improving people and systems - through training at institutions that are accredited for continuing cyber education; employing more people with IT skills into the IT workforce. Determine how to improve future efforts against malicious actors.[5] Ensure team

---

[3] 'Understanding Patches and Software Updates' <https://www.bu.edu/tech/support/> accessed 20 July 2023

[4] Richard Arrignton. '7 steps Police leaders can take today to prevent crime tomorrow' <https://www.police1.com/chiefs-sheriffs/ > accessed 17 February 2022

[5] CyberEdu. 'What is Incident Response?' < https://www.forcepoint.com/cyber-edu/> accessed 24 December 2021

members are aware of the latest developments in the cybersecurity field of threat assessment.

The responses you have resolved to adopt will strengthen your systems against future attacks and pass the message that you have taking ample steps to protect your networks, curb any potential misuse of data and determine the source of the attack. Equip ourselves, internalise the knowledge and the initiatives to handle cyber threats whenever you see them approaching. Ask yourself the following questions: Are we aware that government has issued warnings to organizations to get proper grips with risks and cybersecurity? Are we aware that government has legislated a requirement for Company boards to employ or hire an IT expert that understands technology and risk? Are there policies that can enlighten the populace about coping mechanism when there is an attack? Response mechanism means that we need to establish regulatory framework to create good industry conduct, invest in risk-based cybersecurity framework, secure data privacy, invest in key staff to man our technology, invest funds in cybersecurity incident reporting and response, continue to identify threats so as to gather relevant information and put the collective data into context, share knowledge and adequate information, encourage processes that will deter criminals and punish perpetrators.

Being proactive through the interventions encompassing cyber awareness and educational curriculum is vital. In doing this, Companies can reach out to professionals that are referred to as the 'red team' or 'blue team' groups to intervene whenever they encounter cyber-attacks. A red team is a group of people that are hired to pretend as cyber-attackers in order fight back hackers who have intruded into the security networks of an organisation. The red team will thereafter report back to their engaging organisation and advise them accordingly as to improve the security of the organisation. A blue team on the other hand is engaged to defend against the cyber-attacks and respond to incidents when they occur.[6] These two teams are co-opted from the pool of information systems security, software engineering, cybersecurity or threat intelligence experts since they already possess electronic investigation knowledge. Those who have non-tech backgrounds can also work in a cybersecurity industry if they go for basic IT

[6] Coursera. 'Red Team vs. Blue Team in Cybersecurity' <https://www.coursera.org/articles> accessed 18 September 2023

courses that will equip them with the knowledge to ensure the safeguarding of computer systems and databases which all form a part of securing our desktops, laptops, and mobile devices. These devices are the endpoints which create entry points for cybercriminals to manoeuvre. Endpoint detection and response (EDR) are used to protect end-user/end point devices such as desktops, laptops and mobile devices and are designed to quickly detect, analyse, block and contain any cyber-attacks that are in progress. The EDR experts are in the best position to respond to cyber-attacks, mitigate damages and implement recovery plans thereby protecting these entry points from further malicious attacks. It is thus important that the incident responses must be done within the ambit of the law. Another aspect of cyber-response mechanism is by engaging the tool of Artificial Intelligence (AI) to detect crime. AI is machine learning. Organisations are using AI to prevent and detect crimes such as employee theft, fraud, money laundering and child pornography amongst other cybercrimes while predicting and helping to solve crimes committed by humans. There are two ways AI is helping cybersecurity as a much needed tool that could help stem the tide of cyber-attacks. AI helps automate many tasks that a human analyst would often handle manually, detecting unknown intrusions faster than humans by ensuring no step is forgotten and no minor details are hidden, AI can detect patterns within large quantities of data that human analysts cannot see, such as the key linguistic patterns of hackers who pose emerging threats in the dark web and open source software platforms. AI in addition alerts system analysts.[7] It is important to note that a single data breach can cost businesses loss of customer trust and reputational damage. Companies can also publish a message on its website stating that it is aware of the security concerns, but taking corrective measures to rectify the problem.

In conclusion, a response plan recognizes that the three pillars of cybersecurity are people, process and technology. [8] In ***Australian Securities & Investments Commission v. RI Advice Group Pty Ltd***,[9] the Federal Court in Australia held that a financial institution has obligations under the law to manage cyber resilience and cybersecurity risks adequately.

---

[7] Sagar Samtani. 'How AI is shaping the cybersecurity arms race' <https://the conversation.com > accessed 24 February 2022

[8] Tamarian Del Conte. 'The 3 Pillars of Cyberscurity' <https://blogs.blackberry.com/en/2020/10/ > accessed 24 January 2023

[9] (2022) FCA 496

2. INTERNET FILTERING

In this age of unrestricted flow of information where majority of people post on the Internet, any action aimed at cleaning or clearing the Internet of 'bad' content will amount to an act of filtering the Internet. The word *filter* means a porous device for removing impurities or unwanted material from somewhere. In other words, to filter a substance means to pass it through a device which is designed to remove certain particles contained in it.[10] In China, they call it the '*Jingwang*' action. *Jingwang* means 'clean the Internet. The initiative is aimed at investigating and preventing illegal activities in cyberspace, such actions include screening online live streaming, removing harmful online information and cracking down on illegal publications among others.[11]

In computer security, Internet filtering is a key component of enterprise network security. It is a common security measure conducted by network administrators as a programme or software used to restrict or control the content of the Internet. The filter compares the contents of a web page with a set of rules provided by a person who already installed the Internet filter software. If the contents of that web page are in conflict with a set of rules, the site is likely to be blocked or unavailable at search request. The filtering could be on websites, keywords and profiles, apps, block URL filters, and other files and extensions.

In addition, Companies often use content-based filtering, also known as information filtering, as part of their Internet firewalls. Content filtering helps companies execute corporate policies on the use of Information systems – for example, the filtering and blocking of employee access to social media platforms. Network administrators can configure firewalls, mail servers, routers and domain name system (DNS) to filter unwanted or malicious content which are security threats. Email filtering is the screening of email for spam and other objectionable content. It may also include potentially harmful applications (PHA) such as misbehaving apps, fake apps, high risk apps, imitation apps and counterfeit apps which are apps that could put users or devices at risk. Parents also use web filtering to screen or exclude objectionable content from their children's home computer undesirable

---

[10] See:<https://www.collinsdictionary.com> accessed 23 February 2023

[11] Susan Xuanfeng Ning and Han Wu. 'Cybersecurity Laws and Regulations China 2023' <https://iclg.com/practice-areas/> accessed 27 July 2023

content that is criminal or pornography. The advantages of content filtering are protection of individuals and organizations against harmful content, minimizes the risk of malware attacks, improves employee productivity, and reduces potential malware exposure and acts as further protection of children from accessing content that is inappropriate for their age or function.[12] However, content filtering is not a stand-alone security tool. It has to be accompanied with other security measures like using the highest privacy settings on our online accounts, enabling an MFA and firewalls and installing other security tools on our devices.

Network scanning is another form of filtering which ensures that our devices are functioning healthily. The purpose is to detect inconsistencies or vulnerabilities and protect the network from attacks.[13] Code Obfuscation also prevents all forms of hacking and tampering. It eliminates debugging loopholes. It slows down hackers trying to re-engineer programmes and applications. Finally, it helps protect intellectual property.[14]

Some companies may also use the period of 'Network or Internet Downtime' to filter their website. The term downtime is used to refer to periods when a system is temporarily interrupted or unavailable for the purpose of carrying out their routine maintenance. Downtime falls into two categories: planned and unplanned which gets in the way of network functionality. Planned downtime is notable because it offers advanced warning and gives users a chance to prepare. This is usually done for upgrades or maintenance to the network infrastructure. Unplanned downtime, on the other hand strikes suddenly with no warning. This can occur at any time and could be due to human errors, understaffed IT department, incorrect configurations, equipment failure, power failure, security attacks and natural disasters.[15] Whatever the reason might be, people have to cope with network inconveniences when they occur.[16]

---

[12]Peter Loshin & Andrew Zola. ' Content Filtering' <https://www.techtarget.com/searchsecurity/> accessed 23 February 2023

[13] 'What is Network Scanning? – 4 Best Network Scanning Tools' <https://www.dnsstuff.com/network-scanning/> accessed 31 May 2023

[14] 'Does Obfuscation Affect Code Performance' <https://www.premptive.com/> accessed 17 February 2023

[15] Andy Patrizio. 'Network Downtime' <https://www.techtarget.com/> accessed 17 February 2023

[16]David Anders. 'Internet Down Again? Here Are 5 Possible Causes and How to Fix Them; <https://www.cnet.com/home/Internet > accessed25 August 2023

A web crawler or spider could also qualify as an Internet filtering tool. This is a search engine, bot or software agent which visits all URLs one at a time and identifies all the hyperlinks in a website that is publicly available, until all the pages have been read. It then saves a copy of all the information on index servers.[17]

3. CYBER HYGIENE TIPS

Cyber hygiene literally translates to what we should do and what we should not do online. The world is currently grappling with cybersecurity challenges even though the Internet technology has made a profound impact on the development of the world by making our everyday operations faster and easier. On the other hand, research says a new cyber-attack is carried out every 39 seconds.[18] This is because the Internet has opened opportunities for cybercriminals who threaten our livelihood and security. So we should not leave ourselves susceptible to cybercrime. Keep the following cyber hygiene information handy because the safety tips have to do with how we are to protect ourselves on the Internet.

1. Learn the basics of Internet, cybercrime, cybersecurity and devices that compromise privacy, as new informative literatures keep coming up. The knowledge or awareness can protect us from cybercrime and other malicious attacks because the more we know, the better we can protect ourselves and educate others.
2. Identifying what causes cybercrime and the solution to cybersecurity risks is the aim of law and science.
3. Cybercrime is an unfortunate by-product of the digital age. That is why cybercriminals keep searching for vulnerabilities on our systems. Cybersecurity for Industrial control systems (ICS)[19] is necessary for safeguarding the environment, people and economy. This includes the hardware and software system as well its operators use.
4. Computer hacking is not automatically a crime. In ***United States v. Van Buren,***[20] the Court held that the Anti-Hacking Law shouldn't cover

---

[17]Cem Dilmegani. 'Web Crawler: what it is, How it Works & Applications in 2023' <https://research.aimultiple.com/web-crawler/> accessed13 October 2023

[18] 'Does Obfuscation Affect Code Performance' <https://www.premptive.com/> accessed 17 February 2023

[19] ICS ensures all processes are well protected from cyber threat. See: 'What is ICS Security?' <https://www.fortinet.com.resources/cybeglssary/ > accessed 22 May 2023

[20] 940 F.3d 1192 (11th Cir. 2019)

misusing systems people are allowed to access otherwise that would amount to criminalising a breath-taking amount of everyday computer use. But if you are accessing another person's private information without his consent, or accessing parts of a system that are specifically forbidden, then you are breaking the law.

5. Be mindful that criminals can install software to monitor your network traffic if you are careless. So, ensure you download anti-virus software and use firewall techniques.
6. There are malicious software that can steal a user's credentials on Android devices and computer systems, intercept notifications and new SMS and perform attacks. Try to use a malicious software removal tool on your computer.
7. Build digital forensics capacity. Computer forensics entails seeking professional experts that can help investigate cybercrimes.
8. Diligently police your own affairs on the Internet so that web attacks will decline.
9. Be knowledgeable in computer education and build your cybersecurity capacity.
10. Keep changing your password from time to time. Do not use a similar password on all your networking sites. A strong password secures your privacy. Your static password must be strong and unique with 14+ characters.
11. Make use of a unique password which can only be used once. This is called a one-time Password (OTP) which is not vulnerable to replay, repeat or playback attacks. That way, hackers cannot log in into your email or intercept your security protocol and data after you have concluded your transaction.
12. The fraudulent act of asking for money for a non-existent relative or faking a charity scheme online to help vulnerable children or women is increasing daily. Adopt the three core principles of Zero Trust Security which are – *Never trust; Always verify; and, Implement Zero Trust security* for your business.
13. You can help protect your family's safety by removing their personal data online. Keep low profiles on the Internet networking sites as well.
14. Do not open e-mail attachments from unknown users. Check the source of e-mails before opening it because hackers can send email with

snooping or spying software such that if you click on it, the access would allow the hacker to infiltrate your system.

15. Do not be caught off guard. Install a security software solution and operating system updates as they become available.
16. Use trusted antivirus solutions and always update them regularly to their latest definitions.
17. Do not download pirated software cracks or key generators as they commonly lead to ransomware and information-stealing Trojans.
18. Do not expose internal services to the Internet, such as remote desktop and Network-Attached Storage (NAS) devices.
19. Use secondary channels and turn on your two-factor authentication to verify requests for changes in account information.
20. Be alert to hyperlinks that may contain misspellings of the actual domain name. Remember a secure connection does not guarantee a secure site.[21]
21. Information security is crucial. Monitor your personal accounts on regular basis for irregularities, such as missing deposits.[22]
22. Beware of public WI-FI where hackers can see everything you are reading or downloading. Use VPNs.
23. Stop downloading random apps which are unknown or unspecified.
24. Do not use another person's USB charging cord/cable or power bank. Hackers can exploit the devices to access your sensitive information.
25. Rectify and audit websites where personal data is compromised. Invest in Internet Engineering Task Force (IETF) tools that provide authentication, privacy and data integrity between two communicating computer applications. Use upgraded version of SSL that fixes existing (Secure Sockets Layer) SSL vulnerabilities.
26. If someone tries to talk to you on the phone about any of your online account and asks you to help them by clicking on a link, just say No and hang up!
27. Contact and report to your social media support team for help or rescue when your account is hacked or after a hacker tricks you into clicking a bad link.

---

[21] Yaroslava Ryabova. 'HTTPS doesn't mean safe' <https://www.kapersky.com/blog/20725/ > accessed 28 February 2022.

[22] Bill Toulass. '2022 may be the year cybercrime return its focus to consumers' <https://www.bleeping computer.com/news/security/> accessed 28 February 2022.

28. Be cautious when you send out your information. Always verify identities whether they are legitimate, being mindful that there are no stringent rules.
29. To ensure cyber stability, it is essential to bring perpetrators to book. But you have to report to the Police or make use of their reporting portal.

4. WHY WE SHOULD CARE

There are lots of expectations from the citizens. Nobody feels comfortable when cyber criminals intercept our e-mails, read the content of the mail and extract our information. Cybercrime is growing exponentially and criminals are benefitting financially from it. When our online identities or information are stolen online, they can be used to perpetrate cyber fraud. Moreover software testing is never 100% and with attackers or hackers getting sophisticated or creative by the day, online users and regulators must also be up and doing. A random click on some links can be our greatest undoing because, most hacks start with a victim making some mistakes, for instance entering his password on a convincing-looking phishing page or accidentally downloading a malicious attachment on his computer or even visiting a real website. These are called 'watering hole' attacks and the name comes from the idea of poisoning a central water source that consequently affects anyone who drinks from it. Watering hole attacks can be difficult to detect because they often operate quietly on legitimate websites whose owners may not even notice anything amiss as to how many victims have been attacked or how many devices were affected as well or how long an attack has been going on. Unfortunately, attackers have gotten increasingly skilled at minimizing their digital footprint that makes the attacks easier to set up and harder to trace.[23] We should be worried about the fact that cyber-attacks are conducted on a scale that is not possible in the physical world. For example, a traditional armed robber may only hit one or two banks at a time, but an online cyber-attacker could potentially hit hundreds or thousands of websites at once! The cyber-attacker does not even need to show himself but he can attack the world from his living room just by going through many peoples' personal information on the Internet. The speed a

[23]Lily May Newman. 'Hacker Lexicon: What is a Watering Hole Attack?' <https://www.wired.com/story/> accessed 08 January 2022

hacker uses to commit his crime can happen in just few minutes. So in terms of the speed, the reach, the scale and the effect, cybercrime can be deadlier than traditional crimes.[24] Every day we read about the arrest, prosecution and conviction of Internet fraudsters who impersonate different persons to defraud them on WhatsApp, Messenger and Facebook accounts. In Nigeria, apart from sentencing these fraudsters to jail or given them an option of fine, the Court would also confiscate their devices, auction the items and order the proceeds from the auction to be paid into the Treasury Single Account (TSA) of the Federal Government. What is the lesson here for us especially when you consider the challenges confronting us? Make cybersecurity a priority. Make it a lifestyle. Do not think that cybersecurity can only be understood by scientists otherwise that can overwhelm you. Encrypt your e-mail such that only you can read it. Practice careful and safe messaging on your computer network and don't click on any links in texts, even if they come from a trusted person.

Be vigilant and wary that the Internet space is vulnerable to different cyber-attacks. For example, if you suspect your e-mail account has been hacked, do not panic at first. Check your account activity or login activity. Check your security settings. Is your two-factor authentication or password still the same? Check whether there unusual messages in your e-mail inbox or sent messages. You may also have to scan your computer for viruses. If you are convinced you need further assurance that your email account is safe, you may have to seek professional help from a trusted tech expert or the Police.

The Internet is not a tightly-knit landscape as we think. Be mindful that some fraudsters fake terminal illness, suicide and death on the Internet just to defraud vulnerable people. Do not accept all computer printouts as 100% truth because some information can be inaccurate or misleading but shared deliberately or by mistake as patterns of information sharing to cause online harm. Truly the Internet has magnified both good and bad acts and claims, but there is a need to maintain peace and security in the cyberspace, otherwise everyone and every organizations or governments which rely heavily on ICT to function are at risk. Embrace the three core principles of

---

[24] Loris Miller. 'What is the Difference Between Cybercrime and Traditional Crime?' <https://www. .nеguard.com/> accessed 08 January 2022

Zero Trust Security which are – Never trust; Always verify; as well as, Implement Zero Trust security for your business.

5. REDUCING YOUR CYBER RISKS

Following cybersecurity best practices will help us in many ways. Abusing the Internet for illegal purposes can manifest in many ways. Ransomware attacks are real. Attackers want to prevent you from accessing your data and extort money from you before you are given access. Cultivate a cybersecurity mindset by building a cyber-defence system around your computing, digital and mechanical IoT devices such as desktops, laptops, mobile phones, smart security devices. Anticipate threats because there are always security vulnerabilities such as malware, viruses, trojans, worms or content that can damage computer systems or devices. Cyber-attack can take place anytime and anywhere. Recognise there are ethical issues in Internet technologies and apply security updates. Information security staff and network administrators should be proactive in looking out for any potential threats. Equipping ourselves in cybersecurity education is imperative. The below-listed recommendations will provide a robust strategy or enable what is called 'Zero Trust Security' in cyber-risk reduction. Having a zero trust on the Internet means you do not trust everyone inside or outside your network except each has been verified before allowing them to gain access into your system. It is a shift towards cultivating a more comprehensive and proactive cybersecurity approach aimed at pushing a user-centric approach which objectives are, to treat every user and device as untrusted until verified and leveraging technology like multi-factor authentication to protect against advanced threats.[25]

1. Only connect to the Internet over a secure password-protected network. Stay away from unsecure public access point.
2. Computer criminals know that the password to open your e-mail address could be related to your date of birth, marital status, gender and occupation. Do not be predictable. Be unique. Go with new and stronger password.
3. Install monitoring software on your computer and check your software flaws.

[25] Sonali Pawar. 'Cybersecurity Forum Initiative; published 02 July 2023 on Linkedin

4. Beware of unsolicited calls, voice notes and messages from unknown numbers.
5. Download apps only from their official sites and application stores to avoid malware which can still spread via third-party Android app shops.
6. Avoid sensitive activities that require passwords or credit-cards.
7. Check your Internet footprint. Perform an external vulnerability scan of your whole Internet footprint.
8. Phishing response: Ensure that your staff knows how to report phishing emails.[26] Let your IT staff participate in organizational measures and training.
9. Be extra vigilant and be alert. Some malware disguise as educational apps for their victims to study. Do not be too quick to download free software and don't blindly trust anything you read online.
10. Invest in cyber insurance. The policy will cover your financial losses caused by a cyber-attack.
11. Apply network segmentation – the process of splitting your network into different sub-networks.
12. To avoid being misled by a fake website, always look out for the HTTPS lock symbol in your browser address window when making an online purchase.
13. Install a Firewall to add an extra security layer.
14. If someone changes your password of your computer without your consent, consult a data recovery expert to help you reset the password.
15. Do not accept friend requests from strangers because there are Internet criminals who pose as females or children on social media, as well as posting morphed photographs of their social network friends.
16. Avoid answering calls from unknown numbers which are mostly used to contact victims of voice cloning. In order to avoid bring picked out as a potential victim, try to avoid posting your phone number online or that of your family member. Always verify the identity of your callers on Truecaller.
17. In case you are planning to dispose your phone, "use your phone under the assumption that somebody else might later become its legal owner. Set a passcode that is hard to guess, minimize the private information that

[26] Liam Tung. 'Cybersecurity: 11 steps to take as threat levels increase' <https://www.zdnet.com/article/cybersecurity/> accessed 10 July 2023

is easy to access, and remotely wipe your phone if it is lost or stolen. Otherwise it will be easy for someone to gain an incredible amount of access to your private information."[27]

18. Generally, do routine cybersecurity audits to prevent spooling attack, USB keyboard attack, Internet-connected UPS attack and other attacks that can harm your system.
19. Invest in cybersecurity education and research to deter threats or mitigate human cyber-risk. For example Google is supporting the expansion of the Consortium of Cybersecurity Clinics to introduce thousands of students to potential careers in cybersecurity, while also helping defend small government offices, rural hospitals and non-profits from hacking.[28] In effect, it is better to invest in cybersecurity than part with much more money to recover your data from a hacker or a ransomware criminal. Think about the additional cost of investigating, remediating and restoring the IT infrastructure of the whole business after the hacking incident.[29]
20. Manage your digital footprints online by using a computer with a VPN or proxy network like ToR. The main reason why people prefer to use VPN is because of the need to stay private while online. A VPN will hide you from hackers, marketers and network administrators and secure you from public Wi-Fi. With ToR, it will be hard for anyone to track your digital footprint. Make your social media account private if you don't want random strangers to know your activities. When using public computers, delete your browsing history from the browser. After visiting a website, delete the cookies in order to prevent further tracking. However one thing is for sure, you cannot prevent your data from being collected.[30]
21. There is an urgent need for strategies to be mapped out to confront cybersecurity changes by equipping the youths with computer programming, information tech and engineering, AI ethics and usage, digital forensics skills and techniques, including general cyber education.

---

[27] 'Researchers Uncover Privacy Risks in Phones Purchased at Police Auctions' <https://www.forensicmag.com/598578/> accessed 19 July 2023

[28] Associated Press. 'Google Backs Creation of Cybersecurity Clinics With $20 Million Donation' <https://www.securityweek.com/> accessed 25 June 2023

[29] Danny Palmer. 'Bosses are reluctant to spend money on cybersecurity. Then they get hacked' <https://www.zdnet.com/article/> accessed 10 December 2021

[30] Vincent Tabora. 'Digital Footprints-Leaving Trails Behind For Cyber Forensics' <https://medium.com/the-infosec-journal/> accessed20 May 2022

The range of contemporary cybersecurity field is broad, thus embracing many fields such as extensive expertise in fraud detection, cyber defence, technology ethical hacking, disaster recovery, data protection and privacy both as a safety measure and a career, data encryption and authentication, advocacy for global cooperation in combating cybercrime; implementation of proactive safety measures to digital forensics, ethical hacking and threat intelligence that helps organisations facing cyber-attacks and data breaches.

22. Report all suspected cyber fraud cases and credible threats to the appropriate authorities. On reporting cyber victimization or suspicious cyber activities in Nigeria – "The Inspector-General of Police while calling on users of online banking platforms to be vigilant with regard to their personal information, urges all citizens and residents in the country, as stakeholders in ensuring maximum security, to report all suspicious cyber activities via your country's cyber designated numbers, email and portal.[31]
23. As cyber threats and imposter social media accounts become more sophisticated and regular, there is need for us to support regulatory bodies for operational efficiency and digital transformation because recent research says digital evidence has overtaken physical evidence.[32] The integrated approach enables a more holistic and proactive cybersecurity management.
24. In today's fast-paced world, having experienced professionals and the right skillset is essential. Outsource your security operations to a cybersecurity company. Their experts will play an integral role in tracking cybercrimes and helping to retrieve information or money that is stolen by scammers. These professionals provide specialized knowledge, critical expertise, critical operational support and a solid ground for digital capabilities. They can find the indicators of a compromised data as well as trace and track other online illegal activities of cybercriminals. They should avoid harbouring the cyber-optimism bias because it makes them underestimate risks, therefore causing more security problems. Regular

[31] <https://dailyfocus.com.ng/cybercrime-police-burst-pos-network-fraud-syndicates-responsible-for-over-n16m-theft/> accessed 07 December 2022

[32] 'Survey Says Digital Evidence is now more important than DNA' <https://www.forensicmag.com/5927/> accessed 18 November 2022

trainings on cybersecurity threats and awareness should be conducted. Sustained advocacy and a constant review to meet current realities. Increase capacity and capability to address the skills gap in the cybersecurity sector. Invest in cyber forensics trainings and technical knowledge which will have capacity for organisation. Recruit more technology expertise because a shortage of technical workers in the cybersecurity industry will have an impact beyond the industry.

25. Tap into cybersecurity precaution by leveraging AI and machine learning for threat detection. Patronise international and domestic consultancy outfits that assist companies to comply with personal data privacy regulations based on constant legislative and market updates.

26. There is a need to simplify cybersecurity. A lawyer author has once advocated that to improve cybersecurity, we need to understand how hackers really think, as well as how they code. By so doing, we'll be able to know how the world works and how to effectively tackle cybercrime.[33] A bug bounty hunter has also said "cybersecurity research is about finding and understanding how a programme works. If you are interested in web application security, networking, reverse engineering or programming, you should learn the language used."[34]

27. DROWN is an acronym for 'Decrypting RSA with Obsolete and Weakened eNcryption'. Note that the RSA in cybersecurity means 'Rivest-Shamir Adleman'. This is a type of public-key cryptography widely used for data encryption of e-mail and other digital transactions over the Internet. DROWN is a serious vulnerability that affects HTTPS and any other services that use SSL and TLS, the foundations for privacy on the Internet. TLS on the other stands for Transport Layer Security. The function of TLS is to ensure that eavesdroppers and hackers do not see what we are transmitting. This is particularly useful for private and sensitive information such as passwords, credit card numbers, and personal correspondence. The DROWN attack exposes inherent weaknesses in how companies manage their systems and infrastructures. To avoid the DROWN attack, good security hygiene would require an

---

[33]David Adam. 'The cyber-lawyer who wants to teach everyone how to hack' <https://www.newscientist.com/article/mg2583439/> accessed 16 May 2023

[34]Kevin Townsend. 'Hacker Conversations: Youssef Sammonda, Bug Bounty Hunter'<https://www.securityweek.com> accessed 02 August 2023

organization to audit its servers for obsolete or unused protocols, services and software and remove what is not required; Perform frequent vulnerability assessments to identify any obsolete or vulnerable software and services and; monitor its network traffic for unwanted or undesired.[35]

6. LAW ENFORCEMENT OFFICERS AND CYBERCRIME

The challenges of modern cybersecurity are here to stay for we cannot simply assume we are safe on the Internet even after taking precautions. In today's rapidly evolving world of Internet-facilitated crime, law enforcement officers must harness the power of technology to checkmate crime more effectively and efficiently. The rise in cybercrime has no doubt complicated matters for law enforcement agencies trying to stay ahead of emerging cyber threats because we hear how law enforcement officers contend daily with cybercriminals who are arrested on daily basis. The reality is that today's cybersecurity issues demands strategic solutions that must go beyond a one-size-fits-all approach where traditional methods of crime-fighting have proven inadequate against to tackle online criminal activities and as much as the responsibility also lies in our hands, it does not prevent us from reaching out to the Police for help because they are the most appropriate agency that are statutorily empowered to prevent, detect and investigate criminal activities that takes place online or physically. In policing, it is important to gain an upper hand over cybercriminals and mitigate the risk of online crime or minimize the damage caused. To contain cyber-attacks, law enforcement agencies can send repeated warnings to citizens, leveraging cutting-edge technologies, including AI, facial recognition, video surveillance and search technologies. The fact is when Police investigate cybercrimes enabled by tools of technology; they can identify threats or easily mitigate damages. However, law enforcement agencies should strive to be guided by the following information:

- Develop a cyber-defence plan, policy and practice which must align with assessing the areas of urgent, after assessing its current technology. Although the cybersecurity field is often focused on tools and techniques, the human element is also a vital security strategy and that is, are they trained and re-trained for capacity build-up? The next feasible step should

[35] Dick Bussiere. 'Top takeaways from the DROWN vulnerability' <https://techbeacon.com/security/> accessed 20 May 2023

be to develop a cyber-defence plan and determine what penetration testing tools to use. They should take inventory of the technologies in their establishment. Can it meet their needs and what is the cost involved? The answers can provide valuable insights into the patterns observed in cyber-attacks and whether the technologies were adequate to deal with investigation of cyber-attacks and even phone hacking;

- After assessing their current technology, it is important for the Police to invest in the right technology, employ and train their personnel, and find ways to overcome their budgetary challenges and educate the community.[36] Inter-agency collaboration is also important. Collaboration is building a network of like-minded agencies that involves working together within a process in order to achieve a shared or common goal;[37]
- Leverage intelligence tools to 'shine a light' on the darknet - Agencies must be able to trace cryptocurrency on the darknet and quickly identify instances in which data may have been compromised. To spot potentially online criminal activities, law enforcement has a key role to play in building multi-disciplinary threat assessment teams where different professionals can use their digital forensic tools such as facial recognition, data-extraction software and open-source intelligence instead of manual sorting.[38] Law enforcement agencies can further investigate and analyse context such as historical attack patterns, user behaviour, system and network configuration, device status and current threat intelligence.[39] By recruiting AI for better insights and faster resolutions, the data emanating from these connections can be forensically collected, analysed and turned into actionable intelligence that can profoundly impact investigations;
- Apart from the lack of strict regulations on the Internet, untrained police agencies indirectly encourage criminal behaviour on the Internet. Therefore technology can be used as a means to help officers do their jobs better and more efficiently because Police officers will always be needed to make sense of the information provided to them and use it to

[36] Dalton Webb. 'Leveraging Technology in Policing; <https://www.police1.com> accessed 20 September 2023

[37] Valentine Enedah. 'The Agile Mindset: A Path to Personal Fulfillment and Growth' <https://hackernoon.com/> accessed 20 September 2023

[38] Joshua Lee. 'How technology can help law enforcement fight human trafficking' <https://www.police1.com/investigations/articles/> accessed 26 May 2023

[39] Matt Wilson.'Protection is No Longer Straightforward – Why More Cybersecurity Solutions Must Incorporate Context' <https://www.securityweek.com/> accessed 08 August 2023

protect citizens, through proper identification and tracking.[40] Every latest technology should be utilised to help solve crime.

- The UN Economic and Social Council (ECOSOC) Resolution 2019 urges Member States to encourage the training of law enforcement officers, investigative authorities, prosecutors and Judges in the field of cybercrime, including training them in relevant skills pertaining to evidence collection and information technology, and to equip them to effectively carry out their respective roles in investigating, prosecuting and adjudicating cybercrime offences.[41] This is because "when it comes to understanding security risks, knowledge really is power and at a global level, we want to collate as much of that knowledge (intelligence)...and when you share information and expertise through partnerships and cooperation, you remove technological obstacles which helps boost the effectiveness of the cybersecurity sector."[42]
- In the fight for privacy in the digital era, the recent case of ***Facebook Inc. v. State of New Jersey,*** [43] has become a win for digital privacy rights in New Jersey where Facebook users are now entitled to a greater constitutional protection, where the case sets a limitation on Police conduct and access to digital communications. This means it is no longer permissible for the New Jersey Police to obtain a Facebook user's private messages easily unlike before. Now they would have to apply for a wiretap order and prove more than a probable cause before the Court can grant the order to compel Facebook to provide the contents of users based only on probable cause.[44]
- A man was arrested by the Police for allegedly impersonating the Vice-President of India, after he started seeking favours from senior government officials through WhatsApp. The suspect lived in Italy and created a fake WhatsApp account using the picture of the VP as his profile display to dupe people. His friend was also arrested for allegedly creating a one-time password (OTP) for the said WhatsApp account. The

---

[40] Tiffany Goddard. '3 strategies to mitigate cybercrime' <https://www.police1.com/investigations/articles/> accessed10 December 2022

[41] <https://www.unodc.org/rddb/document/crime/resolution/2019> accessed 12 November 2022

[42] Derek Manky.'Cybersecurity Public-Private Partnership: Where Do We Go Next?' <https://wwww.securityweek.com/> accessed 26 July 2023

[43] 251 N.J. 378 (2022)

[44] Julian Melendi. 'New Jersey Just Made It a Lot Harder for Police to Snoop on Social Media' <https://slate.com/news-and-politics/2023/07/ > accessed 07 July 2023

Police got the details of his WhatsApp profile from the social media platform while the Internet protocol address was traced to Italy.[45]

- A former Police Officer better known as the Cannibal Cop, became involved in a Dark Fetish Net – a forum dedicated to sexual fetishes and fantasies involving torture, rape, murder and even cannibalism. He started using fetish chat rooms, and shared his fantasies about kidnapping, torturing, raping, killing and even cannibalizing various women he knew, including his own wife. His online activities were eventually discovered by his wife, who reported him to the Police. The man was thereafter arrested and charged to Court. At trial, he was ultimately convicted of violating the law and conspiracy to commit kidnapping, after raising a defence that the chat room communications were merely fantasy and that he had no intention of acting on them. However the presiding Judge later acquitted him of the conspiracy charges, ruling that the man's online communication were simply "fantasy role-play." In light of this case, the limits of free speech and the appropriate use of law enforcement resources were called into question.[46]
- The Internet's First Serial killer – His name was John Robinson and his modus operandi was to promise jobs, money and love to women, only to later meet them and kill each of them. He would create fake companies, personas and stories that would attract women who struggled emotionally, sexually and financially. He would make promises of high paying jobs, relationships or BDSM[47] experiences. He would lure them to his hometown and isolate them, control them and eventually kill them. Thereafter he would dump their bodies so the Police would never discover them. The case of this this Internet killer highlights the dark side of the Internet and the extent of online interactions. Therefore when we go online, we need to practice safer cybersecurity practices meaning we have to be vigilant when we meet strangers and always be wary of possible predatory behaviour displayed by other online users.[48]

---

[45] Express News Service. 'Man held for impersonating the VP of India on WhatsApp' <http://indianexpress.com/article/ > accessed 28 February 2023

[46] Liam Hall. 'Inside the Dark World of Fetish Chatrooms: The Cannibal Cop' <https://zeph456. medium.com/> accessed28 July 2023

[47] Aspects of sex that involve physical restraints of Bondage, Dominance Sadism and Masochism

[48] Lawrence Lease. 'John Robinson: The Internet's First Serial Killer' <https://thecrimewire.com/true-crime/> assessed 27 February 2023

7. JUDGES AND CYBER-SEXUAL ASSAULT CASES

The modern world is getting more complex and unpredictable with this ever-evolving technology starring at us daily. The social networking sites where pornography sharing, cyber defamation, blackmail and cyber stalking which operates freely on the Internet have become a cause of concern in the society. Much of the information we are bombarded with on the net can sometimes be confusing to us including Judges. In cases involving online-related sexual assault cases, it has been said that the complainant's fate may depend on the Judge's awareness of how various online platforms' work. The reasons are not far-fetched. It could be due to a generational gap and lack of basic social media awareness leading to lack of competence on evidence of social media communications. It is difficult to wish away a Judge's pre-existing beliefs, cultural values and ideologies because if a Judge does not understand a how online platforms work, chances are that the case is likely to be thrown out, except the victim can connect the perpetrator's digital footprint to the crime. For example, a Judge could not understand why a woman could be groped online after he Googled the offending platform within a manner of minutes. Another Judge said there was no reason for a woman to be fearful on X (Twitter) because he had no idea of how X (Twitter) works. Similarly, a Judge was reported to be unfamiliar with the workings of the LinkedIn network because his impression was that the professional networking site was basically meant for arranging hook-ups. Some Judges do not even understand how Facebook posts, Instagram photos and Snapchat should concern the Courts. According an Advocacy Organization, the Court is so behind when it comes to holding Internet offenders accountable for Internet-related crime. Regrettably, offenders are latching on to the ignorance of few of these Judges. This has implications on the society as offenders become more emboldened, making them more dangerous and willing to take further risks, thus leaving survivors unhappy.[49]

Nonetheless, Internet technologies and AI has come to stay. Judges therefore need to be competent in technology and use of social media tools. In this digital age, they must be equipped with better skills to meet the growing demands of lawyers and litigants enabling them to better deal with the complexity of the Internet. Judges should appreciate the fact that digital

---

[49] Carly Lewis. 'Survivors Suffer When Judges Misunderstand Social Media' <https://www.wired.com/story/judges/> accessed 04 March 2023

communications preserve records of transactions that are of evidential value. Judges who are still weak with the workings of Internet can be guided by experts or they can as well read books that would broaden their knowledge for researching case elements on social media.

www.ingramcontent.com/pod-product-compliance
Lightning Source LLC
Chambersburg PA
CBHW050521240926
51846CB00003B/643
9789786061719